Secrets In The Sanctuary

Author's Signature:

Kametra Laqueal

Published by Teardrops Publishing

No part of this book may be reproduced or transmitted in any form or by any means, electronic or mechanical, including photocopying, recording, or by any information storage or retrieval system, without written permission by the publisher, except for inclusion of brief quotations in a review.

Secrets In The Sanctuary
Copyright © 2018

All Rights Reserved.

This book is a work of non-fiction. Names, characters, places, and incidents are the product of the author's imagination or are being protected. Any resemblance to actual events, locales, or persons, living or dead, is coincidental.

ISBN 978-0-9831444-1-0

Printed in the United States of America

Additional copies of this book are available
By mail.
Send $15.00 each (includes S&H)
Refer to the PO Box on
Teardrops Publishing's Website
Kametra Laqueal

www.TeardropsPublising.net

Acknowledgments

I would like to thank my heavenly Father for giving me the gift to write, and a mind to do it.

Thanks to my beloved daughter Re'Ana Dion. Birthing you taught me how to love another human being unconditionally, patience, and unselfishness.

Thank you Vanessa Hollis for knowing the value of my writing and waiting on me. You are appreciated.

A special thanks to all the beautiful vessels that encouraged me instead of discouraging me, complimented me instead of criticizing me, and all those who prayed for me. You know who you are and I thank God for crossing paths with you on my journey. K.L.

Scripture

"For nothing is secret, that will not be made manifest; neither any thing hid, that shall not be known and come abroad." Luke 12:2

...Intro

My name is Mina Wright. The name Mina means "life" in the Persian culture. Recently divorced, single mom, currently living with my man. *I love me some him*, but when weakness presents itself, I would love on someone else from time to time.

I'm extremely active in church! I know you probably think, *oh my goodness, she's such the hypocrite*, but trust me my heart wants to live a righteous life. After all, I have been through, prayed through, cried *through*, I thought I was finally *through!* I mean, *through!* I'm *through* with life and all the blows that were thrown my way. I knew there was something better for me than having the continuous pain. I knew there was an abundant life out there for me. I knew that God had a plan for my life and I knew I was ready for a change. A change of scenery, a change of career, a change in my finances, I wanted a change. God answered my prayer and I was forced to make a change.

I just turned forty and have been through *hell* for the last past decade. But, through it all, I still trusted God with all my heart. I was raised in the church, sung in the choir, paid my tithes, prayed without ceasing, fasted every Monday, was obedient, but still living with my man. After all the hardship I encountered, I begin to build a relationship with God. I am ready to start living an acceptable and pleasing life for God. I prayed for Him to give me something new. I wanted God to show himself and show up in my life like never before. I knew he could because he brought me through a divorce, death, loss of jobs, eviction, repossessions, foreclosure, heartbreak, you name it, and I had been there. I realized after my various trials, and after I had been through the fiery furnace that the answer was getting back home to Charlotte to start over, and to join a well-grounded church was the answer for me and truly live the righteous life. What I didn't know is the start of a new journey in my life would change my life forever. Let me say this, some church folk, or also known as, saints, were very similar to the world folk! You see I often thought of church to be a like a hospital, you go there because you are sick, and you receive healing, forgiveness, or deliverance and when you are healed you then help others on their path to recovery. I never thought the leaders of the church, or the doctors and nurses of the hospital, were sick also. I didn't think they too needed a few prescriptions written by Jesus named healing, forgiveness, deliverance...etc. Well let me say this, I walked into a whole other level of trials. Oh yes God gave me something new, that he did, and what I would soon realize is there were **Secrets in the Sanctuary**.

Chapter One God or Man?...

I remember my leg could not stop shaking. My palms were a little sweaty, and I was extremely fidgety. I sat at my desk in my office patiently waiting for the long-awaited announcement along with another group of employees, who sat in their offices also. We nervously texted one another back and forward. We all received the same memo week's prior and also attended the same mandatory meeting the very next day after we toasted and screamed "Happy New Year's." We talked about the emails leading up to that date. What did yours say? Do you think you'll lose your job? I thought the company made enough money. But I guess this is why we didn't receive a raise last year. We all exchanged our share of thoughts with one another. I, on the other hand, looked at it for what it was... *bullshit!*

"We regret to inform you, but due to the new year budget, recently released, we will be downsizing this year and you will probably be laid off, let go, or terminated," that is what the email really meant to me. The real scripted version released which read,

"We sincerely regret to inform you, and we value you as an employee, but due to budgets..." and the rest is history. This is why I was so nervous and drinking cups of coffee one after another each morning, drinking glass after glass of wine every night of the week, and liquor on the weekends. But, I still worked like a commander leading her soldiers to victory. Even after my supervisor was, "regrettably laid off," along with her boss, I still worked diligently. Deep down inside I didn't think I would be let go. I had been a faithful employee for five years and my columns were always the most commented on by readers. But even better than that I had a personal relationship with my heavenly father and I knew if God decided that this car ride was over, he would then send me something better like a jet plane to ride on. I was working at the same pace and the same place month after month leading up to the 1st day of 2015. I was still writing my spiritual columns and they were given to my editor no later than 7:49 am every Wednesday morning ready for editing, and ready to be published by the Friday morning weekend edition.

I would arrive an hour early and the first email I would read at 7:55 am was from Terrance D. Boyd, my Editor and Chief, and son of the president of the publishing company.

He had not been at the company for more than a year at this point, but for an odd reason, he seems to break every record. One record was for *Achievement in Revenue Sales for all local news publications,* whatever that meant. All I could remember is standing, clapping, and keeping a fake smile just like every other employee in the room when his name was called at the annual awards banquet.

The email read:

Good morning Mina! On behalf of the company, I am happy to inform you that layoffs are finally over, and we are excited to still have you as a part of our team. I would like to schedule a meeting with you today at 2:30 pm in the conference room on the 3rd floor, to discuss new opportunities and your future with our company. I look forward to seeing you and working with you this year! Please confirm your scheduled meeting time.

*Best Regards,
Terrance D. Boyd-Editor and Chief*

Yes! I knew it. I knew it! Whew, God is so good! I clicked confirmed immediately! I prayed, the church prayed, Mamadoll prayed, and our prayers were answered. I felt safe and secure. I had been through so much and the Lord knew I could not deal with any more bumps in my road anytime soon. I needed a smooth ride. I knew this was promotion and increase. I went from sweaty palms to butterflies in my tummy. 2:30 came too soon. I stepped off the elevator onto the 3rd floor in my fitted black pencil skirt, white blouse with the collar high, and red bottom heels. I didn't mean to walk with a twist but, it was natural for the hips, and the Spanx helped them. I approached the door and slowly I opened it. The first person I noticed was Terrance. Our eyes met instantly. He was reserved. He smiled at my appearance, and I smiled at his. He looked good as usual and he reminded me every bit of a Venti Vanilla whipped latte with my name written on his cup. I caught myself immediately and remembered where I was.

He stood up to greet me with his hand out. "Hello there, Ms. Wright, please have a seat." He said as he pulled a chair out for me.

"Thank you Mr. Boyd," smiling as I replied.

As he sat back in his seat, his eyes began to go up one side of me and down the other. He then gave me a little smile. Clearing his throat, he pulled a few papers from his briefcase; he proceeded to lay them on the table and slowly handed me a ballpoint pen. I was ready to sign and initial next to my new annual salary and new title. I was smiling from ear to ear and so was he.

"Mina I first want to say I commend you on your efforts in continuing your columns. Encouraging people, at the most tragic time of your life. I think that was so brave of you." He said and I jumped right in to comment.

"Thank you, Terrance. I love writing and encouraging people. I was called to do this. This is my calling to encourage people and spread the love that lives inside of me."

"You don't have to tell me, Mina. I feel the love you have for others, and I can see it all over you." He paused and stared at me for a minute. He then gave me a sneaky devilish smile. "And after talking with the committee and of course reviewing your work, I am truly proud to say we were able to offer you another position."

I stood up smiling like a first-time bride at age fifty-five. I was so happy. I quickly sat down so I wouldn't split my skirt. I grabbed his hand and he grabbed mine and shook it real slow.

"Thank You so much. Thank You, Terrance."

"No, thank you, Mina. You have brought so much to our company and have contributed a lot to the success of this company." He paused and kept shaking my hand. "Now let's talk about your new position."

I sat straight up in my seat. "I am ready."

With a slight chuckle in my voice, I replied, "yes, let's talk."

"This position will not require you writing, or staying late nights anymore, Mina. It will only require handling our valuable clients and prospective customers on a daily basis." There he was with that sneaky fake smile again.

"Uh, I'm a little confused. Did you say, I will not be writing?" I giggled nervously.

"Well, only as needed."

"What do you mean, *only as needed*?" My voice grew a little loud and began to shake. "I am the featured columnist for the paper."

"You were the columnist, Mina." He put enfaces on the word *were*.

My eyebrows rose to the roof as I begin to talk to myself. *Calm down Mina. Let him finish Mina. Don't curse him out, Mina. Think about your child Mina. You need your job, Mina.*

"Sooo, what is my new position, Terrance?" I asked in a nice calm voice after I held the word *so* for approximately twenty seconds.

He smiled at me for the third time. "You will be my receptionist." He smiled even bigger this time. "I know this is unexpected but, I fought very hard for them not to let you go for some time now."

You would have thought I was jumping on a trampoline. I jumped up quickly. "*Receptionist! Not to let me go!*"

7

"Mina please, calm down. There is no need to be so defensive and please lower your voice, and sit down."

I immediately calmed down. I pulled my skirt down. "Terrance I apologize, but I want my voice to carry."

He inhaled and then exhaled. Stood up, as he began to say, "Ok, you want to take it there, let us take it there. Mina, take a good look at your columns. We have received a lot of negative feedback from the readers, and to be honest no one wants to constantly read about prayer and fasting, and miracles when the majority of our readers are adults who want to enjoy life by partying, shopping, and drinking and talking about reality shows. I'm sorry Mina."

"They are the ones who need to hear about prayer, fasting, and, miracles. It only takes one person to hear about Christ. Just one. That one can spread the good news to thousands, millions."

"That's your opinion, and also very judgmental of our readers. We're moving in a different direction with the paper, period. My father wants to see growth and move away from the religious section of the paper. He feels that bringing in different avenues and topics besides a religion column will offer the readers what they need. And we have to give the readers what they want, not what we want, even if it compromises our religious beliefs. I'm sorry, but you still will be a part of the team."

Obviously pissed, I asked, "As a receptionist?"

"As myyy receptionist." He said in a low tone voice, while licking his lips.

"Ok. Ok. What will be my salary to still be part of this team and your receptionist?" speaking in a low tone voice, mimicking his.

"Well, it will not be the same as you were currently making of course. But you will still have your benefits, 401k, and stock in a great company etc."

"How much?" I asked aggressively.

He cleared his throat again…and paused. "Please stay calm Mina."

I got louder…."Howww muchhh?" As if I was echoing.

He cleared his throat once again. "Twenty-nine thousand a year." And went on to say, "But when we need you to write a column, you will get a bonus."

I placed my hand over my ear. Did he just accidentally say twenty-nine thousand a year I asked myself, as I stared at him, with confusion? I thought to myself well damn he couldn't make it an even thirty thousand? I shook my head from side to side like a baby learning how to say nooo, nooo, for the very first time. My current salary as of

8

today is, eighty thousand. That is a fifty-one thousand dollar cut in pay; because this damn company is so cheap he couldn't make it an even thirty thousand.

I couldn't believe my ears, but then on the other hand, yes I could. This daddy's boy who thought I was going to catch that cheap ball he just threw. I'll let this one fall. NEXT!

I begin to grab my purse and place it on my shoulder and placed the pen neatly on the table.

"What are you doing Mina? You're staying with the company right?"

I cleared my throat, and kept it professional. "Not right now Terrance. God is directing me in a different direction. But, should you have a position designed for me, and a salary comparable to my work, then we can talk, and that's when you can place the pen in my hand. Until then, I will be seeking other employment."

His mouth dropped wide open.

"Mina! You know I was thinking I could help you. I know a lot of influential ministers. If interested, maybe you can seek employment with one of their larger congregations in the city. That may be able to help you."

I froze. I mean the world stopped for me at that moment. Then he kept going. And going. And going.

"Mina as for now we are not interested in publishing the weekly religious columns anymore. Although I hate to see you leave us, Mina this is the only position we currently have to offer you. Why don't you think about it? You will still have a job with a reputable company, with great health benefits for you and your daughter." Rambling, with a hint of sarcasm in his voice.

I had to take it to another level.

"When did you think of that speech Terrance? Huh? Large congregation. Benefits. You know Terrance, I have thought about it over and over again. This is about last night. Oh yes, it is. I walked past you and your group of friends and you smiled at me this morning, but you never talked directly to me, you talked around me. You talked to everyone else, but me. It was obvious when you called me this morning and I wouldn't respond to your invite."

"What are you talking about Mina? I'm confused. What does this have to do with your position and the company, if I talked to you or not?"

As I grabbed my things I begin to walk towards the door. "My columns were always #1. Always! The readers loved the motivation and encouragement I brought to the paper. But the truth of the matter is; I am being let go, because of what happened on New Year's Eve. That's right, last night."

He looked over at the camera hanging from the ceiling. He begins to stutter and turn red. As he wiped away the small sweat beads from his forehead, he called out my name a couple of times with a nervous chuckle. "Mina. Mina, what are you talking about?"

"I laughed also Pinky. I'm sorry...Terrance.

"Pinky!" Terrance asked.

"Oh yes, you see every-time I think about it. I mean there we were fondling all over one another. I was horny and so were you. We both had been through so much and not to mention our relationships with our significant others, were horrible. We needed one another that night, and we both needed a good time."

"Mina, please stop this. You forgot how you missed a lot of work due to dealing with all your trials and tribulations you were going through, amongst other things." He became very, very defensive.

"Oh, nowww I missed a lot of work. You know what Terrance, I'm not disappointed about this situation today, I'm mad about the *BIG* mistake I made last night. Or, was it the *little* mistake I made. I promised I would not tell your secret to anyone. I mean the handsome, blond, tall, rich boy who penis was mistaken for a finger. I asked you a simple question. Remember? Was it in there? Your body was doing all this moving. You were humping and bumping on top of me and I was confused. I thought, surely, he is not maneuvering his body like this with a finger? Oh, my goodness…I could not identify the difference between the two. I mean you had your finger in their one-minute, and the next thing I know you were putting a condom on, and it felt the same way. I'm just saying…I was not going to tell anyone Pinky. Hell, I was embarrassed for you, and mad as hell, at the way I started my new year off."

My eyes looked directly at the pinky penis, and I shook my head as if I was disgusted. I left his ass standing there holding his mouth wide open, and his skin red as a damn apple. I opened the door, twisted my way out, and never looked back.

Part 2: How All This Began...

"Hello, Mamadoll. Happy New Year's Eve!"

"LOL…Hi baby, this is another day, and a few more hours till another year to give God thanks." Mamadoll said in a way only she could do.

"Yes, ma'am it is," I said.

"Were you busy? I didn't disturb you, did I? " She asked.

"No ma'am. I was just sitting on the couch browsing through some old photos and getting excited about tonight,"

"Well isn't that fun. What are your plans for New Year's Eve and where is my other baby?"

"She is over to Naiomi's house. Damien and I are going to our favorite restaurant tonight where we first met, it's our anniversary."

"Oh really? I never knew how you two met. What restaurant is that?" she asked.

"I never told you, I thought I did. The name is *Café Amir Dolce*, they serve the best Middle Eastern and Spanish cuisines in the city."

"Oh, ok. Have you two decided what you were going to do?"

"Well, since it's our anniversary I really don't think I want to talk about that tonight. I want it to be special. I don't want to argue. I want it to be just him and me celebrating and bringing in the New Year on a happy note."

She was quiet. I needed support from her. Not to be criticized right now from she and I know she could feel that. "Mamadoll can you believe it was five years ago today, when we began dating?"

"Wow! Has it been that long? That's a long time to be someone's girlfriend," She said.

I paused for a second or two, because I really don't believe I have time to hear a sermon. If I say what I really want to she will end up rebuking me. "Anyway we're not going there today, ok. Let's stay on the subject," I said.

"You never want to go there, sweetie," Mamadoll said with a smile in her voice..

"Anyhow, as I was going through my photos I was thinking about at the beginning when Damien was trying to "win" me. He called and called me every day for weeks until I finally said yes I would go out with him. I wasn't even interested in dating anyone do you remember?" I asked.

There was pure silence on the phone and I continued talking.

"I had only been divorced for two months. We never became friends first we jumped right into the boyfriend/girlfriend thing after the first date." I said.

"There isn't a time limit on becoming a girlfriend or boyfriend. But, I will say this friendship, in my opinion, is always best first," She said.

"Oh! I thought you hung up on me. You were so quiet. Why is that, why do you feel that way" I asked?

"Well for one me and your uncle were best friends first and we grew into a relationship slowly. We shared stories with one another about past relationships. He would tell me what he didn't like in women, and I would tell him what I didn't like in a man, and we both knew what we were looking for. Later on, we both told one another, all the while, we were taking notes, learning one another, and enjoying each other's company, as friends. I feel if a person is intimate with you from the beginning, they will tell you what you want to hear. But if it's a true friend without intimacy first, there's no holding back, they will tell you the truth good, or bad.

The intimate part will come later, and that will be the icing on the cake and make it more beautiful." Mamadoll said.

Lord, she is ancient. It's about to be 2015. "I guess I never thought of it from that point of view. I didn't realize until years later when I reflected on what's maybe missing in our relationship. It's as if, I don't have the answer, were so different now. We are not the same couple you saw years ago," I said as I exhaled deeply.

"May I share my thoughts with you Mina and talk to you woman to woman, real friend to real friend," she asked.

I am truly thinking, I can't believe she's asking, she usually just tell me what she thinks. Let me put on my protective gear, because I hear a verbal beat down coming. "Go ahead, I'm listening," I said.

"There is no perfect relationship first of all. There is no such thing. Don't let movies fool you, don't allow celebrities and their relationships fool you, your friends, or the world we live in. But I will tell you the truth because I love you. You have allowed that man to have his way in many different ways, and your living arrangement is no doubt number one, and many other reasons. I really don't think I have enough time."

I'm asking myself, *did she say she didn't have enough time? When have you ever not had enough time to tell me about me? But I will stay respectful.*

"My living arrangement among other reasons, I'm confused by that comment. I truly don't feel you know the reasons why we're having so many problems Mamadoll," I said.

"Excuse me honey, I'm 71 years old, and still in my right mind. I know what you have told me, and I also know what I have seen from him. And know this Mina Wright, right is right and wrong is wrong, there is no in between when you are truly living for God." She said.

"Things are different between us, I'm not saying they're not. I can't put my finger on it. I don't know if it's because we have been through so much these past few months, or because I am trying to live for Christ. I know we have grown apart. Honestly, I feel I still have a bad taste in my mouth from the episode he pulled on me by canceling our trip to Paris without asking me or telling me he did it." I got quite and my voice cracked a little. "Also, when he didn't show up at the hospital after I had the miscarriage to see me, I couldn't look at him the same way."

"You know every time I think about you at that hospital having a miscarriage, and that Negro couldn't drive his…. (She pauses) "Help me, Jesus, to speak holy words," she says. "Did you say ever say something to him about what he did? Did you tell him how you feel Mina Wright?" She asked.

"Yes. I have tried over and over again to talk about it. Every time I try and talk to him he says it was a miscarriage Mina, you didn't have the baby, I was at work and I spoke with the doctors and they said it was ok for you to drive yourself home, I didn't have to come. I'm like whatever Damien, you always have an excuse," I said.

"He is a lie Mina! God forgive me if I'm wrong. But what doctor in their right mind will tell a man he didn't have to come to pick his woman up after she had a miscarriage, huh? I wish he had said that to me. I would have told him the next time you fall and break your leg and arm again on your motorcycle, I can't come and pick you up because the doctor said you can drive yourself home with the other one arm and one leg."

All I could do is laugh at myself. "Mamadoll I'm not going to do evil for evil. You always taught me that vengeance was the Lord. It will only give him a reason to use the word he always uses against me," I said.

"What word is that?" she asked.

I cleared my throat and answered, "Hypocrite."

"Hypocrite! Does he know how to spell hypocrite?" She screamed.

Oh Lord, why did I say that word, and to her. Sometimes I wish my mouth were stapled together when it comes to talking about my man, and my business. I wonder will I ever learn. But sometimes I think God allows you to continue to talk about your problems or situation, so someone can help you, or you can help someone.

"Mamadoll, now you know before I gave my life to Christ, I was clubbing with him, drinking, having sex, and smoking weed. I don't want to make him feel he is doing something wrong now, just because he's still indulging in those activities, and I don't anymore," I said.

"Mina you know I love you to death. I've had you since you were 18 months old, but I want you to listen to me baby, and listen good. If he was a real man that truly loved you he would have been at the hospital. If he was a real man he would sit and talk to you and with you, to solve whatever problems you two are having. You know I have always felt that he was immature. Mina, I don't understand you, or this generation. People just do what they want to do. Let's move-in together first, then get married. Do you honestly think you can truly live for God, and play house with a boyfriend, not your husband, and expect there not to be problems? Do you believe God is going to say to you, *'go ahead Mina you do whatever you want to do, and I'm going to let you have a great relationship...have what you want with no consequences'*... no ma'am it doesn't work like that?"

"I appreciate your concern and I thank God for your knowledge," I said sarcastically. "But I will never ever pressure any man to marry me, and one sin is not greater than the other."

"If he loved you, and was the man God designed for you, created for you, sent to you, Mina you would never ever have to pressure him to do anything. And as for your comment about one sin not being greater than the other, you are correct. But there is a word that can help you with that and it is conviction" She said.

"I feel convicted, but who said I wanted to get married again?" I asked.

"Are you saying you don't? Mina, you love God too much to not want to do what is right. I'm not someone you just met; I'm your Aunt. You told me you were giving him only a year, and that was 4 years ago when you moved in with him," she said.

"I know what I said, but also look at everything that has happened so unexpected to me. I lost my job, I had a miscarriage, and my ex-husband died, my child's father. Hello? Remember? I have been through hell and lost so much I don't want to lose Damien too! I'm tired of losing. I want to win. Can *I WIN*?" I yelled.

"Ok. There it is. I see." She took a long pause. "There it is Mina, you are scared he will leave you if you continue to ask him about marriage. I see now. You rather take a risk of losing your salvation for your flesh?" She said.

Ouch! Did she go there? I felt that punch in my stomach, my head, and all over my body. I don't know how to respond. Before I do, let me pick up my mouth.

"What I said was, I didn't want to lose Damien and that's not being afraid," I said. That's so weak Mina I'm thinking.

"Yes, it is. Mina, look how far God has brought you, and your child. I mean you have been through major storms in your life. I mean storms where people that do not know the Lord surely would have lost their minds, and not made it through, and even those who know the

Lord probably would have needed a therapist and every drug on the market out there to cope with their situation so you have won."

"There is nothing wrong with therapy or medication to help you cope. God gives those doctors and therapist knowledge."

"I never said it was. My point exactly, everything you have been through in your life. You fasted, you prayed, you read your bible, you kept trusting and believing that God would bring you through it and he did. So why would you not trust him to bring a man into your life that will give you Agape Love, a man that will marry you first? Not one that wants to play Ken and Barbie first? God has kept you in your right mind and excellent health right there is enough to make you want to do right."

"Ken and Barbie were married I thought." I said sarcastically. "You bought me bride Barbie and groom Ken."

We both laughed. Mamadoll can be funny at times. Everything she is saying is true. Always have been. I'm shaking my head right now thinking to myself she sure will tell you how she feels, she doesn't hold back, no faking, straight in your face no matter how it hurts your feelings.

"Your right Mamadoll. I thank God for being God. I thank God every day for me and my daughter well-being since the day she lost her father," I said.

"Whew! I'm still praying for God to give me strength and the words to even talk about it. His death just blew me away. I can't believe it's only been one year. I tell you, I think about Ryland every day, in how God called him home so suddenly. I mean he wasn't sick or anything. He was such a good dad. I commend you both on the way you all co-parented. You both acted like adults. You hear so much negative stuff about our black men and ex-wives or baby mommas not getting along but you two got along well. I was just so proud. I told everyone about you two relationship after the divorce it was such a good example." Mamadoll says.

"Thank you. We were better off divorced, sounds funny, doesn't it? We both joked about the fact that we liked each other more apart from one another. He was truly a good daddy. We would laugh about how the church made us marry when I got pregnant with Rylie. We weren't even ready, we were so young, but we both learned a lot from that marriage." I inhaled deeply then exhaled. There was silence on the phone, "I think about his mom all the time. Last time I spoke with her she said this was an unexpected storm, if she didn't know the Lord she would not have made it."

"Shuga, I know she's right. You never know what kind of storm is around the corner, that's why you should pray without ceasing like the bible instructs us to do. I do know this; you can be confidant that Jesus can and will handle it. He will see you through and keep you. God takes care of his children" Mamadoll said.

In my mind, I'm hoping she is about to end her daily sermon with me because I'm tired of getting fed this spiritual knowledge, and my situation not changing, but that's my fault. The funny thing is half the time she's usually right about what she's talking about. I guess all that wisdom has to be shared.

"Yes God does take care of us, Auntie. That's why I want to be obedient, and do his will and not mine."

"Baby how are you doing his will and you living with a man that you are not married too? What are you showing your daughter she's thirteen years old?" she asked?

"Mamadoll this is between me, and God, I repent daily," I said.

"Oh, oh, then you go back and do the same thing every day? The scripture says he that finds a wife finds a good thing, not he that finds a girlfriend," she said.

"The scripture does not say, "not he that finds a girlfriend", what book is that in?" I asked sarcastically. "I know, everything you're saying I've said to myself, and I do feel convicted.

I don't enjoy living together without being married, but I didn't want to move in after I married him, I needed to see what he was like, what he lived like. It's not like I haven't been married before. Also, I have grown accustomed to this house, it's so big, and I don't want to take Rylie out her comfort zone. She's been through enough. We have a nice lifestyle.

"Mina! Mina, stop the pity party and excuses. I know you have been through a lot. I have been through a lot. Everyone has been through something, and if they haven't, one day they will its called trials and tribulations or some say *LIFE*. Baby, you can do whatever God gives you the strength and grace to do. Your situation of being unemployed is temporary and it will pass.

"Don't you ever say, *I can't*, the devil is a liar? You can do all things through Christ. Don't forget who you are. God will provide, and while he's providing he will send you the right husband," she says.

"Oh my goodness you and this marriage thing can we talk about something else," I asked?

"Is that what you call marriage, *a thing?* She asked. "Marriage is ordained and designed by God. It's a ministry. Also, baby girl it only takes thirty minutes to drive to the county courthouse, and get married I looked up the mileage from your house on Google" She says.

With a slight chuckle, I replied, "I didn't think you knew what Google was at seventy-one."

"I can find what I want to find,"

"Mamadoll I love you, but please let's change the subject, it's our anniversary and plus I really need to start getting ready it's already 4:15, our reservations are for eight o'clock," I said.

"Anniversaries are for husbands and wives, not girlfriends and boyfriends. Ok. Ok. I will stop, for today." Mamadoll says.

"Hahaha, you're sooo funnyyy."

"I tell you what Jesus loves...and that's the *Truth*," she says.

"Ouch! The truth hurt, but that's why I love you because sometimes a girl needs to hear the truth. It gives me a little push"

"Remember God correct those he loves," Mamadoll says.

"I remember that's a scripture from the book of Proverbs,"

"You better know it straight Bible," Mamadoll said.

"Well let me start getting pretty, Damien will be here shortly, and I want to be dressed and ready to go, I don't need any drama" I explained.

Drama! If he is a real man like he says he is...well, let me not go there. Kiss my baby girl for me when you see her. I'm praying God will lead you back home to Charlotte because ain't nothing in Dallas anymore. LOL," she says

Oh now she doesn't want to go there, "Mamadoll I don't think you will ever like him," I said.

"I stop liking him when he didn't come to the hospital, because Mina you know I have kept my mouth shut about him all this time, but I will forever stand with Christ, and the commandments we are to follow."

"I understand," I said as I paused. "I will call you tomorrow. I love you and I'll tell Damien you said hello."

"Baby, do me a favor, don't lie to him. Bye-bye, I love you, but remember God loves you more," she says

I feel like I just walked out of a Sunday morning service. Whew! Mamadoll is something else. It's all-good I can take a fussing from her because she adores her God, always have and always will. I can respect someone who stands for what they believe. That woman loved me before she knew me. After my parents were in a car accident and died, her and my uncle begged to adopt me. She knew my mom and dad from the church, not even a week. Look how God did that. They weren't related to her. That's love. She told me she always wanted me to call her Mama, but she wasn't my mom, so you know how people pretend to have this certain kind of life with dolls; I then gave her the name.

Mamadoll. Because I had a mother and she was an angel sent to me on this journey by God, so I wouldn't be alone, and she was beautiful like a doll. She and my Uncle Merle re-named me Mina. They decided to give me that name because when the police arrived at the scene of the car accident I didn't have a scratch on me although the car was totaled. I was sitting in a car seat. As for my parents, they were thrown out of the car. That was 39 years ago and I was there only child.

Mamadoll has never missed a day calling me since the day I left Charlotte North Carolina. I moved to Dallas Texas fifteen years ago. My ex-husband got a promotion in Dallas, and it was best for him and me financially to make that move. Dallas has become home to me, and it is home to Rylie, because she was born here, but I truly miss my family. I feel alone often although I have Damien and best friend Naiomi, and her husband Javier. The two of them have been there for me more than anyone will ever know.

I sat down at the kitchen table and reflected on every word Mamadoll said to me. I thought I had my life all figured out, and did it the way I wanted too.

What I should have done was, trusted God, to not move-in first and waited until I was married that's what I said I was going to do after my divorce. I would never live with a man, without him marrying me… first.

The older I get. The wiser I get. I'm beginning to open my eyes and see the situation differently now. I am beginning to grow closer and closer to God and see things differently especially since I turned forty. I feel as if God is pulling me in a different direction, I feel like I'm supposed to be in a different place in my life. I don't know. I pray for a revelation. I guess it will come.

Now as for Damien Ross, Lord knows I seriously love me some him. That's my Bae. Although we have had numerous problems, this man is what I prayed for. I didn't love my ex-husband the way I love Damien. I think every woman has that *One Man*, that comes into your life, and just make you go crazy and lose yourself whether you marry him or not. Every woman has had one. If you haven't, you must be a lesbian, or he has not arrived in your life yet. I will say I met that man. I really don't know sometimes about him though, and Lord knows, we as women want to know everything half the time, that's our problem. I thought we would be married by now I can't lie after dating for five years. I thought he would have been more supportive when I had the miscarriage. I guess since so much has happened I have seen the real him. I haven't had time to talk to him about anything. I was still sad after the funeral and hurt to see Rylie heart-broken after her father's death. I was so depressed after the miscarriage I became isolated. Who has time to think about getting married? I must say living with someone before marriage does help. I have learned a lot about Damien since I moved in with him four years ago, both good and bad. But, the positive side outweighs the negative.

You see sometimes a woman will get accustomed to a man and his ways. I guess you can call it comfortable, because to be honest, I'm not satisfied. And ladies and gentleman there is a difference. The way he holds you, the way he treats you, and the way he talks to you. The little things you two do together. It becomes a part of your relationship. It is your relationship. You choose not to go through the preliminary stuff anymore and start over with anyone else anymore after you have given this man three to five years of your life. Also, I will say it over and over again I don't want to lose anyone else, I have lost enough, I am ready to win and I sure as hell don't want to train another man. Sometimes, I feel like I'm settling, I ignore what is right in front of my face even if I know it's wrong. See ladies and gentleman, Damien is a well-educated black man with a Bachelor's degree. He may be a little crazy as hell sometimes, but the brother is smart and has a very established career. He has tried to encourage me through all my trials, although, this is new to he and I. Damien was never encouraged by his parents. He said his dad criticized his mom all the time and his mom actually criticized him. I can say this, we may have our fights, our issues, our battles, but his lovemaking will make a sista pull her Bohemian or Malaysian weave straight from India, six hundred dollar sew-in, out her head two days after the sew in.

Sex is beyond wonderful, but we haven't been able to have it because of the miscarriage, there's a waiting period I told him. I really don't want to continue making love to him because I feel like if I stop some of the things I've been doing, I will get what I deserve. Even before the miscarriage, I was making up excuses not to have sex with him. I was avoiding him all the time. Damien is a good catch, he is super fine, caramel skin I call him *caramel latte*. Bowlegged, bald-headed, no kids well established with a nice *big* house, and note free on his two cars. Rides his motorcycle, plays dominoes, exercises with me, we text each other all day, and he is not a down-low brother! He also gives me his credit card every now and then. Oh yeah, he's a keeper! We also have similar backgrounds. We both love diverse foods and music; we both are goal oriented and both divorcees. He lost both of his parents ten years ago. I think he wants the same thing I want when it comes to marriage, but sometimes it's hard for men to express themselves. I really don't know what he believes. And I also don't know what Mamadoll is talking about. Every relationship has problems. He loves Rylie and I and begged us to move in with him, so we could grow together in our relationship. So, I decided to sell my house and move-in with him.

On the day I moved in he placed a *Tiffany* diamond ring on my finger, he said it's not an engagement ring, but that was coming soon. That was only four years ago. All I could say was it takes time. I can say that since I have moved in with him I have done a lot of soul-searching. I started attending this very nice, small church with maybe one hundred members. I begin to grow active in the ministry. Since I obtained my degree in communications, I created the church monthly newsletters. I chose to not be compensated to do the Lords work. I feel God will take care of what I need for helping his kingdom. I've also begun volunteering at hospitals and schools, or wherever I'm needed in the community. I enjoy keeping myself busy and I have a deep desire to help people that are going through tough times. Also, those who don't believe there is a way out. I see it as an opportunity to talk about the goodness of Jesus and what he's done for me, and how he will do the same for them if they will accept him. I believe this is why my lifestyle has convicted me. When it comes to religion or simply believing there is a God, Damien and I are opposite. He has never attended the church with my daughter and I. I honestly don't think he has been to a church since he's been an adult. Not to mention that he's 44 years of age. I ask him to go with Rylie and me, but he constantly refuses. He says he prays, but he never prays with me. The most important thing to me is his belief, because light and dark don't work well together. Also, how he interacts with my child, that's very important, and he is very good with her. When her father couldn't get her from school, Damien was always there. He gives her real nice gifts for birthdays and holidays. He teaches her how to cook, helps her with her homework, plays play-station, in the past, we always did family events together. For some reason, she is not very receptive to him. I often ask Rylie how she feels about him. She just says *'he's ok mom.* As long as you're happy, I'm happy.' I can appreciate that. I'm glad my well-being is a concern of hers, but I'm not selfish, it's not about me I often tell her. I glanced at my cell phone and the time is getting closer.

I'm so happy because the past few months have been hell for both of us. I think we both deserve to be happy. I pray for the situation to get better. I do know and believe prayer changes things, whether we like the outcome, or not of our situation prayer will change it regardless.

I decided to turn Pandora© on to listen to me some ole-school while I began getting dressed. It's going to be a wonderful evening, I keep telling myself.

I could hear the sound of the garage door open, and a sexy voice calls my name.

"Mina, Mina, baby girl where you at" Damien yelled.

That's the voice of my man. I love the sound of his voice. I ran downstairs of course to greet him.

"Hey, there handsome," I said with a big grin on my face. "Happy Anniversary and Happy New Year's to You!"

"Thank you and same to you doll face. You look so edible in that chemise," He then walked over and grabbed my face with both hands and gave me a passionate kiss, "Mmm, damn your kiss taste delightful."

"And your kisses taste like a chilled glass of red wine."

"Your kisses taste like, (he pauses), there isn't a word out there that can describe it," he said.

"That's your anniversary kiss stay tuned; more to come to you," channeling my version of a seductive voice.

"Oh, yeah! You mean to tell me, Mina Wright, I'm finally going to get me some. I can't believe it. I guess a brother only get some on holidays and anniversaries?" he replied sarcastically.

"No not holidays because remember you didn't get none on Thanksgiving or Christmas." Giving a little chuckle, Mina went on to say. "And don't start Damien. Baby you know these past months have been challenging for me."

"Mina, you don't start! I can't take the crying and emotional spats, not today," He said.

"Emotional spats? Excuse me. You haven't seen me all day and I am not having any emotional spats. You haven't seen me cry, you said it yourself, and plus there's nothing wrong with crying," I said.

"True, not today, so please change the subject," he asked.

"Sure. I've been trying to get ready since 4 o'clock so please allow me to continue," I said.

"Interesting." He became really quiet and looked confused then asked, "What held you back?"

I hesitated, because he and Mamadoll are not the best of friends. So I lied. "Laundry, and looking through some old photos of you and Rylie. I spoke very quietly and added, "And talking to my Mamadoll."

"Back down memory lane, I suppose. As for Mamadoll, I know she preached a good sermon today." He began to laugh loudly. "Yes, sir Mamadoll. Wait don't tell me, you two took up the offering, and had the alter call after her sermon. Let me guess now you are saved and sanctified," he said.

"Whatever Damien, she didn't save me for your information, Jesus did that," I said.

"I hear ya. I really don't feel like getting religious tonight; let's leave that for Sunday's. Now baby would you please play me some music that I want to hear and let me feel you, I just want to feel you? Put on my boys Jodeci and pour your daddy a drink, let's celebrate up in here, its New Year's Eve!"

I wasn't aware there were certain nights to be religious. He can be so funny at times. I quench at the thought of me some Damien. How I love these times. Rylie's gone for the night. I am happy. He is happy. We deserve this. I'm going to make him his favorite drink.

But which one would he like? I'm thinking is it Patron and sprite or Crown and coke, or straight, Grey Goose? I decided to make him a nice smooth drink, just how he likes it. Hennessey and Coke Cola!

"Here you go, hot chocolate," I smiled and said.

"You're not drinking? Come on Mina," he said.

"Okay. Okay. I'll have a glass of wine,"

"See, that's what I'm talking about, chilling, relaxing, pleasing your man, that's all I ask for, now come dance with me baby."

I walked over to dance with him. We were dancing having a really good time…for a minute or two.

"Oh yes. It's our anniversary," he said.

So we begin to dance with his drink in one hand and my glass of red wine in mine. He grabbed my hand that was free and smiled at me while he begins to pull me closer to him. We danced through one, no two, or maybe three songs. I was feeling kind of tipsy now because I was drinking my glass of wine as if it was a bottle of water and one hundred degrees outside. He looked into my eyes then he kissed me. This kiss was a deep passionate kiss, more intense this time with force and it felt soothing and delightful.

Then his tongue moved to my ear, then back and forth from my ear to my neck. Then he continued down to my breast, and he licked around my nipples, then down lower and lower to my waist, then my navel, then on my thighs. He opened my legs and placed them apart as he allowed his tongue to travel to my other lips. I was standing there with my eyes rolling in the back of my head. Jodeci song *Forever My Lady* begins to play. He looked up at me as he continued to enjoy himself. He stopped, but his hands continued to move. He asked, "Don't I make you feel good baby girl?"

I looked down at him into his eyes and responded, "Yes." I responded in a real soft voice.

Then he continued to lick faster and aggressively. He said, "Say yes daddy you make me feel good."

I was a good girl and obeyed his request, "Yes daddy, you make me feel good."

He then replied and asked; "You know you are forever my lady don't you?" So then I begin to kiss and rubbed on his baldhead. He put his finger in my mouth, and I begin to suck it. Before you know it, we were on the living room floor.

I caught myself and then I took his finger out my mouth real slow, and I asked him in a seductive voice, "Baby, since you say I'm forever your lady, why can't you make me forever you wife?"

Why did I go there? Jodeci stopped singing, and the drink didn't taste good anymore to Damien. He let every part of my body go. Then he looked at me with a *stank* look on his face, and I returned the same look waiting for an answer. Now here comes the real Damien.

"Party's over Mina. I'm going to take a shower," he said.

"C'mon answer me, Damien," I asked.

He turned around and looked at me like I was in a strait jacket. "No. I will not, you are always spoiling the moment Mina; we were having a good time, damn. Why did you have to take it there?"

"Why not?" I raised my voice and yelled, "Baby we are in a relationship Damien. We live together. We do everything together. Why can't I be able to ask my man whatever I feel like asking him?"

I can't believe I raised my voice. I am not afraid of the outcome and could care less or how he feels at this point. I want an answer.

"Mina, do you have a problem with your hearing? I said I was taking a shower, and change your tone in my house." He said.

"Your house?" I asked.

"Yes, my house, you sold yours, remember?"

Wow. How rude of him. Now I'm really angry.

"I have been living here for a year, and I helped you pay this house off remember? I think I can also call this my house." I said

"Truth hurts Mina. I know sweetie, but your name isn't on the deed." He said while he poured himself another drink.

WOW! I literally had a vision of slapping the shitaki out of him. Lord, please let me calm down. I will not allow your words to ruin this night for me. I begin to walk up the stairs.

"Mina would you like to have another drink, you seem a little upset," he said. I continued to walk upstairs.

"Mina, can you hear?"

I turned around. "I'm sorry. I was ignoring you. Did you say something? I asked.

"I called your name. You know every time you talk to Mamadoll your ass act funny, this is not Mamadoll's house, or relationship, this is mine. Now would you like a drink?"

"No, I don't want another drink."

"What? You done drinking?" He asked sarcastically. "The party was just getting started. Because I don't want to talk about marriage you walk off. You need to go on with that mess," Damien said.

"With what mess? I don't understand that statement, what are you talking about."

"What do you think I'm calling mess? You're holier than thou...I love the Lord, but I am having sex and giving my man whatever he wants, and I'm not married. Oh, but you are the first one in church every Sunday. Screaming to me on a Saturday night, I can't miss church," Damien said.

"You are being judgmental! At least I go to church."

"That's exactly what you do. You go to church, and come home, and do the same thing you did before you left for church...hahaha." He said.

"I haven't had sex with you?" it became quiet. "How about this Damien, maybe I should change everything I'm doing, including my living arrangement,"

Damien stands up and walks over to me. Now we are face to face. "What are you talking about now hypocrite!" he said in a slow mean voice.

"Do you know how to spell hypocrite?" I asked.

"I'm so tired of that ghetto sarcastic mouth of yours, you always act like you're going to leave me or something, change your living arrangement Mina go right ahead, do you boo," he said.

"Damien you always want to pick a fight with me when I ask you about marriage. Be a grown man, and just say either you do, or don't, instead of picking a fight. It's very immature and I'm tired of it." I said as I turned to walk up the stairs.

"A grown man?" He asked surprised. "What the hell you mean you're tired of it? Come back here now Mina and explain yourself," he yelled.

"Oh goodness, here we go. It's our anniversary." I turned around and took a step down the stairs. "You never let me finish Damien when I bring up marriage, you never want to talk about it."

"I'm not going to talk about it now," he said.

"Dammit Damien, stop. Stop it. This is childish. We are no longer children. We are adults. I don't want to keep shacking, and I'm not going to keep shacking with you. There you have it," I said.

Damien was quiet. I turned to walk upstairs. "Mina, no need to get dressed, I'm not feeling you or your attitude. Change of plans, we're not going anywhere and I'm not giving you your gift; it will not be a Happy New Year's for neither one of us now. You ruined it!" Damien said.

"I ruined it?" I cannot believe him! NO! I'm sick of this shit. I'm not staying here tonight. NO! It's New Year's Eve?

"No, no, no sir.... you are wrong…you mean you aren't going anywhere. But as for me, I'm going upstairs to get dressed, and you feel in the blank." I said.

He didn't say one word. He mean-mugged me out the corner of his eye as I walked up the stairs and away from such ignorance. I wanted to cry, I wanted to scream, I wanted to slap the shitaki out of him, but I couldn't. At this moment all of these emotions on top of other emotions are going through me right now.

It's an *I hate you emotion* + But *damn I love you emotion* + Oooo *I can't stand your ass emotion* + I'm *sick of his shit and this relationship emotion* =a sum of What's *keeping me here then emotion*?

I know for a fact he picked a fight with me on purpose, and I know my feeling is right. God does not allow his children to be ignorant. I went into the bedroom to finish getting pretty, not for him, not for anyone else, but for myself. It's not an anniversary, I'm not married, and I'm tired of someone who can't appreciate my worth. I am Royalty.

As I stand in this mirror I'm thinking you are a strong beautiful queen, if I don't see the queen in me, no one else will either. People, whether it is a woman or man will treat you how you allow them too. I'm going out tonight with or without him and I will have me a good time.

I texted my best friend Naiomi to let her know everything was still as planned. I don't want her to worry, and I really don't want her to know what just happened. She is like a sister to me. I know God put our friendship together. She and her husband are the best. Their marriage, their relationship is beautiful. We both attend the same church and her daughter and Rylie have become the best of friends. I met her fourteen years ago when I was working part-time at the bank. We have been friends ever since. She has been married for eighteen years, they have been through their ups n downs, but through it all, and they maintained their love for one another and stayed together. I believe that is what a true relationship is about. When you truly love someone you both fight, the bible said two is better than one, you can't fight in a relationship alone you both have to want it, and that's including marriage.

I'm all dressed now and looking stunning If I do say so myself. I walked out the room looking like a ten-in-a-half, not just a ten. I wore my long, fitting black maxi dress, with one shoulder out and a gold buckle belt. I wore my Jimmy Choo black pumps. My makeup is flawless with a mixture of Nars, Anastacia, and MAC. My hips standing at attention, and my twins (breast) are saying heyyy...in a good way. I walked downstairs and I never looked his way. He was sipping on his drink undressed sitting naked on the couch. Uggg. He makes me sick. I know he didn't think I was going to come down these stairs to give him some, shame on him.

As I approach the front door I see him out the corner of my eye. This brother thinks when he uses the restroom, gold comes out his body parts. No, wait a minute; I'm sorry platinum. I walked past him stepping real loud in my stilettos on the hardwood floor. I wanted him to look at what he was going to miss tonight. He never turned around to look. ASSHOLE! I opened the door to walk out, and out of his mouth, he called my name.

"Mina," he said in a low baritone voice.

Something on the inside of me known as my spirit told me to continue to walk out the door, and do not turn around. But this is my man, we have history, five years history, and It's only an argument, and I know he loves me and I know he is going to want me to stay with him while he gets dressed, and I'm so tired of the word, *and* because I have used it so many times. That means I'm just making excuses. I am the bigger person. I turned around and looked him into his eyes.

"Yes, Damien," I said nicely.

He stood up then turned around as if he was going to walk upstairs. This brother said. "I hate that you're going to miss out on this super-hot link basket," he says as he looks down at his penis. "So I guess my DVD and my hand will be taking your place tonight and screaming Happy New Year's."

As I rolled my eyes up in my head, reaching for the front door. He called my name again. "I have to be somewhere, I have reservations," I said

"Don't get in too late, or you will be locked out."

I was thinking, Lord, bless me to hold my peace, "The LORD is my shepherd; I shall not want" (Psalm 23). Ye though I walk through the valley of death I should fear no evil, God is my fortress, my refuge a very present help...I stood there and quoted every scripture I could remember to keep from sending this man home with his maker, the enemy. But I couldn't hold it for long, me and my mouth.

"You can lock whatever door you want too, boo, boo. Because who said I was coming back tonight?"

I turned and proceeded out the door; again, me with my big mouth. "Oh before I forget, have a Happy New Year with your hand and your DVD."

I jumped in my vehicle. I'm so glad Rylie is over Naiomi's house and didn't witness this mess. I turned the radio up as loud as I could. How convenient Big Sean, "I don't f…with you" was playing on the radio. I rolled the windows to my car down, as I drove out the driveway! That's how I feel. I'm so angry and fed up I couldn't cry if I wanted too. I hear my phone ringing. I know it's him, and I am not going to answer this phone. I look down… and it's not him, its Mamadoll calling me. I'm thinking I love you to death Mamadoll but now is not the time. I don't feel like going to church right now. I sent her to voice mail and ignored the call and kept driving.

I drove up to the restaurant where we had reservations. I valet parked. I want to be pampered tonight. My emotions settled down. I glanced up at the sky as it was dark crisp blue, and the moon is shining brightly. I hear soft jazz playing as I approached the door. A text message sound came through my phone; I knew he was going to text me.

Hey girl, I know you're having fun…love you. I know you're going to respond to that important wedding date it's about time...IM WAITING…LOL. If I don't speak with you, have a Happy New Year and tell Damien hello for me!

It's my bestie, Naiomi. I almost burst out in tears, but again could not cry. There comes a time in your life where you can't cry anymore after so many trials and so many struggle. You are simply fed up! My soul is tired. So as for tonight, I'm leaving that situation outside, this situation will not be going on the inside of the restaurant with me or into the New Year. Good-bye Issues. Hello to a beautiful night and Happy New Year!

As I walked into the restaurant there were couples everywhere. Coupled up, smiling! Shit! Here I am alone. Oh well, it's too late. I'm here now. A gentleman greeted me with a big smile and, "Happy New Year," I liked that part, but then his first question out his mouth is, *will you be dining alone?* It sounded as if he was echoing, *ouch! I didn't know if I wanted him to call the ambulance now for the question, which felt like a bullet, or wait until later after I answered.*

"Yes, I will be dining alone," I said with the biggest fake smile.

"Oh no, I didn't expect that answer. Well tell me beautiful do you have reservations?

"Yes, I have reservations the name is Mina Wright?"

"Mina Wright? Where do I know that name from?"

"I don't know." I paused. "Maybe because I come in here often for lunch." I said with a slight chuckle.

"No, No it's probably from the best well written religious columnist in the city of Dallas." A voice appeared out of no- where. I turned around and surprisingly out of all restaurants there stood my editor and chief, Terrance Boyd. Why tonight Lord?

"Terrance! What a surprise."

"Mina! I was thinking the exact same thing. I'm surprised to see you here tonight?"

"Is there someone else dining with you tonight Ms. Wright? Is there more to your party?" The hostess asked you the same thing." Terrance said with a big grin on his face.

I giggled nervously. I ignored the host and answered around Terrance questions.

"Well, this is one of my favorite restaurants'. I love the food here and of course, the atmosphere is wonderful on a night like this and I thought I would grab me a nice dinner."

"Alone?" He responded.

"Why would you think I would be dining alone?"

"Because you used the noun "I" when you said you would be grabbing a nice dinner."

I didn't want to answer him and didn't feel I needed too. I was embarrassed. I cleared my throat. I looked away for a second in hopes that maybe, just maybe, after five years Damien would put aside his anger and walk through the door. But there I was hoping. I said I wouldn't bring that mess in here and I'm not.

"I enjoy being alone, and I had a change of plans tonight, so here I am." Dammit, Mina that was terrible, I mean terrible answer.

He stepped a little closer to me and whispered in my ear, "Well would you like some company? There is a gentleman standing in front of you that would like to have dinner with you."

I looked over at the entrance door again. Hell, it's a new year. I didn't hesitate. I looked over at the hostess, "the other party is here now."

The hostess smiled. "Well, let's get this party started, follow me you two."

He led the two of us to the back of the restaurant to a quiet dim area. A young woman appeared out of know where playing the saxophone.

We sat down in a booth with candles lit on the table. He didn't hesitate when it came to the questions.

"Why are you alone tonight?" Terrance asked.

"Excuse me? Well, I chose to be."

"But why? It's New Year's Eve. Why would someone so beautiful like you be alone?"

"I said the same thing about you. Why would someone so handsome be alone?"

"Because I'm tired of the bullshit. Ready for something new." He responded without hesitation.

"Oh, you too?"

"Of course! Everyone gets tired of arguing and shit. You want to have a good time and chill, I mean its New Year's fu…. Eve."

"I agree, but I'm not here to talk about how I got here, the fact is I'm here and I'm ready to enjoy my night."

"Let's enjoy it together. What are we drinking beautiful?" Terrance asked.

"I'll take two Cosmos, double shot of Grey Goose in each," I said.

"Whoa, I like it! I'll have the same." Terrance told the waiter.

He then moved a little closer to me. "Damn you look good. I remember looking at you at work and fantasizing about you. I've never been with a black woman before."

"Terrance I see you are not afraid of words and you didn't waste any time."

With a slight smile, Terrance replied, "Why would I be? If the opportunity appears in front of you, reach for it and grab it."

"Oh is this an opportunity?" The waitress brought over our drinks.

"Mmm, yes it is, sweetie. For the both of us."

I blushed. I was admiring the compliments, even if it was bullshit flowing out his mouth, he knew the right thing to say, but don't they all in the beginning. I must admit Terrance was extremely eye-candy. He was at least 6'3. Blonde hair, smooth tanned skin, and built like a professional athlete with a nice low haircut. He always dressed in those expensive suits.

"I never knew you paid attention Terrance. You were always about business and so busy when I would stop by your office."

"Well Mina, we had deadlines to meet, and I knew you had a boyfriend. Besides, I knew my situation was complicated as hell."

"That's right, you are dating Raquel, the Human Resources Coordinator."

"We were dating. We took a break." He winked at me. "If you know what I mean."

"Oh, I know what you mean?"

"Cheers!" He said as we both took a drink. Then we had another drink, and another, and another.

"Terrance tell me why are we having a meeting tomorrow on New Year's Eve? Couldn't that have waited until next week?"

He took another shot. "I don't want to talk about work. But I will say this. You don't have to worry about anything, Mocha Mamma."

Did he just call me Mocha Mamma? It was two minutes till midnight and we both were tipsy. We were having a great time. Laughing and reminiscing about old times, and of people we once worked with. The countdown began and Terrance rubbed my leg underneath the table and then his finger slowly progressed to my inner thigh.

"Let's go party. I want to bring in the New Year with a smile on my face."

"Let's go."

We proceeded to the dance floor as he grabbed my hand to lead. Before you knew it, everyone was screaming, "Happy New Year's!"

We danced to the music and I was tipsy as hell. Terrance was also.

He begins to dance closer and closer to me. My body against his body, his body against mine, rubbing those hands and moving those hands. The music was playing and his hand was moving all over my body and I was enjoying it. To be honest, I forgot I was on the dance floor. We made our way back to the table and I began taking more and more shots and he was too.

"Hey, Mina and Terrance." I heard out of no-where. We both looked around to see who was calling our name.

"Hey, Cain. Happy New Year!" We both said loud, as we smiled and waved.

Terrance whispered in my ear. "Mina I will be right back." He then kissed me on my cheek.

"You drinking Cain? I got you."

"Oh yes T, get me a Scotch straight up."

"Got you, Cain. And I got you, Ms. Mina." He licked his lips and walked away.

Cain pushed me on my arm. "You sexy bitch you. What are you doing here? Are you here with Terrance?"

"No, No Cain we saw one another. We're just enjoying the music. Having a good time," I'm thinking he is so messy.

"Oh, really I couldn't tell the way his hands were all over you on the dance floor, and the way you were smiling," Cain giving a slight chuckle as he went on to say, "I said this Bitch trying to keep her J.O.B."

"What? Oh please, I was never worried about my job."

"Oh really. Well, I am, bitch. I need to keep my car, I am already two notes behind."

"Well, they said it's just an announcement."

"Mmm...that's what they said. But girl you know, we are the last ones left, and we're Black."

"Cain, don't worry, we will be fine. Our color has nothing to do with it," she said with a smile on her face.

"Boo, please. Oh shit, here he comes."

We both smiled big, and in one voice. "Hey, Terrance."

"Alright lets party. Cain you joining us?"

"Well, I hadn't planned on it. But I can, or I can just see you both tomorrow." Cain then laughed nervously.

"Well at least have a shot with us."

"Of course."

We all toasted and sipped up. Cain coughed a little.

"Whew! I will not have a throat left if I continue drinking that sh…"

Terrance then begins to whisper in my ear. "Stay with me tonight Mina."

I was tipsy as hell. But is he asking me to stay with him? I continued to bounce to the music as his eyes were glued to my movements. I gyrated even more in my tight fitted dress on the seat of the booth. Terrance's tongue waddled out his mouth. I was already feeling myself, and this New Year. I kept sipping on my drink having a good time. Then I noticed Cain staring at me.

"I'll be back." Cain said.

I kept having a good time. Then suddenly I felt something wet, and it was moving fast then slow. It began moving up and down my leg real slow and then closer to my inner thigh. It felt so good, as the music slowed down. My bounce began to slow down, as I gyrated my body to the beat of the music. I looked over and didn't see Terrance. Then this warm, but wet feeling continued to move further up my thigh and even closer to my private area. As I lifted the tablecloth up, I could see the top of Terrance's blond hair moving up and down slightly. I was speechless. I didn't know what to do. I was hoping no one saw us as I took in this amazing, but oh so guilty feeling. Looking around, I noticed everyone still partying. Cain was nowhere in sight. I began to squirm a bit, because it felt so good. I had never experienced this before in a public setting. My goodness, he was very hungry down there.

I noticed the waiter approaching the table. "Would you like another drink?"

I couldn't speak in that moment, because he was hitting my spot. "Oh, oh, oh," I moaned as he continued. I tried pulling away, but he took his hands and gripped both of my butt cheeks from behind and pulled me in closer. Closing my legs a bit, I paused and responded, "Nooo sirrr," I said while breathing deeply.

"Ok. Do you think the gentleman would like something, I can have it ready for him when he returns?"

I wish he would go away.

"Yes, I would like one more drink," this voice cried out from underneath the table.

I was so embarrassed. Oh my God! I am speechless. I turned beet red as the waiter glanced down at the table with a smirk on his face.

"I'll be right back to watch," shaking his head, "I mean, with his drink." The waiter said as he walked away.

I'm at a loss for words, to describe how I was feeling in this moment. Terrance lifted his head and came from underneath the table. He wiped his face, from the milkshake he siphoned from out of me. As the waiter was making his way back to the table, I glanced over at Terrance. He smiled at me as the waiter placed his drink on the table.

"I brought you a drink as well. It's on the house." The waiter said, as he gave this eerie wink.

I took that drink and tossed it back as if it was a shot glass.

"You tasted wonderful. Come to my room. I have a room upstairs. Let's get this New Year started right."

Without hesitation, I asked, "What's the room number?"

"Two, zero, one, five!"

"Room twenty fifteen," I asked.

"Yes."

"I will see you there."

"Waiter. Check please." Terrance said as he signaled the waiter.

I can't believe I'm doing this. I have never cheated on Damien. I sat there as Terrance walked away. I went to the restroom for a second. I looked down at my phone. No calls. It was 1:30 am. No Happy New Year's.

I walked slowly out the restaurant and to the elevator. I pressed the button for the 20th floor. I walked down the hallway, stopping in front of room twenty fifteen. I paused. Then knocked. He opened the door. As I made my way in, Terrance began taken his clothes off. I had myself another drink. I wanted to feel good and good I felt.

Terrance asked me to lie face down. And I did. Terrance took his hands to spread my butt cheeks apart. He began licking me from behind. His fingers were everywhere his tongue was. I gripped the sheet tightly. After, what felt like a lifetime of four-play; it was time for the real deal. I asked him did he have a condom, he continued to lick the middle of my assets. He stopped and then began again with his finger, again, and again. Now it had been close to an hour of four-play. But who's counting it was feeling good. I gave him a shower to the face and then he turned me over I breastfed him like a newborn baby. He had both of my hands bonded together, as he held them. Eagerly waiting to have some of his prime ribs. He continued to eat away at me. He rose up, grabbling for the condom. Oh Yes. It's going down. I thought to myself.

He took his fingers and kept fondling me. I sort of glanced over at the clock on the table and an hour had passed. He was still licking and sucking. He went from the breast to the toes. Another hour had passed and he was still licking. I guess his tongue doesn't get tired. He rose up a little and then put the condom on. It was dark. I began to talk to him.

"Let me ride you baby," I asked. He didn't answer. Before I knew it, he was humping on top me so fast, and then he began to shake, quenched and screamed. I wanted to scream too, but I didn't have a reason to. I was confused.

"I'm ready Terrance. Baby put it in. I want to scream and shake too."

He then went back downtown licking. I became real aggressive at this point. "No baby, I want some meat."

He looked up, "I just gave it to you. I came. Didn't you?"

"You what? You put it in?"

"Yes Mina, I'm sorry. Let me make it up to you. It was so good darling." He said as he continued to give me oral sex.

Oh, my goodness. My first time cheating on Damien and the fact that I haven't had sex in months and this is what I get? Is this a joke? He tried to use the 'it was so damn good' line. Fine as his body is. He then got up. "I need to use the restroom," he said smiling, "I'm still on hard so stay here sweetness. You are great. My goodness. Whew, what a way to bring in the New Year!"

As he got up, I got a real good look at his penis. He was still on hard and it was the size of one Oscar Mayer Wiener still in the package, uncooked. This is why I didn't feel it. I quickly gathered my clothes and began to wipe myself off with items in my purse. I was not impressed at all. I was going home. He served his purpose.

"Mina where are you going doll, its four am?"

"We have had a great night but I am going home. You know I still live with someone?"

"I do know that. I do also, but not for long. Can I walk you down the stairs?"

"I would like that."

"You know I enjoyed your company. Thank You."

"It's all good. I think we both needed that." I didn't want to tell him the truth about how I was really feeling.

He walked me down to the elevators. "I can take it from here," I said.

"Are you sure? When can I see you again?"

"Well, you will see me later today."

"I'm not talking about at work Mina. I want to see you away from work. I want some more. Sweetie, I enjoyed you."

"We will talk Terrance."

"I'll see you at the office." He smiled as the elevator door closed.

Wow, the Pinky penis man, smh. I finally made my way home. It was 4:31, as I pulled into the driveway. I went in through the front door instead of the garage. I decided not to go upstairs. I walked in the house and didn't attempt to go into the bedroom. I grabbed a blanket from the closet and lay on the couch. Kicked those stilettos off and plopped down on the couch fully clothed and fell into a peaceful sleep.

Chapter 2. Are you fed up Now?...

The sound of my cell phone woke me up. I opened my eyes to the bright sunlight shining in through the window. I looked at my phone to see who was calling me and of course, it's my aunt, but I saw I had also had 4 smiley faces text messages from Terrance, the pinky man.

"Good morning, Happy New Year!" I said as I answered the phone.

"Good morning sunshine," Mamadoll said.

"Oh Lord, what time is it?" I screamed.

Detecting the excitement in my voice, Mamadoll replied, "Calm down, calm down, its 9:13 my time, and I believe we are on the same time zone."

"I'm sorry Mamadoll. Oh my goodness. I overslept. I need to get ready for work. I have to be there at one," I said.

"At one? On New Year's Day?" She asked.

"Yes, remember, they have an announcement and I have a deadline for the New Year's football game. It needs to be completed by tonight for the early edition tomorrow." I said.

"I understand. Well whatever happens Mina, you can always come home. How was last night?"

Here she go again, early in the morning. "It went great," I said.

"Well did he propose?" she asked.

I looked around the house to see if Damien was around. "I don't want to talk about Damien. Not this morning, I haven't brushed my teeth, or had my coffee." I said rudely.

"Mina, I know you just woke up, but I felt funny in spirit last night, I could not stop thinking about you, I prayed for you all night. Is everything ok, are you, and the baby ok?" She asked.

I was thinking I know you felt funny in your spirit, because I was a very bad girl. "Yes, we're fine. I have decided to make some changes."

"Change is mandatory sometimes, and good in most cases," she said.

"Mamadoll you have your life, and I have my life, let me handle my situation. No disrespect, but I blame myself. I already told you too much, and I need for you to support me, I need support from you, can you give me that please."

"Yes, I can. We are going to start the New Year off right. I feel like I'm supporting by giving you the right advice." She said.

My other line clicked. I looked down at my phone. It was Terrance. What does his ass want?

"Hello," I said in low tone voice.

"Good morning beautiful. I can still taste you," He said with a smile in his voice.

Oh Lord, did he just say that! I cleared my throat and changed the subject quickly, because I don't know if Damien is here or not.

"Are you ready for today? For this big announcement?" I asked.

"I know I'm ready to put my tongue in you again. Are you ready for my tongue, baby?"

Is he serious? His tongue? I'm glad he didn't ask me about his penis. I guess he knew better. He didn't give me time to respond.

"Didn't you enjoy me, last night?" His voice became deep. He started breathing heavy and hard. "I wanttt youuu. Meet me before heading into the meeting?"

I was thinking hell no! I cleared my throat. "I can't. I really need to take a shower and get ready for today? We can talk later, ok."

"What's the problem?" he asked.

Damn, he is aggressive. Before responding. I begin to walk around the house to see if Damien was anywhere in sight. I started upstairs. He was nowhere around. I should have known, because that brother wouldn't miss a day of work if Jesus were returning today.

As I continued to look around the house, doesn't look as if he slept here either. The bed was perfect. The bathroom is spotless. It looks the same as it did last night.

"Mina?"

I forgot he was holding. "I'm here. I tell you what. Let me see you at the office."

"Are you going to meet me?" Terrance asked.

"Look. I will talk to you at work. I just woke up and last night was good." I begin to whisper. But not now."

"After work. No exceptions. And where your heels to work by the way?"

Is he serious? "Ok." I tried to hurry him off the phone.

"Why are you rushing me, sweetie? Was it good to you?"

Oh Lord is he serious. He is annoying me right now.

I thought I heard a noise coming from the kitchen area.

"Let's see each other at work,"

"Fine," He said as we both hung up.

I ran downstairs and it was the trashcans that fell over leading to the alley. I shut the garage door, which Damien apparently left open, and ran back upstairs to take me a hot shower. On my way to work I thought about going back home to Charlotte and just moving my things out of Damien house and putting them in storage, and when he gets home he will see I'm gone. I'm leaving him. I will start the New Year off right, hopefully, after last night Terrance will promote me. I will find Rylie and me, a nice rent house. I thought well maybe I will text him, and ask him to meet me for lunch after the announcement, and I will tell him I'm moving out. Mina, stop thinking about it, think about something else and just do it. I am going to be a lady, and do it decently and in order, and I'm not going to play that game of, can we still be friends. I know he will be home around 8 o'clock. I will tell him tonight once Rylie is sleep, because I don't want her to see any drama if this Negro act a fool on me. Hell, he probably is going to say ok, no problem, the way he's been acting. I drove down the highway and a few minutes later, my thoughts begin to change. I started thinking on good things, and wondering what if I did move back home to Charlotte? I know Mamadoll would see that we had a roof over our head without a doubt. I could probably get on with the local newspaper there and write columns. Kia is still one of my best friends and the biggest evangelist there, and I would love to hang out with her and help her with her ministry. But, I sure would miss Naiomi and Javier. They are my family. Then again, it also would be a new beginning for the both of us.

  I pulled into the parking lot of my job. I feel good. And whatever happens- happens. I will stay calm, I thought to myself. Well we know now That was a lie. Not even two hours later, I let Terrance have it verbally, packed up my office, and walked out. That's right, the pinky penis terminated my ass, or did I fire myself by not taking the receptionist position? Either way it's done.

  After it was all over, I drove around town for a while. I wanted to start my New Year off on a good note, not in a bad mood. Once, I finally make it to Naiomi house as I pulled into the driveway I instantly saw my baby girl running out the house.

  "Momma how was your date night? You and Damien getting married?" Rylie asked as she gleamed into my eyes.

  Kids and teenagers say and ask whatever they want. Why did that have to be the first question out her mouth?

  "Can you say hi first, and give me a hug?" I asked.

  "Sorry. Hi mommy,"

  "Did you enjoy yourself?" I asked

  "Yes, we had a lot of fun. I watched an old video of you at my baby shower, you were so happy momma and your stomach was huge." She said.

"It sure was. That's usually what happens when you're pregnant with a turkey."

"Well hello, there missy," Naiomi said. "I only text you ten times, and you didn't respond, I thought I was going to have to call 911."

With a grin on my face, I responded, "No. I knew it wasn't an emergency. You kept texting me smiley faces and saying wyd?"

"You look great Mina. I made us lunch. Let's sit down, and please give me some details about last night and the big announcement they had at the job today. I pray all good." Naiomi said.

I looked at Rylie, Naiomi looked at her daughter. Both understood it was time for grown-ups to talk.

"We will only be a minute girls, I promise,"

"Yeah, right mama," Rylie replied.

I sat down at Naiomi's table while she made some ice tea. "Damien canceled our plans last night, I brought in the New Year with my boss, aka pinky penis. I go into the office this morning to discover that he demoted me. So, I then quit."

Naiomi didn't flinch. She walked from the kitchen, over to her bar, and went from making ice tea with lemon to ice tea with a shot of my favorite.

"So I guess it was good to him, but not you," Breaking out into laughter.

I also began to laugh. I kept laughing. For a minute, it seemed as though I couldn't stop..

I began to tell Naiomi about my night, "Well first off I did not have dinner with my roommate. Actually, my night did a whole 360 turn on me. I ran into someone you would never believe!"

"Wait a minute, wait a minute," Naiomi stands up with both her hands in the air. "I'm confused, what happened, you didn't have dinner with Damien." Was he in one of those moods again Mina?" She asked.

I paused for a second and gathered my thoughts. I saw Naiomi drop her head and exhaled a really deep breath. I really don't want to talk about Damien and his unexpected behavior on our anniversary night. The more I talk about Damien, the more I begin to dislike him, my situation, and it makes me very emotional and I'm tired of crying.

"Please have a seat. There was a disagreement. That being said, you know how my mouth is girl. One thing led to another so he decided not to join me for dinner, but I went anyway." I said

"Alone?" She screamed and stood up again with her hands folded.

"Yes ma'am alone," I said.

"Good for you, and I'm not saying this because you are my best friend for life, I mean it. You have been through too much these last few months, and he needs to be more supportive, not the one causing problems," she said.

"You know the funny thing is it didn't even bother me this time like in the past times. Remember how I would act after an argument whether or not it was my fault? I would cater to him, text him all day, always the first to apologize. I think out of the five years we have been together he may have apologized once, maybe twice.

Before I knew it, there I was talking about Damien. "I don't care anymore, Naiomi. Do you know I have not spoken to him since I left last night?"

"So, since you haven't talked to him, he doesn't know you lost your job?"

"I fired myself. I didn't want to be hisss receptionist."

"Same thing," Naiomi said with a smile on her face.

"No. He doesn't know. This morning I didn't see him. I went to the office and met with Terrance, and here I am."

"Here you are. Looking fabulous. Feeling fabulous. Started your year off right.

"Off right?"

"Haven't you been praying for change?"

"Yes."

"There you have it."

"I didn't want to lose my job!"

"Well, you should have been hisss receptionist," She said in a sexy voice.

"No. I was not about to be his receptionist." I said as the silence began to take over the room for a minute. Then I began to glance out the window.

"You are tired. But also, you are growing Mina. And with growth comes pain. You have grown spiritually I can see it. You're not afraid to be alone anymore, or, of what the outcome will be if you don't cater to him, or apologize to him, or if you end up alone for a few years. Remember our talks. Sometimes that is the way God designs it. He has to get our attention with no distractions, when he is trying to fulfill his purpose for your life. He will remove those that do not belong in your life or those that cannot go with you on your journey. It will be painful, but we know that all things work together for good, and for those who love the Lord" She said.

Naiomi, to be honest, I did not want to hear people say I told you so. It will never work if you live together before marriage. I just wanted to believe that Damien was the one for me, and I've seen many couples live together before marriage and it worked out."

"You said you didn't want to hear what people had to say. Ha! Who are these people?" she asked. "Honey please allow me to tell you about people. People will go through hell in a relationship, and you will never know. They will not tell you that part, and Mina we know what the bible says so stop looking at what others do. This is your life, your journey, your purpose, this is what God is doing with YOU!" she said.

Whew. I wonder if she's going to call a timeout now and decide to take a water break. "You're right Naiomi, geez. You sound like Mamadoll, and your only 45 years old. You ladies have a lot of wisdom," I said.

"It comes from growing, and learning from making mistakes, but also following Gods lead. We need to allow him to order our steps. The reason I say, allow him, is because when you allow him, that means you trust in him, not yourself. It's like telling an experienced airline pilot move over I can fly this plain when the pilot has told you, he can get you to your destination, if you just trust him. But you get in the seat and want to fly anyway. Then you wonder why you never get to your destination. Maybe because you are not the pilot," she said.

"Wow Naiomi, I like that. I never thought of it that way."

"You know why?" she asked.

"Why?" I asked.

"We want what we want no matter what God has told us or showed us. It's like God is saying trust me, and do it my way and I will give you what you need. I will give you the right man, the right career, peace of mind, joy, and much more," she said.

I gave her the biggest hug. "We love you and Rylie. Mina, it's not fussing, it's love."

I grabbed Rylie and proceeded to the car. As I drove out the driveway I looked in my rearview mirror. Naiomi and her children were waving goodbye from their front yard. I thought about God, and how amazing He is. I didn't have any family here in Dallas, only Rylie's dad. And God hooked the two of us up as friends; he knew I would need someone like her. God always has our best interest.

Raindrops began to drop on my windshield before I was out of her neighborhood good. I looked over at Rylie; she was looking out the window with a smile on her face. It feels so good to see her smile again.

"What are you smiling about gorgeous," I asked.

"God. He is smiling at us," She said.

"Yes, he is," I said.

"How was your anniversary?" she asked.

"It was ok," I said.

"Just ok mom." She asked with a look of curiosity on her face.

I cleared my throat. I am not about to talk about this again, and especially not to a thirteen-year-old.

"You know Rylie you are not to live with a man you're only dating and call your boyfriend before marriage," I said.

"Yes, I know. Daddy told me. And you say it all the time mom. So why did we move in with him," she asked.

"That's a question I am asking myself, watch and learn from momma," I said.

"Well is that the reason you two argue a lot," She asked.

"It could be, or maybe we're just not meant to be," I said.

It was quiet for a minute, "its ok mom to be alone. That just gives us time to be together more," She smiled and said.

"Your right baby. Rylie, I have asked you this before, how do you feel about Damien?"

She didn't hesitate, "He's ok mom, I tell you that all the time," she said.

"Just ok?" I asked.

"Momma he is nothing like my dad, but he is nice to me. I really don't like the way he talks to you sometimes, and when you talk about getting married he always changes the subject… always mom," she said.

Wow, she said that like she was waiting for me to ask. Kids pay attention to everything when we are not paying attention as adults.

"Well, once we get home I want you to start packing some of your clothes and putting some items in boxes. There are boxes in the garage. I'm about to make some changes, I hope you understand, I know you have been through a lot but it's best for the both of us." I said.

"Mom I'm ok. I know I will see my dad again in heaven. I feel it. Momma just does what's best for us, and I know you will. I just hope the change is for the better, and I hope the school will be fun," She said.

"We will cross that bridge, when we get to it. And change is good baby-girl. The best is yet to come, you just wait and see, God is about to do something big in our life," I said. We looked at each other and smiled. It started sprinkling once again, as I drove into our subdivision. As I turned the corner, down the street I saw cars slowing down and hitting their breaks.

What the hell! I screamed.

Chapter 3: It's a Done Deal...

  I ran the car on the curb in a panic. I cannot remember placing the car in park, but what I do remember is my eyes and the unbelief they were seeing. My eyes locked with Damien's as he stood in the driveway of our home. As I ran towards him I remember running by every piece of furniture and clothing I owned. My sixty-inch plasma flat screen television, my ninety-two thousand mink coat, Gucci shoes, Louis Vuitton™ luggage, all my clothes, Rylie's clothes, and other items sitting in a wet yard. He put everything I owned in the yard. EVERYTHING! But, to make matters worse, of all the things, my daughter's expensive bedroom furniture her daddy bought her two weeks, I mean exactly two weeks before his death. I lost it. My mind is telling me it's real, but my heart does not want to believe it, or receive it. You want to believe an argument, a disagreement, would not go this far because that is not the way you would have handled it. You would have simply talked with your other half, your man; you're boo, by sitting down with him like a forty-year-old woman and a forty-four-year-old mature Adult would do. BUT, when you are dealing with, half man/half teenager, spoiled, selfish, immature 44-year-old, ladies and gentleman this is what you get in return. Also, ladies and gentleman, this is the definition of a woman who is not thinking clearly.

  "DAMIENNNN! I yelled his name so loud I believe the house windows cracked. Not far behind me is Rylie walking.

  "Mom, our stuff, my furniture, my iPad, my TV, and PlayStation, MOM do something." Rylie is saying hysterically.

  "Rylie get back in the car right now. Dammit, Damien what the hell have you done? Huh? You asshole! Its Over! Over! You put my child and my belongings in the yard? Really? You are such a coward! Why would you put my shit in the yard huh...ANSWER ME?" I was screaming.

  Damien walked towards me from the garage. He had a sarcastic smile on his face and was shaking, from side to side, his finger at me. He begins clapping his hands as if he was at a show applauding.

  "My, my Mina you appear to be angry," he said.

  I gave him a real nasty look; I mean a stanky look. I calmed down and took a deep breath, "Oh really? Do I seem angry to you? I mean you only put my belongings in the yard, now why would I be angry huh? Do you know that REAL MEN communicate with their mate? But that's a trait that you evidently don't know anything about since your dad whopped on your mama ass, all the time and then said I love you." I said.

He had that evil I know you want to slap me smirk on his face again. "Are you sure I don't know anything about communication? Or is it that you know how to talk to everyone else, but me." He said.

"What the hell are you talking about Damien? Everyone else?" I asked.

He turned around and began speaking to a few neighbors who was standing outside as if he was on stage performing. "Everyone, everyone, I mean everybody I have an announcement to make, so listen up. I decided not to go to work today." He looked back at me with an evil smirk. Mina assumed she was at home alone, that's her fault for assuming. Mina thought she was so smart when she decided to communicate with her new boyfriend. I called him, mayonnaise man. Her newbie, whom she explained, how unhappy she was. The boyfriend she allowed to perform sexual acts on her in a public place. But I'm not done, Mina says she loves the Lord…I wonder was God smiling down on you then Mina?" He then turned and smiled at me then continued.

"Since she wasn't woman enough to come to me first, since she was so unhappy." He paused for a moment. "The noise you heard today coming from the alley, was not wind sweetie and you didn't wait long enough to see if I would show up at the restaurant."

I was stunned. I didn't move. I stood there in shock…for a moment. But what do I have to lose? NOTHING. I turned around, and saw the few neighbors that were standing in their yards staring. They had family over because of course this a holiday. I've never been so embarrassed in my entire life. I thought I was having a nightmare. All I could do was think wow you didn't give a damn about my child or me. All the shit I put up with from this man. Then I had a thought. I decided if you want to be on a stage, by any means don't do it alone. Please allow me to join you.

"Yes everyone, listen up, he's right. Everything he said is about right. But from the looks of what this wannabe man has done, now you all can understand why I cheated and why I wanted to leave, right?"

"I mean really who eavesdrop and hear their woman talking to another man and runs away from their own home, down the alley, turning a trash can over and shit, and does not say a word? Oh, I'm sorry please don't let me forget he watched another man taste how sweet and good and satisfying his woman was and he does nothing. You know ladies and gentlemen I can't even call that a bitch move. I know bitches that would have whooped my ass for that!" I said.

"Wannabe man? I was man enough to get you to sell your house and move-in with me without a ring. I bought the ring after you moved in after you sold your house. I still have my house as you can see. Now, what can you say? Can I get an Amen?" He shouted.

"Can you get an Amen? Can you spell Amen? Well, he's right everyone. I did move-in with him without being married or obtaining a "ring," but that was before I realized he likes the feeling of his hand on himself better than feeling a real woman. I mean really, people he purchased porn DVD's before he paid his mortgage. That's why I had to help him financially after I moved in. Now can one of you great neighbors come and get this dog and take him to the pound." I screamed.

I could hear voices in unison saying, "Oh my God, what's going on? Someone should call the police. This so embarrassing. I feel so sorry for her and her daughter. On and On."

Then Damien responds, "Well you know sometimes a brother hand just feels better than what he has at home, and furthermore I needed to catch up on my mortgage, so I suggested you move-in. I told you what you wanted to hear. Now I'm caught upon the mortgage. Oh wait a minute, I don't have one, and my house is paid for, debt free you can now go. Goodbye."

I froze. I didn't know if I wanted to go to my car and get my gun to shoot him, or run up the stairs in the house, get his gun, and shoot him with his own. Five years and this is what I get. All the mess I have been through these past months. I wonder did I mean anything to him. Did my daughter mean anything? He is less than a man. I turned around to walk to my car to get the gun he bought for me when we first start dating. Why not cease the anger he carries on the inside of him. I could always plead insanity. Truth be told I was insane for staying with someone this long. I walked to the car went straight under my seat.

"Mama!" "Mama!" I hear Rylie's voice.

"Mina!" I hear another voice.

"Mama, Mama!" I hear my name screamed with a mixture of trembling and fear in a voice. I lost it. Whatever "It" is; it's no longer with me. I felt the presence of a body standing behind me while I am face-to-face, eye-to-eye with Damien. Although, he is 6'3, I can't remember if I was standing on an object or if the anger within me made me rise above my 5'7 height. I feel a hand touch my shoulder.

"Mina honey." Another voice called my name. As I turned around to see who it was, my adrenaline is so high that I screamed, "What!" To my surprise, I was performing to a sold-out crowd. I thought I saw maybe two or three neighbors standing outside, but I thought wrong. Every single neighbor in the neighborhood and their friends, and their friend's friend was standing in my yard. I looked around for Rylie. My baby damn near had every piece of our belongings piled in the back seat and trunk of my 2001 Chevy Tahoe.

What amazed me is was she wasn't alone. All of the neighbors that waved at me every morning and attended all those cookouts were helping her also.

"Mina sweetheart calm down. We will help you where do want your belongings to go?" Mrs. Ratcliff, my neighbor across the street, asked me.

I held my head down for a second and then I remembered whose I was. I could feel the Holy Spirit with-in and Gods presence all around me. He sent his angels to protect us and to help us. And they kept coming. Before I could answer Mrs. Ratcliff questions, to the right of me walking up the driveway were Naiomi and her husband, Javier. Apparently, my child had called them.

After I came to my senses, I remembered I was my child only living parent. I quickly realized Damien or the things he placed outside wasn't worth it. "Everyone I am sorry this had to happen in our neighborhood. I apologize for the way I have reacted."

I then smiled a little. "That being said if you all could help me load whatever items, furniture, clothes in my truck and best-friend truck I would be so grateful."

I never looked back at Damien. He grabbed a patio chair; he then opened a can of beer, and yelled "awww...relief."

"Shut up Damien. You shut the hell- up. All you put her through. You think you have done something? You ain't shit." Naiomi yelled.

"Naiomi, don't do this. Let's wait until we get the majority of my things in the car; then you can say to him what his daddy used to say to him and his mama." I then winked at him.

Damien stood up immediately and pointed his finger at me. "You and your tamale loving friend need to finish getting your shit and get off my property." He paused. "Listen everyone I was provoked to act the way I acted today. She cheated which gave me the right to do it." He begins pounding on his chest,

"I'm a good dude, I provided a roof over her and her kid head. I'm a good dude. I took care of them. "

Naiomi's husband Javier, walked over to Damien and said, "D-Man who are you trying to convince? Just go in the house and let us finish. Whatever happened between you and Mina, regardless, Rylie is innocent, and you put your business out on the street and this where you have to continue to live."

Damien never said one word again he stepped back in the garage so he wouldn't get rained on and watched.

Naiomi walked over to me, "Mina it's starting to rain we have to get going."

"Come on mom, Mr. Javier has gotten our furniture, our clothes and TV's loaded up. It's a thunderstorm warning; please let's go." Rylie shouted.

I couldn't move. I don't know why I just stood there in the yard. I was numb. What's funny is I feel free. I opened my arms wide, held my head back and twirled around in the yard as the rain began to drizzle on my face. The spirit of being alone was gone, the sense of feeling rejected left right behind it. No, I am not crazy, I'm not a hypocrite, and I am no longer someone's girlfriend. I'm a child of the highest God. All this time I thought I could not handle it emotionally if another person that I loved died, or walked out of my life, so I thought. But in an instant, the feelings are gone. I ran to my car in the rain, and my spirit told me not to look back, and I was obedient. I jumped in the car with my hair and clothes-dripping wet. I shut the car door and looked over at Rylie to apologize to her for all this chaos but, to my surprise, she had a smirk on her face.

"Mama before you start blaming yourself let me say something. I'm so proud of you. You are the best mom a girl could ever pray for. I saw you stand up for yourself even though you were hurting and embarrassed. You didn't continue to argue with him, and we don't even know where we're going. You don't have a job. You weren't afraid that's what I'm trying to say. You stood in the yard and started praising God mom, although all this was happening to us. It's like you knew God would come and help us or something."

"Rylie, God has and will always be there. He had his angles (our neighbors) in the right place at the right time. That's not a coincidence. You should be proud of yourself, look what you did! Thank you, baby. You were smart enough to call Naiomi and Javier, LOL."

"I was so nervous, mama." I was saying think Rylie. I remember dad telling me whenever you are in a situation, and you don't know what to do, to start praying. I was like, Jesus help my mommy and I, please, LOL."

"Well he heard you my dear." I said.

It began to rain harder and harder as I drove away from the horror house. I glanced in the rearview mirror and not far behind me were Naiomi and Javier. Some of our clothes, shoes, electronics, and other belongings were piled in the back of my SUV. Naiomi and Javier carried Rylie's furniture, along with her mattresses on the back of his flatbed. His Dodge Ram truck is only two weeks old. God bless them for helping us. As we pull into their driveway, the rain slowed down and before we get out the car it had stopped altogether. Javier and Naiomi walked over to the car and knocked on the window.

"Mina I'm so sorry Hun, I don't think we can save the furniture or mattresses," Javier said.

"Javier I'm not worried about that stuff, you two are amazing people," (I paused as my voice begin to crack).

I got out of the car, and before I knew it, the sun was coming out of the clouds shining. That's Texas for you I thought.

"Mama, look there's a rainbow," Rylie said.

It had to be the prettiest rainbow I had ever seen. "Beautiful!"

"Do you know what the rainbow symbolizes Mina? Naiomi asked.

"Yes I do. It symbolizes the covenant or the promise God made with Noah after the worldwide flood was brought to remove sin and evil-minded men. God promised Noah that he would not bring this kind of flood again."

"He's giving you a new season Mina. Now starts your new season." Naiomi said.

"Ladies forgive me but let's talk about this in the house. I have a great meal in mind that I am going to prepare for us. All of us are going to put this behind us, eat, watch some movies; we're going to have a good night" Javier said.

"You're right honey, let's get in the house," Naiomi said.

"I need to grab some of our clothes out of the car, and Javier do you think my tv will be ok?"

"Stop your worrying Mina. God has proven that he's got you. Your things will be fine quit worrying sweetheart, rest my child take a deep breath, take a warm soothing shower, and rest." Javier said.

"Ok, ok, your right. I don't know how I can repay you guys, but I will. Naiomi, I am so grateful for you both. You have a good husband and companion Naiomi God has blessed you."

"Yes, he is. It has been a difficult journey for us, and our marriage to get to this point but we made it." Naiomi said.

I thought to myself, as long as we have been friends I've never heard Naiomi say much of anything about her marriage. As I finally enter Naiomi's home I immediately went for the stairs to the guest bedroom. Before I could close the door, Naiomi stopped it with her foot. She handed me some of my things. I feel exhausted emotionally and mentally. I plopped down on the bed. "Wow what a way to start the New Year! I feel like Job in the bible. I have lost so much. If this has been a test for me these last few months, I do believe I have passed. I have never have drawn so close to God, I mean never."

"Girlfriend, I have been there and back. How do you think I'm able to work in ministry and encourage others, I had to go through something. You are not going through this for nothing I told you that before Mina" She said.

"Yes you have, but I don't recall ever hearing you talk about your difficult journey, I mean not in detail."

"Well in the beginning before you joined the church I told my testimony in front of the church. I spoke for at least an hour," She said.

"I remember you were telling me about that."

"Javier and I were not going to walk down the aisle if we would not have used wisdom and followed our hearts. Javier desired to be a preacher at the age of 20. We started dating a month after we both turned twenty-one. I knew he was heaven sent, but anytime you have a calling on your life, the enemy attacks, and his attacks are not easy to handle, but if God allows it, then you know he got you. I also discovered that God allows trials because he will test our faith. That being said the enemy first attack was using my parents and Mina I truly loved my parents. It broke my heart into pieces, and it was tough to except because I'm an only child.

My dad did not approve of Javier being Puerto Rican, and I, of course, being Black, so he refused to walk me down the aisle or except my decision to marry Javier. He never spoke a word to Javier.

My mother was old-fashioned and took my dad side. They both did not speak to me nor did they come to my wedding. They were not there for my baby shower, nor when I gave birth to Javier Jr. A very trying time of my faith." Naiomi said.

"Oh my Naiomi, bless your heart. Your dad is so sweet and loving towards you. I would have never known."

"He is now but, you are witnessing the "now" effect of my life, there also was a "then" effect that's a whole other subject. We have all night let me tell you about one trial at a time. LOL." Naiomi begins to tell me their struggles one by one. I thought I was the only one again. That's always what the enemy wants you to believe. She went on to tell me how and why her faith is so strong in the Lord to this day.

"I was determined to marry Javier. We both accepted Jesus as our Lord and savior and was in church every time the doors opened. I was anxious, and you know the bible tells us to be anxious for nothing. I wasn't obedient had to have it my way, so we moved in together before we got married. That was the worst decision I have ever made."

"Tell me about it...it seems we as believers of Christ get punished more because we know better. LOL." I said jokingly.

Naiomi sat down on the bed. "That's true! We know better that's why the punishment is harsh. Mina everything went wrong. Javier lost his job, so money was tight. We lost our cars. I had to quit school to get a second job because Javier couldn't find a job. I couldn't get any assistance with rent or food. I was making minimum wage at a fast food restaurant of $6.30 an hour.

On top of all of that, I found out I was pregnant in my tubes. I was having severe morning sickness. I missed a lot of work and eventually got fired. So now neither one of us had a job. Before they could take the baby out of my tubes, I miscarried. The very next week we received a letter we were being evicted, and Javier had a minor stroke and nearly died. It was a challenging year for us."

"No way! A stroke at twenty-one years old?" I said in unbelief.

"Yes! By then he was twenty-two. The trials and problems took a toll on him. He survived. We survived. We moved out of the apartment into his parent's house. We slept in separate bedrooms, we both eventually were blessed with great jobs, and Mina, we didn't have sex or touch one another again until we got married six months later, and we grew closer in our marriage. When problems would come up we had the attitude we've been here before and dealt with it," She said.

I'm speechless. If you were to see them today, you wouldn't believe it. Naiomi works heavy in the ministry assisting women and men with finding housing and jobs, and they have a very successful landscaping business. Now I know why. They have a beautiful home, sixty-seven hundred square feet, five bedrooms, four-in-a-half baths, three-car garage, pool, Jacuzzi, and a movie theater that would make Cinemark want to lease it.

Two adorable, smart children. Javier is the associate pastor at the church. Look at God! "He does give you back triple for your trials," I said.

"Oh yeah, he does. He will do the same for you, Mina. We stayed with God. We kept fasting; we kept praying, we kept believing until something happened" She said.

"I believe he will," I said.

At least 2 hours had pass and before we both knew it, Javier had finished his dinner. Javier prepared a wonderful feast. We had chicken and steak fajitas, beans, rice, salad, ceviche, tamales, tortilla chips, salsa, and Naiomi's famous pecan sweet potato pie for dessert. I laughed. We get the best of both worlds.

We sat around the table eating, laughing and talking. No one brought up what happened, we just enjoyed our night like Javier said we would. After dinner, the kids put a movie on, but I decided it was time to take a long hot shower. I was alone for the first time since it happened. The steam from the hot water, felt so refreshing. I prayed while standing in the shower and received my answer from God of what to do next. I know I was in the shower for at least forty-five minutes, if not longer, but before I knew it Riley comes in the bathroom unannounced. There goes my time alone.

"Sorry to interrupt mama, but Mamadoll have been trying to get a hold of us, she's called everyone phone she knew to call including the church. I told her we were fine and at Naiomi's." she said.

I smiled, because I'm not surprised. I grab the phone, "Hello Mamadoll all is well," I said laughing.

"Hello!" She said yelling. "I am a nervous wreck, but before I go into that let me tell you this. I have my car loaded up ready, I'm on my way to Dallas, but before I come and get you and the baby, I'm going to stop by Damien's house and send him back home to hell where he belongs. I told the Lord to send me I'll go. I accept the assignment." she said.

I laughed so hard I thought I was going to pee on myself. I know I laughed for a few minutes. Mamadoll began laughing too. We both laughed and laughed.

"I'm very serious Mina," she said.

"No, no God said vengeance is his,"

"I talked to God about it and what you mean No? Mina, I bought me a plane ticket." She said.

"I thought you said you had the car loaded up?" I asked.

"Oh! Lord, forgive me. LOL. But I am going to send him back to his maker…Satan. He is waiting with open arms. He can't stay here on earth Mina, it's not Damien's home."

"Ha ha ha, I've already used that one. You taught me well." I took a deep breath and paused for a moment, "Mamadoll I lost almost everything. He placed our things in the yard, it started raining, Naiomi and her husband came," I began rambling.

"Mina, Mina, Mina, stop it! You lost things. But baby you are still breathing. You stand. Do you hear me? I don't care what you do, stand baby. God can and will replace things."

"Mamadoll you know what. You don't have to come here; I'm coming there. I'm coming home."

There was a loud scream, but no tears this time. "This is the day, this is the day that the Lord has made, that the Lord has made, I will rejoice and be glad in it," she sang.

"Ha ha ha... I'm leaving tomorrow morning, so therefore, we will see you tomorrow before dark appears, Lord say the same," I said.

"Oh, he is saying the same. I'm going to get the house and your rooms ready. Yes, Jesus. I tell ya, Mina, he will never fell you. He won't, man will, but Jesus won't. I love you two, and I will see you tomorrow."

I thought she was going to start preaching. But she didn't.

I put some comfortable clothes on and proceeded to walk downstairs to say goodnight. I noticed Javier and Naiomi talking quietly in their bedroom with the door opened slightly. I didn't want to disturb them but before I made it to the staircase they both called my name.

"Yes."

"Javi and I were just talking and we decided that we have plenty of space for the both of you and we would like to extend your stay with us. You can stay here as long as you need too and still have your own bedrooms," Naiomi said.

I'm not surprised. That's just like the Santos family, always helping people. "I thank you both so much and God bless you for that offer, but I have decided to move back home, to Charlotte," she said.

"WOWWW Mina, oh my God, you're leaving, you're going back." Naiomi asked.

"Oh, Mina. We respect your decision. Go where the heavenly father leads you," Javier said.

"Thank You. I feel led. I don't know what it is, but the entire drive over here I saw those signs that read H.O.M.E." I said.

"Well God speaks to us in many different ways," Javier said.

"Have you told your aunt? She is going to be so excited about you coming home." Naiomi asked.

"Yes, I have, she just started singing."

Naiomi walked over to me and gave me the biggest hug. "I am going to miss you girlfriend. The both of you."

"Fourteen years we have known each other. You and Javier drove me to the hospital when I went into labor, because Ryland was at work, then you threw me my baby shower, then you would drop Rylie off at school for me and pick her up sometimes, and that's only a few things I can name because you are always there Naiomi Santos, always" I said.

"Mina you are my friend. That's what real friends do. You planned and gave me the best 40th birthday party anyone could ask for. You picked up my kids from school for three months when the bank changed my hours. You gave us our anniversary party with your own money. You let us stay with you and Ryland for a whole week when our house flooded, and loaned me your MasterCard, that I charged to the limit, and couldn't pay you back. I can on and on about God using you in my life." Naiomi said with emphasis.

"I forgot all about that. I was so pissed at you about my credit card did I ever tell you that?"

"I don't believe you did. I apologized to you Mina."

"Wait, wait a minute, you charged up her credit card and didn't pay it? Naiomi?" Javier asked.

"Oops. You remember Javi, sweetheart? I went through that season when I was trying to figure out what I wanted to do in life, find my purpose type of thing. You were trying to start your business, all that good stuff and Mary Kay cosmetics kept calling me, and the rest is history." Naiomi said.

"Naiomi, we should have paid her back." He said.

"No Javier its ok, that was over ten years ago," I said.

"Has it been that long? Was it ten years ago, are you sure?" Naiomi asked.

"Yes, I'm sure because that was the last time I ever loaned you anything, again. LOL."

We all stood in the hallway and laughed. That's what real friends are for through thick and then, through the ups and downs. What's so good about it is, we can go through all that we have been through and still love one another, show love to others, and laugh.

The next morning I woke up early. Prayed then organized the truck. I wanted to leave early because I knew I had a lengthy drive ahead of me. Rylie was excited and saying her goodbyes to Javi Jr. and Nicholette. They are like sister and brothers.

"Well you two," I said to Javier and Naiomi "it's been a journey and a pleasure having you two join me on it, but I must enter the next phase of my life."

"We understand." They both said in unison.

"You take care of your mom Rylie," Javier said.

"Of course I will, if I don't Mamadoll will, don't worry. LOL." Rylie said.

Everyone laughed. "Let me get myself together, get settled in, and then I want everyone to come and see us in Charlotte ok."

"Ok, we will be there," Naiomi, said as a tear fell from her eye.

"I'm just moving to Charlotte we will forever be besties," I said.

"I know. But it just won't be the same. I am used to driving 20 minutes down the highway to see you, and who am going to sit with at church now?" She asked.

"Well, now you will be quite in church and you will have to hop your butt on an airplane. Just grab the credit card from Javier and charge you and the kid's tickets." I said.

"Oh no. She will not be using any credit cards anymore no ma'am." Javier said.

"Let it go, Javier," Naiomi said sarcastically.

We jumped in the Tahoe, started it up and I looked at the Santos family and said, "You guys, please pray the Hoe get us to Charlotte ok."

As we drove off, I looked in my rearview mirror, and there was my bestie, her husband, and children waving and smiling holding a poster board that read, *If God be for you, who can be against you!*

I looked over at Rylie and said, "buckle up baby girl here we go!"

Chapter 4: Home is Where I belong...

Thank God, we finally made it to Charlotte after a few stops on the way and a quick nap. It's 7:01 am, and the sun has just begun to rise. I don't feel tired at all; I feel excited. As I continue driving I can finally see the beautiful skyline of Charlotte. It's been 14 years since I lived here and Lord knows I have some catching up to do and I'm ready. It appears my GPS says we have at least another 35 minutes to Mamadoll house. She and my uncle decided to move on up like the Jefferson's and moved far away from the city. The house was a gift to her from my uncle on their 50th wedding anniversary. The neighborhood is called Vine Heights a very established one, and all of Charlotte finest live there. Mamadoll said its maybe twenty houses now ranging from two hundred to four hundred thousand dollars. Now that's a very nice house in Charlotte. They were the first to build on their street and didn't have any neighbors for at least a year. It's a beautiful subdivision. Only retirees with a nice annual income, professional athletes, politicians, and prominent pastors live in this neighborhood. Everyone knows everyone. There is a gate attendee standing at attention as soon as you drive up keeping a watch on everything. Mamadoll said mistresses often try to sneak in, but for some reason, if that happens, they never leave out, and no one ever asks any questions. My Uncle made sure Mamadoll and I would be taken care of after he passed away from kidney failure six years ago.

    I traveled the world with Rylie and tried my best to save as much as I could, but things happened. It's funny because the entire drive from Dallas I thought about my Uncle and how he treated me like he birthed me himself. He was my daddy and my best friend. I remember how at a young age he advised me to stay with God. He used to say it's going to get a little rough and tough through life, but baby stay with God. I now understand what he meant. I talked with God the entire trip to Charlotte, and I know he heard me. I said before he does anything else, I asked him to lead me to a good church home where I can be used, and I also thanked him for sending me back home. I know this is where I belong I can already feel the blessings and a wonderful season ahead that God has for me.

    Once I took the exit to Mamadoll's house, I saw a very familiar face on a billboard. The pearly white teeth and a huge smile, was oh so familiar. I realized it was my best friend from high school and roommate from college, Kia St. James; excuse me Evangelist Kia St. James. WOW! I heard God was using her, and from the looks of the billboard, she is doing very well. The last time I saw her was at my uncle's funeral, and we had a few words and of course said we would keep in touch and we never did. Then she reached out to me after Rylie's father passed while she was in China for a gospel conference. People grow apart; it's life.

Once I get settled in, I will try and visit her church. I heard she is the Lead Evangelist (whatever that is) over a congregation of twenty-two thousand members one of the largest in the Southeast.

I've heard a few of her sermons on DVD's, but I have never been able to watch her on television because she preaches Saturday night service, and it's not televised. She has no idea I have moved back so I will probably need to surprise her.

I finally make it to Mamadoll subdivision and the gate attendee is ready for work standing at his post. It's the same attendee that has worked here since my aunt and uncle moved in.

"Good morning Mr. Davies, long time no see."

"Mina. Oh Lord, Oh, Jesus. Is that you? I thought I was seeing a pretty ghost girl." He said.

Ok. I thought to myself, whatever he means. I guess he is trying to say I'm pale. So, moving right along. It's too early to entertain him.

"Yes, sir it's me. Can you please let me in the gate?"

"Mina I wish I could but Mamadoll didn't tell me you were coming and I'm going to need to see some identification ma'am." He said

Identification! No, he didn't! Now you know who I am because I didn't even have to tell you whom I was here to see, or my name. Ok, 2% rental cop it's too early to be playing with me, and I have been driving for 15 plus hours. I sure hope they give him his promotion.

"Sure, no problem here's my ID, and I'll call her myself," I said with a big fake smile.

But, I didn't need to call her because before I knew it, I saw Mamadoll headlights from her car headed toward me down the hill. God is always looking after us. I could not wait, so I hopped out the car and ran up the hill while the gate was still opening. "Mamadoll we're home." I screamed.

She jumped out of the car as if she was 30 years old and opened her arms wide to hug me "Thank God. My babies made it safe. You made it Mina, you made it home," she yelled.

"Yes, we did, I'm so happy to be here."

"You're happy? Honey, I couldn't sleep last night, I was so anxious." She said.

"I didn't either. I had to drive. How did you know we were here?"

"Mina you know me, they have their cameras all over the neighborhood watching us, and I have my cameras all over my house watching them. Now come on in so you can get some rest." She said.

That's Mamadoll for you always one step ahead and always looking out for us. I finally made it into the house. I paused in the foyer and sat some of our things down. I begin to get a little emotional. Mamadoll has lived here for seven years alone. But you would think we were away on vacation from the looks of the house.

I looked at the wall to the left of me and saw pictures of Rylie and me when she was first born. She still had my wedding photos up. There are so many good memories in this home. From the moment I stepped into her house I felt the peace and the presence of God. She had our rooms all furnished and decorated. The dressers in both of our rooms had our bibles with our monogrammed initials engraved on them from years ago. Our rooms were ready for us to take over. Our beds had the prettiest duvet covering on them with matching drapes. Our bathrooms stocked with toothpaste, body wash, fresh towels, and extra toiletries. It felt so good to be here, and I wanted to be here. I should have listened and come here sooner, but I can't live in the "I should have." I thought I would be tired from the drive, hell it's already 8:30 am, but I am too excited to sleep. After I got our things out the car and took me a long hot bath I could hear Mamadoll in the kitchen, and the smell of her homemade biscuits made my stomach growl, but that smell of black coffee brewing was on my mind. I headed downstairs to the kitchen.

"I thought you were going to sleep suga. I know you are tired," Mamadoll said.

"I can't go to sleep, and I had to have me some coffee, I am addicted. Mamadoll, you know we love our coffee."

"Where's Rylie?" she asked.

"She went back to sleep. She loves her room and I love my room. Thank you so much."

"Thank you, for what?" She asked.

"For being you. I feel so welcomed here. I realized I hadn't been home in three years. You were always coming to Dallas." I said.

"I know I know. I had to get a break from this house sometimes, and this city. And I missed you even more after your uncle passed, you know it was always the three of us." She said.

"And it still is the three of us."

"Sure is. Look at God. He gives us the desires of our heart." She said.

"I guess so," I said.

"You guess so?" she said confused, "He does in His time, it's his time and his plan."

"I know." Let me not get her started on her daily sermons, so I changed the subject. "I was thinking about shopping around at some private schools on Monday for Rylie."

"That sounds good. You only have seven more days before school starts after the New Year." She said.

"Oh ok, I'll start Monday. I think I'll rest today. I can't remember when I rested on a Friday, I'm always on the go."

"Well now you have the opportunity to do just that, but don't forget we have your aunt wedding on tomorrow. She asks that we all dress in the colors black and white, or black and red, or did she say red only. I can't remember," She laughed as she continued preparing breakfast.

I would forget too. I mean, she is on her 5th husband. I cannot believe she is even having a wedding ceremony. Wait a minute we're talking about Aunt Bae who was asked to leave her church because she slept with half the congregation, married or not. Then every time she was hired she slept with her bosses, and I've never heard of a hospital asking can you check out early? I heard she was sleeping with the patients and some of the men were going into cardiac arrest. You would think after a certain number of marriages, it would be against the law to continue to have a ceremony? I poured me some coffee and sat at the breakfast nook to get ready to clock-in @ imbeingmessy.com.

"Where did she meet this one?" I asked.

Mamadoll looked at me with a smirk on her face," I didn't tell you?" She asked.

"No. If you did, I probably forgot. But in all honesty, I do not recall hearing you talk about him."

"She's marrying Dr. Gene Calhoun." She said.

"Dr. Calhoun!" "He is still alive? I mean how old is he?"

"Ha ha ha...Mina, he is only 81. He looks like he's around sixty years-old."

"Only!" I tell you the truth men don't stop. "Wasn't he married for like fifty years?"

"Yes, his wife died a few months ago." She said.

"A few months ago?" "Anyway, I'm not going there," I said.

"Yes, Mina a few months ago. You know some people can't be alone they are accustomed to having that other person around. Let's not be judgmental of people. They are really in love his son told me." She said.

"His son told you? I thought he didn't have any children," I said.

"Yes, he has one he claims from his wife. He's the only one that carries the Calhoun name. Do remember Bryce Calhoun?"

"No, I don't. But that name sounds very familiar." I said.

"He is our county commissioner. He is running again also, and I work with a few sisters from this church he attends on his campaign, so I talk to him quite often. He's a very nice young, single, handsome, no kids, educated, accomplished, Christian man. God has favored him." She said

Oh Lord, there she goes. The titles don't impress me. "I saw a few signs and a billboard on my way here. He is handsome. Small as this city is you would think I would know him. You didn't tell me you were working in a campaign office?" I said.

"I just started this past Monday. I'm so excited. I will be doing all the marketing. I will be visiting nursing homes, schools, churches, getting people to vote for him. You know I like to stay busy. You had so much going on this week, so I didn't mention it. He is the same age as you."

"Hot 40! Good for him. I'm glad you have something to do Mamadoll, you would think you were my age." I paused. "Speaking of billboards, I saw my old bestie, Ms. Kia St. James all over the city billboards. You didn't tell me that she was on billboards." I said.

She was quiet, very quiet. She seems to be in deep thought, and then she responds. "Yes, she is very popular. She blew up so fast. I tell you, she and Pastor Kincade have so many members. I know at least twenty thousand or more."

"Talk about favor from God. Mamadoll, have you ever heard her speak?" I asked.

"I've heard her speak maybe twice. She hasn't been preaching, teaching, evangelizing, whatever you want to call it for very long. I believe she maybe start sharing her calling with the world three or four years ago." She said.

"All those members in only four years?"

"She doesn't have those members alone. She is the associate pastor. Pastor Kincade is the head Pastor and founder. God gave that man at least eighteen to twenty thousand before Kia came along, then, of course, the ministry expanded." She said,

"Now that's a lot of power, those two together," I said.

"Yes, they are anointed, and the Holy Spirit lives in the both of them. That has to be the best pastor I have heard." She said.

"Oh really?" I don't think I ever heard her speak that way about anyone but Jesus. "Do you ever visit?"

"I have been a few times. But you know I love my church. It's only the 10 of us, but we have some church up in there. I'm old school Mina, traditional. I want to sing hymns. I want to walk around and put my offering in the bucket. I want to hear people stand-up and share their testimonies, and most of all I want to be able to speak with my pastor one on one, and see him walk around and talk with his congregation." She said.

"I know Mamadoll. Did you see her when you visited? I plan on visiting." I said.

"Oh, Mina you should after you visit my church." She smiled. "She would love to see you. She only talked with me briefly at the church there were so many people around her, but from time to time I ran into her at the home depot when she was remodeling her home, and she would talk with me. She misses you all's friendship." She said.

"Aw, she did? She never kept in touch really, but I didn't either. I will definitely visit her church, and I would love to talk with her to see what she has been up too over these past years," I said.

"I know she will love that Mina. They have three services, which is great. They have Saturday service that starts at three o'clock p.m. and two Sunday services which start at nine o'clock am and one PM."

"A Saturday service? That's nice I don't think I have attended a Saturday service before." I said.

"Yes, it is. Your Aunt Bae attends regularly and Commissioner Calhoun along with nearly the entire city. Speaking of your Aunt Bae, she will be over to see you later today along with other people that missed you."

"Other people?" I'm thinking when were you going to share this with me? "That's cool Mamadoll but people like who?"

"Your cousins like Zi'lah and her daughter and son, your Uncle Henry and his wife. Everyone was happy you were coming back, you are loved and was missed," she said.

I was speechless. All this love from people I love. I haven't felt loved in so long. I forgot what it felt like. "That's good to know Mamadoll, I would be happy to see them as well," I said.

We sat at the Breakfast nook and finished our breakfast and drank our freshly brewed coffee. Then we talked and talked, and talked then looked at photos from over the years for I know hours. Before we knew the time had passed, and it was past noon. I finally felt a little tired, so I decided to lie down and get me some rest. Once I laid down, Rylie decided to wake up, and it was time for her to hang out with Mamadoll. They went grocery shopping, shoe shopping, and shopping for an outfit for the wedding. I slept so good and for hours. The feeling of this bed felt so good I didn't want to wake up. I didn't realize how tired I was, but my body did because I couldn't seem to get out the bed. I could hear voices afar, talking and laughing. When I did wake up, I looked at my cell phone, and Naiomi called and texted me twice. She wrote, *we already miss you guys: I know you made it safe and sound. Don't forget about us*, with nearly ten to twenty emoji's. I responded.

"My bestie, how could we ever forget about you guys? The trip was great. We made it. I'm just waking up I will call you later, Love you all-ways."

I could smell the smell of good cooking from downstairs. Before I opened the bedroom door, Rylie opened it for me.

"Mommy, you're awake! I said to myself you were probably up by now. I had so much fun with Mamadoll. We went shopping and everything." She said.

"That's great honey. What did you two do?" I asked.

"We went to some boutiques, and we got some ice cream, and then the campaign center where she works and I made some signs." She said.

"Nice. Show me what you got. I smell food." I said.

"Yes, mommy Mamadoll cooked so much. You have to see." She said.

I headed downstairs with my daughter hand and hand to the kitchen that reminded and smelled like a soul food restaurant. Mamadoll prepared a meal for us that will probably put ten pounds or more on you, but that meal is worth the ten extra pounds. It was like old times. She cooked southern chicken fried chicken, fried catfish, smothered pork chops, fried corn on the cob, southern mashed potatoes, collard greens, macaroni and cheese, cabbage, cornbread muffins, homemade buttermilk rolls, and for dessert baked banana pudding and peach cobbler. I am truly at home.

"Hello everyone! Oh, my goodness, look at all this food. Let me grab a plate." I said.

"Mina Mina, give me a hug. It's so good to see you, sweetheart." Aunt Bae said.

I was shocked at the sight of her. I didn't even recognize her. I know Mamadoll said she looked young, but she is 69 years old, and she doesn't even look a day over 50. Her face doesn't move…at all. I had to get my composure together.

"Aunt B, it's been years, you look so, (I paused), young," I said.

She gave me a stanky look with her eyes, without her face moving. Then responded, "Well thank you, Mina, you look great like always. Look at your curves girlfriend. My, my, you still have a nice shape. Don't lose it with eating all this good cooking from my sister. You better be careful if you want to catch you a new man, cause you need one after all you been through." She said while shaking her head as she sat at the table.

What the hell? Now, what does she mean by that comment? I glanced over at Mamadoll and she was stirring that pot of greens a long time and never looked up. I tell you the truth every family has at least one member of the family who knows the five w's, of who, what, when, where, and why. Who got divorced? What time they had the affair? When their spouse found out about it? Where the spouse was once he or she found out and why they did it? She didn't stop there. She continued.

"I prayed so hard Mina. I said Lord I hope Mina grabbed her mink and her Louis Vutton luggage." Then she paused and began batting those eyelashes. "Did you get your Mink baby? And that luggage?"

I wasn't surprised. I responded in a respectful way, "Aunt Bae thank you for your concern, and just so you know, I still run at least three times a week and yes I have my…" before I could even tell her I got my mink she interrupted me.

"Mina it's so good to hear you still run. Then you won't have a problem finding another man now will you?" I cringed at her comments and Mamadoll froze. She has always been so messy and nosey, total opposite from Mamadoll.

Now that I'm older I know how to handle her. Back in the day when I was younger I would have snapped her head off with my mouth. But I'm not falling for that now.

This is how you get someone out of your business without them picking you apart, because that's what she trying to do, get me to say something. I'm thinking, why would I be looking for a man, 24 hours later? Probably because that's something she would be doing. I looked over my shoulder to see what Rylie was doing. She looked very uncomfortable.

"No, I won't have a problem finding a man because he found me." I lift my hands in the air. "His name is Jesus. I'm so glad he came in my life. He is the best thing to happen to me." I winked at Rylie, and she smiled big at me.

Aunt Bae was quiet for a moment and then all of a sudden she blurted out loud, "That's right Mina. Hallelujah! I love me some Jesus. He is a mighty good friend. Yes, he is."

Yep, all you have to do is start talking about the Lord, people either walk away and say, "oh Lord there she go talking about the Lord", or they will start talking about him with you and they still will not know your business it works every time.

"Mamadoll I heard you and Rylie visited the campaign headquarters," I said.

"We sure did. Rylie did so well. She helped make the signs and met her some friends. She is just like you when you were that age simply friendly and outgoing."

"Thank you. Mama, we had fun. I got to meet Mr. Calhoun." Rylie said.

"Really. That's good Rylie I hope you enjoyed yourself."

"Doll you mean to tell me Bryce was there. He told me he wasn't going up there. I needed to see if he was going to wear his tuxedo or a suit," Aunt Bae said.

"Well, he came up there for a minute. I invited him to dinner tonight, and he said he would try to stop by." Mamadoll said.

"I'm going to call him. Mina, baby, do you have your dress. I need you to wear red on tomorrow, look pretty, I like the short haircut by the way" Aunt Bae said.

I don't want to answer her. "Thank you, but I thought you wanted us to wear black?"

She stood up dramatically waving her hands, "no, no honey, no ma'am, Doll I told you I wanted you and the girls to be in red. Red is the color of love, and since I am in love, I wanted my family to wear red. He doesn't have any family but Bryce, and he looks good in a bag. Oh yes ma'am he is fine. Honey he is F.I.N.E.! Wait until you see him, Mina."

Lord, have mercy. Is she talking about her soon to be son-in-law like that? She is so ridiculous. She is on her fifth husband and has the nerve to be picky about what colors we wear. Red is the color for love. Excuse me, but I want to wear black because this marriage will be dead and gone by next month. I'm going to need a lot of prayers when dealing with her.

"Aunt Bae its fine, I have plenty of red I can wear. No worries."

"Oh good, I thought I was about to have a heart attack, honey. I was saying, Lord, I'm not ready yet, I'm getting married to the love of my life finally."

I raised one eyebrow, she shouldn't tell a lie to God like that. *Love of my life*; please exit stage left, Aunt Bae. I was saved; by the doorbell as I attempted to walk into the living area to watch a show on Netflix.

"Hey everybody." I heard a familiar voice and looked around to see it was my cousin Zi'lah and her children. I haven't seen her in years.

"Well hello there Zi'lah, longtime no see, cousin," I said.

"Mina, look at you. You look so good, darling. What have you been up too I haven't seen you in forever, and I'm so sorry about your ex-husband." she said.

"Thank you. I have been up to a whole lot, but I'm slowing down now that I'm home."

"That's good to hear Mina. I'm going through a divorce did Mamadoll tell you?" She asked.

"No. I didn't know that." But before I could say another word, Aunt Bae interrupted her. Isn't it funny she wanted me to talk about what happened to me, but wants Zi'lah to be quiet?

"Let's not go there, Zi'lah. This is a happy occasion your cousin is home, and it's time for a wedding in the family finally." Aunt Bae said.

Zi'lah and I looked at one another for I know ten seconds. Zi'lah rolled her eyes up in her head then smiled at me.

"Let me fix you a plate baby," Mamadoll said.

"Thanks, Mamadoll I am starving," Zi'lah said.

"I'm going to pour us a glass of wine I needed one yesterday. You do drink wine Mina right?" Aunt Bae asked.

"Occasionally, I will take a glass tonight," I said.

"Good. I'm getting a little nervous before my big day." She said.

Nervous? Everyone was quiet. Again, Zi'lah and I looked at one another and smiled. She rolled her eyes up in her head again.

"Mina, have you talked to Kia?" Zi'lah asked.

"Not since Rylie dad passed. I was telling Auntie earlier I couldn't wait to see her. She has gotten so famous around here. I have heard some of the DVD's," I said.

"Oh yes! You have got to visit the church at least once. She is anointed, and I mean she will leave you speechless. I joined her church, well not her church, but A Street called Straight Ministries," Zi'lah said.

"You joined? To God be the glory, good for you!" I said.

"Oh, baby that's wonderful I tell you that ministry is bringing more and more people God." Mamadoll said.

"Yes, it is Doll, and that's why I love it. Pastor Kincade is a great man of God." Aunt Bae said.

"Is he?" A deep sexy male voice appeared from out of nowhere and asked. I looked up to see a very, I do mean very handsome black man looking around early 40's standing around 6'3, nice grade of hair in a fine expensive Italian linen suit. The smell of his Creed Irish Tweed cologne swallowed the kitchen. Everyone but me, stood up to greet him. They all just went crazy over him.

"Bryce, I texted you, and then I called you twice today. I was worried, son." Aunt Bae said.

"Oh, Bryce sit down and eat son, I know you're hungry. I made your favorite." Mamadoll said.

"Hey Mr. Calhoun, I like the suit and those shoes. You're looking prosperous." Zi'lah said in a sexy voice.

There I was sitting at the table with my glass of wine thinking geez they were swarming all over him as if they had been on lockdown from a man for ten plus years. I mean he is fine, she didn't lie about that, and he knows it. He locked eyes with me for a second, and then I turned away. The groupies realized I was there then decided to introduce us.

"Bryce this is Mina, your cousin from Dallas. Well, she's from here but she lived in Dallas for many years." Aunt Bae said.

Oh, now I'm his cousin. I reached my hand out to shake his, but before I knew it, he bent down and grabbed my hand to kiss it. Oh, he is something else. Please stop.

He spoke," Mina Mamadoll said you were beautiful, but she didn't use the right word when she described you. Stunning. No, that's not a good enough word. Gorgeous. No, that's not good enough. Alluring. Nope that's not good either. I mean did God make a word to describe you?"

Everyone laughed but me. I mean they laughed so hard they were crying, including Mamadoll. Women, women, please, I see why this brother's head is bigger than his career.

"Thank you, Mr. Calhoun, I've heard a lot about you as well. Glad to finally meet you."

"Oh, what have you heard? Let me guess he's handsome, educated, smart, and single." He said smiling.

"No, I haven't heard those terms used at all," I said sarcastically. You should have seen this brother's mouth, and everyone else's in that kitchen.

"Gotcha!" I said laughing.

He smiled at me then responded. "You have a sense of humor Ms. Mina. I like that in a woman, playful spirit," Then he growled at me and stared at me up and down and all around like I was a 20-ounce steak on the grill.

"Bryce Calhoun you be a good boy, now." Aunt Bae said.

He looks me with a smirk on his face, "I don't think I can now, with such distraction around."

"Would you like for me to make you plate Bryce?" Mamadoll asked.

"Yes, ma'am, please do so. Everything smells wonderful as usual." He said.

"Bryce, are you bringing a date tomorrow?" Zi'lah asked.

He didn't respond right away. He ignored her question as he continued to stare at me. "No Zi'lah. I really don't have time to be bothered, and plus you never bring a car to a car lot, unless it's used and you're trying to trade it in."

Everyone laughed but me, again. I'm sick in my stomach, and I have only been around him a few minutes. I looked at the clock, and it's ten-thirty. Zi'lah got up from the table to go home, and I was right behind her.

"Well everyone I'm going to run upstairs and wind down a minute, or two I'm still recuperating from my drive. Mamadoll I love you and congrats auntie, and good to see you. Zi'lah we will hook up, next week, Bryce, (I paused), nice to meet you cousin." I said.

I turned and walked upstairs to spend time with my child only to hear my name being called.

"Mina, you don't need any help getting in bed, do you?" Bryce asked with a smile.

Is he serious I'm asking myself? I turned around to give him the stankiest look, I mean nasty, but I respected my aunt and responded, "I do not."

Chapter 5: Aunt Bae's Wedding...

Although, its Aunt Bae's fifth marriage; Mamadoll is scrambling to get things in order for her wedding. "Rise and shine my lady and baby girl it's the big day. We have to be at the church by three o'clock, and it's ten already," she said. I slept like a baby and really didn't want to get up. I can smell bacon from downstairs. I hopped out of bed and Rylie met me at the door. We ran downstairs like two kids on Christmas day anxious to open our gifts. Once we were in the kitchen, it was literally just like when I was a child. There was a kitchen filled with breakfast food and Mamadoll singing her favorite gospel song "For the rest of my life, I'll serve him." That was one of her favorite songs she would sing whenever she was going through a trial and even if she wasn't. As I glanced around the kitchen I noticed Mamadoll cooked every body part from the pig, and more. There was a buffet set-up. Eggs, bacon, sausage, fish and butter grits, homemade biscuits, pancakes, rice, hash brown casserole, fruit, with a little OJ and freshly brewed coffee. You would think she was cooking for a family of ten or more, but this is the way she cooked. We walked in the kitchen, and both gave her a big hug at the same time.

"Good morning girls, what's the hug for?" she asked.

"All of this. You are something else Mamadoll, and I love me some you." I said

"Why thank you, I love you both too and just glad you are home, honey. Come on you two let's eat." She said.

"You cooked all this for us?" I asked.

"Of course. From time to time Aunt Bae will stop by and Uncle Henry, Zi'lah, and of course Bryce, he thinks I'm his mom." She said.

I nearly choked on my orange juice. I am not feeling him at all. I don't know what it is. It's something funny with his spirit, or is it I know he thinks he is all that, but really none of that. I will not say anything to Mamadoll for now, because she thinks the world of him.

"This is so good, thank you. I can't wait to put on my dress." Rylie said.

"I'm ready to see you in it baby. Mina, she looked just like you did when you went to the 8th-grade prom."

"Oh no. Not the 8th-grade prom. I thought I was the bomb back then." I said.

"Yes, you did. I thought you were going to give you uncle a heart attack, ha, ha... he was so overprotective of you." She said.

"Like my mom is with me," Rylie said.

"Oh, whatever. It bothers me when her face is always on her iPhone." I said.

"I understand Mina. We will teach her like I taught you." Mamadoll said.

"What's that?" Rylie said looking confused.

"She made me do chores half the day, and play outside the other half, then by six o'clock it was time for church," I said.

"But mama you didn't' have cell phones then I thought," Rylie said.

"I know."

"So how can I do all those chores with my phone?" She asked.

"You can't, that's our point." Mamadoll and I said in unison.

Rylie looked at us both like we were the ones crazy. "Oh my goodness, its 12:30 already I have to be at the conference hall downtown at two o'clock sharp." She said.

"Ok do you need help?" I asked.

"Yes, please put the flowers in your car for me, I don't have room sweetie," she said.

"No problem, where are they?"

"They are in the garage ready to go."

"Sure no problem."

I walked out to the garage. It looked like a museum full of memorabilia from over two decades. With Mamadoll's wedding photos, my baby photos, my high school photos, my wedding photos, my baby shower photos, Rylie baby pictures, and all of Aunt Bae's other four wedding photos. I tell you the truth Mamadoll keeps everything. I do mean everything. I glanced through some of the pictures and saw one of Kia and me from my yearbook from high school she wrote,

"Mina, you have the best personality. My best friend forever and always, stay with God. He will always be there with you. Love Kia."

We were so very close. We were praising God at eighteen years old. Lord knows we didn't know the trials that were ahead of us. Thank God for Mamadoll taking us to church and teaching us about Jesus. She was like a mom to her back then, Kia never knew her mother, and her dad never talked about her. He dated every woman in Charlotte, took their money, and that's how he took care of Kia, I heard. But she was my buddy remind me of Naiomi and me. It's as if God gave me a new friend all over again once I got to Dallas.

"Mommy, go get dressed please, come on hurry up," Rylie said.

"What time is it?" I asked.

"One o'clock, and you have to bring the flowers," Rylie said.

I rushed up the stairs to get dressed. I wore my red fitting dress just below my knees with gold jewelry and gold strappy sandals around my ankles. I grabbed my gold, black, and red clutch. My make-up was flawless. Rylie wore a red dress fitting for a thirteen-year-old. Mamadoll wore a beautiful red and black dress fitting for her age with her Sunday ready for church hat. Before we left, we took selfies with one another. I followed behind her and Rylie in my car to the to the conference hall in case I wanted to leave the event early.

Once we arrived, I saw the most exceptional people of Charlotte getting out of their cars. I'm so confused at this point because I thought this was a sixty to eighty something-year-old wedding. But apparently, somebody knows somebody who told everybody. I'm not looking for anything, but I'm glad I dressed to impress.

We entered the hall, and there stood the sizeable beautiful photo of Aunt Bae and Dr. Calhoun's wedding photo. They looked like they were forty years old and maybe fifty-five years old, with a little touch of plastic. If that's what it takes, to look youthful and you're happy with it, then go for it. There were people everywhere as I consistently smiled and says, excuse me, over and over again. To my surprise, the finest brothers and beautiful sisters God made were here, and I was too busy enjoying the scenery to help with flower decorating, but of course, I did. Aunt Bae had me so busy I was going back and forth from one area to the next. Finally, the flowers were in place, and Mamadoll went to the dressing room to help Aunt Bae finished getting ready. Guest began to walk in the conference area to have a seat. I ran to the restroom to freshen up because it felt like I had worked an 8-hour shift at a fast food restaurant the way I begin sweating.

Before I knew it five o'clock came too quick. I gathered my things quickly in my purse and hurried out the bathroom door.

BAM! This is a day, I will never forget. My body, his body, met unexpectedly face to face. I nearly fell, he almost fell, but we both maintained our balance. My purse and earrings went flying down the hallway. My dress! Let's say he received a nice glimpse of my lace Victoria Secrets undergarment. I was embarrassed, but at the same time glad to see there was no one else around but he and I. I didn't want to look up at him, but I finally did. Our eyes met, and we stared at one another for a moment. He looked at me up and down in slow motion, and then he spoke.

"I'm so sorry young lady. Are you ok?" He said in a very low semi-deep voice.

He was a very intriguing, eye opener for a woman. He was indeed a good-looking man. His light brown eyes were so familiar to me. He wasn't just fine, and he wasn't just a handsome man. He was simply divine, with a smell of the most exquisite cologne made. His suit was black, and it had to be tailor-made. His haircut was trimmed so nice, with thick natural waves laying low.

His goal tee designed to perfection on his chocolate smooth skin. I could not find the words to say, but as I straighten my dress and responded. "Yes I'm fine, but sir I'm the one that is sorry, so please excuse me, I was in such a rush and wasn't paying attention to where I was going," I said.

I believe it was at least five seconds as we gazed into one another eyes again. He looked familiar to me, but I can't figure out from where. I would have remembered meeting him or seeing him somewhere. He then dusted off his suit and gathered himself. He reached out his hand to me and said, "Hello, I don't believe we have ever met, or ever been in the presence of one another."

Lord, have mercy, he speaks so well and must be reading my mind. I exhaled, then inhaled, and then exhaled again. His words were so articulate I had to respond accurate and precise. I licked my lips and batted my long eyelashes.

"I believe you are right sir because I would have remembered you." I then extended my hand out to him for a handshake. "Hello my name is Mina, and your name is," I asked.

He wasted no time gripping my hand firmly. "Very nice to meet you, Mina. My name is Patrick, and I know I would have remembered if I ever met someone like you," he said.

We both smiled and were still holding hands. "Patrick it's very nice to meet you also," I said with my Colgate smile.

He paused for a second and stared at me again then replied, "Likewise Mina."

We finally stopped shaking one another hands, and I glanced to grab a glimpse of his hands, but he placed them in his pockets. I was looking to see if he had a ring on. Dang! All of sudden he went to say a word, but we were disturbed by a voice singing from a distance.

"I do believe that's my sign, the wedding has started. I'm here for a wedding ceremony so I should make my way over there," he said.

Really? I wonder who he's here to see, or who he's with. I should ask him. "I'm here for a wedding also, and I don't want to be late either, so I guess I'll be going too," I said.

"Is that right (he paused). Again It was a pleasure meeting you today, enjoy your ceremony," He said with a smile.

Silence. I want to talk more, get to know him. Are you single? Where are you from? How many kids? Are you from here?

"Excuse me, one more thing. You dropped this." He then hit me with my colorful, nicely wrapped Kotex tampon. Pausing after handing it to me, he went on to say, "And this also." He then stabbed me with the Trojan condom that fell to the floor as well.

I cleared my throat a few times. "Thank You so much. I haven't carried this purse in years."

He smiled. "Again, have a good night."

His spirit is so pleasant to be around, and his presence takes over a room. I responded to him and said, "Likewise."

We both walked away from one another and went in two different directions. As I walked away, I slowly turned back to see if he was going to the same ceremony. I remembered there was another wedding held in the other banquet hall. I turned around slightly to look back at him. He was not only staring back at me with a smile on his face, he stopped again, and spoke from afar.

"Is it Mrs. or Ms. Mina, my God, our God surely smiled on your mother and father when you were created?" He turned back around, and before I could respond, he was gone.

Jesus, Jesus, Jesus. I didn't know another name to call. I smiled so big, and those words felt so good to hear. I was done for the year. I felt great! I walked into the ceremony feeling like a billionaire, not a millionaire. Who is he and where did he go. Brother, come back.

Once inside the banquet hall, Mamadoll truly outdid herself. The décor was beautiful. She had dozens of roses all over, red drapes hanging, red light bulbs in the light fixtures, and black accents to add to it. I sat with Rylie, and Mamadoll, Uncle Henry and his wife, and Zi'lah and her children on the very front row. I glanced around the entire room, looking for "Mr. Patrick," but I didn't see him, but what I did see, was a room filled with young good-looking professionals. I have to say, if Aunt Bae has decided to make this her last marriage, she is doing it big. But, also I must remember everyone in the city knows Dr. Calhoun. The live band began to play soft music after the singer finished her song. Before I knew it, Bryce walked in like he was the President of the United States. He was waving and shaking people hands like this was a campaign site. Guest started whispering, pointing at him, and taking pictures of him. The usher finally walked over and politely showed him to his seat, which was with us. He sat down and of course kissed Mamadoll and Rylie. He gave me a fake smile and winked. I thought Zi'lah was going to jump out of her seat once he sat down. She called his name two or three times before he acknowledged her. "Bryce glad to see you came alone. Would you like to sit here with me?" She asked, as she looked him up and down. "Zi'lah this event, or whatever you

70

want to call it, is already too much for one, and not enough for two. I'll be sitting alone." He then walked away. Then I heard the crowd again whispering, pointing, and standing up. I thought it was time for Aunt Bae to walk down the aisle because it's only 5:45, but to my surprise, before I could get a glimpse of the person Mamadoll turns to me and says,

"Look Mina, there's your friend,"

I looked up, and it was Kia, I mean Evangelist St. James. I was so surprised. I didn't remember Aunt Bae telling me she would be officiating the ceremony. Guest was going crazy. She looked so good in her suit, and she has a glow. I saw the anointing of God all over her.

Before she made her way to the stage Bryce stood-up to hug her. I then stood up to say hello, but before I could say a word, she noticed it was I.

"Is that Mina Wright? My best friend forever and ever, and ever Mina Wright" she said with a huge grin on her face.

"Kia, yes it is. How are you honey, long time no see, in person that is, because your face is everywhere?" I said.

She opened her arms so wide to hug me. I know we hugged one another for at least a good two minutes. She put both of her hands on my face and just smiled at me, "Mina, Mina, it's so good to see you. How have you been? When did you get here? We have to get together. When do you leave?"

I started laughing, "I'm here to stay. I moved back home." I said.

"You did. When? Welcome home, why didn't you call me?" She asked. But before we could continue our conversation, the usher said Aunt Bae was ready. We both said we would catch up at the reception. The band began to play "All My Life" by K-Ci and JoJo.

Dr. Calhoun walked in first down the aisle in a pinstripe red suit and a black fedora with a red feather. He smiled and waved at guest without any jaw or lip movement. Then Aunt Bae is standing at the entrance to the banquet hall door right behind him ready for her grand entrance. The guest stands as she begins to walk. She danced her way real slow down the aisle to the music, and people were laughing and clapping. I was thinking there are way too many stars in this show.

Once Aunt Bae finally made her way to the altar and I had a chance to grab a visual of her attire. I was outdone. She wore a wedding dress that was very red. It reminded you of a 1985 prom to remember. There were ruffles all over the dress. Ruffles and more ruffles and a hint of lace. Her veil was a sheer red, her shoes were red, the gloves she wore were red, her hair accessories were red, her costume jewelry was red including earrings, and her lipstick was red. I don't believe in my 40 years of living I had ever seen so much red. The two of them standing next to one another was surely a site to see. They looked like an 80-year-old pimp and his senior citizen strawberry shortcake. I didn't know if I was surprised at the outfits or the fact that she actually had the nerve to wear that dress. She said she wanted to stand out, and she did just that.

It was time to say their vows, but Aunt Bae surprised everyone and said she wrote her own. Kia handed her the microphone, "Do everyone knows why there is so much red in here today?" She asked smiling at the guest.

Rylie looked at me and giggled. I smiled and winked at her. Mamadoll gave us both the "you better be quiet look."

"Here she go, I should have brought my pop-corn," Zi'lah said.

Then Aunt Bae got a little louder, "People, Red is the color of love. Love is in this room and in our hearts, do you see the love?" Everyone shook their heads yes, then she began with her performance. "I wrote these vowels after our very first date. I knew he was the one and only man for me. My very first, and my last love, you are the world to me." She then stopped and began to giggle a little.

I was thinking to myself even she has to laugh at that sentence.

She continued, "Everyone I'm laughing because I'm so thrilled to become his wife and to be in his life. We will be together until death do us part. I do mean the finale. I will never let this man go. I'm not going anywhere, and I do mean anywhere, and will not allow another woman get his money, I mean get this Man. MAN I said." she got louder.

"She meant exactly what she said," Zi'lah said in my ear.

I looked over to see what Mamadoll reaction was; she was shaking her head from left to right. Then when she noticed me looking at her and she acted like something was wrong with her neck. I couldn't stop laughing. I had to act like I was blowing my nose so the tissue would cover my mouth. Is this for real? Kia quickly took the microphone from her hand and finished her job and pronounced them husband and wife. The beginning of the show was over, and now it was time for the ending, the reception.

Zi'lah leaned over and said to me, "Don't let me forget to tell Aunt Bae how she cheated herself, she could have charged guest to see this...ha ha."

Everyone headed toward the exit door and to the reception hall next door. I sat there for a minute and then Aunt Bae called my name. I grabbed Rylie to walk over but was interrupted by Kia.

"Girl I haven't seen you since you were a little girl," Kia said to Rylie as she hugged her. "Me and your mama were and still best friends. We were closer than close."

"You're the lady on the billboards, and I saw pictures of you from my mom," Rylie said.

"Oh, really I thought your mom didn't remember me." Kia winked at me and said.

"How can I forget my ride or die," I said.

"I know, I know, I'm giving you a hard time. I missed you girlfriend. When did all this happen?" she asked.

"What me moving here?" I asked.

"Yes. You didn't give me the heads up. You didn't call or nothing Mina." she said.

"It's a very long story, and I will save it for later. I didn't know I was moving back until four days ago." I said.

She looked confused, and her smile left. "Is everything ok Mina, is something wrong?"

"Everything is fine. I'm so happy to be back home, and I told Mamadoll, I was going to call you, but it looks like you are very busy Ms. Evangelist."

She took a deep breath, "Mina can you believe this? Girl one day I was teaching Sunday school, and the next day, I was selling out local venues for people to hear me speak."

"That's just like our God. What did the word say in Deuteronomy 28 and all these blessings shall come upon you and overtake you because you obey the voice of the Lord? You obeyed and answered the call." I said.

"I pinch myself sometimes Mina. I have been all over the world. Seen so many places and faces. So many years of seeking God's will for my life and my purpose. All along, my purpose was to serve Him. He's going to have his way regardless."

"Yes ma'am, you just said a whole lot right there. That was a sermon itself. I am learning it is his will, not my own. Girlfriend only if I would have listened to Him and not my flesh. I would have saved myself from a lot of painful relationships." I said.

"Sweetheart that's how we learn. That's how ministries form and grow. If you don't go through anything, He can't use you. We have to be witnesses for Him. We can't tell a world about our heavenly father if every situation is perfect, every relationship is wonderful if we never have gotten sick or had to deal with death. Girl, don't get me started, I will start preaching up in here."

"Whew! I hear and feel the anointing from all over you. I know you tear the devil up when you speak."

"You better know it. Demons flee, and strongholds are broken in the name of Jesus. We lay hands and speak healing, and have some church. You must come and visit." She said.

"Of course I'm there, what time?" I asked.

"There's a ten o'clock service, and another one at two. What service would you like to attend and how many people? I would need to know, so I can have your car valet parked and your seats reserved." She said.

"My car what and seat who?" I asked confused.

She laughed. "Mina I forgot we are from small churches. Well, this is not what you're used to this is the new millennium church. When you have twenty-five thousand members to accommodate, you have to create a seating program, parking agenda, program, etc."

"I guess so. So, in that case, then it will be the three of us attending tomorrow."

"Ok great! I will have everything prepared for you, once you arrive."

"Will you be speaking tomorrow?"

Before she could respond, my daughter interrupted us.

"They are ready to start the reception. Mamadoll said you ladies could continue talking inside the reception." Rylie said as she giggled.

Kia looked at me and said. "I see we have the same Mamadoll always watching us two."

"Ain't nothing changed but her age," I said. We both laughed and walked over to the reception together. When I entered the room with Kia, all eyes were on us. We sat at the table reserved for the family, and before I knew it, we were back talking like old times.

"Mina I forgot to tell you how I prayed and my heart was so heavy when I heard about your ex-husband."

"Thank you. I received your message. We pulled through, but you know it's a day to day process."

"I know sweetheart, and you both always have my prayers. You two are doing so well Mina, and you look so great. What made you finally come back home?" she asked.

"Well, let just say, it was meant for me to be here. I didn't want to see it end this way, but I didn't have a choice,"

"Oh, one of those scenarios." She looked at me with concern.

"Yes. I smiled. It was painful, but for a purpose."

"Mina! I was just talking about writing a daily blog about testimonials from people who suffered from painful experiences, but during that time discovered their purpose in life."

"That's great! Did you need some help? I would love to help you."

"You can. Do you still write?" she asked.

"Yes. I was laid off earlier this week from the newspaper I was writing for. Business was slow. So he said."

"Who is he?"

"The owner's son. Nobody special."

"Oh, one of those. *A daddy's boy*. I'm surprised he didn't try to sleep with you."

"He did."

She looked at me with a smirk on her face. "Well, Mina didn't you know. You were not supposed to sleep with him, and if you did you were supposed to pretend you liked it. You would still have a job. "We both laughed.

"You know what I could use some help with the church newsletter. Would you be interested?"

"Of course I would be."

"I'm thinking to myself, this would be full-time for you. We have twenty-five thousand plus members."

"Yes! I could surely try." I said.

"That's wonderful Mina. We could use your help at the church."

"Really? Ok. I haven't started looking for a job yet, but I will make time to help you."

"Don't worry Mina, I have plenty of contacts for you to work where you want to in this city. You don't have to worry. God's got you. The storm is over now, here come the Sun."

I can already feel God's favor in my life. "Thank you so much, Kia."

"You're so welcome. Let's schedule lunch for Tuesday of next week, are you available?" She asked.

"So far I don't have any plans."

"Great. I know a wonderful restaurant downtown Charlotte."

"Am I invited?" Bryce interrupted and asked.

"Hello Mr. Calhoun that depends," Kia said.

"On what Evangelist St. James?" He asked with a smirk on his face.

"If you can handle not being the only one that gets attention in public." She said.

"You have such a sense of humor Evangelist St. James. Who knew?" He said sarcastically.

I wanted to respond for her, but I know Kia can handle this herself. She didn't entertain him, because, she was saved by her cell phone.

"Excuse me I need to take this call." She said as she walked to the back of the room. I turned to look for Mamadoll and Rylie hoping he wouldn't bother me.

"You look like a deli-cioussss apple in that red dress," he said.

I continued to look around the room as if I didn't hear him. Then Aunt Bae's loud voice began to speak from a microphone.

"Please take a seat everyone. It's now time for our toast." She said.

I saw everyone walking to his or her designated table. I finally saw Rylie and Mamadoll. They came to the table with smiles on their face. "What are you two smiling about?" I asked.

Mamadoll responded, "I'm happy Mina. When I saw you and Kia together, it was like old times. Where is she?"

"She had a phone call. She's coming back." I looked over, and Zi'lah came and sat down.

"Did I miss anything?" Zi'lah asked.

"No. Where have you been?" I asked.

"Girl making my rounds. Do you see all the fine men in here?"

"Yes, I see them," I said. The lights dimmed in the room and then turned red. The band begins to play a song by Sade. "What is this? I don't think I have ever been to a reception where the lights turned red?"

Zi'lah responded, "Well you know your Aunt has a little freak in her."

I looked over at Aunt Bae, and she was smiling at her sister. I know deep inside she was laughing.

Aunt Bae approached the microphone and then cleared her throat to grabbing the guest's attention. "Everyone, thank you all for coming to witness me and the man God has joined me with for the rest of our lives. We couldn't have done it without you. There will be waiters walking around to pour you a nice tasty drink in your glass. Our choice of drink tonight is Grand Marnier and Sprite. For my pastors and spiritual brothers and sisters, remember what Jesus did at the wedding to the water. Now please lift your glasses, take a sip, and toast to this union!"

I'm wondering who throws a reception and have Grand Marnier and sprite as the drink to toast with, and not Champaign, or wine?

"Ok everyone let's have a good time with good eating, good drinking, good dancing, and some good flirting. I know one of you ladies have it in you and one day you can be like me when you get older and get you one of these." Aunt Bae said as she flashes her ring rubbing on her new husband's arm. The band stopped, and the DJ started playing. Nearly every guest ran to the dance floor from men, women, kids, preachers, husbands, wives, and hoes. We were all getting our groove on. The song selection was on point and the very first song of the night was Montel Williams *This is how we do it*! My Uncle Henry and Aunt Doris were dancing on their canes. Zi'lah grabbed her a handsome young man that was maybe from the Islands. The next song was, *Back that Azz* up, by Juvenile. And here comes more people to the dance floor. I thought every woman with a big butt was going to knock the other women down, to get to that dance floor.

I saw weave, wigs, and big booties jiggling begging for Spanx everywhere. Waiters continued walking around pouring more and more every time a cup looked empty. Everyone was backing it up, and brothers and sisters were choosing who they wanted to back it up with. I was about to sit down, but the DJ hit me one last time with *The Wobble* extended version. Rylie grabbed me by the hand, and we headed back to the dance floor.

We wobbled and wobbled. The song finally stopped playing then the DJ started playing another one immediately. *The Cupid Shuffle*. Oh, Lord! I haven't danced like this or had so much fun in so long all I could do is smile, laugh, clap, smile, laugh, and clap some more. There was one part of my body that wasn't smiling or laughing, and that was my feet. After the song finished, I decided to take a break from dancing with the family and guest. I sat down at the closest table near the dance floor. I was out of breath of course, but ready for a nice glass of wine. I don't believe I have seen any wine tonight, just liquor. The waiter brought over a bottle of water to my table, and I was thinking; how did he know what I desired right now. I guess the sweat on my face gave me away. I glanced over my shoulder and saw my Aunt smiling and chatting with renowned local preachers. My baby was smiling and laughing getting her dance on with Aunt Bae and her new husband. I started massaging my feet under the table to give them a little understanding. After the fifth song, it was time for the slow jams. I knew Rylie would sit down then. I saw Aunt Bae and her husband walking over to mingle with the crowd. I noticed Bryce and a little girl that seems to be about nineteen-years-old getting cozy on the dance floor. I guess he takes them young, old, blind, crazy; he doesn't care as long as they can vote. The DJ's first slow song of the night was Keith Sweat, *Make it last forever.*

Zi'lah limped over to the table I was sitting at singing loud and sipping on her cup. "Mina, my feet are screaming for help. Please call a doctor."

"Ask your new uncle. Aunt Bae's husband," I said laughing.

"Ha...Ha... Mina, I need a doctor to massage my feet, not foot Botox."

"Girlfriend where's that handsome gentleman you were bumping and grinding on, he was a cutie. He looked like he was from the islands."

"An island? Girl please, I didn't want to dance by myself he was pouring me a drink. I pulled him on the dance floor."

"Pouring you a drink? Zi'lah, is he one of the waiters?"

She looked at me with a big tipsy smile, "Yes girl. He's from one of the island in Mexico. He did not understand a word I was saying." She said laughing.

We both laughed. "You cannot have another drink Zi'lah."

"That's fine with me. I might fall." She said laughing.

The music faded, and I noticed guest making their way to the buffet area. I thought I would grab me a bite to eat, so I decided to put my shoes back on my feet. I think I can do this, but it seems one shoe was missing. I bent my knees a little lower to look under the table. I heard someone call my name.

"Mina, Mina,"

It was Kia. "Kia, where did you go?"

"I had to meet with someone. What's under the table?" She asked, while laughing.

"I couldn't find my shoe for a minute. But I finally found it." I leaned under the table to put it on.

"Mina, I have someone I would like for you to meet."

"Ok, who?" I said with a big smile.

Her guest back was turned to us as he was talking to several other people, "Pastor this is my best friend that I was telling you about." Kia said.

He turned around, and my mouth dropped, and my heart stopped. "Mina this Pastor Patrick Kincade. My pastor, my mentor, and my big brother."

He didn't flinch, and I didn't flinch. He was so smooth, as freshly brewed coffee. I stood there staring at him. It was the mystery man I ran into coming out of the bathroom, Patrick. What a coincidence. He smiled at me, and I smiled back. Kia stood there looking at the both of us in confusion.

"Did I miss something?" she asked.

He cleared his throat, "Kia it seems me and your best friend have already met and said our hellos. But there is nothing wrong with speaking again. Hello Ms. Mina."

"Really how?" she sounded shocked looking at the both of us back and forth.

I ignored her. "Hello, Patrick. Oops, I meant to say Pastor Kincade, you didn't tell me you were a pastor."

"You didn't ask. He said with a smile. "Patrick is fine you had it right the first time. How did you enjoy the wedding?"

"The wedding was interesting," I said. He is so fine and Lord I hope my breath doesn't smell like wine.

"I believe interesting is the right word to use. I didn't see the entire ceremony. I caught the ending. I had another engagement to attend." He said.

"I remember you mentioned you had a ceremony to attend."

"Good memory. Yes, I did. It was next door, and I promised the bride and groom I would stop by and I'm a man who believes in keeping his word." He said.

Lord have mercy on me, he talks so well. "I believe your word is sometimes all you have," I said.

"Not sometimes Mina, all the time. It is an essential part of one's character. If you say with your mouth, you are going to do something, try your best to do it. It's a sign of maturity."

"I agree, Pastor Kincade," We both were quite, again, just like when we first met. He smiled, and his voice got a little deeper and lower, "remember it is Patrick to you."

I smiled, "For me? Thank you! I feel so special."

"You should feel that way because you are. And you will, for now on." He said and winked at me.

"How can you be so sure?" I asked and winked back.

"I can feel it in my spirit," he said laughing.

"Well, shouldn't I also feel it in my spirit," I said.

"You should and you will once you believe it," he said.

I was speechless. I now remembered why he looked so familiar to me. I couldn't respond, because I didn't want to sound stupid. He intimidates me, and now I'm intimidated by his title. This is a man of God. I've listened to on the radio, watched on television and commercials, and saw his books on bookstands in different cities. Here

I stood flirting with him. I genuinely believe I am attracted to the calling on his life. I am never intimidated by anyone. I have often felt intimidation comes from the enemy, because God has made every being, equal, and He is no respecter of person, but the good Lord knows I am not myself right now. I continued to smile at him, and before I could say a word, Kia stepped closer to the both of us and interrupted our conversation.

She whispered. "You two look at me, you have an audience. Pastor, please remember where you are." I didn't understand what she meant.

I guess because I've never been a situation where it mattered to anyone, but my Mamadoll who I talked too. I turned around to see jaw-dropping women, men, the waiters, waitresses, my aunts, (the both of them), uncles, cousins, and whomever else in attendance were all staring.

The DJ didn't help the situation either. He was so, star struck; he had to give him a shout out. "Everyone look, we have Pastor Kincade in the building tonight. Hey Pastor P. I got that Fred Hammond, Kirk Franklin, Tamela Mann on my playlist for you, tell me what you wanna hear, I got it. You helped me in so many ways pastor, if you only knew," He said.

Pastor Kincade smiled, and everyone else also did. He shouted back at the DJ. "Thanks my brother. I couldn't continue my calling if I didn't see a change in people like you and the strength of God enabling me. But I'm good, please continue," He said.

How he responded was indeed a humble comment. "That was nice of you to say. Let him play a song for you." I said.

"Thank you Mina. I really can't think of a song I would like to hear. Plus I am enjoying my conversation with you."

Oh my. I didn't know how to respond at this point, but my mouth always comes up with something, "I'm enjoying you, I mean our conversation as well...LOL"

Kia leaned over and said, "Pastor Kincade I think you should mingle a bit. There are people that would like to meet you." To my surprise Pastor Patrick didn't respond are flinch at Kia's comment. It seems he could care less. He continued to stare at me as I looked around the room. He looked away at Kia with a smile.

"I am mingling." He said with a flirty smile.

"You're right Pastor my apologies," she said, with a look of concern.

"No need to apologize Kia. You are just protecting the both of us, thank you." He said.

Protecting us? Before we knew it, our conversation came to an end. People begin to approach him, and he was lost in the crowd, and once again gone. People swarmed around him like he was an art exhibit. I walked away to the buffet table without a goodbye. I saw my child and Mamadoll waiting for me. Mamadoll wasted no time.

"I see you met Pastor Kincade," Mamadoll said.

"Yes, I did, he is a very nice gentlemen," I said. She smiled at me and never made another comment. I didn't notice Kia was right behind us.

"Hey lady, were about to head home?"

"Yes I need to get Auntie and Rylie home before it gets too late." I said. "Oh wait a minute! I forgot I drove myself."

Kia smiled and stared at me for a moment, "Mina Wright, we will chat later." She paused, and went on to say, "So, I will see you and these lovely angels in the morning, right?"

"Yes, you will, and again it was so good to see you. Do you have far to drive?" I asked.

"No, not at all, I live in Walton Park." She said.

"Oh, my how nice! Be careful honey, Love Ya!" I said.

I said my goodbyes to everyone, and we all headed out the door. I could feel eyes all on me, but I wasn't bothered by it.

Once we finally made it home, we all were tired, and it was time for me to enjoy a hot steamy bubble bath. I sat in the warm water and soaked my feet, legs, arms, and every other part of my body. I couldn't stop thinking about my night, or Pastor Patrick Kincade.

This night has caught me off guard. I wasn't thinking about him in a lustful way, these were thoughts of his persona, his cool, down to earth demeanor. To be a very well-known man in this community, he was an approachable gentleman. I must admit to myself I was quite attracted to him. What is puzzling my mind is I've never been attracted to a preacher before. Not one, in my lifetime that I can recall. I also, never saw if he had a ring on or not. The funny thing about this whole scenario is, I don't think I've ever heard of him having a wife. That is not normal. Something is wrong. He is too fine, too successful, and too established, not to have been married. There are two facts I know that is true, number one, he was flirting with me, and number two, I loved it! I am such an over-thinker at times. This is a conversation I would love to have with my bestie, Naiomi. We are going to have some catching up to do. One thing I can say, it's already looking better and I haven't been home seventy-two hours yet!

Chapter 6: Sunday Morning Service...

I drove up to the gate at what seems to be one of the largest churches in the USA. It took us at least 40 minutes to drive there, and at least another 15 minutes to get to the gate and then to park. I pulled up to the gate and a gate attendant asked my name as he approached my car. "God Bless you my sister in Christ, is this your first time visiting with us?"

"Good morning and God bless you, my name is Mina Wright, and yes it's my first time. Evangelist Kia invited my family and me." I said.

He typed something on his iPad then responded, "Yes ma'am. Please drive forward to the young man in the black suit straight ahead. Welcome and enjoy the service, God has a blessing for you and your family today my sister." I smiled and proceeded to the young man. Once I was there two gentlemen walked over and opened my door, then another opened Mamadoll's door, then another walked over and opened Rylie's. They were all smiling, and once we stepped out of the car, they reached out their arms and hugged us.

"Welcome sisters, we are happy to have you here. God has a blessing for you today."

We all smiled and proceeded to walk towards one of the entrances to the church. "Mom this looks like an amusement park. Are you sure this is a church?" Rylie asked.

I laughed. "Yes, it is a church baby. It's beautiful, isn't it? I asked.

"Yes," Rylie said.

The church was unbelievable. Once we made it on the inside, I think we all were speechless. It was nothing like I had ever seen before. There was a tall statue of Jesus, identical to the one in Rio de Janeiro, with his arms stretched wide in the entrance area of the church to greet us. There were also greeters at the doors with programs and a welcome kit.

"Welcome ladies to a Street Called Straight Ministries," she said. She then handed each one of us a program and welcome kit. In the kit was Pastor Kincade's book, a t-shirt that read *Don't turn to the left, Don't turn to the right, but walk straight with Jesus,* there was a journal with the church name, and a pen. All items came with the church name inscribed on them. We were taken around to the other side of the church, and as we walked, we were able to get a small tour. There were a few small chapels' inside the church as well such as a chapel for Rylie to attend with others her age. Near the children's chapel were a children and teenager area reminiscent with a carnival theme. There were a few rides, popcorn and cotton candy stations, and billiards.

The area also provided a pizza restaurant, go-cart riding, and a small rollercoaster. It was unbelievable. The usher said this is where children come to play and to some of them this is the closest they would ever get to an amusement park.

She mentioned as we toured how Pastor Kincade wanted the children not to miss out on an opportunity because of a temporary situation they were placed in, or their parents. There were pictures of the sky, clouds, and the sun throughout. There were video's playing of Pastor Kincade and Kia sermons. Pictures of Noah's Ark chiseled in the walls, David and Goliath art hung high, and the last supper as well. I think the most stunning photo of them was a statue of our savior Jesus Christ carrying the cross on his back. It brought chills to me my body, and brought me to tears. We all stopped to view it amongst many other visitors, "Rylie you see what Jesus did for you and I, and your mom and the people of the world?" Mamadoll asked.

"Yes ma'am. I know he died for us." She said.

"That's right and don't you ever forget it," Mamadoll said.

"I want I promise," Rylie said.

It felt like we had toured a city before we made it to the sanctuary. Once we finally reached the sanctuary, it was worth the drive. I do not believe I have ever seen this many people in a sanctuary in person, perhaps on television. From the looks of it, there were at least fifteen thousand to twenty thousand people, or maybe even more. The spirit of the Lord was high, and I feel his presence. I instantly forgot everything, and every being around me. It felt so good to be in the presence of the Lord, to hear the choir singing, and to witness saints praising God. The usher led us to the very first row with another family. I have never liked sitting in the front row, but I accepted the invitation from Kia, so this is the price I had to pay. Rylie looked amazed. There was a screen directly in front of us similar to the one's you only see in a movie theater. There were cameramen all over filming and at least one hundred ushers. The choir had at least five hundred plus members, and there were two musicians for every instrument. Kia appeared out of nowhere onto the pulpit and ready to go.

"Good morning Saints of God. Let's give God some praise this morning. Yeah! I want every believer in this sanctuary to repeat after me. I will leave my problems behind. I am giving them to God today! This is for you devil and all your demonic forces you have been deleted, destroyed, and devoured in the name of Jesus. I know who I am and I know whose I am. I am the child of the highest God. I am more than a conquer, I can do all things through Christ who strengthens me. I am the head and not the tail, I am above and not beneath, and NO weapon formed against me shall prosper! Now give our God some praise, Hallelujah!"

Whew! I felt that, and I repeated it in my head again after I said it. The choir began singing another song, and you would have thought I was a member of the choir because I was singing to every beat and drum. After the song, a gentleman took over the pulpit and said a prayer.

Kia appeared again and asked for all the visitors to stand. She welcomed all the visitors and ushers a long with members walked around and gave every visitor a welcome kit. I know there had to be at least one thousand visitors. Rylie and I stood up, and the camera immediately came over and there we were on the big screen.

Kia grabbed her microphone and walked over to us, "Saints of God I want you all to know I am over-joyed this morning,"

She then walked over, took me by the hand and I grabbed Rylie's. I looked back and read Mamadoll lips, "it will be alright Mina, don't be scared, let God use you."

My heart was pounding faster and faster. I was extremely nervous, and my skin turned red as a tomato. Sweat began to come out of my pours. Once we were on the pulpit, I turned around slowly to face the congregation, and my body froze. I was so glad I wore my Sunday best outfit. I looked over at Rylie, and she was smiling from ear to ear. I have never found myself in front of so many people. I prayed to God she would not ask me to say one word.

"Saints this is and will always be my very best friend. This is her first time here with her daughter and Mamadoll, but what's most important is they just moved back to Charlotte, and God has restored our friendship. This woman has a testimony saints of God and she's a living witness that God will see you through the storm." She said.

I was thinking I love Kia to death, but she better not ask me to say one word, because Lord knows I am never coming back here to visit.

"Mina, please share with us, just a little bit of your story."

I was speechless. I grabbed the microphone with nearly twenty thousand people staring at me. "Thank you, Kia, for such very kind words and for inviting us here today I could not think of another place I would have wanted to be but in the house of the Lord, I want to be a great saint, because I'm ready to hear a word from God. I have dealt with some storms in my life over the past year; I mean challenging storms. One after another, (I paused), I didn't see a way out, but God did, and I had to learn how to trust him. I had to come to realize that trials come to make you strong; they are not a form of punishment from

God. In fact, in the Bible, he tells us to count it all joy when we go through various trials. Over the past few months, I've dealt with so much loss, that I wondered if I would ever win. I'm here to tell that someone out there you probably can't see a way out and is wondering wills the storm ever end, and when it ends will you be the winner. I won in the most crucial area of my life, and that was accepting Jesus Christ as my Lord and Savior. No matter what comes your way get this in your sprit God is a good God, and he will never leave you or forsake you. He will carry you thorough the fire, flood, rain, snow, tornado, hurricane, whatever it is. He's good every day, all day, every night, all night and he loves you. Remember this many of the afflictions of the righteous, but God will deliver us from them all. Don't give up you will win with Jesus! May God bless and keep every one of you. Thank You." I handed Kia the microphone and hugged her. We were welcomed back to our seats by a standing ovation from the congregation.

Mamadoll had tears running down her face as she hugged the two of us so hard while praising God. I started crying, Kia was crying and then she spoke again.

"No matter what you're going through today he's a good GOD, and he is worthy, I do mean worthy, I said worthy to be praised. Amen."

It was time for the offering, and I had yet to see Pastor Kincade. This particular offering is helping those in need who are members and also those that are none members. The church uses this offering to support at least 20-30 families in need of assistance with rent, food, shelter, clothing, school supplies, gas in their car to get to and from work, and any other needs to be met Aunt Mag said. The musicians began playing; *God is my Everything*, by the Chicago Mass Choir while the buckets made their way around the sanctuary. I looked over my shoulder, and there was Bryce, his dad, and Aunt Bae all sitting together, and all dressed in the same colors, but thankfully not red. Bryce was staring at me, and once he noticed I saw him staring, he smiled and waved, I waved back and smiled at Aunt Bae. She blew me a kiss and said I love you. I turned around in my seat and sitting on the pulpit was Pastor Kincade with both of his hands up in the air singing along to the music. He had the most beautiful, suit that man could tailor on. He approached the microphone and began to speak.

"While the buckets come to an end of being passed around, I want every one of you to know you must trust God. I was sitting in my office listening to Sister Mina's testimony, and I nearly ran out here to get me a seat. I was going ask her to preach." he laughed and said. The entire congregation clapped and laughed. I could not believe what my ears had just heard. I laughed, and at the same time I was blushing, and the camera was in my face, and there I appeared on the big screen. "Ushers, camera crew, Evangelist St. James, thank you all, please be seated." He said and then continued. My ears were ready to receive a word. "Saints of God thank you for being here in attendance today. I appreciate you, and I love you with all my heart. I want to let you know that I will be giving out more cars." Before he could finish, the congregation started screaming and shouting Amen again. He smiled and looked around and started again. "Many of you know I am not the type of man that is not stingy, tight or wants to hold on to every dime I have in the bank. I give cars away to those who are riding the bus, or those that cannot afford a car note, insurance or gas, because you are a single parent trying to provide for your children, but is also working and trying to improve their situation. God has placed it on my heart to always give. Like praying without ceasing, give without ceasing. We are blessed to be a blessing. I am not bragging or boasting, I am clearly advising you; that if you can help someone in need, do it. You perhaps may be the answer to an ongoing financial trial or financial stronghold that will not cease, Amen." Everyone said Amen, and he continued.

"I want you to know there is not one person exempt from trials and tribulations. If I don't know anything else I know this, they will not stay. Like any situation in life there is a beginning, and also there is an ending. I am here today to give you a word from my God, your God, our God to encourage and strengthen you. No matter how it may look in the natural please allow yourself to take a look into the spiritual because God is behind the scenes writing, directing, producing, casting, and completing his purpose for this particular season in your life." He said.

Before he could continue, the congregation began clapping and shouting Amen, Glory be to God, and Hallelujah! He then took a deep breath and began to speak again.

"God has not forgotten you and in the book of Isaiah 49:16, God said, "See I have inscribed you on the palms of my hand."

Then he put his palms together, and I was like a child at Chuck e Cheese, longing for more.

He continued, "The Lord said your destroyers and those who laid you waste shall go away from you." Then he began to clap his hands and speak louder, "I am here to tell you if you have a piece of paper, or if you want to write this down, the sermon topic is T4YT then write dot, dot, dot, and the title in which it stands for is Triple Four Your Trials. He will give you back triple for all the troubles and trials you have gone through. That means Triple joy, triple peace, triple good health, triple in your finances, triple cars, triple houses, whatever it is that you lost or went through, you are going to get back Triple, look at your neighbor and say Triple."

That was my confirmation. That's exactly what Naiomi said to me. He preached all over the pulpit. Lord knows I couldn't move and I if he didn't say anything else that was enough for me He gave the best sermon that I had heard in years. This man preached and traveled from one end of the pulpit to the other end. He was preaching in one moment, and in another, he was teaching. He came down and moved from one aisle to the next aisle, I was moved. I was so glad I came to this church to hear this sermon. I couldn't stop thanking God for knowing Kia, and her inviting me. The sermon came to an end, and he called the alter call for those who wanted to become members. Before you knew I walked down the aisle to become a member with Rylie's hand in mine. There were at least a hundred to two hundred souls at the alter that day. Pastor Kincade walked over and gave me a long hug and then whispered in my ear.

"I am so glad to see you become a member and a part of this ministry, God bless you sister."

I didn't have a chance to respond, he quickly moved on and let me go. Once the service ended, Kia walked over with pure excitement in her eyes.

"Mina Wright, you are my girl. I am so happy you joined. Girl wasn't that sermon for us?"

"Kia, it was a sermon I needed to hear yesterday. Girl these past months I was discouraged. I feel rejuvenated." I said.

"You and I both. Did you hear what the pastor said about you?"

"I did. I was shocked and couldn't stop smiling. And I must say, I was truly flattered."

"As you should be, that was a compliment. He said you sound that good. Good enough to preach." She said.

"Oh please. I wouldn't go that far, I was too nervous," I said.

Mamadoll joined I conversation, "But Mina God spoke through you, and only God knows how many people you helped through your testimony today." She said.

"Thank you, Auntie. I believe I learned from the best," I said.

"I believe I learned from the best and that's Jesus." She said.

"Amen Mamadoll," Kia said.

"Sisters, God bless you all." Bryce said, as he walked over.

"Bryce I didn't know you were here today. Did you enjoy the service?" Mamadoll asked.

"I always enjoy Pastor Kincade messages he brings the word, but I also enjoy Evangelist Kia, when will you be preaching, its' been quite a while. You know what, I don't know if I ever heard you preach." He said smiling.

Kia was quiet and looked at him with a not so nice look, then she said. "I preach all the time Commissioner Calhoun just because I am not preaching on a Sunday, that you decided to attend church services, at this church, does not mean I do not preach. I'm glad to hear you enjoy hearing me. How is the election going?"

Bryce got quiet, and his smile left, "Well as you know it's very early, but I will trust in God, and I know that he will give me favor and I will be the commissioner again. I'm not worried at all." He said.

"Yes you will son." Aunt Bae walked up and said. "We are rooting for you, and we will be marketing and getting voters to get out there and vote. Mina, I loved your speech on today."

"You were not the only one Bae. Pastor Kincade did as well." Bryce said with a smirk on his face.

I ignored him, and I realized why I didn't like him. He is messy. He is a member of messymen.com, and I cannot keep company with a messy man. "Thank You, Auntie. I was so nervous. I pray I helped at least one person out there going through a hard time. "I said.

"You did baby. You helped me." Aunt Bae said.

"Thank You that makes me feel so good,"

"That is beautiful for you to say, Bae." Mamadoll said as she smiled.

"Mina I would like for you to come to my office with me for a minute. If you have time." Kia said.

"Of course, I will. Mamadoll can you and Rylie wait for me?" I asked

"No need Mina. You go with your friend I will take them home." Bryce said.

I quickly responded, "I will take them home, I will only be a minute." I said.

"Mina, take your time. Everyone will be over today; you know I'm cooking a good meal. Bryce can take us. He is at the house every Sunday. Baby enjoy time with your friend, Rylie is fine were fine." Mamadoll said.

A change is coming he does not need to be at Mamadoll house every Sunday. "Thank you Auntie, so much, I won't be long. Rylie sweetie, behave. Thank you, Bryce." I said.

"No problem Mina. Mamadoll is like a mom to me. So, it's like were sister and brother. You do what you have to do and then come on home. You will be longer than a minute." He winked and smiled.

Do what I have to do? Longer than a minute? Where is he going with this? Why is he such a hater? "Bryce, I don't understand your comment, and I'm not about to try too. Again thanks for giving Mamadoll and my daughter a ride." I went on to say. "Mina, we will see you at home honey." Aunt Bae said.

"She's coming too." I'm thinking? *I thought she will be honeymooning, but I guess not after your fifth husband.*

Kia and I began speaking to members and visitors of the congregation. She was hugging so many people, and I begin to do the same. So many people came up to me saying how I touched them in a way and how I helped them. God truly used me today. We walked over to Kia office. It was a huge office with beautiful modern day décor and sheik-style furniture with the color of silver, turquoise, and white. She had a huge painting of her and her father over her clear glass desk. Her phone rang, and she had to step out to answer. I could see half the congregation walking to their cars through the big bay windows in her office and the skyline of the city of Charlotte.

"Mina, hello again and it was good to see you today. Is Kia around?" He asked.

It was Pastor Kincade. He looked so good in his suit. I mean mmm mmm Campbell's soup good. He wasn't as social as he was last night. We are in the house of the Lord, and I respect that, and even better he didn't have a ring on.

"Hello Pastor Kincade," I said smiling. "She stepped out, she had a phone call."

"Ok. Please tell her I need to speak with her." He said.

"No problem Pastor, I'll let her know," I said. He then turned to walk out the office. He was so sharp and looked so good. Lord help me, please. I couldn't stop smiling, I feel like I'm 15 years old again, and this was my first crush.

"Mina I haven't had the chance to thank you." He walked back into her office and said. "Thank you for becoming a member of a Street Called Straight Ministries, and also you blessed me today with your testimony." Pastor Kincade said.

I assumed he had left. "You are so very welcome. You blessed me today with your sermon." I said.

"Thank You I hoped it helped someone in some type of way."

"Of course it did. Look at all those souls who joined, but also all those members you have." I said.

"That's good, but we have people that join our church all the time, but they never come to church. We need members who are for real about God, not fair weather members, not those who come every now and then. I'm sorry, I am rambling. And Lord, forgive me for complaining. I of all people shouldn't say those types of things. I am very grateful for the favor God has given us." He said.

"You're human, right? So why can't you vent? And also, I joined, and I'm not a fair weather member, you have me, and I will be here." I said.

He smiled with those bright pearly whites. "I think part of your statement is wrong Mina, you are a member, but I do not have you yet." He said.

I cleared my throat, "When the time is right you will." *Oh, oh, oh. Did I just say that out loud?*

"Sorry about that I had to take a phone call." Kia walked in and said.

"I stopped by to see if you were going to host the event on next Thursday?" Pastor Kincade asked.

"The Hope for Hugs event I completely forgot about it. Can I please get back with you Pastor by Tuesday I have so much on my plate, and I was coming to talk to you about Mina." She said.

"About Mina?" I said.

"LOL...Mina calm down. You remember the position we have coming available in the ministry." She said.

I was on the defense. I can't lie, probably because I'm guilty as hell of being attracted to this man, now my pastor. "Oh yes, I remember I am still interested," I said.

"Ok, ok. The position for a writer for the upcoming weekly newspaper were putting together. Do you write?" He asked.

"Does she write? This girl wrote for our college newspaper, and for a professional newspaper. One of the fastest growing and largest in Dallas." Kia said.

"Talented and gifted. I love it!" He said.

"I haven't been able to use my gift. I was laid off."

"That's alright it still there so let's put that gift to work." He said.

"Ok, when do you want me to start?" I asked.

Everyone got quiet, and Kia looked over at him, "You will need to complete an application, background verification, and go through an interview process with me. We treat everyone the same around here. It is the way I do business." He said.

That is not a problem with me. Let's keep it business. "Not a problem. When would you like to interview me?"

"I'm available tomorrow. But I'm going to sleep in a little late. Therefore, I would like to interview you around 1:30 pm. Can you be here at that time?" He asked.

I wanted to ask, would you like for me to sleep in with you, but I didn't. I kept it professional. "Yes, I can be here at 1:25 pm," I said.

He laughed. "Very good. If you are hired, we will then discuss pay rate, benefits, shift, and your duties for the position. This is the business part, not church," he said.

I'm still trying to digest the part when he said, *if you are hired*, and *this is the business part, not church*.

Ok brother it's a business. I'll remember that, and I need a job, and I'm not tripping. "Not a problem Mr. Kincade." *I change to mister from pastor sense this is a business*, "Sounds like a plan. I'll be here."

"Good, good. This is going to be great for us and especially for the both of you," Kia said.

What does she mean by for the both of you? "Well I am going to head home my aunt is cooking, and it's already 1:32 and a sista didn't have breakfast," I said.

"That sounds good girlfriend. What is she cooking?" Kia asked.

"I have no Idea, but you know Mamadoll, she will have a roast in one pot, baked chicken in another, and a brisket. You name it. You both are welcome to stop by." I said.

"Thanks for the invite, but I have plans. I will catch you next Sunday for sure." Kia said.

"Absolutely. The invite will be there." I said.

Pastor Kincade had a look on his face like he was in deep thought. "I would love to join you and Mamadoll, I'm sure the food is delicious, but I have to answer my calling. I have to be at another church after the next service is over." He said.

"You still have to eat." I blurted out before I knew it.

"I know. I will grab me something from the café downstairs. The cooks take care of their pastor." He said.

"Café? I didn't see a café!" I said.

"Well, that means I will have to take you on a full tour of the church." He said.

"I guess so. Whenever you have the time." I said.

He smiled. "I wouldn't know what to do with myself if I actually had time on my hands. Speaking of time, I need to get out of here. Mina, I will see you tomorrow. Kia, I will meet with you on Wednesday."

"No, Tuesday Sir," Kia said.

Patrick didn't respond.

"Thank You both for a great opportunity and considering me," I said.

"Not a problem Mina, you should know I was going to look out for you and Rylie. I'll call you tomorrow." Kia said.

I walked out her of her office, and the both of them were staring at me. I have had quite a day and a week. God is throwing out blessings, and I have my hands ready to catch them. I am excited about my future and ready to be a part of this ministry. My life is moving in a direction that I was not prepared for so quickly, but I am willing to go wherever God takes me. I jumped into my car so excited I started screaming thank you, Jesus, for opportunity and putting the right people in my life. The entire way home I thought about the message and how it blessed my soul. Triple For Your Trials continued to ring in my head. And the fact that I opened my mouth, actually said what I said in front of twenty thousand people in the sanctuary, and online viewers. Who would have thought just two weeks ago I was crying and didn't have any direction on which way to go, and now here I stand in front of a church encouraging people and letting them know about the goodness of God. It's simply amazing. I cannot wait to talk to Naomi. We have so much catching up to do. Once I made it home, I saw cars lined up in the front yard and driveway. Rylie is such the social butterfly. She was playing outside with the neighbors and her cousins. It's been some time since I have lived with my aunt. I forgot how she enjoys spending time with family. I could smell her home cooking from outside.

I walked in the house and acknowledged the familiar faces present. "Hello everyone. It smells so good up in here Mamadoll, what are you cooking?"

"Hey suga, you know me I just threw something together. Glad to see you made it in time to eat with us." Mamadoll said.

"You just threw something together, Pork Chops, Meat Loaf, Macaroni and Cheese, smothered potatoes, fried corn on the cob, black eye peas, and homemade butter rolls, and you call that throwing something together?"

"Mina, you know my sister. Girl, you blessed me today for a second time mmm, mmm, I kept saying thank you, Jesus, for Mina sharing her story with us." Aunt Bae said.

"Thank you for a second time." I said with a slight chuckle.

"What took you so long to get home? We had been here for at least an hour or two." Aunt Bae asked.

I tell you the truth if it's not her asking the questions, its Bryce. But like I said every family has a messy Aunt, cousin, or somebody. Why isn't she at home with her new husband? I should ask her that. "I stayed behind to talk with Kia. I'm a head upstairs to change. I'll be back." I ran upstairs to my bathroom and pulled out my phone to text Naiomi. Hey BFF all is well, and life is going good. I am so glad I moved home. I joined church, and I have an interview with the same church, I just joined. And I must tell you more. I miss you all. Tell Javi hello. I'll call you later.

Naiomi didn't hesitate to respond. Mina OMG you forgot about us already! LOL. I'm so happy for you. I never doubted God. I knew he was going to take good care of you both. I will be waiting for my call. Love you girl.

I changed into something comfortable and headed to the kitchen. Everyone was talking and having a good time.

"Mina baby, uncle enjoyed you with all the other folks in church. And you were wearing that skirt," Uncle Henry said.

"I agree Uncle Henry. You looked delightful." Bryce said.

"Thanks,"

"We weren't the only ones who noticed. I noticed when you were at the alter the Pastor gave you a real long hug." Aunt Bae said giggling.

Here she goes. "I believe he hugged everyone," I said.

"No, no Mina, he only hugged you, we all witnessed it!" Bryce said as he was sipping on his drink.

"I know I saw it." Aunt Bae chimed in.

"Me too." Zi'lah walked in and commented.

"Me three, and I thought I saw his hand move below the waist." Uncle Henry said as he chucked aloud.

"No, you did not Uncle Henry. Stop it that's how rumors get started, and I don't want Rylie to hear you all saying those type of things about me and the pastor," I said.

"She saw it too." Uncle Henry laughed and said.

Everyone thought that was so funny. "Anyway, Zi'lah where did you sit at in church?" I asked.

She responded all dramatic, "Well, unfortunately, I sat wayyyy way in the balcony. I couldn't get a seat in the front row, and sure couldn't get a microphone in my hand, or a camera in my face and I've been a member for five years." She laughed.

I responded all dramatic also, "Of course you can Zi'lah, you just need to be on time for church and not come an hour late, and you wouldn't have to sit way wayyy in the balcony." I laughed.

"Ok, ok, I deserve that one. I was up late last night." She said looking at Bryce with a smirk.

Damn, I sure hope she did not give him none of her inheritance down there, she must realize she is worth more than that.

"Zi'lah if you had what the pastor wanted, you might get a microphone in your hand and camera in your face that's what Mina really wanted to say." Uncle Henry said.

Uncle Henry is too old to be so messy. He was laughing so hard I thought his false teeth was going to fall out his mouth again. "Uncle Henry, Pastor Kincade is a man of God and now my pastor that's all," I said.

"Pastor Kincade is still a man that God made." Uncle Henry said.

"That's enough Henry. Everyone leave Mina alone. She is a beautiful woman, and of course, men are going to flirt with her, let us stop the gossiping and get ready to eat." Mamadoll said.

"Honey if that was me, and that man was looking at me like he is looking at you, and hugging all on me, I would be searching for me a wedding dress by now." Aunt Bae said.

"We know you would Aunt Bae," I said.

We all sat down again at the beautiful table and ate a beautiful meal prepared by Mamadoll. I ate and immediately headed to me some alone time before it was time for to return and clean the kitchen. I needed to pray and seek God about this situation. I also wanted to find me a nice professional outfit for my interview tomorrow. I got on my knees to thank God for what he has done in my life, and what he was about to do. I am grateful for being surrounded around believers, and for having a praying woman of God in my life, like Mamadoll. After about an hour of alone time with God, I decided to see if my Mamadoll was ready for me to clean the kitchen.

Bryce was sitting on the couch lounging as if this was his new address. Mamadoll and Aunt Bae was sitting on the front porch swinging and enjoying the nice weather God had given us.

Rylie, of course, was on her iPad. I noticed no one tried to lift a finger in the kitchen beside me. I begin washing the dishes and mopping the kitchen floor. I was humming to the sound of gospel jazz and was in my own little world. Rylie came in to help me out. She had her headphones on, and I had my earphones in. We were almost done before someone joined us by tapping me on my shoulder.

"Mina I was wondering would you like to come down to the campaign office tomorrow and join us. We could really use your help and your lovely spirit." Bryce asked.

I will be nice and not respond sarcastically. "Bryce, I would love too, but I have plans for tomorrow."

"Well what time will you be done, we will be there past the evening, and sometimes we don't leave until around eight or nine pm." He said.

"I don't know Bryce, but if I am done in time, I will try to swing through, ok," I said.

"Sure thing. I was only asking because Mamadoll told me you were going to be looking for work soon, and I was going to help you out, I know a lot of people in this city, and my name goes a long way." He said.

He is so full of himself. *My name goes a long way.* Oh whatever, go home. "Like I said, I'll try to swing through if time allows."

"I hear you, sweetie. Mina just be careful, this is not the same Charlotte, and it sure isn't Dallas." He said sarcastically.

"What does that mean Bryce?" I asked.

"What does it sound like it means?" He sounded serious. He walked over to me and got a little too close to my space. He continued to speak. "Sometimes we enter a new place, and we are the new face. So, therefore, we receive the attention we have longed for, and we think that it will bring much more. Newsflash Mina, its only attention. It is nothing more, or nothing less. It will not turn into a relationship or a marriage. It's only attention, and it's only to entertain one's desire, because it is what he or she is missing at home. But when he or she begins receiving that attention again, from the significant other, you want be needed."

Whoa! I didn't pause or hesitate to respond. This is another damn Damien. Does he know my words cut also? God is still helping me in that area.

"Poor Bryce, are you speaking from experience?" I asked.

You would have thought I slapped him and cursed him out. He had an evil look on his face as if he wanted to take me and throw me away somewhere. I gave him the same facial expression right back, because I am not afraid of him, or his title. From his comment he made, he is a 3BM, a broken, bruised, bitter man. He told it on himself. I do not care how much money he has in the bank or his pockets, or the fact he doesn't have any children, his title, or how handsome he is. Someone has ruined him, and he is still hurting. I left him and his feelings standing in the kitchen.

My Interview

I left the house at 12:15 to be on time for my 1:30 interview at the church. I knew it would at least be a forty-minute drive, but I found myself stuck in traffic that was unexpected. I wore my black suit with a pencil skirt and lavender sheer, but silky blouse, with my jacket button, closed. While sitting in traffic, Kia called me to confirm our lunch appointment on Tuesday, the one I forgot about. I have been moving non-stop since the day I got back into this city. I confirmed with her because I really would like to know what she's been up to besides preaching and teaching, and also how she came in contact with Pastor Kincade. I am curious about what kind of relationship they have. Being that we are still great friends I would have thought she would have given me a little insight on him, but that's just me being nosey.

I arrived to the church earlier than I anticipated even with the traffic jam. Once I pulled into the parking lot the gate attendant said he was expecting me. He then pointed me in the direction of a personalized parking spot that read: This spot belongs to a *Future Employee of a Street called Straight Ministries*. Now that's pretty professional. When I walked in the church; an older woman who looked to be in her late 60's, smiled at me frequently as she escorted me upstairs and away from the church. We entered another building that read, *you are now entering the Business Area* followed by a name, *PAK Corporation and Investments*.

She pointed me to the couch and asked me to have a seat. She then said someone would be with me shortly. This was definitely, the *Business Area*. There was a huge receptionist desk in the center of the floor. The décor had a modern and sheik style to it with very stylish wall art throughout the entire floor. I saw PAK on nearly every pen, pencil, cups, mugs, and the walls. From afar I saw an enormous 20x20 framed photograph of a beautiful little girl who seems to be maybe five or six years old. I walked a little closer and right beside the photo was another one, this photo had Pastor Kincade alongside the little beauty. At the bottom of the photo inscribed read, Pasha Kincade age five, and her father, Pastor Patrick Allen Kincade. Well there we go; he has a daughter. I wonder how old she is. I wonder if she's his only child. Where is Pasha's mother? I thought to myself, as I asked these questions in my head,

"Ms. Wright, Mr. Kincade will now see you." Said the older woman.

I walked into the not so regular size office, which looked like a penthouse suite. He was not dressed in a suit, as a matter fact, I like him even more with this look. He wore a recreational type of outfit. A black, white, and red Nike jogging suit with the latest edition Jordan tennis shoes, and a matching baseball cap. He was casual and comfortable relaxing on his plush couch watching Family Feud on the, oh so nice seventy-two-inch plasma television imprinted into the wall.

"I love Family Feud. It's my favorite game show." I said. He never turned around. He grabbed the remote and turned the television off. He slowly jumped up and then turned around. You would have thought the man saw a ghost.

"Whoa." He quickly caught himself and began to clear his throat. "Ms. Wright you look very professional."

I responded, "Thank you very much." We both laughed.

"Excuse my appearance I am normally not dressed so casual at work, but I forgot I took the day off. I didn't have your phone number to call and reschedule, and I am a man of my word, so here I am." He said.

He could have called Kia for my number, but I won't go there, I'm glad he didn't.

"Well thank you for coming in on your day off. I feel special." I said. Smiling like a little teenager.

"Here we go, remember you are special my dear. Will I have to remind you all the time, or every time we see one another?" He asked.

He walked a little closer to me, and I smiled. "I am special, and that's why you came into work today," I said.

"Is that right? How can you be so sure?" He said with a big smile.

"Because you told me, I always remember? Now, do you want to start? (I paused), this interview Mr. Kincade?" I asked then winked at him.

"I wanna start alright." He said in a deep sexy voice...this interview, Ms. Mina," he said smiling from ear to ear.

"When you start, you want be able to stop," I said.

"How do you know I will want to stop? I think I will enjoy it." He said.

I nearly undressed myself, but quickly realized what I was saying, and how I was behaving. I was behaving seductively, and that is not the person I wanted to be. But I was longing for a hug and to be held, but that is not what I am here for.

"Give me the first question," I asked.

He hesitated then responded. "Where are you from?"

"I'm from Charlotte, North Carolina," I said.

"How old are you?'" he asked.

"I am forty years old," I said.

"How many children?'"

"Only one, from my first marriage," I said.

"What happened to your marriage?" he asked.

"Just different. No understanding, No communication."

He looked at me with a confused look. "Do you ever want to be married again?"

I paused. "If it's the Lord's will."

He smiled. "Good answer."

"Do you have a boyfriend?" he asked.

"No,"

"Why Not?" he asked.

"We broke up?"

"When." He said.

"A week ago,"

"A what?" he shouted.

"A week ago, but it was over before the finale," I said.

"Why?" he asked.

"Wasn't meant to be."

"What college did you go to?" he asked

"I went to a college in Dallas," I said

"Dallas, Texas?" He asked.

"Yes. I moved there when I got married. My ex-husband had a job transfer."

"So you are a Cowboy fan?" He said.

"I like football. Yes, I do like the Cowboys" I said.

"Really? I get tickets all the time to games. Would you and your daughter like to go sometime?" he asked.

"We would love too?"

"Good, Good. Maybe someday someone will take you, I'm a Redskins fan."

"Ha, ha, ha. Bad for you."

We both smiled. "Sense of humor," I said.

We both starred at one another briefly in silence.

"I like that." He responded. "Now, let's get to business. This job is a writing position. It's for a writer." He added.

Now he wants to talk about the job since he has found out everything else he wanted to know. "Great. I love to write." I said.

"Good. Share your gift then and write about what people experience and how the Lord has brought them through. Let those who know the Lord, and those who don't know God grab a newspaper in the airports, coffee house, convenience stores, college campuses, neighborhood doorsteps, hospitals, bus stations, train stations read about his victorious miracles. It will consist of you visiting hospitals and nursing homes along with members who are sick and shut-in, or those who have recovered. You need to meet with them, get to know them, know their testimony and so forth. You cannot be in this ministry without being part of what people are going through. You cannot have a heart, or a passion, for those who are in need without feeling their need, or their pain. I love God; I'm crazy about Jesus and Jesus is about people. I love how God has used me to be an influential person in my community and communities around the world. I can help them when they feel hopeless, preach a good sermon, or share a scripture with them that will turn tears into laughter. I'm sorry you have to excuse me I get excited about helping people." He said.

I didn't know what to say, he went from flirting to talking about his love for people, but this is what makes him so attractive. He is just like me still a human being with a desire for the opposite sex, and not afraid to show it even with the title he carries. "I love giving. I love how I feel when I give. But sometimes people take advantage of a giving spirit." I said.

He stopped and looked at me for a moment, "Use discernment, give, and let God handle the rest. God will not allow his children to be ignorant. You might not see what the person's motive is in the natural realm or, whether they are good or bad at first, but God will expose what is hidden remember that. So what are your thoughts on the newspaper?" He asked.

"I think you have a great idea," I said.

"It's not about me. It's not about you. I'm not speaking of me. This is bigger than me." He began speaking with passion. He jumped up out of his chair and continued, "I'm speaking of the ministry, God's Ministry, the kingdom, God's kingdom, and the need of the people Mina."

"Your right! It's not about me, or you, it's about the people and about our children as well. They are our future. We need leaders, motivators, imitators of Christ to build a village, or whatever it is we are striving to achieve in this kingdom business." I said.

He smiled. "What would the layout look like? What would you talk about? What would you name it? With all the social media out here, how would you get people in today's society to read it? Where would you market?"

I thought about his questions. But before I could answer he responded.

"Oh yes! Thank you, Jesus. I knew when God spoke to me about you he had a plan. Let's go and achieve what God has told us to do. When can you start?"

"When do you want me to start?" I asked.

"Tomorrow."

"Are you serious?"

"As a heart attack."

"Ok. I'll be here."

"Let's start after one. Say around one-thirty." He said.

"That's fine with me," I said happily.

"Good, Good, give me a second, let me grab the paperwork for you to complete."

I couldn't believe it, I haven't been home a week, and there I was with a job, not a job but a career working in the ministry of one of the largest non-denominational churches in the world. I knew God was going to bless me; indeed, he is on time, and he knew just what I needed like always.

While I sat waiting for him to grab my paperwork I noticed several pictures of him and his daughter. I thought this would be an excellent opportunity to begin probing and throw a joke in there at the same time.

"Is that your daughter?" I asked.

He didn't answer right away. "Yes, that is daddy's angel."

"She is a beautiful angel. I was sitting here wondering, if she looks more like her dad or her mom?" I said joking.

He laughed really hard. "You have to guess Ms. Mina? Haven't you seen her daddy?"

He dodged that bullet real smooth. As soon as I went to ask another question he changed the subject.

"Alright, Ms. Mina here is all your paperwork. Please bring it back by tomorrow, so you can receive your passcodes to the building, badge, parking space number, discount card for merchandise, (he paused), and I will get your name tag made for your office door and whatever else is needed." He said.

"My office, my badge, and my own parking space. Wow! You forgot something." I said.

"What was that?"

"My salary."

"Yes, Yes I knew I forgot something. Okay. We will sell the paper for two dollars per copy. You will receive all the money that is generated from the sales of the paper and an annual salary of ninety-five thousand."

I begin doing the math in my head. "Let me understand this. If the paper sells twenty thousand copies a month, I will receive all the money from the sales. Did I hear you correctly? That would be forty thousand! Along with my salary." I said.

"I know what I said, sweetheart. You are the creator, managing editor, and writer. It's your newspaper." He said.

I jumped up and nearly touched heaven's door screaming. I was so happy, as tears begin to flow slowly on my face. Before I knew it, I wrapped my arms around him and proceeded to give him a big hug. To my surprise, he hugged me back. "Thank you, Jesus! Thank You, Jesus! Thank God for you Pastor, I mean Mr. Kincade. Thank you so much, I will not disappoint you." He didn't want to let go, so he continued hugging me with a very tight grip, and our bodies drew closer and closer. In a deep voice, he spoke as his lips touched my ear.

"I'm ready for change Mina, I need a change, I've been praying for change." His warm cheek pressed against mine, his arms, everything felt so good. Then we were looking at one another face-to-face, eye-to-eye.

"I've been praying for change also. Change is mandatory and often necessary," I said.

Before we knew it, our lips said hello, nice to meet you, and our tongues said how are you, where have you been? It was not only a kiss, this man was kissing me on a whole other level, and I was enjoying it. But we both knew this was not the right place. I gently pulled away from him real, real slow. I shook my head.

"We can't do this, not here, and not like this. This is still a church," I said.

He smiled at me and pulled me back close to him. "What are we doing Mina?" He asked me confused. "We were having a conversation, and we kissed, and this is my office in another building, not church." He began to kiss me slowly on my neck, and his hands begin moving to my waist. "I am attracted to you, and I know the feeling is mutual. I was attracted to you from the moment you spoke to me after you bumped into me and nearly knocked me over." We both laughed standing there like two teenagers. "But on a serious note I know my position and who I am maybe challenging for you to deal with, and I understand." He paused, and I begin thinking now I know why I am so attracted to him. He is so down to earth and funny, and I can't believe I kissed this man. He has made me feel so good about myself. We are human, and it's not easy to ignore our attraction towards one another, I was ready to hear more, and I had my words ready to respond, but then his phone rang. He answered, and his voice got very low. He sat down on his couch, took his baseball hat off and rubbed his head with his hand back and forth. He then spoke loudly. "I'm sorry to hear that, and you know you and your father are in my prayers, what do you need from me?" I couldn't hear the voice on the other end, but whomever it was the call disturbed him. "Well let me finish up here at the office, and I will call you once I get settled in, tell her I love too." He said. From the sound of it, that was a call from probably his baby mama, but I didn't want to go there and assume. I turned and begin to stare out the window at the far skyline of Charlotte. Rain was in the forecast, and I did not want to be in five o'clock traffic. It was already 3:15. I heard his footsteps walk up behind me, and the heat from his body was blowing on my mind. "I am sorry for the interruption Mina, can we finish?" I turned around, and we smiled at one another. He took his hand and rubbed it through my short curls then kissed me on my forehead slowly, our foreheads touching one another with both hands on my face.

"You are truly an answered prayer Mina Wright." He said. I was not dry anywhere on my body at this point.

I responded, "How can you be so sure?" He rubbed his hands against my face looking romantic and sexy, but serious at the same time.

"Because I know what I prayed for, and I believed God would answer."

"Then what are you going to do with your answered prayer?" I asked.

He smiled and said, "Take care of it and show God how grateful I am."

Lord, have mercy on me. I will take two of him. This man has got me already. We went to kiss again, but his phone rang again, and someone knocked on the door at the same time. I was nervous. Oh Lord someone is at the door. I straightened my clothes, and he answered his phone a little aggravated and real short.

"This is Patrick. Hello. Yes, she told me. I'm so sorry. Yes, sir, I will. Bye-Bye." He said. Then he hung up the phone, and then answered the door.

"Mr. Kincade you had a four o'clock appointment with the Fathers R Us program, they called to see if you would be there by 4:15, because they have something special for you planned." The beautiful older lady who greeted me said.

Patrick glanced over at me, and he exhaled with a deep breath, "Please let them know I will be there, thank you."

He is such a busy man. "Were you going to continue where you left off before we were interrupted? Are would you like to continue another time?" I asked.

He paused then walked over to me and grabbed my hand. He then kissed it. "I would like to continue our conversation away from here, because as you can see I'm supposed to be off day, but I'm still working and I…"

I interrupted him, "Because you are always needed."

He looked at me with a serious yet seductive look in his eyes. He was quite for a moment, "I have needs too. Can you, no, I'm sorry. Will you fulfill my needs, Mina?"

I began to melt literally, and lust grew stronger all over my mind and body. Lord Jesus you know I'm trying to do right. Please get me out of the office, give me an exit right now, or I will give in. "We can fulfill each other needs," I responded.

"I like that, and yes we can. May I have your phone number?"

I didn't hesitate, "Sure."

"I'm calling you now." He said.

"Is this your number?" I asked.

"Yes, my personal number, and you are now one of the seven people who have it. You actually make number eight." He said.

"The number eight represents new beginnings." I said.

"I know my dear, and that's not a coincidence." He said with excitement in his voice.

Then his office phone rang again, and at this point, I grabbed my purse and proceeded to make my way to the door again. "I am going to let you answer your calling. It is already four o'clock and you have somewhere to be, and I do also. "I said.

"I am man of my word, remember?" He said.

"I remember PAK, words of wisdom," I said.

"Oh, now I'm PAK. Ok, ok, ha, ha, ha, someone's getting comfortable around here." He said smiling.

I looked around and asked, "Who would that be sir?"

"Who would that be? He asked. "That would be that owl...who. Who." He said.

"Well someone made me feel comfortable," I said.

"That was maybe someone's plan." He said smiling then he winked at me. "So tomorrow we start."

"Yes sir," I responded and headed out the office door. I walked down the huge hallway to only see more and more pictures and awards. There were a group of older women smiling at me once I approached the elevator.

"Have a blessed day Ms. Wright and welcome we all are excited to have you here." She said. I was surprised. How did she know my name and that I were hired?

"Thank you," I replied then she continued. "Your testimony encouraged me on Sunday."

"That is very kind of you to say." I reached my hand out to introduce myself. "I'm Mina, and you are?"

"I know who you are sweetie. I'm Hazel Schroeder, Pastor Kincade personal assistant." She said.

Now that explains it. "It's very nice to meet you."

"You also, I look forward to us working together." She smiled and said.

"Like wise," I said with a smile.

Once in the car, I had to regroup. There were so many. I couldn't believe going through my brain I needed to breathe and relax. I wish at this moment there was a drive through nearby where you could grab you a few glasses of wine and a designated driver. I have not been home a full week, and I couldn't believe every positive thing that has happened to me. I couldn't believe he offered me a job position doing exactly what I love to do such as writing.

I couldn't believe the salary he offered me, and I cannot believe I kissed him, and he kissed me. Most of all I couldn't believe I didn't want to move back home. I must learn to trust God more. I have to realize his plan is so much better than we can think or imagine. God has an amazing purpose for my life.

I'm sitting in traffic thinking; *how this has all came together. I must get to a place where I trust God.* I made it home to see I was alone. No family just me myself and I. I saw a hand written note left for me on my bedroom door. Mamadoll is old school for sure. She didn't bother texting me.

Honey me and Rylie are on the campaign trail for Commissioner Calhoun, there is food in the kitchen ready to be eaten by you. We love you, see when we get home!

Wow, she is serious about helping Bryce and his campaign.

I decided once I arrived home I would unpack my luggage and sort my belongings around my room because they have not been touched since I made it home. I can't stop thinking about Patrick and how we kissed. I forgot he was a pastor and my pastor, after the way he kissed me. It was seductive and aggressive like he had not kissed anyone in a while. His hands felt so good while he was holding me. I walked around my room-straightening things up talking to myself, and out loud to God. What am I going to do? How am I going to work with him every day and stay dry down there and not lust after him?

I am just being honest with myself, and God. I need self-control. I am still human God. My conversation with God was interrupted. It was my bestie Naiomi, and I remembered I promised I would call her back.

"Hello, my best friend forever," I said.

"I don't think we will be best friends forever from the looks of things. I thought you were going to call me back Mina Wright?"

"I know what I said, missy. Girlfriend I have not rested or sat down but a few minutes, then I'm doing something else and going from here to there, and everywhere. I'm so very sorry." I said.

"Yeah, yeah, I hear you. What's been going on lady? How is it being back home? How is Rylie and Mamadoll?" she asked.

I remembered in my luggage I had a bottle of wine. I ran downstairs to grab a glass and poor me some because I knew this was going to be a long conversation.

"Mamadoll is wonderful, and she and Rylie have bonded. Lawd have mercy. There is so much to tell I don't know if we have time." I said.

"We have plenty of time, Javi and the kids are at the movies."

"How are Javi and the kids?"

"They're fine, everyone is fine, give me the scoop woman!" She said yelling.

"Ok, ok let me go sit out on the patio with my wine, this going to be good," I said.

"I have my wine too, and I'm already on the patio, just like old times," she said.

I begin to tell Naiomi about my week at home step by step but immediately jumped into the most important part. "First off I found and joined a great church, and I have a job with a great salary," I said.

"What! Already Mina you just got there. Where, when did this happen?" She asked."

"Remember me telling you about my friend I grew up with Kia St. James who is an evangelist?" She remembered. "I ran into her at my Aunt Bae wedding, and she invited me to her church on yesterday, and I got up to tell my testimony, and then there was an interview set-up, and then I went to my interview. I was offered a job to be the editor of the up and coming church newspaper with a salary of ninety-five thousand annually. And then I was so excited, I kissed the famous pastor and he kissed me back and I didn't want to stop, but I knew I had to, but I didn't. Did you get all that?"

"Hold up, hold up! Did you say you kissed the famous pastor?" She asked in shock.

I responded, "Yes that's what I said. I know it's hard to believe."

"Wait a minute Mina. Hold up." She was silent. "Didn't you just lose your job, after letting cotton man kiss on you?"

"I fired myself."

"Same thing. And didn't you just get put out the house, in the rain, from someone you loved for five years?"

"My things were placed outside. So I guess, yes."

"And not even two weeks later you move back home, you join church, you go from being jobless to having a job paying ninety-five thousand a year, and you kiss a famous pastor?"

"I guess you can say that. Yes, that's true."

She was quite. "Girl, want he do it? God will do it. I bet if someone asked you where is Damien what would you say."

"Damien? Damien who? "We laughed hard. That's my girl. Gotta love her.

"First of all who is the pastor? How did you kiss him? Did you go out with him? Jesus girl you got me over here on pouring another glass of wine." She said.

I took a deep breath. I know Naiomi will never tell anyone what we talk about. She never has. "Well we did not go out, or should I say we have not went out yet, but anyway he offered me the job writing for the newspaper like I mentioned at ninety-five thousand a year, and I will receive all the income from the papers we sell." I took a sip of wine and continued, Naiomi was so quite I had to say hello twice. "The papers will sell at two dollars each," I said. I heard a scream a loud scream.

"Whew, ooohhh. Mina. Girl, I would have had that man on the desk, the floor, in his closet. "

"Wait a minute Naiomi. We almost went there. We were all over one another." I said

"Was there tongue action? Any clothes come off?" She asked probing.

"Yes and no," I said.

"Yes and no what?" she asked.

"What's up with you? You're the one always quite I'm surprised at you and your questions?" I said.

"I know you have needs and wants Mina and especially after what you have been through. You deserve it. I want to see my BFF happy, that's all." She said.

Naiomi always has the nicest words to say, always wanting to see me happy. "Ok, shall we continue?"

"Where were you when you and he kissed?" she asked.

"His office attached to the church. We kept getting disturbed by phone calls etc." I said.

"His office attached to the church? What's the name of this church? Who is he, Mina?" She asked.

"He is known here in Charlotte and surrounding cities nearby, but I don't know if he was as popular in Dallas. The name is a Street called Straight Ministries. His name is Patrick Kincade." I said.
I heard her sipping on her wine then she spoke. "The Patrick Allen Kincade?"
"Yes. That's him have you heard of him?" I asked.
"Anointed, prophetic, oh so handsome and FINE, Patrick Kincade with twenty thousand members, yes anyone in ministry has heard of him, I'm surprised you have not." She said.
"I heard of him, but I didn't realize who he was here in Charlotte. I didn't pay attention to how many members, blah, blah, you know all that stuff." I said.
"Mina this is amazing. I'm speechless. You went from shacking with no good devil Damien to locking lips with a pastor." She said.
"Damien who? I keep asking." I replied.
"I know that's right. You are hilarious Mina. That's my girl. So, Mina, he's not married? Well, I guess not, because I know you are not going to mess with a married man." She said.
"He didn't have on a ring on his finger. I only saw pictures of he and his daughter. If he were married, surely he would have pictures of he and his wife. Or family pictures?"
"You would think he would, and definitely have his ring on. I don't know these days Mina. It's not traditional anymore in some of these churches. Girl church folk are a trip." She said.
"Well I am traditional, and if we are married, I want everyone to know were married and I am the first lady of my church. I would want my husband to have pictures of not only he and my daughter. I would think he had something to hide." I said.
"That's true, but think about it from this point of view if he is married maybe she doesn't want to be seen. He has twenty thousand plus members. Everywhere he goes he is noticed, hardly any private time. Then you have the atheist, other non-believer groups, thieves, straights, gays, etc. Who may not like him and what he stands for, so he has to be careful? That position is not for everyone. That's why God chooses them." She said.
Damn, Naiomi is always on point. I love that we share and talk about everything. "I guess I didn't think about it like that."
"Honey we can always find out, it's called Google." She said.
"See, I should not have to do that? If you're married dammit wear your ring and stop flirting with other women. I guess I'll Google him tonight."

"You don't have to. I got your back. I have the iPad in my lap, and Google pulled up. I have begun my search. I love you too much to see you to go from bad to worse."

"Thank you, Naiomi, because Lord knows I want my own husband, and no one else's," I said.

"That's right. Ok, I have him pulled up." She then paused and continued. "Mina he is so handsome. I can see you two together. This is a nice picture of him in a suit, he not only looks good; he looks wonderful. Ask him can he send my husband the suits he can't fit into anymore?"

"Naiomi can you be serious?" I asked.

"Sure I can. Ok let us see what Google says about Mr. Kincade," She said.

"OMG, I'm nervous. This is snooping. Google is not the truth. You know?" I said.

"No it isn't, but it will give you a little insight on the past and present of the man. Here we go.

"Patrick Allen Kincade born on February 22, 1964, in Denver, Colorado to Patrick Charles and Mara Ilene- Kincade. He is their only child. He was the NFL's first round draft pick in 1985 and signed to a twenty-five million- dollar contract over a four years period. He retired after the fourth year to answer his calling to become a preacher. He moved to Charlotte, North Carolina in 2006 and the same year begin his ministries now known as A Street Called Straight Ministries with only three hundred twenty-five member that grew to twenty thousand and became one of the largest non -profit, non-denominational ministries in the world." She stopped reading and took a long pause. "He married Tish Kincade in 2005 and the two added to their family after Tish gave birth to a daughter, Pasha in 2009. He has an estimated net worth of two hundred eighty million dollars. He is currently working on his biography entitled, Priceless Perseverance scheduled to debut on bookshelves winter of 2016." I stopped her before she could continue.

"Alrighty then, I believe I can stop guessing now. I knew it! There are not any good men in this world! I believe they live on another planet where they are faithful to their wives, good fathers to their children, excellent jobs with benefits, and really do have the fear of God living in them." I said.

Naiomi was quite. She never spoke once or interrupted me. I felt like she was saying here we go again. "Hello?" I said.

"I'm here, are you finished?" She asked.

"Well say something," I said.

"I can't. I am over here thinking about that two hundred eighty million dollars. Ha, ha, ha," She said.

"Naiomi please be serious."

"Ok. Ok. First thing you should do is calm down missy. You just met him. Mina, you haven't been around to see what's really going on. There are several ways to look at this. That man is not that bold to approach you the way he did, and do what he did in his office to be a (a) married (B) a well-known pastor. He hasn't known you long enough Mina to act the way he is acting. What if you were to go to the press on him? What if you were to lie on him? What if you were to tell the entire congregation? Would he risk all that God has blessed him with for a piece of your pie, or like you say your inheritance? I don't know the man, but I know he is too smart for that."

Naiomi does have a good point. But I'm sitting here thinking about the fact that Google© also did not say a word about a divorce. "Your right Naiomi I totally agree with you, but what if the wife doesn't care about him seeing other women. Let's look at this outside the spiritual realm and look at this from the world point of view. What if she is there just for the money and has the mentality as long as I'm getting paid do whatever you want, there are women like that. Maybe they both are pretending in front of the congregation and people?

"But why would someone go that far? Just be honest and divorce?" Naiomi asked.

"I feel the same way you do Naiomi, and it blows my mind why couples stay together. I see it all the time. People usually stay in relationships for finances, children, reputation, etc. And we don't know for sure. He's Innocent until proven guilty." I said.

"Mina, Mamadoll never said anything about him being married, or your friend Kia?" she said.

"Not a word. Mamadoll or Kia, and we flirted at the wedding in front of a crowd of people. It's not like he was hiding his attraction towards me." I said.

"Surely Mamadoll would have told you. She doesn't hold back and especially when it comes to you." She said.

I heard the sound of another call coming through my phone. I looked to see who it was and to my surprise, it was PAK, aka Pastor Patrick. "Naiomi he's calling me," I said surprised.

"Who? The Pastor?" Naiomi shouted.

"Yes girl, this is unexpected," I said.

"Answer the phone. Answer the phone" Naiomi shouted.

"Hold on. No, let me call you back." I said.

"Ok, ok," Naiomi said.

"Hello,"
"Hello dear, how are you this evening?" He asked in the sexiest low baritone voice.
"I'm well and you?" I said.
"I am blessed my dear, did I disturb you?" He asked.
"No, not at all I was just chatting with my best friend," I said. He sounds so sexy on the phone.
"Who is that Kia?" He asked.
"No, another friend of mine in Dallas. Speaking of Kia, have you talked to her?"
"I spoke with her briefly today after you, and I met."
My mind began to race. I wonder did he tell her we kissed. Surely he didn't tell her. I hope he didn't tell her. "That's good. I know me, and her are supposed to meet tomorrow for lunch, prior to you and I meeting."
"Good. Good. I wish I could join you two, but like always, I have to answer to my calling and attend a funeral out of town." We both were quite for a moment. I could hear what sounded like smooth jazz playing in the background. He is always so busy. Maybe this is why he is single if he is single.
"I am sorry to hear that. I do not like funerals."
"Well my dear Mina I don't enjoy them myself. But funerals are a part of my calling, and I accepted the calling so, therefore, I must be obedient and answer." He said.
"Yes you must Patrick, and the people need you." It sounds so funny calling him Patrick and not pastor.
"It's a coincidence you said that because actually, that's is my reason for calling you, well one of my reasons." He said.
I took a deep breath to hear whatever it was he was about to say, but I tried to remain optimistic. I began to say a quite prayer to myself; Lord, don't let this man change his mind on me about my job offer. I want this job. All the negative of what he may say to me start weighing in on my mind, but my spirit quickly reminded I was in a new season of my life and to leave the past in the past. The past is not allowed in the present. I took about two more sips of my wine before responding.
"Really, well I guess let's start with the first reason let's just get it out the way," I said.
"Do you have time?" He asked.
"However much time you need," I said.
"I need a lifetime."
"If it's meant to be you will have a lifetime,"

He giggled then responded. "Mina I don't know how you are going to take this, but I do not want to start off any relationship, friendship, partnership with lies. That's not who I am." He stopped then started again. "When I met you I was instantly attracted to you, but I know at the same time I must be very careful with you, and myself. What happened today was mutual. I don't want you to feel as if you did anything wrong, but I do want to put it behind us and move forward because I want to be your pastor, your boss, your friend. Can we start by being friends?" He asked.

Interesting, I always prayed for a man to be my friend. I knew it! Here we go. I want to say brother cut the "Bu**Sh**" I have already read about you on Google. But I didn't. I kept my composure. I was thinking about my salary amongst other things. "I agree with every word you just said. Let's start fresh and eliminate the flesh move we pulled today. So tell me whatever it is you need to say I am sure I can take it."

He was quite. "Mina Wright. I am so ready to get to know you I couldn't stop thinking about you, what you wore today, your lips, your smile, your personality, the way we kissed, just everything about you since you left my office today."

I was shocked. I squatted to pick my mouth up off the floor.

"That feels so good to hear because you left a very good impression on me as well. I am happy to hear I'm not alone." I said.

"No baby you are not alone, I'm right there with you." He said

"I like the sound of that."

He giggled a little then responded, "Good my dear. Here's the second reason I called. Unfortunately, I had to change your first day to start work to this following Monday, because I will not be back until late Saturday night. Is this ok with you?" He asked.

"Yes of course. This will allow me time to find Rylie a good school, and finish up things I need to do around town. What time do you want me to start on Monday?" I asked.

"I would like to start early because I have plans later that evening. Let's say ten am until three pm."

Here we go. He has plans. He always has plans or something to do because he has a wife. Stop thinking negative Mina I began to tell myself. I'm not tripping its all-good. "That would be a great time. I guess I'll see you on Monday?"

"Yes, you will. I hope you're not disappointed?"

"Of course not. I understand."

"Then it's official. We will meet at my office. One more thing."

"Yes, Patrick. What is it?"

"I wanted to get off early because I would like to take you to dinner that night? Will you be able to attend?" He asked.

Without hesitation, I responded and began thinking. I do not care if women say you are not supposed to be available every time a man want do this or that. If I don't go, someone else will. I want to be wined and dined. "Yes. I would love to have dinner with you?"

"Ok great. I will call my colleague, and give him the ok to make the reservations." He said.

I was a little speechless but also a little tipsy, so I had to gather my words. "I guess I will see you on Monday then."

"Yes, Monday it is."

"Where are we going for dinner?" I said.

"To a special place. I can't wait." He said.

I responded in a seductive tone. Chardonnay had got the best of me.

"Me either be careful and have a good night."

"You do the same and thank you, sweetheart."

"Thank You? For what?" I asked.

He didn't speak right away. I could still hear the jazz music in the background, and it sounded like he was driving. He is so cool. "For giving me an unforgettable kiss today. I can still taste your lips, and the taste is so delicious. I can't wait to taste them again."

I didn't know how to respond to that comment, so I took the fact he was a pastor out of the equation and remembered he was still a MAN. I responded like a women trying to please her soon to be man should.

"But you see I need, and I want you to wait for me because I don't need you giving your good..." (I paused then I laughed) "Kisses to anyone else. Can you hold tight until Monday night?"

"I don't know if I can do that, but I know it's what I need to do. I can wait until Monday at ten am." He said laughing.

"Good, it will be worth wait," I said. He was like a kid waiting in line for ice cream at the neighborhood ice cream truck.

"How can I be sure it will be worth the wait?" He asked.

"Because I know what I am capable of giving," I said. He was quiet for a while. He didn't say a word, so I continued to speak. I guess I left him speechless. "Again good night Patrick."

He spoke real slow and in a low sounding voice, "Good night Mina until Monday then."

I hung up the phone and sipped me another glass of wine. That felt so good. I mean real good. I haven't flirted like this in a long time. It feels so good to be desired and wanted by the opposite sex and someone who has it going on. Not stuck up, but down to earth, a real man who sees what I am worth. I love how he says, dear or my dear. I know without a doubt I was blushing so hard MAC cosmetics would have given me my own personal blush name and named a blush brush after me. I was flattered from my head to my toe, but also a little confused. I know God is not the author of confusion, so this confusion mentality is not coming from him. I have to know is he with this woman, married, or what's really going on? I need a long hot bath after speaking with him but I have to call my girl Naiomi back. Every women should have another trust worthy women in their life she can confide in.

"Mina, what happened? What did he say?" These were the first few word out of her mouth when I called her back.

"He moved my first day of work to Monday, and asked me would I like to go out on a date?"

"He what? What did you say?"

"I said ok I will be there on Monday, and I will join him for dinner, and he said he will make reservations, and end of story."

"End of story. No ma'am, no sir, that's not the end, that's just the beginning. This man is into you."

"You think so?"

"I know so. Girlfriend he gave you a job with a very nice salary, and you are about to receive all the revenue from a very successful newspaper, yes I said successful, and he wants to take you on a date. He is not married."

I didn't say a word. I thought about everything she just said, and I am so very grateful for the job offer and the opportunity, but I will not be second, or third to any other woman. "I don't know Naiomi, but I am going to ask him when we go out to dinner. I am not going to play the guessing game. It's not worth losing who I am, or who I am in Christ."

"I understand Mina, and I believe you should get that conversation out of the way. Just be who you are. You are so observant girlfriend you can learn everything you want to know about just a person by watching and listening. Just go. Have a good time. There is nothing wrong with going out to dinner. Whatever you need to know remember this, God does not leave his children ignorant. He will reveal it to you. It's up to you to except what he's showing you. I love you girl. And like I always say, use wisdom."

"I Love you too. In all my getting I hope to get an understanding. I refuse to walk out of one door, and into another door that looks good on the outside then it opens and says, *Hi you have now entered the door called worse*, welcome."

I finished my small bottle of wine and placed Rylie and my belongings in order around the house. It wasn't until about 9:30 when Rylie and Mamadoll arrived home. They both were excited about working for the campaign and wanted to know all the details of what happened on my interview, the rated G version. I sat on my bed with the two of them and told them all the details about my new career. Mamadoll was extremely happy; because she felt on the inside I was about to enter one of the greatest seasons of my life. She assured me over and over again that she would help with whatever Rylie or I needed. Although I am nervous, I am confident in God and that he will give me the tools I need to build this community newsletter and all new relationships. I know for sure if God is in the midst of the situation, or occupation it will succeed no matter what. I began preparation for Monday my first day. I want to be ahead, not behind. Although it was six days away, I started laying out and designing the way I wanted the newsletter to look. How I wanted it to appeal to both believers and those who were not. To young and old, rich and poor, I wanted it to be diverse, with a touch, a hint, of God's word all over it. Sometimes that's all it takes.

Kia texted me early the next morning, confirming our date for lunch, she moved it up an hour because she wanted to have brunch downtown. She said she was asked to speak at a nearby women's shelter. I agreed and met her for brunch. We met at a very nice restaurant downtown, but it was extremely packed with people. When I arrived, the host took me to a very private area in the back. "Hello my friend," I said as I approached the table.

Kia smiled, stood up and reached out her arms to me to hug me. She has always been full of love. "Good afternoon Ms. Mina."

"It is a good afternoon isn't it," I said smiling.

She smiled back at me. "So I have not spoken to you in a few days, I was meaning to call you I have been so busy how did your interview go?"

I hope she is not probing. I am not comfortable with her about talking about him because I don't know if she will say something to him or not. "My interview went wonderful. I have to thank God for you because I got the job."

"Hallelujah! I am so glad in more than one way."

"Thank you. I'm excited."

"You're not the only one. PAK called me the minute you walked out the office. That brother was Mina this and Mina that. I said what did she do to you?"

"Do to him! I did nothing to him I just interviewed with him." I laughed nervously. She starred at her menu smiling then the waiter came over to our table.

"I was only teasing you Mina. Girl what are you so defensive about. PAK said you two had a really good interview and he enjoyed your company."

I'm defensive because I am guilty. "We did have a great interview. I got to know a little more about him and the job position."

"Really? He said the same about you."

"How long have you two known each other?"

"Girlfriend many, many years? He is my brother from another mother. I love him so much. He deserves a new chapter in his life."

"What do you mean by that?"

She didn't get a chance to answer. "You look so familiar. Where do I know you from?" The waitress asked Kia.

Kia smiled. "Well, sweetie do you watch gospel networks or maybe a little local TV?"

The waitress looked confused, "no I don't; unfortunately, I probably should. You remind so much of my mother's neighbor. Do you live in Grayson Park?

Kia looked down, up, and all around, and acted very uncomfortable with the young women asking her where she lived, "No I do not. You must be thinking of someone else sweetheart."

"That's so weird and a coincidence because the neighbor next door is a preacher or something like that my mom was telling me and I see her in the yard from time to time, and she looks just like you, and she has…." The young women could not complete her sentences before a very uncomfortable and responded aggressively.

"Sweetheart now you know all black people look alike." The young woman laughed nervously.

"I'm sorry if I offended you." The waitress was silent. "But your outfit is identical to the one I thought she was wearing this morning."

Kia was getting agitated by the minute. Kia cleared her throat.

"Maybe I have a twin now can you please take our order. Thank You" Kia asked.

"Are you ok Kia?" I asked.

"Yes Mina, but I really don't want everyone to know where I live. But, I guess it doesn't matter, I am trying to move anyway. The house is way too big for me and too far out. It takes me an hour to get to church and any other place around the city and two hours to get to the airport. Now that I am traveling that is a pretty far drive."

"Yes, it is. I have got to come out there to see it. Those homes are beautiful what made you move out there?"

"I will be honest with you Mina since were friends, I was dating a guy prior to answering my calling, I don't think I even knew Pastor then, at any rate, he bought the home, and I thought we were going to get married, but it did not work out that way. God had a different path he wanted me to take, and we went our separate ways, and that's that.

"I'm sorry to hear that, but God path is always the best route, look at you now. How did you meet Patrick, if you don't mind me asking?" I have to know some things about this man.

"It's funny because I was really going through a challenging time in my life and I was out there Mina. Not too bad, I was just seeking and desiring what I thought was love, but it sex, and I was fulfilling my flesh needs. Pastor was speaking at huge convention, and I walked down the isle, and he laid his hands on me, and I felt the holy spirit move, and my life was changed, and I joined his ministry and began teaching Sunday School, and it's been moving non-stop since then, and that was four years ago."

"What a great testimony. He seems like a person who truly loves the Lord, and that kind of love develops a desire to help people. He also is very good looking I might add." I had to throw that comment in the conversation.

She smiled as she wiped her mouth. "Yes he is, and women throw it to him. When I say throw it, I didn't know so many women knew how to play the quarterback position." We laughed.

"I can imagine. He is a looker. The daughter was absolutely adorable. I saw pictures of her throughout the hallway. I was wondering, what his wife look like." I asked. She didn't move. I kept eating my food and smiling at the same time.

"Pasha is adorable, isn't she, PAK's little angle. As for Tish, his wife, she's attractive. They are two totally different people. I do mean different." Ok here we go I was thinking. I thought she was going to elaborate more, but she didn't. She is loyal to him I have observed that.

"Honey let me tell you Mina that man will give you the shirt off his back. He loves helping people and does not expect anything in return. My prayer for PAK; is that God bless him with his heart desires, whatever he wants, he deserves it. That man has done so much for me, the church, and for this community, and what you two are about to do girl you haven't seen nothing yet. No other ministry has created a community gospel newspaper to reach out to people all over the community and the city and spread God's word."

I listened to every word she was saying, and it was true from what I have witnessed. "That's very true. I was thinking how the world has a newspaper to share depressing events around the world and there's nothing wrong with that. We need that. But, we also can hear how good God is to us in spite of it all. I know it may sound funny, but I'm nervous Kia. I don't want to fail you or, Patrick. I want to succeed. I want to win. I pray it's successful." I said.

She grabbed my hand, "Mina, it will be fine. You don't have to worry. Worrying is not from God. God has put you in both of our lives for a reason Mina. We will see that you get what you need to be successful. I know Patrick will. If God be for you baby, who can be against you. No one."

"Thank you both so much. I'm grateful. I am walking into a new season, and my emotions are all over the place. Change can be risky, but it's worth the risk. Usually, that's when my faith steps in most times for me."

"Me also Mina. I'm walking into a new season as well. I need to make changes in my life, my surroundings. I have to move into a different environment soon also." She hesitated as we begin to eat our lunch. "It will work out for everyone, and hopefully for the best."

It will, I agree. Where are you moving to, may I ask?

"I don't know yet, maybe a loft in the downtown area. I really want to finish what I started. I would really like God to open doors for me in this area. I want to help women out of prison find a good stable job, a roof over their head, and help them every way possible. That's how I started Hope for Hugs.

"Oh yes, the event on Thursday. I remember you talking to Patrick about that." I said.

"Yes, that's the one. Our motto is, you can give someone hope by simply giving them a hug. They feel the loved. They feel like someone truly cares. You don't even need to speak a word. Just a hug." She said.

"I get it. I like the sound of that. Do it, Kia!"

"I am. When the time is right. I am all over the place right now. I want to give it my full attention. That's going to be a ministry in itself." She said,

"Let's toast to it with our papaya tea," I said. We both lifted our glasses and toasted.

We continued our conversation, and I got to know a little bit more about her and what she was going through. I feel like she is struggling in her call, but I didn't know why. She continued to vent about what she had been going through over the past years, and months.

She admitted she was lonely, and sometimes wanted to walk away from her calling, but she knew what God called her to do and he would give her the strength and grace to do it. Now I have grown to know them both a little bit more. The human side is shown very clear. Often times Pastors, evangelist, and spiritual leaders are put on a pedestal where they experience the same trials we do, but they feel they cannot share their trial with anyone because of their calling. I think that often times we as people in the body of Christ have made them feel that way. We look up to them, instead of looking at the God that dwells in them. Although people say, they know you are still human. Can you share your deepest most sincere thoughts and desires with someone, and not be judge, or have a stone thrown at you to knock you off your thrown? I don't believe so because we live in a society where if you are a spiritual leader, people don't really want to hear about your troubles, they want to know how God brought you through those troubles. But what if you are preaching and teaching, and you still are going through, or dealing with a stronghold you have not been delivered from? I could relate to her and feel where she was coming from because although I was not in her position, I had in-fact been in her position, it's the loneliness feeling, but still working in ministry and encouraging others.

The feeling that still haunted her of being neglected by her mother, watching her father use women, and also being mistreated by men herself was still very present in her thoughts and feelings, although, she was being used by God in a supernatural way. I could hear the conviction in her voice, but yet she would never tell me what was troubling her.

After my lunch, with her, I made my way to the local office depot to grab some office supplies. I wanted to start creating a draft of what my newspaper would look like. I knew I had a few days left before my first day, but I was determined to start early so I would get accustomed to working on the newspaper daily, whether I was at the office, or not. Rylie and Mamadoll, of course, was working at the campaign headquarters, so I had a little time to myself when I made it home. I decided to cook for them since Mamadoll had cooked for us every night. I had mixed emotions. I was excited about everything that was going on. My first day to work with him, and the fact he asked me to dinner. I wasn't excited about the fact that to the world and his members he was still seen as a married man, and I don't know really know if he isn't. If I could only forget about the taste of his kiss and how his hands felt against my body. If we didn't kiss and if I wasn't so attracted to him it would not be so hard to tell him I can't go to dinner. But, the reality of the whole situation is I want to go. He is still my boss, and he invited me, and I really do not see anything wrong with an innocent dinner. Just when I'm thinking about him, he calls me; and my voice changed to sexy immediately.

"Hello there. What a beautiful surprise." I said.

"Hello, gorgeous. How are you?" he asked.

"I am good. How are you?"

"I'm ok. I take that back I am actually much better now that I hear your voice. You always sound so good, and happy Mina." He said.

"I am happy. You always sound happy also Patrick. What are you up to this evening?" I asked.

"I am on my way out of town. I have the funeral to attend, and I thought I would stop by." He said.

What the hell? Stop by where? How does he know where I live? I'm not about to allow him to start dropping by. Now he is out of line. I don't live alone. I cleared my throat and allowed my eyebrows to be lowered to their normal position.

"I wasn't aware you knew where I lived," I said.

"You weren't? You completed an application and gave me your resume." He said.

"Ha, ha, ha. Your right but I live with my Aunt, and I wasn't expecting any visitors, and also I don't want to be dis-respectful." What am I doing? Its only 5:30 and they want be here until nine, and I'm forty-years-old.

"You know what, you right and I apologize. I am out of line thinking I can drop by your house whenever I want. I should have called so maybe some other time." He said.

He thinks I don't know what he is doing. I cannot start this. He is married, I think; and my pastor for the one-hundredth time. "It's all good. Maybe some other time." It was silence on the phone I thought he hung up on me. He wasn't expecting that type of response.

"I guess so my dear. I will talk to you later." He said.

He hung up the phone and was gone. Damn! But I did what was right. I put the bake chicken in the oven and grabbed my bottle of Pinot. I poured me a glass of wine and then the doorbell rang. I looked out the peephole. I opened the door.

"I can't handle rejection, especially when I am used to having my way," Patrick said smiling holding two twelve dozen fully bloomed red long stem roses in crystal vases. The vases were engraved with the letter "M."

I must admit I was impressed. "You hit the spot." Not the spot I was hoping for, but he did hit something. "Who could reject these beautiful roses? Please come in." I said.

He walked in the door all calm and cool. "Beautiful home you, your Aunt have hear. Did I surprise you?" He asked laughing.

"Yes, you did. I was very surprised. The roses are my favorite. How did you know? I love them. Thank You." I said.

"I guessed." He said.

"You guessed? Whatever Patrick." I said.

"What? I did. You look like a woman who deserved rose's weather, or not you liked them. I want be too long, and I really didn't mean to stop by unannounced."

"Are you sure about that?" Because I would say, this is a stalker move…LOL"

"Oh I know you didn't just say that. Stalker move? In that case, I guess you open the door and let stalkers in your home?"

"Ha…ha. Know I do not. It's you." Did I really just say that?

"It's me? It's me? He said.

"You know what I mean. I know you. Come on don't make me answer that." I said.

"Alright, I'll let you off the hook. I was on the highway and the florist called me. The flowers were ready now. They would have been dead by Monday for our dinner. So I turned around and grabbed them." He said laughing. "What? It's true."

I stood there shaking my head from side to side to let him know I'm not buying it. I want to be friends he said. Why do men lie and say that? He sat down on the couch, and I walked over to him and sat in front him on the coffee table.

"I hear you. It's ok to say you wanted to see me or wanted to taste my sweet kisses before you went out of town." I said.

He looked at me with the biggest smile then leaned his body comfortably on the couch. "I wanted to see you Mina and taste your…" He paused. "Sweet kisses, before I went out of town."

I smiled back at him, "Now you see me." I said. He grabbed my hand and kissed it. Then he kissed it, and kissed it some more, and moved up to my forearm, then shoulder, then my neck, then my ear. He whispered, "It's good to see you again. I'm going to go my sweet Mina. I'll see you on Monday." I began rubbing his smooth, silky waves with my other hand back and forward slowly. I was thinking to myself. I don't care where we are the next time he will get all of my inheritance down there. I will sign it over, and he can have the entire estate. "Thank you for stopping by. I hope you have a safe trip." I said.

We hugged. He hugged me again so tight. We kissed, and I wrapped both my arms around his neck. I really didn't want him to leave.

I wanted him to stay. I wanted to spend time with him. I didn't want to sneak or be in a rush.

"Before I go I have something else for you." He walked out to his car and returned with bags.

"What's all this?" I asked.

"I stopped by the office store and grabbed you some supplies so you will have here at home, and so you can start working on your newspaper if you wanted to before Monday."

I could only smile. How thoughtful of him. "Great minds truly think alike. Thank you."

"Yes, they do. You know that adds a little more to success. Two minds are better than one."

"I agree." He kissed me on my lips and turned and walked away. He jumped into a "oh so" nice black Mercedes Benz AMG G 65. It was so pretty. I frowned and shook my head. A SUV should not be that pretty, or a man driving it. Someone has got to be ugly. He left me speechless as usual. I sat down on the couch starring at my roses. They were beautiful. My vases with the letter M engraved I loved. The office supplies were thoughtful, and the kiss was great. But what if this man is lying to me about his marital status. I refuse to date a married man; it's not what I believe in or stand for. I am against it. I repeat this so much you would think by now I would have told him to stay away. So why am I allowing him to into my space? Why do we as women come out of one situation, and go right into another? I finished the dinner I had prepared for Mamadoll and Rylie. I started working on my newspaper to take my mind off things. Im old school so I'll leave the laptop for last. I begin with writing topics and sorting different sections for the newspaper. I started with designing the cover and writing down different name suggestions for each topic then breaking them into different parts into how they will be laid out. I know I wanted to spotlight testimonies and the word from the Pastor. I felt there was a need for local employers to advertise to continue to help God's people have a stable income and benefits. I wanted to have members birthdays listed, those who had just given birth and those soon to be married. I wanted events such as gospel concerts and advertisers such as dentists, doctors, and many other entrepreneurs to advertise their business. I wanted listings of home that were for sale and for rent. Last but not least, I needed a name for my newspaper.

A name that stood out and related to the gospel and our purpose, so I wrote and read the bible more and more to achieve this goal. I was anxious and ready for Monday to come and it was only Tuesday. I had five days. I stayed focused. I was almost done with every task I had planned to do for the week before I begin my assignment. I found Rylie a good school and scheduled her doctor's appointments for physicals. I worked every day for three hours on my newspaper like I said I would do. I helped Mamadoll clean and organize the house. I set-up my office space at home and re-decorated my room so I would have plenty of space. I browsed the Internet daily for ideas but also to make sure no one had the name I had in mind for the newspaper. I finally came up with a name that I believe was designed for the newspaper, but also for the meaning of it, and what it stood for. I was so busy with my own business that I felt a little selfish. I knew I had a deadline, but I also knew I promised Mamadoll I would stop by the campaign center before the week was out, and I kept my promise. She asked me daily to stop by because she was so proud of me, and she wanted her co-workers to meet me. It was Friday evening, and I decided to go to the center to visit with Mamadoll and Rylie. I was determined to help her with whatever she needed done. As soon as I walked in, I saw nothing but women ranging in all ages. It was loud, and everyone was running around, hanging posters, and answering phones. I walked around to a more quite area down a hall. An older woman approached me.

"Hi ma'am, are you lost? Can I help you?"

"Yes, I'm looking for Mamadoll." Before I could finish my sentence, she interrupted me.

"Oh my goodness I know who you are. Child you look just like your daughter. You are just a beautiful caramel donut."

Donut! Wait a minute did she just call me fat? "Well I guess. Thank you, ma'am. I've never been called a donut, but thank you."

"Ha, ha, ha. You know you have that nice little round donut booty back there. That's why I called you that." She laughed so hard at her own joke I just stood there and smiled. Older people will say anything.

"Hello, Mina it's been a few days where have you been hiding, the church," Bryce said sarcastically.

He is so messy. "Yes, I have. Church is always a good place to be." I said sarcastically.

"Only if your there for the right reason." He said smiling. I didn't have time to respond to his silly comment.

"Mina baby congratulations honey. I heard you are going to be working at the church." Aunt Bae said.

"Thank You, Auntie. It's not the church it Pastor Kincade business." I said.

"Is that right? My goodness, Mina you just joined the church, and your already working for the church? What's your secret? Do tell us?"

He is such a jerk. I cannot tolerate him. If it weren't for my Mamadoll, I would curse him out. "Well Bryce if I tell you my secret, then it wouldn't be a secret anymore." All the women started laughing.

"That was funny sweetie." The woman said.

"Ms. Shirley I believe your fifteen minute break was over fifteen minutes ago," Bryce said to the women that greeted me. Then he snapped his fingers. "If I were you I would say good bye to Mina, and hello to my work."

She stopped smiling. "I'm sorry sir. Mina, it was a pleasure meeting you."

"You also Ms. Shirley can you take me to Mamadoll?" I asked.

"I sure can."

"Mina, please allow me. Ms. Shirley has work to do." Bryce said.

"I was done sir I don't mind. I'll take her," she said.

The look on Bryce's face, if looks could terminate you, Ms. Shirley would be filing for unemployment right about now.

I walked down the hallway laughing on the inside as we left Bryce standing there. I walked into the workstation and saw Mamadoll and Rylie working. Aunt Bae wasn't far behind Ms. Shirley and I. Mamadoll walked over to hug me and begin to introduce to me, everyone. They all had heard so much about me. I begin assisting Mamadoll with whatever she needed.

The employees were searching the Internet for phone numbers and addresses in certain neighborhoods to obtain more votes for the Commissioner of the city. I wonder what type of commissioner is he. I wonder how he treats the people in the community. He comes across as such a jerk. But, from the looks of it, he must need the votes because they are working all night and its early January. But who am I to judge I know nothing about politics. It was almost eight o'clock and I had been there for two hours. I felt like that was long enough, and it was time for me to go. I made my rounds to see if any of the women needed help. Ms. Shirley was the only one. It's always one, who will answer what I have been asking on the inside.

"What is it that you need help with Ms. Shirley?"

"I need help with stuffing the rest of the envelopes." She said.

She would want me to help with something I dislike doing. I sat down and begin to stuff the envelopes one by one. From the desk area I was sitting in there was a view of the front rear of the building. I saw Bryce talking on the phone, and then a woman pulled up in a late model black BMW. I couldn't see her face only her arm with a few beautiful diamond bangles. I noticed how he looked around to see if anyone was looking then he leaned over in her car. She drove off fast then only a few minutes later I saw Zi'lah walk over, and they began kissing. I knew it. She was all over that man at the house. Why is she interested in him? He is no good. I thought I was going to throw up.

"He is a snake. I do mean snake?" Ms. Shirley said as she was also looking out the window.

"Why do you say that?"

"Look at him. His spirit ain't right. I have heard so much about that man. He has so many enemies in this city. He is not for the community. He is not going to win this election this time you watch and see." She said.

"Well, how did he win the first time?" I asked.

"That's a question you need to ask your infamous pastor?" She said sarcastically.

"Pastor?" I asked surprised.

"Yes Pastor Kincade. That man is admired and loved in the city and the pastor endorsed and supported him. The man has almost thirty-thousand members, and Mr. Calhoun attends the church, so members are going to listen to their leader, and if he tells them to vote, then the rest is history."

I didn't say a word. The best thing to do when you want the answer in any situation you are not sure about is to listen to someone who has been in that environment. Although she may be exaggerating, or she may be making a story up, gossiping, or whatever you want to call it, what she is saying make a lot of since. She continued.

"I'm so ready for this to be over with. I really needed the money. He's a snake, but he pays really well. I just don't like his spirit, and what he does. They said that man have slept with so many married women and have torn so many families apart. Rumor has it that he has ran through some women in that sanctuary over at the church. I couldn't understand why Pastor Kincade supported him. Pastor is such a good person, that man will give you the shirt off his back. He has saved schools and businesses in this city not to mention everything else he does. He gives so much money to homeless shelters, battered women, adoption agencies and he has all those members to answer to. He will come to the hospital and visit your love one. That says a whole lot. What does this man do? He hangs around sniffing women, and other men women." She said.

Very interesting. I knew my instinct was right about him. This is why he in everyone else business. He does not want to see anyone happy. I sit here thinking how I would really like Mamadoll to excuse herself from volunteering at this center. I am surprised Mamadoll likes him so much. She is usually a pretty good judge of character. I also wonder why Patrick would support someone like him. Something is not right. I finished stuffing the envelopes and grabbed Rylie to head home. Mamadoll said she was right behind me. I probed a little on the way home to see if Rylie saw anything strange or felt a certain way while she has been volunteering there. One thing I have learned about children is they see all and know all. She did not say one negative word about volunteering there; actually, she loved it. Although, she did mention Zi'lah and her children are there every day all during the day. Which was strange to me because she has a job. I will pray about it and let God reveal to me whatever it is I need to know. I don't want to be a busy body.

It was Saturday evening, and I had accomplished what I set out to do this week. I washed all day and cooked to give Mamadoll a day off. Later that day Rylie and I hung out and went to a local movie and the mall. It was around seven when we returned home. I had not talked to Patrick since the day he stopped over with roses. No text. Nothing at all. I thought I would give him a call being that it was Saturday night. I figured he would be on his way back from out of town by now since we had church on tomorrow. He answered after the second ring.

"Hello, beautiful. What a surprise! How are you? What's up?" He said.

He sounded very excited to hear from me. "Hello, Mr. Kincade what's up with you?"

"Nothing much on my way back to Charlotte from the funeral. What about you?"

"I figured you were. I'm actually just returning home I have had a busy week, and I thought I would give you a call. Thought you would need someone to talk to while driving." As if I knew he was driving.

"How thoughtful of you. I'm actually about thirty minutes from Charlotte. I'm starving, have you eaten?"

"I...I... ate earlier."

"Well, I would you like to join me for a bite to eat."

"Really? I would love to join you for a bite to eat. Where are we going?"

"My restaurant; on Daniels Island."

"Your restaurant?"

"Well I haven't closed the deal, but I'm speaking it into existence. Can you join me?"

Can I join you? Hell yes. He is on the move, with newspapers, and restaurants. Go get it then. I don't know how I'm going to do this without Mamadoll all up in my business. She will have put me in hell by midnight if she knew. I will have to meet him. I'm not about to have her questioning me with his marital status.

"Yes, I can. Can you send me the address?"

"No need I can come and pick you up, and we can ride together."

No, we cannot either I wanted to say. "I just prefer to drive Patrick. Can you hold on for a second?" I heard someone knocking on my door.

"Mina baby," Mamadoll said.

"Yes, ma'am."

"Tell Mamadoll I said hello," Patrick said.

I whispered, "Patrick not now stop playing."

"I'm going to go to bed I'm so tired."

"Ok, I'll see you in the morning."

"Rylie is knocked out sleep also," Mamadoll said.

"Is she? Ok, I love you. I'll talk with you in the morning."

On second thought, "Patrick I'll be ready in about thirty minutes. Are you still coming?"

"Yes, I am. I'll be there in twenty-nine."

Yes! Spontaneous. I love it. I know I put on the cutest outfit I had in my closet. I took me a real quick shower and fixed my hair. I put a little make-up on and a pair of stilettos. I kissed Rylie goodnight and tiptoed down the hallway. I felt like I was sixteen-teen again. Before I knew it, I saw his shadow from my upstairs window approaching the front door.

I must have leaped downstairs to stop him before he rang the doorbell. As soon as I opened the door, I could smell his cologne. Damn, he smelled good. I love a fine man that smell good.

"Is that all it took? Thirty minutes for you to look like that?"

"Well, actually twenty-nine minutes," I said smiling and whispering.

"Ha, ha. Hello sweetheart you look radiant. I'm glad you could join me."

"I wouldn't have missed it."

"Why are you whispering?"

Did he really just ask me that? "Everyone is asleep."

We walked to the car, and he opened the door for me. The car smelled like him, mm mm good. It was immaculate from the top to the bottom. He started the car and turned the volume on the radio a little louder. The song, *Heaven* by KEM begin to play, and he was singing right along with it. The ride was so nice and smooth. We both were enjoying each other company and the music. I looked out the window at the beautiful sky just enjoying the moment. We chatted a little off and on until we got to the island. It was so nice and peaceful. There was a full moon on this night, and it was shining bright. The reflection off the water was breath taking and romantic. I don't believe I had witness such a sight before in my life, and surely not on a date. He opened my door and grabbed my hand as we walked toward the restaurant, which to my surprise was on a yacht. Once we entered the lights were dimmed, and we walked to a table that was set with candles and twelve full-bloomed roses placed in a vase in the middle of the table. We were the only ones on the entire yacht. Patrick said he would be right back he was going to the restroom. I was in a different frame of mind. I was at a loss for words. The waiter pulled my chair out for me, and there was an envelope sitting in my chair with my name written on it. I looked around. I proceeded to open the envelope and begin to read it.

"From the moment I met you, I knew you were special. Not only to me but also, more importantly to God. I don't know what this feeling is, but I know I would be satisfied if it stayed, because there is plenty of room for it. I watched you dance at the wedding reception that night, and I wanted to ask you could I dance with you but I didn't have the opportunity, but now I do, so I'm asking you now Mina, will you dance with me?"

I turned around and there standing on a small dance floor on the deck was Patrick along with a band behind him. It was only the band and us. I put my sexy walk on for him and walked outside to the deck. He bowed to me then grabbed my hand, kissed it, then walked me to the dance floor. The band begins to play Jesse Powell, "You." Neither one of us said a word.

We slow danced, and our eyes wouldn't look anywhere else but into one another's. This is the type of man I have prayed for. I know he is, I mean I know it is. I rubbed my hand against his cheek, and he held his hands on my waist. I was in another world. I couldn't gather the words to say. I then laid my head on his chest as we continued to dance. Once the music slowed down and we continued to dance slower. We finally stopped and walked hand and hand back to the inside of the yacht. I was blushing so hard, and he was to. He let my chair out for me to sit down, and then he sat down and grabbed the menu. As he glanced

the menu, he looked up at me every now and then and then we both smiled at one another.
"Do you know what you have a taste for sweetheart?"
I was at a loss for words, and I couldn't stop blushing. Deep on the inside, I wanted to thank him for making me feel like a true queen.
"I have no idea. I haven't had a chance to look at the menu. What do you suggest?"
"I love it all. The salmon, mahi-mahi, trout, white fish, it's all good, but my favorite is the ahi-tuna." He said.
"I love ahi-tuna."
"Good I'll let the waiter know. What would you like to drink?"
I would love a cosmos, or vodka and sprite, or margarita but I'm going to stick with wine. "I'll take a glass of red wine. Do you drink?"
"Water, juice, milk. Ha, ha," He said.
"I hope you don't mind. But you know what I'll just drink some water."
"No. Be yourself. Don't do that Mina. Enjoy yourself."
"Ok, I will."
"Adrian were ready he said."
"You all are on first name basis."
"Of course that's my family."
"No way."
"Yes, the band and all."
"That's right you're buying this right?"
"I'm thinking about it. Should I?"
"You're asking me?"
"Yes, what do you think?"
"I...I...think it's gorgeous and very romantic. You can have weddings here, along with many other events like anniversary dinners, proposals. You can do a lot with the place."
"I was thinking the same way, but with more like christenings and baptismal in mind. We think so much alike. It amazes me some of the things you say."
"Baptismal, Patrick no, not on a yacht baby. I don't think I want to attend a baptismal and the directions lead me to a yacht, and they are being baptized in the island. You're not John, and the ones getting baptized is not Jesus. Keep it in the church we don't need anyone drowning."
"Ha, ha, ha...you are so funny... I mean hilarious. You say the funniest things. Ok, OK I will keep it at the church. I so enjoy being with you and around you. Let's toast." Patrick said.

128

I raised my wine glass, "To our future, what God put together let no man put asunder." We toasted, and I begin sipping on my wine and him on his water.

"Patrick there is something we need to talk about," I said.

"I know it is, and now is not a better time before we go any further." He said.

I wasn't ready for that response, but since he already knows what I want to talk about, I will let him finish. "Since you know then tell me," I said.

He continued to look at the menu. The waiter walked over, and he proceeded to order. His attitude changed and he was much more cool and relaxed. And he is ordering for me, I mean us. "Mina would you like an appetizer?

"Yes. I like the fried calamari."

"Great that's my favorite. We'll have two orders, one for her and one for me. And bring some ranch dressing and hot sauce please." Damn that's my kind of man, I can eat ranch dressing with anything. "Would you like anything else to drink?

"No thank you. I'm good." I know one thing he is going to tell me about his marriage situation tonight. I can't get caught up. I just can't.

"As for the conversation we started prior to the toasting, shall we continue?"

Damn is he inside my mind. "Yes, Patrick we should. I wasted no time. There is no need of getting my hopes up high. "Can I ask you, what is your marital status?"

"I guess you don't waste any time. Just jump right in there and ask, huh?"

"Why should I?"

"You shouldn't," he said.

"So answer then?" He wiped his mouth and took a sip of his water. He cleared his throat and begins to speak.

"There is not too many people I feel comfortable around, and I surely don't feel I should share some of my deepest secrets or personal life events and experiences with. First and foremost I am a man Mina let that be established. I understand, yet I'm misunderstood. I love yet not loved. I'm often encouraging but yet encouraged. I can apologize, but yet never receive an apology. I can forgive, but if I make mistake I am not forgiven, and people will not forget. But yet and still because of the God in me I can get up and preach every Sunday morning until I'm out of breath, lay hands on people and they are healed, marry them, bury them and their mamas and fathers, brothers and sisters, visit them in the hospital, but I can't stay married for five years." So he isn't married? He then excused himself from the table. He walked over to the deck and look to be in deep thought. I then I walked behind him.

"Does anyone know this? Did you tell the members of the church?" I asked confused because I am.

He giggled and then turned around to speak to me. "I have not."

"Why not Patrick."
"Why not what Mina."
"Why haven't you shared this with your congregation?"
"The timing has not been right and I am not..." he stopped in the middle of his conversation.
"You're not what... ready?"

He turned around, and we were facing one another. "Maybe."

"So let me understand this. They meaning your members, society, people, think you are still married?"

He took a deep breath. "Look, Mina, only God, myself, you and my staff know the truth on earth. I would like if it stays that way until I'm ready to face my congregation, society, and people. I don't even know why I'm telling you this. I know some women that don't care if I am married, or not."

"That's because they don't know what true love is. When love live on the inside of you, you are not selfish. You consider the other person and their household, their children, not your own selfish gain." Oh Lord, I sound like Mamadoll.

"Wow!" He said. He then starred at me for a minute, or two. "I love my heavenly father, and he knows that I am grateful for the blessings he has bestowed on me and the gift he has instilled in me to preach the gospel, but he also knows I am human and he knows my struggle, and I can't, and I won't let his people down. They need me."

"They need the truth, Patrick. I said calmly. "They need to know that you are called by God, and you fall or fell too like they have before. But, because we serve a merciful God, he is there with arms open to give you the grace and strength to get up, dust yourself off, and tell twenty-thousand plus people my marriage did not work out. But I serve a God who is a restorer, and he will send to me the wife and help mate he wants me to be with." I was really loud.

He looked at me like who are you talking too? Then he got loud. "That's easy for someone who is not in my position to say. I have people looking up to me. I have at least three hundred to four hundred couples looking to be married in my seminar every other Saturday, wanting counseling. I cannot let them down. I want let them down."

I was speechless for the moment, but because I was blessed with a big mouth, I responded "Unfortunately Patrick you already have." I turned at walked back to the table.

I sat down and begin to eat my calamari. I was disappointed with this man, this leader, this person God has blessed to lead the people. I looked up and saw him headed to the table also. He looked upset.

"Mina you kissed me in my office and have flirted with me since the first day you met me, yet you never once asked me was I married? But, I never judged you; I never said a word to you. Did I?"

I thought about what he said. I did inquire about his marital status, but it wasn't to him. "Your right, but it bothered me, and I wasn't comfortable with it."

"And I am? You think I'm comfortable with not telling my members I'm no longer married? Is that what you think?"

"I didn't say that Patrick. I do feel at some point you want to be honest with yourself, and also honest with your members, that's all."

"Mina there is no perfect person, and there was no perfect person in the bible to walk this earth except for Jesus. We all have our flaws. That's one of the many reasons we need God. Mina don't you know I struggle with this every day. This is one of the many reasons why only a few people know. People feel like because you are a spiritual leader you can't make a mistake, or you are not supposed to make a mistake. Everything has to be a secret."

"When people see you make mistakes they are shocked then you hear the, "I can't believe it," so you feel like you can't talk about it. This is the first time I have ever talked to anyone. I do mean anyone about this situation. Not even my dad who I buried a year ago, who I loved so very dearly ever knew I was divorce. He was so proud of me, and what I have become I didn't want to let him down. I don't want to let the people down. I never ask to be what I was called to be. I just wanted to play football. God chose me. Maybe I wasn't ready."

"If you were not ready he would not have called you. Patrick I understand. I worked in the ministry, and I lived with a man I know had no desire to marry me. I stayed because I didn't want to hear what people had to say. PEOPLE! I'm so tired of PEOPLE! I'm not here to condemn you, or convict you, but I am going to tell you the truth. I would not be a friend if I didn't. I know it's hard because so many people look up to you and love you. But, Patrick sit back and think about who on earth you really want to please and who you have to answer too."

The waiter brought our dinner, and the yacht began to move as we toured the Island. We both begin to eat. It was quiet at our table. I had another glass of wine, and it was still quiet. The band started playing another love song, and neither one of us moved.

"I guess that's our first argument." He said.

"If that's what you want to call it." We both continued to eat.

"Mina listen, I respect you. Most of all I appreciate your honesty and your passion when defending what you feel is right. I got to hand it to you, you believe in what you're saying."

"I'm supposed to. The bible does say be ready to take defense."

"You were the defense, offense, the coach, the owner...Ha, ha... you played many positions on team Jesus."

"Well, that's the best team to play on, so I got a little excited...excuse me." I said.

"It's all good. Out of the seven people who know about my situation, I don't think any of them ever (he paused) said anything to me about how they felt or gave me any advice. As a matter of fact, they just accepted my situation and kept it moving. I like it. I like the feisty in you. I like the honesty. You don't hold back."

"Not anymore. I've been through too much. Why hold back now, there is no telling where this may go."

He stopped eating and placed the napkin down on the table. "Be patient with me Mina, please. In time it will be taken care of. I'm not trying to manipulate anyone or deceive my members. The situation is not only about me. There is more to this and more people I truly love involved, and I don't want to see anyone hurt."

"I understand, your daughter. I have one of those. Patrick, thank you for being honest with me. Thank you for feeling comfortable enough to vent to me."

"Yes, Pasha is one of those people and thank you for listening to me. Mina I seek God daily, and I believe he put you in my path to push me to tell my members, so I can be free, the past two years I never had the desire to speak about it or tell my members, but God is working. I don't know, but it's going to fall in place. Can I get one more dance with you tonight?"

I don't know what it is, but it's something about Patrick that loves, that I couldn't resist so I put the fork down and stood up to dance. "Yes, you can. You sure you're not going to be tired tomorrow? You have church in the morning remember?" He grabbed my hand, and we headed to the dance floor.

We smiled at each other and slowly began to dance again as our foreheads touched. "WE have church in the morning, and no WE shouldn't be tired."

The Next Morning

I woke up to the sound of a message coming through my cell phone. *'Have a good time at church today…PAK'.* That's what Patrick wrote. It was time to get ready for church. I smelled breakfast from the kitchen and I knew Mamadoll was up and cooking. She was playing those old spiritual hymns. I woke Rylie up, and I begin to get ready for church. This time I wanted to be sharper than the last time. I woke up smiling and smiling. Mamadoll decided to attend her church this Sunday, so we headed out the door without her. We arrived right on time at church, and I decided to sit in the middle section and not on the front row. The spirit was high, and the music begins to play, and the choir starts singing. We were getting our praise and worship on. Kia walked out, and she was hyped up for Jesus this Sunday. She asked us all to sit down, and she asked a young man to the pulpit to speak. He was a tall white gentleman, clean cut and wore a very nice black suit. She handed him the microphone, and he wiped what seem to be tears in eyes and begin to speak.

"Good morning saints of God on behalf of my family, your first lady, our family we would like to thank you for your prayers and thank everyone who attended the home going service of our beloved sister. Cancer may have attacked her flesh, but it couldn't have her spirit. We will see her up there, when it's our time."

What a surprise. Rewind in my mind. Did he say, first lady? Yes he did. I looked back at what the crowd was looking at, and the congregation begins standing up and applauding. Walking toward the pulpit, in my opinion, was a Miss America look alike. A very tall, attractive, well dressed, white brunette head woman, with the biggest pearly whites and very large boobs. She waived and hugged members as she walked down the aisle like this was a pageant. She approached the young man with a big hug, and he begins to speak again.

"A Street Called Straight Ministries' this woman was there for our sister every day. She never left her side."

The congregation began to applaud.

"She moved back home the past few months to take care of our sister when no one else was there. Please give Tish Kincade a warm welcome back home."

There she was. There was the first lady. She wasn't what I thought she would be. She was Caucasian. That was surprising to me, and I don't know why. She had a rock that is also known as a ring on her wedding finger. I so happened to glance over at the pulpit and, their standing was Patrick looking right at me. This big church and he finds me. I stared back at him, and he smiled at me. I smiled a little and turned my attention back to her. She threw her hair a few times around before she begins to speak.

"Good morning everyone I want to thank you all for your prayers and my brother for that beautiful introduction. God has dealt with me these past few months about my life."

She then looked over at Patrick. He didn't make a move and he didn't smile, he didn't make any facial expression.

"You have a wonderful pastor, leader, and he's your friend. He officiated the funeral on yesterday, and I thought about why I married him."

I looked at Patrick, and he looked confused while staring at her. I saw Kia with a confused look as well.

"I married him because he is such a great person. He stopped in his busy schedule to do the funeral at the last minute when my sister pastor couldn't do it. This is why everyone loves him."

She went on to speak. She was very extra. After she finished, she was escorted to her seat. Patrick begins to speak then it was time for the offering. While the offering buckets were being passed around, I glanced at the pulpit. Patrick was staring at me. I glanced away without smiling. This felt awkward to me. I reached for the bucket on my row. As I turned around to hand it to the next row, Tish and my eyes locked. She was staring at me from afar. I wasn't tripping and know my mind wasn't playing tricks on me. I was thinking is staring at me? I glanced back again to see. As I turned around, she was still staring at me. I wonder does she know who I am. If she does know, who told her? Who should I watch my back, around? And anyway, if they are divorced why in the hell does she cares? So many questions and not enough answers. I need to be cautious.

Chapter 7: My First Day, Our Second Date...

I gathered my supplies and headed to my car. I kissed Rylie good-bye and hugged Mamadoll. I was ready for my first day. I was ready for a breakthrough and an opportunity that's been sitting still waiting to explode. I knew this was not just about me so therefore I was dedicated and committed to doing the best I could to make this position the best for not only me, not for Patrick, but for Gods people. I drove in the parking lot, and my name appeared on a parking spot, *Mina Wright*. I loved looking at the look of my name on the sign. I felt like this was my time, and I was prepared. I hopped out the car, and damn near ran through the entrance. I was dressed for success and dressed super professional. I arrived at least twenty minutes earlier than I was scheduled. I have learned that early is always better than *I'm almost there, or I'm only a few minutes late.*

I stepped out the elevator and sitting at the receptionist desk was Ms. Doris with a bright smile. She stood up, and instead of greeting me with a handshake and smile, she gave me the biggest hug. I hugged her back, and I felt like more than an employee, but a family member. We walked down the hallway, and adjacent to Patrick's office was mine. The name imprinted on a small piece of the wall before to the wall was my name, Mina Wright, Creator. As I entered my office, I was stunned. There were at least eight dozens of red roses everywhere in vases engraved with the letter *M* on them. Identical to the ones delivered to me by Patrick. I guess the florist had time to make these. The décor was priceless. It was very similar to Patrick. There were red, black and white colors throughout the office with a few of my favorite colors added. Paintings all over the walls. Beautiful light fixtures, hanging down a huge chandelier as a centerpiece. A 60-inch flat screen television on the wall. Wood flooring with a priceless 16x16 rug with red, black, white colors and designs lying in the middle of the floor. My desk had a huge window view. It was a white color. My chair was suede red. The couch that sat to the left for clients was black leather with red and white pillows. I looked to my right and there was a 20x24 photo of Rylie and me hanging, I was speechless. I just stood in the middle of the floor in amazement.

"Welcome to your first day, Mina. Are you ready?" Patrick said.

I turned around, and he was holding a cup of coffee. "I'm always ready and Good morning," I said.

He smiled then handed me the cup, "This is for you. I hope you like coffee."

"I love coffee. Wow! Someone knows a lot about me. Where did the photo come from?

He laughed. "The photo was donated by Mamadoll."

"Oh really? I guess she was in the giving spirit. And how did she get this picture to you?"

"If I tell you all my secrets Mina, then it wouldn't be a secret, now would it? I have to leave some things, only for Mamadoll, God and me."

"No, it wouldn't. But when it's dealing with me and my personal belongings, I wouldn't say it was a secret."

"You're right. But we can talk about that some other time, it's too early now. Moving forward, we will meet in the conference room at 11:30 sharp. Please have your presentation ready for us to see."

"Ok. What do you mean for us?" I asked.

"The committee and staff. I didn't tell you?" He asked.

"No, I don't believe I was informed of a committee."

"Oh, I'm sorry it will only consist of me, Kia, and the other seven staff members. We all are anxious to see what the newspaper will be like. Remember Mina, this is the business side."

I wanted to say damn couldn't you give me a little heads up, and tell me I was going to be in front of people talking about something I created two days ago. But, like he always reminds me this is a business. He turned to walk away then turns back around.

"I hope you like the flowers and coffee, and by the way you look stunning, see you in a minute."

I grabbed my things out my bag. Geez, I thought it was only for him and me. What do I do now? I said I was always ready and I need to be for whatever he has. He is very spontaneous. I gathered my materials and began to section them off and design them and print them in order. Before I knew it, it was eleven o'clock. My door opened. I thought it was Patrick. But it wasn't.

"Mina are you ready?" Ms. Doris said.

"Give me ten minutes." I yelled.

She closed the door and I began to scramble. I was trying to get myself together. And I was trying to not be so nervous. It was 11:11. Doris was at the door again. Damn, she is an on time employee. "Let's go Mina, chop, chop." She helped me grab my materials and lead me to the boardroom. I felt like it took an eternity to get there, but once I arrived I had indeed arrived. The door opened and all the staff members sat at their designated spots at the conference table. Kia sat at the very front and she immediately turned around with a big bright smile. Patrick stood by the window with this sexy look in his eyes and smirk on his face. I saw some members there that I had not met but it didn't bother me. I smiled back at Kia and nodded at Patrick. I wasn't nervous anymore. I felt this sort of confidence come over me all of a sudden. I wasted no time I just jumped right in and begin to speak.

"Good morning everyone and thank you for having me. My name is Mina and look forward to working with you all and making this newspaper a success. Before I begin can you all stand so we can pray together? Everyone stood up and smiled and I led them in a powerful emotional prayer. After prayer without hesitation before I presented the newspaper I had one more thing to address.

"I know social media is very dominant in this day and age and I know, nearly 25% of people read the newspaper and the majority of them are 55 and up. I also know that many of you wonder; how will this be effective in our community with so many people addicted and obsessed with social media, blogs, and websites. I'm here to inform you that although much of that is true about social media and the statistics, I am convinced when you are doing something for Christ no matter what it may look like in the natural, the spiritual realm has an argument and that argument says you will succeed. I don't know how this paper will turn out, I just know when God says do something you do it, because he has a better plan no man can imagine. Failure is not in my destiny, but winning is. That being said let us begins." Everyone was silent but smiling.

"The first highlight the reader will see once they open the newspaper is:

A Word from our Pastor

Page 1: This is where Patrick will give his bi-weekly word and/or scripture for the members and community. I will have a small inspiring word and motivating scripture from the editor/writer/co-creator of the newspaper just down below him.

Page 2 and 3: You will see a section for those who are getting married in the congregation. There will be photos and dates of ceremonies provided with a little insight of how they met and so on. This section is:

Two is better than One

Page 4 and 5: This Section will consist of those who are about to conceive and there also will be photos available and this will be titled:

First Love, then Marriage, now Diapers

Page 6, 7, and 8: This section will be much longer because it is advertising. Readers will begin to enter the *members' corner* and it will consist of focusing on the needs of our members and also others in the community. This is where the local businesses will advertise their businesses, and also career opportunities for those in need of a job, or a different career move. We will also allow Politicians to speak here because election time is approaching. It will be titled:

Your needs being Met is our Business

Page 9 and 10 will be the section where we solute our members' birthdays for the month. It will have balloons and birthday cake designs all over it with special high light of those turning 60, 70, 80, and 90 and so forth it will be titled:

There's a time to be Born

Page 11 and 12 we will highlight our members who are graduates of high school and college along with photos. It will be titled:

For I know the plans I have for You

Page 13 and 14 will consist of the members who want to share their testimonies and so much more about the goodness of Jesus, and how God has brought them through various trials and storms in their lives. This will be titled:

Hear my Hallelujah!

Page 15 and 16: We then will have a memoriam of those who are called home, because we all know earth is not our home there will be photos. It will be titled,

Absent from the body is present with the Lord

Page 17: Last but not least because the number 7 is Gods number of completion. We will end with a word from our associate Pastor, Kia St. James. It will be titled,

Hugs 4 Hope

It will spotlight women out of prison and women around the city who are changing their lives for the better. But also this will open a door for Kia to have a chance to talk about the organization and educate people around the city so we can get this organization moving to and give the women the opportunity they need."

Everyone was on mute as they all sat in their chairs around the boardroom glaring at me. I paused and then spoke again. "I know you all are thinking. What is the name?" I walked around the table with my ruler in my hand. "Well, I thought about magazines names like Ebony, Essence, and Time just to name a few. And the name fell into my spirit. The name is something that means a lot to me and defines who we are in Christ and also to the world. I introduce to you, *A Street called Straight Ministries*. The city of Charlotte first ever religious news publication…. drum roll please", I pulled the cover off:

It was soundless in the boardroom. You could hear a pen drop, if it fell right next to you. I grew a little nervous. "You get it? Servant, because we are servants of Christ, and we serve one another, *Well done thy good and faithful servant*. The numbers represent non-stop serving 24 hours, seven days a week. And since it's a gospel newspaper, I used the format of how scriptures are written in the Bible with colons, and of course the *t* stands out to symbolize the cross." I finally heard clapping and Patrick stood up. He clapped and walked over, near to where I was standing.

"BRAVO! Mina! Mina, Mina. I thought you were going to come in here and have ten pages of a colorful newsletter with a calendar and recipes…" He paused. "I don't know what I was thinking to be honest. Now this is what I'm talking about. Good job servant!"

Kia stood up, "I love it. I love it. I love it! Girlfriend you got a gift that lies in you! Forget the newspaper; let's do a magazine…. Servant, which could be available twenty four seven."

Every one begin agreeing with Kia and congratulating me and complimenting my work.

"Wait a minute everyone. We start small. Remember small beginnings then God will lead us to more. Let first see how the newspaper does. I say we celebrate. Lunch is on Kia."

"Celebrate!" Ms. Doris said surprisingly.

Kia looked surprised as well. "You mean we get a break?"

"Of course you do. Only today." Patrick smiled and said.

"Mina I love working with you already girl." Ms. Doris chimed in.

"Thanks Ms. Doris I think we are going to be great co-workers."

"I know we are. You just keep doing what you doing. I need my lunch's sweetie."

We all walked out the boardroom and back to our offices. Kia was right behind me. On the way to my office I glanced at Patrick and his face was buried in his work that fast.

"He is all about work. That man doesn't stop." Kia said.

"I see. How are things with you? I know the last time we spoke you were going to move," I asked.

"I'm still moving. Actually, I'm going to leave a deposit on a place I viewed near downtown. They are opening right before the summer begins."

"Good. Did you get someone to purchase your home?"

"I have some people coming to look at it next week. Hopefully it will sale fast."

"Well maybe we can have a garage sale."

"That sounds good. Maybe we should. Let's make a date to start planning." Kia said, with excitement in her voice.

"Ok, what's good for you, with your busy schedule?" I asked.

"During the week, because the week is so busy."

"Sounds like a plan. We can always have it at Mamadoll's house. She loves garage sales. Let me know if you need some help, because I'm here. Rylie and I can also help you move some things in the Tahoe. The hoe specializes in moving."

"Ha ha ha thank you girl. But, I'm getting all new furniture. I am only taking my clothes."

"Nice."

"I know you are about to be so busy with this newspaper. You probably won't have time."

"I will make time. I still have a life. Kia and I are ready for the challenge."

Patrick appeared from out of no-where. "Are you ladies going to do any work today?" He said with a smile.

We both looked at each other.

"I'm only teasing ladies, did anyone at least order us food?"

"I'm ordering right now PAK." Kia said.

"Let me take these things to my office and I'll call you with my order." Patrick said as he grabbed everything from my hand. "I got you." He said.

We made it to my office and he closed the door. I turned around and he was just standing there looking at me. Before I could speak, we both began to smile at each other like we always do.

"Can I tell you how impressed I am with you right now? I knew you had it in you, but I didn't give you enough credit. Mina your newspaper, our newspaper and you are going to be so successful. I pray you can handle it. The criticism, the judging, the pressure to meet deadlines, and the notoriety around the community."

"I can handle it. I'll be fine Patrick. Don't worry. I have been through a lot. I'm pretty tough."

"I'm not worried. And I know you are a tough sista. But sweetheart, this is a whole other ballgame. This game is not for second string, this game is for starters who came to win."

"How many rings do you have coach?"

"Too many to count."

"So I should succeed."

"That depends on your effort."

He then smiled and started walking towards me. "Also, did I tell you how wonderful you looked at church yesterday?"

"Yes you did last night on the phone about four or five times. But I want get tired of hearing it from you."

"You look good at church yesterday. Did you enjoy the service?"

He asked me the exact same question last night. I wonder does he think I want to talk about what happen at church. Does he want to see how I responded to the fact that his ex-wife is white, and the fact she stared at me the entire service. She is not important to me, and today is my day, and I will enjoy it. Let me get this out the way. I turned and walked towards the window. "Patrick, I was sorry to hear about your ex-sister-in-law. I know losing someone is hard on a family. I thought it was very kind of you to step right in and officiate for them. But if you are probing to see how I felt about seeing your ex-wife for the first time, it really didn't affect me at all." I said.

"Are you sure about that Mina? Because your body language showed me differently."

"Would you like to hear Yes I'm sure."

"I would like to hear the truth. We have to say honest with each other. I have already told you the secret Mina. So there is no need to lie about anything like something simple as a feeling."

"No I'm not sure. I felt uncomfortable. I was jealous when she reminisced about why she married you. I'm feeling some type away for a man I met almost one month ago, and I don't know where this is going to go, or where my heart will end up."

"Mina, baby turn around and look at me. Look into my eyes and let me look into yours."

I turned around.

"You never know where anything in life is going to end up. You never know how a job will end. You never know how your child will turn out. You never know if you will wake up in the morning, but you still go to sleep, you don't stay up all night and say to yourself, I wonder if I'm going to wake up now do you?" He walked over and grabbed me slow by the waist. I put my arms around his neck. We hugged and then I gave him a kiss on his forehead and then his lips.

"Mina you have to trust God. You have to be honest with yourself and me. I haven't dated anyone in two years, and I haven't held a woman In God knows how long but I'm not afraid of the outcome. I'm divorced. I'm not sleeping with her, or anyone else. I want you. I want to get to know you. So, please give yourself time to except the situation I'm in. Let's get past the launch. I will address the church of my marital status when I am ready, not when you are ready for me too. I will."

"Ok, Patrick. Now, we have work to do."

"I don't know how I'm going to work with you?" He said. "I don't need any distractions, and you distract me. In a good way."

"Oh do I? I promise to stay in my office."

"That will not help me. I will just walk over."

My phone rang and I saw it was Kia. I pressed the speaker button. "Hey girl I forgot to call you, sorry."

"It's ok. I guess you are going to pass up lunch. I need your order?"

While I began to place my order, Patrick starting unbuttoning my blouse and kissing me on my chest area. I started giggling, because he caught me off-guard.

"Got it! Have you seen PAK?" Before I could respond he responded for me.

"Kia just order me; what I always get." Then he started licking my nipple.

"PAK I've already ordered for you, that's not why I'm looking for you. Your 1:30 appointment is here."

"It's already 1:30?" He said.

"Yes sir. Time flies when you're having fun." Kia said laughing.

"Funny Kia. I'm on my way." He then looked at me, "we will continue where we left off tonight."

"Yes we will." I replied.

It was forty-five minutes later, before the food finally arrived. Everyone grabbed their order and headed back to their offices. I decided to go to everyone's office and ask them to eat together in the boardroom, except for Patrick, because his door was closed. Everyone said yes. We all sat in the boardroom talking and getting to know one another. I realized Kia rarely spent any time with them. She's like that, very private. But, we are too small of a group, and we can at least spend an hour with one another. The door opened and Patrick walked in.

"I didn't get my invitation." He said.

Everyone was quiet, but me of course. "You were with your appointment." I pulled a chair out, "have a seat."

He sat down beside me and began to eat his lunch. He was eating as if his last meal was a month ago. He then took his hand and began to rub it slowly up and down my thigh underneath the table.

"I'm glad you could join us. Mr. Kincade." Doris smiled and said.

"I am too."

He began to get closer and closer to my zipper. I stopped eating for a moment and glanced around the table. Everyone was enjoying their lunch. He began to unzip my pants slowly. My mind raced and I was thinking, what is this man doing. I had to slow him down. I needed to think of something to say.

"I know it's my first day, but I think we should all take out time to sit and have lunch with each other every day if we can. Relax, unwind, and just have us a good ole time for 1 hour. Life is so short. That's all."

"Sounds like a plan to me. I'm in." Patrick said.

"Me too." Kia said.

"Me three." Doris said.

"Me four" Elaine shouted."

"Me five."

"Me six."

Patrick and I smiled at one another like we were the only ones in the room. I looked away and of course all eyes were on us and they were smiling too.

"I'm going back to my office. Thanks for lunch Kia." I said.

"Thanks PAK." Kia said smiling.

"Thank you Patrick."

"Anytime. Anyplace. Anywhere." He said to me.

I cannot believe what he was doing in there or just said in front of them sitting there. Can you say embarrassed? I kept walking as if I did not hear him. I started immediately working once I made it to my office. I got so much accomplished when I finally looked up it was 4:30. I called and contacted at least twenty to twenty-five advertisers. But, the bad news is I didn't have enough room for everyone to advertise. I only had enough space for twenty advertisers. I begin to come up with a different type of strategy and thinking of different ways for all the advertisers who wanted to advertise to have an opportunity to be featured in the *SerVant24:7*.

My phone was ringing off the hook I had to send a few of them to voicemail and the other ones Ms. Doris had to catch. I had scheduled to meet with the photographer this week and I had already completed my inspirational word for the first edition. I looked up and it was four o'clock. Ms. Doris walked in and handed a few papers to me. One was from Patrick and the other from Kia. It was there inspirational words. Great! Then I received three e-faxes with the advertiser's information for their products.

143

Then by 5:30 I had received seventeen advertiser's information for their section of the paper. I only had room for twenty. This means I had completed the section for advertisers in one day! Yea! I had so much drive in me I didn't want to stop.

"Knock. Knock."

I didn't have to look up because I knew that voice and the smell of that cologne. "Yes sir"

"Wow. Somebody is busy." Patrick said.

"Yes, that somebody is. How can I help you?"

"You can help me by calling it quits."

I looked up. He had changed in some jeans and very nice polo shirt. His tennis shoes looked like they were purchased a few minutes prior to him standing in my door. "Quits? Already?"

"Yes. It's 6:45."

I looked over at the time on my computer. "I didn't even realize it. Let me wrap things up hear and change into my clothes. I need to call my child and check on her and Mamadoll also."

"No problem. You remembered to bring a change of clothes, I like that. Take your time. I'll be in my office waiting."

I freshened up in the restroom, changed in some relaxing clothes, brushed my teeth, watered my garden down there☺, sprayed on the perfume he complimented me on, and headed out the door. When I walked out he was leaning against the wall looking like a tall double dipped German chocolate ice cream on a waffle cone, that I wanted to lick. Lord, help me please.

"I'm ready." I smiled and said.

He smiled and grabbed my hand as we walked in to the elevator. He glanced over at me with sneaky smirk on his face. I looked up and around and there were no cameras. I was thinking to myself Lord don't let this man touch me in this elevator…I will give in, but too late for that request. He pressed the stop button on the panel. The elevator stopped. He turned and walked towards me. He lifted me up and sat me on the bar in the corner of the elevator, where I was trapped. I was caught off guard. His hands moved from my face to softly around my neck. He began to un-button my blouse. He took his hands and began massaging my breast real slow. We gazed in each other's eyes while his hands were putting on quite the performance. He then took one hand and grabbed the both of my breast. He pressed them together tight, then begin sucking both of my nipples at the same time. His other hand was working also. It was unzipping my jeans slowly and began moving all around my garden, which by now was dripping wet. I forgot I was in an elevator. He stopped kissing my breast and began kissing my abdomen and as he began moving his extra-long tongue below my navel we heard a loud voice.

"Mr. Kincade is everything ok sir?" A voice appeared out of no-where on the elevator speakers. I damn near jumped through the closed elevator doors. I was so damn paranoid. I thought I had a vision of the two of us on TMZ titled, *Pastor and the Tramp*.

Patrick wasn't fazed at all by the voice. He didn't flinch. "That's my security Mina. They look out for a brother."

"I see." I straightened up my clothes, my hair, and every other piece of evidence on my body that was tampered with. He smiled at me and asked was I ready. He pushed for the elevator to start again. I was at a loss of words. I continued smiling. My pastor, my boss, Patrick, is something else after hours. Lord I am going to need your help with this one.

We walked out the elevator holding hands and smiling like two teenagers. Security was tighter than a maximum-security prison. There were codes to use and badges just to walk out the building. We walked to what I thought was a different car, it was, but it was still one of his cars. He popped the truck open.

"Hand me your purse Mina?"

"My purse?" Now I know he did not just ask a black woman for her purse. He must think he is still with his ex. I clutched my purse as if I had just robbed a bank and there was a million dollars in there. I shook my head no. "I can't do that Baby. You are fine as wine, but I can't do that."

He laughed. "Mina stop tripping. I got you baby. We are about to get on my bike and you will need to leave it here. You are something else. It is secure."

I prayed and then I handed it to him slowly. I mean real slow. He grabbed it placed it in the trunk. Someone drove up on a Harley Davis motorcycle and parked it.

"Mr. Kincade it's ready for you, enjoy."

He turned towards me and asked, "Are you ready, my dear?"

"For?"

"An adventure."

"Were taking a ride on a motorcycle?"

"Well of course. Not many people know but this is what I love to do when I'm not working or pastoring. I love to just ride my bike, and think. I love to be outdoors especially on a night like tonight with this nice weather and a beautiful woman holding on to me, I couldn't ask for anything else."

"First time for everything." I said.

"Before we leave I have something for you." He turned around and pulled a leather jacket, along with a helmet, out of a box. They both read SerVant24:7, on the back of them. I became overwhelmed with flattery. I got so emotional. Damn, this man right hear is something else. How did he have time to have this made so quickly? He placed my helmet and jacket on me; and he then put his helmet and jacket on which read the same thing. We hopped on the motorcycle and I placed my arms around his waist. I held on to him so tight. He grabbed my hands; then whispered in his sexy voice, that I could barely hear him say, because of my helmet.

"Don't be afraid, I got you."

I closed my eyes as we rode off into the night. We rode around town for at least an hour, if not longer. The ride was so needed, and felt so relaxing. He pulled up to a Japanese restaurant which looked like a hole in the wall, but that was ok with me because those are always the good ones. We walked in and it was stunning on the inside, it was very romantic. The lights were dimmed in red and there were beautiful chandeliers throughout. There were drapes that separated each individual table area. You could hear an acoustic guitar playing jazz in the background. There was a Japanese man who greeted us at the door. He was so happy to see Patrick. He hugged him two or three times then a Japanese woman appeared and hugged him the same way.

She was very emotional. They spoke to him in Japanese and he spoke back to them in Japanese. I watched how he enter-acted with them. This brother is a jack-of-all-trades. I see why so many people love Patrick; he sees no color, no race, no ethnicity. Before we sat down we handed them our shoes. I was thinking no purse, no shoes, why don't we just take off everything. That was my flesh thinking that way. As we followed the host to our eating area I noticed we were the only ones in the restaurant just like our date on the yacht. I have to remember his situation and his occupation. We were led to our table, which sat behind drapes. We then sat down on the floor on pillows and Patrick proceeded to order our drinks for us.

"Nice restaurant. I didn't know you could speak Japanese. I'm impressed."

"I didn't tell you. My bad. I can speak a little, learned in college. That was God. He knew I would have to connect with people one day. I'm impressed with you."

"With me? What did I do?"

"Your feet didn't stink."

"Ha, ha, ha, very funny. I do take baths."

"Not baths. I was hoping you took showers."

"I take those too."

"Good that can be our next date."

"Ha, ha. I'll need to check my schedule."

"When you check it, every other day; should have my name on it."

"Is that right Mr. Kincade? I have a child that requires my attention, and a newspaper to build. I don't know if I'm going to have time like that."

"Time will manifest itself Ms. Wright. Some things will just happen."

We were having another wonderful date night. We laughed and talked about everything again, like we always do from childhood to teenage years, to adulthood.

We touched on past relationships; divorce, dealing with death, to careers. I was starting to realize more and more each time, why everything I had prayed for was beginning to manifest in the natural. I always prayed for my next mate to be my friend first. I saw it in the spiritual, but I didn't know if I would truly meet someone, a real man, that I actually could be a friend with, I didn't trust myself. I didn't think I could do it without the intimacy part. I'm not so much lusting after him anymore. I am more getting to know him on a friend level. I flirt with him all the time. That's natural I'm attracted to him. I know we have kissed and touched, and almost went there in the elevator, but we haven't taken it to the other level and I must say I am enjoying being friends and it makes us both desire one another more. I'm now realizing what she was talking about now. He shared with me so many secrets and intimate details of his life. He is very loving and truly cares about people. He ordered for the both of us. The waiter brought us over our appetizers and our drinks. I had me a little plum Saki. The lights grew dimmer and the drapes slowly closed over our table. The jazz was still playing in the background. I continued to sip on my Saki and begin to feel good.

"What did you order?"

"I ordered a volcano roll. Would you like to taste one?"

"Sure." He leaned to grab his fork.

"Let me feed it to you with the chopsticks." He dropped the fork. He opened his mouth wide and real slow. I placed the sushi in his mouth and apiece fell on his lip. I picked up the napkin to wipe it off for him, but instead I licked it off. We both giggled.

"You are something else Mina."

"Why do you say that?"

"Because you are. Someone I want to get to know more and more."

"We are getting to know one another."

He stopped eating. "Yes, we are, but I would like to see what breakfast taste like with you, then lunch, and dinner."

So, what is he saying? Is he saying he wants me to spend the night with him, or what? "Patrick, we probably shouldn't be alone overnight together."

"Who said we were going to be alone?"

"Well maybe I took the statement you made about breakfast wrong."

"You took it right. But I never said we were going to be alone."

"Well where would we be?"

"My home. I have housekeepers, and chefs. Its people there."

"That's cute but you know what I am trying to say."

"Say it then Mina, no holding back, it's me and you baby-girl. You think we are going to be intimate with one another if were ever alone?"

"Well, yes. Did you just see how we were on one another in the elevator?"

"I did and I was meaning to tell you those breast of yours are beautiful and taste delightful."

"They said thank you." We both were quiet. "All jokes aside I know we are going to be intimate."

He stopped eating, "Mina you act as if were teenagers. What's the problem? We are both single adults."

I hesitated and stopped eating. "I can't get the fact out of my head that you're a Pastor and sometimes I am overwhelmed with conviction."

He was quiet. We both were. "I'm a pastor this is true? But, my flesh is not dead. I prayed for God to kill it until he sends me my wife, it was dead at one point, but it was resurrected once you came into my life."

"OMG... so this is my fault?"

"It is always the woman's fault. Remember, Eve ate the apple and Adam followed her. Sarah couldn't wait on baby Isaac that's why Ismael came, and Delilah seduced Sampson, because she had to have those coins. Women."

"You did not just take it there. You really don't want to go there? Now, I know my bible."

"Oh, do you? Hit me with your best shot. Give it to me."

"Ok. Who followed Jesus all the way to the cross? Where were those male disciples at? Who stayed and watched him beaten, hung, and then nailed? His mother Mary, and Mary Magdalene.

The disciples were nowhere around. There is no record of them when Jesus is being led to the cross. And who doubted Jesus, a man named Thomas. Also, who betrayed Jesus, again a man named Judas, but who washed his feet for him, a woman, named Mary Magdalene. I rest my case."

"Baby, baby, I was talking about the Old Testament. Before Christ came." We both laughed.

"We're talking about the Bible in general." He is so funny.

"You made a good point. But listen Mina to me sweetie, If I wasn't trying to keep us from taking this to the bedroom, I would not be wining and dining you, touching, and kissing on you the way I do, then watching walk away and go home. Cold showers do not feel good. I'm tired of them."

"So, you don't like to see me go home?"

He was quiet. "I am starting to want to see and be around you more, so of course I don't want to see you go home."

"I don't want to go home sometimes, but I know that friendship first is one thing I have asked God for in a relationship. Although, I enjoy flirting and having fun with you, without taking it there just yet."

"I agree. You're my buddy. I like hanging with you."

"Thanks, I enjoy hanging with you also. You make me laugh. You are hilarious at times."

"Am I? One thing I forgot to tell you, I was thinking about writing a sermon about you."

I sat my glass of wine down. "You were, about me? What was it going to be about?"

"A Christian woman and her love for the wine, is it right, or wrong? You have almost finished that bottle."

"Ha ha…. Stop it. You better not Patrick."

"I'm only kidding. I wouldn't dare, whatever we do is between me and you."

"You Promise?"

"I promise."

"Were taking it to the grave?" I asked.

"Yes ma'am, six, seven, eight feet under it's going, because it can't stay here." He said.

"Ok."

"Now let's finish up with our dinner. I know you have your daughter, and you have to go home baby, I respect that."

"Speaking of daughters, you have yours also. Do you see her often?"

He paused, and then sat his fork down.

"I do from time to time. But, I don't want to see her mom; so therefore, I have to deal with the consequence. It's a long, difficult, hurtful, story Mina. You wouldn't believe what I have been through with this woman. You think you know someone and then you're hit with the.... You are married to a stranger. I knew it before I married her. God showed me so many things about her. But, when our flesh gets in the way amongst other things. We want what we want, and then we pay the price for it later. I paid the price. I'm still paying the price."

"But have you learned from it?"

"Yes I have. Do you know I didn't have wisdom until after I became a pastor? It was as if I experienced every hurtful emotion a person could feel after I was called to preach. After I started this ministry. I went through so much hurt, I was going to walk away. But, the ministry kept growing, growing, and growing. The more trials, hurt, and pains I experienced, the more anointed I became. I preached harder and harder every Sunday. If a situation occurred that hurt me on Saturday, when Sunday came I lit the pulpit up! My mother always said stay with Jesus baby; he already won the battle for us. So, I stayed. I have my flaws and I have desires, dreams, and goals, like everyone else, but most of all I know my purpose. When the time is right and when I am comfortable, I will share it with you. Now can a brother get a kiss, I've been looking at those lips move all night. And they have been talking to me saying, daddy kiss me."

We kissed and fondled one another. We ended our meal, and continued our conversation. I was enlightened by his thoughtfulness of the fact that I needed to go home. We rode back to the office. The ride was even smoother this time. I don't know if it was the Saki, or, the fact that I was on cloud nine from this date with him. Whatever this feeling was, I couldn't shake it. Life is something else. You never know where it will take you. I never would have pictured us like this. Once we got back to the office, we sat there on the bike for at least ten minutes just holding one another, I didn't want to let go and he didn't either.

He said he respected the fact that I had to be at home because I am an example for my child and I do live with my Aunt. He said it's called respecting her and her home. I climbed off his bike and took my helmet off.

"I love the helmet and jacket in case I didn't tell you."

"Thank you. I had to pay extra to have those items expedited by the time you clocked out."

"You did well, really well. I take that back, you did great Patrick!"

"Thank you Mina. Should I follow you home, it's late."

"No, I'm fine Patrick."

"Are you sure?"

"I'm fine." I said stern.

"If you say so. I thoroughly enjoyed myself."

"I did also."

"I'll see you tomorrow." I said.

"Yes."

He walked me over to my car. "Please promise me you will call me when you get home."

"I promise."

I jumped in the car and drove away. I turned up the radio and listen to smooth relaxing jazz all the way home. The drive was at least fifteen extra minutes from the original time, but it didn't bother me once. I am in a great season of my life and every day for me has been wonderful. I pulled into our subdivision and headed through the gate. It was 10:35, so I know Mamadoll and Rylie are probably sleep by now, because it's already a quarter to eleven. I walked in the house and Mamadoll was watching television on the couch. I walked over and tried to scare her. "Boo!" I said.

She didn't flinch. "Mina now you know I'm old school. If I met you and Rylie at the gate that night you all drove all the way from Dallas, surely I heard my front door open." Mamadoll said as she began to smile.

"I know, I know. I was just messing with you. Where's Rylie?

"Sleep before we left the campaign center."

"I figured. I was going to scare her too I just wanted you two to laugh. To see you smile. That's all. I miss you two already and I just started working again, and I feel like I haven't been spending enough time with you, or Rylie?"

"Mina, how long did I take care of you?"

"Nearly all my life."

"She is fine, and as for me, I'm fine. We're fine. Mina walk into what God has called you do to. You love writing. You have always told me you wanted to write stories to encourage people. You don't know where this is going to lead you. It's only a season and then there will be another season, then another, its call life. You will never know what God is doing, but when he moves you move with him. You run right into your destiny, I mean run. Don't' look at what others are doing stay focus and you catch what God hands to you. It's your time to do what you were born to do. Go and make us even prouder. Give me something else to brag about at the center."

"I will. I thank God for putting such an encouraging, praying woman in my life. Now, you mentioned the center. I have a question to ask you."

"Alright, but before you ask me, I have a question for you?"

I was thinking to myself, oh Lord, what have she heard. "Yes ma'am."

"How was your first day?"

I begin to instantly breathe again. "It was wonderful. Thanks for asking." I said with a big smile.

"I knew it! I felt it deep in my spirit it would be. God gave me peace about it.
Did you see Pastor Kincade? I like him so much, and even more now that he hired you. Sometimes I look at him on television and I want to give him a big motherly hug and tell him how proud the community is of him."

I wanted to say; I gave him the hug and much more for you and the community. "That is so sweet. I did. I work very close with him."

"That's good Mina. I heard he was such a good person."

"He is Mamadoll a very good boss and gentleman. Actually, you will get to meet him at the launch party for *SerVant24:7*.

"For who? A party?"

I grabbed a piece of paper and wrote the name of the newspaper down for her. "*SerVant24:7* is what I titled the newspaper."

"Mina Wright, you came up with this name? *SerVant24:7*? You did this?"

"Yes ma'am. These past few nights in my room."

"This is God ordered. I knew you could do it. You could not have chosen a better name for a gospel newspaper or newsletter. Whatever you want to call it, I love it! I knew God was going to use you. We are servants, all the time, twenty-four seven! Amen! Amen! I wouldn't miss the party for the world. It's a holy ghost party, right?"

"It's the launching of the first issue of *SerVant24:7* newspaper, and this is the business part Mamadoll." I'm starting to sound like Patrick.

"The holy ghost is your business Mina. I'm only teasing you baby. I will be there for you!"

We stood in the living room hugging one another smiling.

"Look at how God has brought you through and to the next level of what He had waiting for you, now what if you didn't move home? Just what if? All you need to do is believe Him when He says He's going to do something. It will be done. Trust Him Mina. That's all it is to it, and that's it!"

Chapter 8: Now it Begins...

We were just shy a month from the launching of the first issue of **SerVant24:7.** We all worked diligently every day, all day. We participated in visiting hospitals, local businesses, neighborhoods, schools, restaurants, airports, salons, barbershops, campaign headquarters, libraries, and bus stops. If you can name it, we visited it. We each would email members to remind them of deadlines and what we received and also what we needed. We all put in our opinions and helped choose the photos for the cover. Each page, each detail, from beginning to end was on-going. I edited, I wrote over and over again for members and local businesses that completed their work with typos, and punctuation out of order and so much more. The phone and emails never stopped. From the beginning when Patrick made the announcement to the end of each week, it was none stop busy. Patrick and I had not been on a date in two weeks although; we worked closely every day and said our good nights every night. We still managed to get us some kissing, rubbing, and touching in between breaks and when he walked me to the car every night after work. Every day I arrived for work, my roses were freshly waiting on me next to my freshly brewed coffee. PAK didn't miss a day of spoiling me. We both stayed focus because we knew we had to make this first issue top priority. We knew we should finish this and then the other would come later. Our friendship grew. It blossomed the more and more we worked together and was around one another. We all were bonding. Kia and I were back talking like old times, and the others were right onboard with us. We ate lunch together and stayed every day late until we finished, then back again the next morning, and every Sunday at church. God was definitely with us every step of the way. There was no mess, no gossiping, no confusion, no one missing work, or deadlines. We were all diligent in every task we set out to do. We were focused and dedicated to get this right. Patrick was preaching harder and harder with force and passion every single Sunday. He was on fire! The ministry continued to grow. I begin to lose count of how many joined. I do know there were so many believers it looked like a football stadium at times on Sunday mornings. I begin to get to know the members more and more. They begin to know me as well. I know I have spent so much time with many of the members to gain insight to what they were desiring from the ministry, their pastor, as well as **SerVant24:7**. Many members, or let me just say the majority of the members wanted to see more from their *First Lady*. They wanted her to be more involved with church and the church activities also they would like her to be seen around the community like

Patrick, and in the sanctuary. They wanted her to speak to them instead of always hiding as if she wasn't part of the ministry. Many of them said they didn't know they had a First Lady. Some members wanted more marriage seminars with both Patrick and the *First Lady* involved. They wanted more service times. They also wanted to hear Kia preach from time to time. They wanted Sunday school back, and programs at Christmas time for the children. It was a lot of to consume and try to create a paper around their needs.

On a more positive note, many of the members were so pleased with the word of God they were hearing every Sunday; they could care less if there was a first, second, or third lady. They just wanted to be ready when Jesus returned.

It was definitely interesting to hear both positive and negative feedback regarding the ministry.

But, of course, I was not going to allow the negative feedback to be advertised in my paper and there is no perfect ministry. We will stay positive, especially, for the first edition. We had accomplished so much in just a months' time who wants to hear negative.

Patrick allowed us to have the week off of the party we could not believe it. Well, I take that back, we could believe it but, our equilibrium could not. We were all needing rest, and we finally got it. May was here quickly. The cool breeze had left, and summer was fast approaching. I desired Patrick more and more, especially being around him every day. I must admit the *being friends first thing* is cool and it is needed and helpful to any two beings wanting to be in a relationship, but I also needed to feel a warm body next to mine and for that body to hold me a little closer and not all the time with our clothes on. Some may say she is a little hot, or horny, but I say I am a woman that is 40 years old, alive, and well, and I have needs to be met. Those needs cannot be met all the time with my toy. Chicken is ok. But, every once in a while, I need beef, well done!

It was getting closer and closer to our launching party for **SerVant24:7**. We had five days until the actual day of the party, so Patrick gave us the week off! The party was that Saturday coming up. He said he knew it would be a busy week for me and he knew she was my first priority. I was able to take my baby to school and pick her up the entire week. She was extremely excited about the paper and the fact it would be on stands in her high school with her mothers' name on it.

She said teachers had already begun asking her to ask me would I come and speak and the newspaper had not came out yet.

The media had a lot to talk about the entire week. Saturday was getting close. Me, Rylie, Kia, and Mamadoll went shopping for our shoes and dresses on Friday. We were pushing it but, we finally all found beautiful outfits. Patrick said I needed to look as if I was going to the Oscars. He said the who's who would be there and he wanted this night to attract the best of the best for our newspaper. He handed me his very black, and I do mean ebony, American Express Card, and off I went along with my crew. That means hair, plus face, plus nails, plus body, plus teeth plus shoes, plus accessories equal radiant! We all had our manipedi done together and then full body massages. Poor Rylie fell asleep during her massage, and I joined her. Instead of eating out once we finally made it home Mamadoll cooked us up a good dinner. Kia stayed with us until late that evening and then decided to go home. Patrick had called me throughout that day and of course to tell me good night. The day of the launching party I was up by five a.m., for prayer with Mamadoll and her prayer warriors. Then I went for a thirty-minute run and hair appointment. I also fasted. I needed this because I needed self-control and to handle the criticism that came along with a project you had work very hard for and then people will come along and tear it to pieces. But, what I have learned is, people who wished God handed them your talent, aka HATERS, will try to bring you down because they like to feel better about the fact they did nothing with their talent.

But I decided to choose the five NOTS: Not tonight, Not tomorrow, Not the next day, and last but Not least, NOT AT ALL will allow them to get me tonight.

You are cordially invited to the Launching of
SerVant24:7

Bi-weekly – Gospel News Publication
1st edition

To be held at Pastor Patrick Kincade Mansion

Please call the number listed on your personal invitation and enter code RSVP to gain access to address.

A private Affair

This is the way the invitation read. We were all ready to leave the house by 4:30, and on our way to Patrick's mansion. He sent a limo to pick us up because he didn't want me to drive, and Rylie wouldn't be able to stay very long. The drive was at least an hour and fifteen minutes. Once we drove into the community, it was only three mansions on the street, and all of them were so large, Rylie thought they were office buildings. This was my first time at his home. It was definitely a mansion. I was at a loss for words. It took at least; I would say, ten to fifteen minutes to reach the front door. It was very secluded. Security was tight! Once we arrived there were cars and professional people everywhere, but it was still very classy. There was a red carpet laid out to walk up to the front door, and a huge tent that led to the back area with lights dimmed all over. I took a few pictures, and many of the people already knew who I was. Rylie and Mamadoll were smiling from ear to ear. There was a kid area similar to a circus theme. It was phenomenal. There was a wait staff dressed in tuxedos. There was every kind of food from every country in the world. A photo of the newspaper cover hung high as the ceiling: **SerVant24:7.** There it was and there it hung, my name, my invention. Wow! I couldn't believe it was happening so fast and feeling good. Everything was in order. The flow of the process was so smooth. I walked around and begin to notice some of the most famous preachers and their wives I had enjoyed watching on television all around me. Local media stations were everywhere. Reporters I had watched on television as a child. This was unbelievable. And of course, just when I wanted to take a tour of this mansion, the party was about to start. I finally ran into my co-workers who all looked stunning. We all mingled and conversed with one another. Kia approached us looking lovely as well, and we all were engaging in some fun finally. We were having a good time hanging with one another and meeting different people.

  I saw Patrick, and we spoke from afar. He smiled, and then I smiled, he winked, then I winked. He had an entourage around him of local businessmen and socialites. He touched his eye and then his cell phone.

  We talked in codes from time to time, so I understood what he meant. That meant look at your cell phone.

  He had texted me: *I thanked God for allowing you into my dream after I saw you standing over there with that dress on. My, my, Mina. #Stunning.*

  I responded: *Was I only standing in the dream? Or was I doing something else with you, because you look so edible in your tuxedo? #ohsohandsome*

  He texted again: *Don't make me drool, please; people are all around me Baby.*

  The music begins to come to an end, and Kia asks were we ready. Too late now we're here, and I have been preparing for months we better be ready. She made her way to the area built like a stage near the pool where a tent sat. This area was also beautifully lit up with candles and lights. Of course, the band waived at me because they remembered me from the yacht. I walked toward the small stage, and my stomach had a city full of butterflies. I was so nervous. I looked around the event for my friend. I had not had any wine, and soon as I saw the waiter, I asked him for Nay, Nay aka Chardonnay, my buddy. He grabbed my buddy real quick and a small buzz joined me after the second glass, or maybe the third, but who's counting it's my newspaper and my party. I got a little emotional when I looked around the room at some of the people I never thought I would be around in my lifetime. Patrick took the stage and began speaking to the crowd, and they immediately were quiet and attentive to what he had to say. He spoke so well. I was engaged in his speech. He was incredibly handsome in his suit. I was in Patrickland. I turned to speak to Ms. Doris and there "she" was staring at me. Tish was here. She was standing not even two feet behind me. Why is she here? Oh! I forgot she is the first lady. She showed up for the show and boy was she all dolled up from top the top, to the bottom. Hair done, (check), nails, (check) face, well I'm concerned. I'm not a hater at all, she wore a beautiful dress and looked very well kept, but she has been to Aunt Bae husband. Her cheeks never moved, and lips were extremely full. She was stunning I will give it to her. She was all smiles; walking through the crowd. It looks as if she was trying to make her way to the stage to join him. Calm down Mina I told myself, and remember you are a lady and most importantly you know the truth. I wonder why she is here and what does she want. I remembered my NOTS! I am Not going to allow this woman distract me. It is my night, Not hers. I looked back over my shoulder, and she was gone. I then noticed walking down the red carpet was Bryce and Zi'lah holding hands smiling and waving. He stopped to talk with a few reporters. I wonder how he received an invitation. No, let me re-phrase that I wonder why he received an invitation? But, I looked to my right in the right direction and there was my baby smiling at me. That picture was all the motivation I needed to Not be distracted.

"I want to thank each and every one of you for supporting our cause tonight." People were clapping. I could not do it without you, the community, my members, other spiritual leaders as well." Patrick paused. "I have been through a lot over the past few years with the passing of parents four months apart, building a ministry at the same, it has not been an easy route to drive. There have been many routes and detours I have had to take, but thanks be unto God who guided me to my destination safe and sound. He has truly kept me. I haven't been the best child, but I also haven't been the worse, that's why my brother and sister, Grace and Mercy steps in right on time to make sure I stay focused and do what God has called me to do.

Everyone clapped and shouted Amen! "He has put some phenomenal and talented people in my life over the past two-years." He smiled. "He has been so good to me, and I am in a good place in my life right now." He looked over at me, "I mean a really good place, and with this newspaper coming out on Monday, I couldn't ask for anything more from God. You know I'm at a loss for words right now." He begins to get very emotional.

"Over the past few months, I have felt so loved. I mean loved like I have never felt before." Tish walked directly in front of him to the front of the stage. She folded her arms and stood there staring at him. I saw the look in his eyes as if he wanted to choke her. He gritted his teeth and gave her blank stare. She was doing this on purpose. She knows something about him and me. I know it. I wanted to stand right next to her to agitate her, but I'm a grown woman, and there is no need for games when the truth has been told. Patrick begins to speak again.

"As I was saying right now I am ready to take this and any other opportunities that present themselves to the next level." Everyone start clapping and cheering. "But it wasn't just about me. Two is so much better than one, and that other half..."

Before he could finish speaking, I was thinking, *I know he is not going to call her to that stage.* I cannot watch this. All of my hard work, I will not watch it. He continued.

"God sent this person to assist me in the areas I needed." He looked over at me again. I didn't smile. I didn't know how to feel. Remember your NOTS Mina, I told myself.

"This newspaper would not have been created and completed if it was not for Mina Wright."

Dammit that's my boy! I was surprised! Damn, it felt good to hear him say my name in front of all these people, and especially in front of Miss America Tish.

"Please give a big hand clap for the **SerVant24:7** Creator, Editor-n- Chief, Ms. Mina Wright. Mina come and join me."

I cannot tell you what happen after that. I would have peed on myself if my dress weren't so fitted. My bladder held it, so I was good.

"Just be yourself, Mina. Go ahead. God is with you." Kia said as she smiled.
I cat walked to the stage and waived, and shook hands on my way there. I was ready to take the crown off Tish head. Patrick reached out his hand to help me up. He then gave me a kiss on my jaw. The crowd was silenced. I never looked over at her, but I could feel her staring at me.

It's a new season sweetie. I felt this confidence arise on the inside of me. I wanted to thank her for standing there, and thank her for the divorce also. I approached the microphone and words begin to flow out of my mouth without hesitation. I'm going to show her how to put on a show but in a Christian way.

"Thank you so much Patrick, for such kind words. I didn't have a speech prepared for you. Patrick surprised me with the invite to join him up here." The crowd laughed. "So that being said I will speak from my heart. Thank you for being here tonight and supporting us. We all have worked so hard to provide you with the best reading material on what's happening in our community, and what the believers have to say. When I began working on this project, I learned so much from God's people. Their desires and dreams. They wanted more besides going to church once or twice a week, or watching preachers and listening to sermons on one or two major networks television five days a week. They wanted to read about God's people and hear a word from him while they are on their lunch breaks. Or, they could be in the doctor's office scared of what the news is from there test results pick-up the **SerVant24:7** newspaper, and read an article about someone's deliverance with the same diagnosis. This is how I created, *Hear my Hallelujah* section. Sharing testimonies with those who are hopeless, we serve twenty-four seven."

Everyone began shouting and clapping. But I wasn't through. "My goal was never about trying to be popular or gain notoriety. I just wanted to use the gift God gave me, and when he opened the door for me I walked in." Several members from the crowd shouted Amen and people clapped. "This project didn't involve only me; it involved others as well," I called them by name and ask them to join me on stage. "We all worked days and nights to ensure the message of Jesus Christ is shared with those who don't know him. I was glad to introduce him and let those who didn't know he was so much more than a carpenter or a prophet. He is our savior, redeemer, protector, provider, healer, restorer, our everything, and we will share what he has done for us in print on every corner store, airport, train station, school, libraries, along with other publications. Etc."

I couldn't finish my speech from the cheers. Everyone start clapping and shouting. Kia and my crew were clapping even louder. Mamadoll was louder than everyone at this event. "I want to thank my team." I thanked them one by one and asked them all to join me on stage. "And most of all I want to thank my Aunt who told me no matter what you may see in the natural, trust God. To my baby girl thank you for being patient with me while God takes me on this journey. Last but not least," I turned to Patrick.

"Pastor Kincade thank you for being a phenomenal leader and teacher in this community. You have become my best friend, and I love working with you." This time I looked over at her, then back at him. "May God grant you the desires of your heart according to his will." I did mean the desires of his hearts. "May God bless you all and keep you." Then I shouted really loud with my fist in the air. "Now let me hear you're your Hallelujah!" Everyone shouted Hallelujah! I walked off stage feeling absolutely wonderful. It's my season I can feel it. My family and all of the invitees met me. Patrick he went his way, and I went mine. The music was playing, and I was enjoying listening. I decided to grab me a plate to eat. I made my way through the crowd and took more and more pictures and shook more and more hands, and answered more and more questions. Everyone wanted to know where I came up with the name, where was I from, was I married, how many kids? Blah, blah, blah. The time was moving by so fast it was already 9:15. Mamadoll and Rylie had so much fun neither could hang for long. Kia said she would drive me back to the car because I still needed to meet with more press and another reporter. I walked them both back to the car to the driver waiting. Mamadoll told me at least one hundred times of how proud she was of me.

    I know the best feeling of the night was my daughter saying, how she wanted to write, to be like me. Mamadoll finally got a chance to talk with Patrick. They sat in the corner and talk for at least an hour. I'm sure Mamadoll let him in on how she feels about me. As we walked to the car for nearly ten minutes, she talked about Patrick. His spirit and how proud of me she was again. Zi'lah came out of no- where and found us. She was tipsy and on cloud nine.

"Congrats, my cousin. Hello Mamadoll." She said slurring.

"Hello, Zi'lah baby we didn't know you were here."

"Yes, ma'am. Bryce and I came together." She said looking at me.

"Well, baby it was so many people here. I saw Bryce briefly, but he didn't say a word about you being hear."

Mamadoll will always throw a little offense in, and boy does she love the game.

"Well, he probably just wanted to talk about the campaign. Speaking of campaign Mamadoll did you ask Mina about a larger section of the newspaper for Bryce election coming up?"

I thought in my mind I know Bryce is not using Zi'lah to get more votes and to get me to add a section just for him? Mama Doll stopped walking and turned to Zi'lah.

"Zi'lah, no I have not talked to Mina about Bryce campaign. It's not for me, It's for Bryce, and he has a mouth." She got in the car and said goodnight and that was that, and that is Mamadoll.

I changed the subject because Zi'lah's feelings were hurt and her face was on the ground. "Where have you been hiding missy?" She was really short with me in conversation and very defensive.

"I haven't been hiding anywhere, I've been with my man helping him with his campaign."

With her man? "I suppose that's Bryce," I asked.

"Yes, it is?"

"Ok honey, good for you. Well, I missed you coming by the house, and I haven't seen you at church."

"I'm looking for a new church, Street called Straight is too big for me, look at all those members. Pastor Kincade don't know me, girl. I need a pastor to talk to me, who knows his members."

"You've been coming for years, haven't you?"

"So what? I went there because it was the church to be at. He's not all that, and Kia either. She doesn't even preach. Like Bryce said, we want a preacher that will congregate with us."

"So if they talk to you and know you personally, that will get you into heaven? If you talk to him, or Kia, they will talk to you Zi'lah. Learn how to think for yourself and go where God leads you, not where Bryce leads you."

"Mina, please. You don't even know. They are not what they say they are, him or Kia. And where is his wife? Why isn't his wife ever with him? Why isn't she visible to the congregation? Why isn't she on billboards and commercials? Isn't she the First Lady?"

I got really defensive and protective of Patrick and Kia. "I don't know if you were a member for all those years you should have ask them those questions. Better yet, you should have asked before you joined. I don't know, and I really don't care where his wife is, I care about where my soul is going. And furthermore, I don't why Bryce is talking, when he has endorsed him."

"Mina I know you don't care for Bryce, but we are in love. We are falling in love more and more. I don't care what you think but that man loves me. We are planning to get married after he wins the election. I will be a First Lady. The First Lady of the city." She said slurring.

I laughed. "I never said he wasn't in love with you. I didn't know what you two were doing. Why are you so defensive?"

"Because I know you two don't get along Mina, and I know what you're going to say like all the rest of the people in this city?"

"What am I going to say since you know me so well? Huh? Is it because you know how he really is deep down inside, and it's easier to blame everyone else because we are not afraid to say it? It's your life Zi'lah you are a grown woman. I don't have to tell you anything about Bryce. But, I will say this, I have only known the man four maybe five months at the most, and every time I see him, he is always in a woman, not only a woman but a married woman's' face."

"You are always in a married man's face Mina. A pastor at that!" She said.

I turned to walk away, took a deep breath, and remembered my NOTS! I will Not entertain this mess. She is a typical woman dating a man that's no good, and what does she do, defends him and get angry with you for telling her what she already knows, so typical. "I don't know where this anger is coming from, and I am not about to try and figure it out. Goodnight Zi'lah. I wish you much happiness. I hope you find Bryce a newspaper willing to support his campaign." I left her tipsy, gullible ass standing there.

I entered the house and made my rounds again. I was invited to everyone's table, and I talk with so many intelligent people wanting me to assist them in many different business adventures. I was all over the place.

I took a sip of Nay Nay every time I got a chance. I still had not been able to take a tour of this museum aka mansion. It was unbelievable. I kept shaking my hand and asking myself, does he needs all this room by himself? It was a quarter till' twelve and my feet were telling me it was time to slow it down. I noticed Kia having a good time throughout the night. It was good to see her smile. She was spending time with a very nice looking gentleman. She said he was also running for county commissioner in the upcoming election. He wanted at least a full page and was willing to pay whatever price. I was willing to give him the full page! As for my man, he walked and talked and shook hands with the thousand attendees, and I allowed him to do his thing. The band started to play a song selection by Pete Belasco, Keep On. I was in my own world, finally some time alone. I sat alone on part of the patio just relaxing.

"Can I join you, my dear?"

I didn't have to turn around. I know that voice oh so well. It always appears out of no-where. "Yes, you can."

"You have been all over the place woman. I look to my left you're gone. I look to the right and you're way on the other side of the room. I had to sneak up on you before you moved again. I haven't been able to sit and talk with you all night."

"I had to be about my business baby, networking, promoting **SerVant24:7,** getting the job done."

"No, rephrase that, you got the job done and where did that speech come from? You just started talking and kept going. It was great. You have a calling to speak I can hear it. I heard it the very first time you spoke at church. The audience loved you. People are so receptive to you."

"Thanks and I meant what I said form my heart. It all came from my heart. Jesus loved people. It's about the people that need it, not you, not me, you know."

"You're right. I know you mean every word you are saying from your heart maybe that is why I'm so into you. I love being around you, working with you every day. Your spirit is just lovely to be around. I'm telling you, my life is great right now! I'm so happy."

"That's good to hear Patrick, and also good to see."

We sat listening to music. It was quiet for a moment. People were still there enjoying themselves. I was very tipsy, and I was feeling really good, and he was looking really good. I looked up really slow from his feet all the way until I got to those sexy lips of his. He was staring at me like I was a fresh Ice glass of water on a one hundred degree, hot summer day. He had a look in his eyes like, only if I could taste it.

"Where's Mamadoll and your daughter?"

"The driver you sent took them home already. Rylie didn't need to be here that late."

"I understand. I love spending time with Mamadoll." He said.

I'm thinking, please cut the small talk. "I was wondering if you were going to feel like taking me home. I haven't seen Kia, and I was going to catch a ride with her."

"Unfortunately, Mina I can't do that. The cars are put up for the night. They have a curfew. But you are welcome to stay the night with me." He said seductively with a smirk on his face as he bit into an apple.

"An apple? The forbidden fruit." I said.

"Then maybe I should eat something different." He said.

I then grabbed some fruit as well from a fruit tray on the table. I licked the strawberry really slow, up and down, and then I bit into it. "We can eat together."

I don't think he realized he was drooling a little. I stood up with a napkin, leaned over the table with my assets in the air, and wiped the side of his mouth.

"Can I come to this party over here, it's seems like it's more entertaining. Hey now!"

As I continued wiping Patrick's face, I didn't even turn around. Patrick sat there with a smirk on his face. It was none other than miserable, messy, bitter, and bruised, Bryce. His behavior was very annoying. He was loud. His eyes were red. He seemed to be high in my opinion, but of what.

"Commissioner Calhoun what can I do for you?" Patrick asked.

I slowly turned around. There we were face to face. It seems as though Bryce brought company with him. Standing next to him was none other than the former First Lady, Tish. She acted out of character as well. She had her arms crossed, and she stood with an attitude. She starred at me with the meanest, and evilest look. I felt very uncomfortable, but I remained calm.

"Well, Well Pastor. It seems as though you have good taste. I'm sorry; we're not at church. Please forgive me. So, is it Pastor, or is this the business time and your name is Patrick?" He asked sarcastically as he giggled extremely hard.

Patrick looked at me and laughed. "Commissioner my name is, (he paused), and will always be Patrick." This time his voice changed into a very serious tone. "I'll ask you again, how can I help you."

Bryce looked at me, and I looked at him. "Mina congrats to you." Bryce walked closer to me, and Patrick stood up. Tish laughed out loud sarcastically. "The paper is outstanding, love the name, and love what it stands for. You two make a great team." Bryce said.

"Thank You, Bryce," I said.

Patrick stepped in front of me as if he was protecting me. Bryce and Tish stood there staring at me with evil in their eyes. What is this about? I began to think. This woman knows nothing about me, and I know Bryce is mad because he didn't get the inheritance. But where is this animosity coming from?

"Did you two need something? If not, Mina and I are about to leave. And you two can stay." Patrick asked.

Tish stepped forward. "What did you say your name was?" She looked at me.

I stepped closer.

"I never said my name," I said.

"Someone has an attitude. No need for that. Let me introduce myself. I'm Tish Kincade." She stretched out her hand out to shake mine.

"No attitude here. There is no need for it. I'm Mina Wright."

"Mina! Ok good, I'm glad we have gotten that out of the way, because I didn't know if it was Mya or Mia." She then looked at me up and down. So, naturally, I did the same to her. Patrick grabbed me by my hand and squeezed it really tight. I guess he knew I would NOT be able to keep calm.

"It's late, and Mina and I were just about to leave. If you two don't have anything else to say, thanks for coming, and God bless you." Patrick and I started walking away.

"We have questions, Patrick," Bryce said.

We both stopped walking. "I have answers, Bryce. What is it?" Patrick asked.

"I really need the front cover 1st edition, I need a full page inside the newspaper to advertise, I need pictures of me and you golfing, hanging out, you know what I mean. I need this to be continued every bi-weekly publication until I win this election." Bryce said.

Patrick laughed again. "Everyone has a sense of humor. I do apologize commissioner, but I hate to break the bad news to you, but it's not my paper, so therefore it's not my decision." He glanced at me, "Mina is in control of **SerVant24:7**, you will need to direct all questions to her. Mina do you have a business card?"

"Yes, I do Patrick." I pulled my card out of my clutch and handed it to Bryce. He snatched it out of my hand, and Patrick didn't like it.

"Bryce she is a lady, and we know you don't know how to respect ladies, but you will respect this one. Don't ever do that again." It was quiet. Patrick looked angry. Tish stepped in and spoke.

"I have a question Patrick for Mya...Mia... Whatever your name is. Are you going to put Bryce on the cover next week that's all we need to know?" Tish asked.

Why in the hell does she care? I thought to myself.

"Good-bye Tish," Patrick said.

"It's ok Patrick." I glanced at her and Bryce. "Bryce knows my name really well, all the times he's hung out at my house." I then winked at him. My flesh was on fire! I was thinking if you two want to play this game, let's do this. "My name is Mina and is it Trish, Tricia...I can't seem to remember yours either?" Patrick gripped my waist and whispered in my ear.

"Don't let them get to you Mina, let's go."

"You don't know my name? I'm surprised." She walked a little closer to me. I had to remember my NOTS. If she comes any closer, I will NOT be able to hold my peace.

"It's Tish Kincade, the First Lady of the church sweetie. Commissioner Calhoun and I had some questions like I said, about the paper for Patrick, not you." She turned and walked toward Patrick who was standing directly next to me. "Two things. Daddy will be endorsing Commissioner Calhoun, and wanted to know will he have a full page for his campaign as promised? And secondly, everyone wanted to know why isn't there, *A word from the First Lady column*, in the newspaper called *Service?*"

She doesn't even know the name. "First of all, the name is **SerVant24:7**. Secondly, like Patrick said, it's my newspaper. Thirdly, Commissioner Calhoun can have a section, I have no problem with that, but he will not have a whole page, it's already taken, and he will not be featured on the cover. Lastly, when the Street Called Straight Ministries gets a First Lady, she will have a column." I said.

I looked at Patrick, and he was smiling at me. I grabbed his hand and walked towards the back door of his Mansion.

"Mina, I needed you in my life. I have been waiting on someone like you."

We walked away. Patrick made a few phone calls, and everyone begin to clear out. It was, and all was clear. Security checked the grounds and all around the house inside and out. We both had enough of mingling, and mess. I don't know what all this was about with Bryce and Tish, but tonight was NOT the night to inquire. I had a good night and was ready for some much-needed rest. Once on the inside, I noticed the 30-foot ceilings and the beautiful crystal studded chandeliers hanging. Chardonnay had settled in, and I was ready to swing from one of them. I allowed him to lead me and I followed him. I felt very comfortable with him like I was supposed to be here. We walked up the spiral staircase to his bedroom. It was the size of a two, maybe three-bedroom loft. He closed the door slowly behind him and lying on the bed was an all lace black camisoles. On the side of the bed a note read, Mina are you ready to take a flight to whole other level? I begin to unzip my dress slowly. I could see him looking out the corner of my eye. I took off everything one by one and tossed it over on the chair except for my heels. He lit the candles in the fireplace.

And I begin to walk around the room, with nothing but my heels on lighting all the candles.

He then grabbed another remote control and turned the Jazz master music station on Pandora. Art of Noise, what have you done with my body begun to play.

I was in my moment of feeling good, and he was too. He took his jacket off, then his shirt. His mussels appeared to be flawless to look at. They ranged from his neck to his waist. All I could see was hot chocolate!

    I think we both were hott! I lie on his gigantic California King bed and begin to touch myself. He came from behind to assist. He kissed me from the back of my neck to the crack of my assets, and the rest was history. I was ready for my flight to take off and hit cloud nine. I got on the airplane, buckled up, and was flying at latitude called *wonderful*. He placed my body on the satin sheets, and his strong grip opened my legs wide and split them a-part. He was hungry, and I was ready for him to eat. Body-to-body, heat-to-heat, and soul-to-soul. I grabbed his head along with his ears so tight, and I lost control. I begin to moan and scream. My legs wrapped around his neck like I was a gymnast. The louder I screamed, the more he enjoyed his entrée. The more I pulled and gripped his head, the more he licked the plate. My body shook like there was an earthquake in the sky. He got his from that introduction, and I was ready to get some more.

    So I took the long route to our destination. He slowed things down and lifted up and begins to make passionate love to me. Real slow, real smooth, and he was really deep. Stroke for stroke, rub for rub, touch, for touch. He held me so tight. The feeling was superb! Up and down. Gripping my assets, legs around his waist, he was flying this plane like a veteran. I felt it was time to allow him to enjoy the flight and take a break. I hopped on top of him and took him to a whole other dimension of the flight. I kissed his chest slowly down to his thighs and then I moved to the middle. Slurp, Slurp, slurping, and then his hands grabbed my head tight, then tighter, his body shook, and shook again, and his rolled in the back of his head. I then rode this plane like it was my last flight. He gripped my hips with both his hands, squeezing them tight as I proceeded to start my flight attendant duties, serving my passenger. Allowing my passenger to enjoy his ride. We couldn't stop until we got what we needed and then we could land. His body shook again at the same time as mine. We landed at our destination, and the rest of this flight is history. I will say this, the wall in his bedroom needed sheetrock repair from the headboard after this was over. Goodnight!

    The next morning I woke up to the sun shining brightly in my face. I rose up and looked around the room. I didn't see Patrick. I looked over and in the trashcan were four condom wrappers. I guess after two years Patrick had an abundance of protein to let out. I grabbed my phone to see what time it was, and it was only 7:15 a.m. It took me at least two minutes to climb down from his bed, and another to three minutes to figure out what door was the restroom. I finally found it and opened the door to find Patrick standing in the shower. I could see chocolate melting through the steamed shower doors, damn. I apologized and closed the door. I don't know why I apologized. I think I was embarrassed for introducing him to, Porno Mina, instead of Prophet Mina, last night. I try to forget that he is a Pastor and my Pastor at that, but the reality is he is also a single man.

"Mina!" he shouted.

I opened the door with the sheet wrapped around me. He opened the shower glass door. "Good morning Patrick."

"Good morning. Come here beautiful and join me."

I desired to join him. But, the conviction was all over my spirit? I guess because I know I am trying to live a saved and sanctified life, and he is still a preacher. But he is also single, and I am too, and he is such a good catch Lord, yes he is, and I am too! The guilt and shame of giving him my inheritance and all of my estate had begun to weigh heavy on my mine. As for Patrick if he had any kind of conviction, he hid it well. He was all-smiles. He was humming in the shower and moving his body from side to side. I walked over to the shower. My sheet fell to the floor, and I stepped in. I laid my head back and allowed the warm, soothing water to fall on to my face then my body. Patrick grabbed the body wash and poured it all over my body. He grabbed the towel, and I could feel his hands beginning to massage my breast. His hands rubbed them continuously. I grabbed a towel and begin to wash his body as well. We moved our towels on one another body from top to bottom then front and back.

"How did you enjoy your flight last night?" I asked.

"I loved it! I enjoyed it so much. I would like to purchase another ticket. Would you like to join me on this trip to Niagara Falls?"

"Of course." We took another flight in the shower that morning.

Patrick handed me one of his robes with his initials engraved on it. I walked out to check my phone. I had fifty-six missed calls. These were calls from numbers I didn't recognize. I know I gave my card to so many people last night, but there is no telling who these numbers could be. I thought to myself they are already calling me. It's a great sign! I didn't have any calls from Mamadoll today, and she figured I was staying with Kia or working. I didn't lie, I agreed to everything she said. She said they were going to her church carnival with Rylie's friend next door, and they wouldn't be back until late Saturday night. That left me with the whole day to myself. I looked over at Patrick, and he was checking his messages also, he looked back at me and winked.

"Ready for breakfast?" He asked.

"Yes."

"What would you like?"
"What do we have in the fridge?"
"I have no idea Mina. Let's go down stairs and take a look." He winked.

He grabbed my hand and kissed me on my forehead. We walked downstairs, and on the way, I couldn't help myself from being impressed by this house. The walls, the décor, the chandeliers, floors, the art, are simply exquisite. We walked in the kitchen, and it look as if it was a hotel buffet prepared for us. There was an omelet station, a waffle area, bacon, ham, turkey, cereal, pancakes, fruit, juices' and my favorite coffee. The table had twelve dozen fresh roses sitting in the middle. "I would like some coffee with cream first," I said. He pressed a button on the intercom and out walked a chef. I tied my robe a little tighter.

"Are you ok?" He asked.
"Yes am but, I didn't know anyone else was in the house."
"Oh, that's just Jeff. He's family."
"The band, and now Jeffery the Chef," I said.
"Oh Yeah. Baby, I gotta keep it in the family. Successes will either bring you closer to your family, or it will take you far away from your family. Remember that." He said.
"I think I got a taste of that last night."
"Why would you say that?"
"Last night was good for me, but it seems my cousin had a problem amongst your ex and Bryce, in my opinion."

He waited, and then spoke. "My ex and Bryce is not a concern, and I do not consider that family, on the other hand, you mentioned cousin. What is that about?"

"My cousin was rather rude to me. I mean downright defensive when it came to Bryce."

"Wait a minute who is this cousin? And what does this have to do with Bryce?"

"My cousin is Zi'lah, and I guess she and Bryce are in love and suppose to get married and.... I don't know what's going on, but she was rude. She was saying things like; *I know you don't like him*...blah, blah, blah. Just being silly."

He continued to eat. "Why don't she think you like him?"
"'Because I don't."
"Why?"
"Because I don't like his spirit. I don't like men who are always in women face and married women at that. That's a selfish person."
"What about the women?"

"Selfish and trifling. The bible say have your own husband."

"Mina the bible says a whole lot. But you can't dislike a person for being who they are. You don't condone what they do, but you have to still love them. This is what Jesus required us to do. It is your cousin's problem, and not yours. You pray that God will give her revelation on their situation and see them through. I was once the same way, protective and defensive when it came to my loved ones, but I realized that it is their life and they made the choice to be with that person, or to do drugs, or to be the way they are, or not to believe God exist. They will to answer to God for their actions just like you and me."

"But I don't like him flirting with me."

"What is he doing? Is it out of line? Has he touched you?"

"No Patrick. It's nothing."

He stopped eating. "Mina, talk to me. I don't want to start with lies and secrets. Talk to me."

"You talk to me, Patrick," I said loud. "I mean I'm a little confused here. Bryce shows up with your ex-wife. I don't even know if you are really divorced."

He hesitated and looked out the window. "Mina can you enjoy this day and let your past go. Can you release it? Baby, please. We had a good time last night, and I don't want to talk about those people."

We both continued to eat.

"Are you worried about Tish?"

"I'm not worried about anything or anyone. But I must admit I don't appreciate her approaching us last night on our time the way she did. I mean if you two are divorce, then she should not be concerned about me and what we are doing."

"You are absolutely right. And you shouldn't be concerned about her. This is our morning. Not the church, not Mamadoll, not members, not the newspaper, but our morning, so that means our time." He grabbed the both of my hands." Listen Mina, you know I have a lot of influence in this city. Everyone wants a title or to be successful, but they don't want to work for it, so if they see a cracked door, they ease their way in without putting forth the effort to push it open."

"I don't understand that language. Please talk to me." I said.

He was silent. "Mina, can I trust you?"

"Of course you can Patrick."

"There are things that go deeper than religion, or church. It's more involved than members, or even money. It's all about image, reputation, and your name. In most cases, it's just about winning. I have endorsed Bryce before, but I will not this time. This is between you and

me only. Remember your Not's Mina." I couldn't believe what he said. He continued. "Not Kia, Not Mamadoll, or anyone else ok?"
I was a little disturbed. "Ok. I understand." I responded.
"Mina we're going to date. We are dating. And I am going to make you my woman. You are my woman." That was a first for me. "But, you have to trust me and not listen to what others say, and I will have to trust you. Stay with me, baby. Just stay. We will have our trials and situations that will arise where we don't know what to do, but God is in control of this. He is working for us. I feel it, and I know it. Remember what I am saying to you on this day, Bryce and my ex, are God's children also, but they mean nothing to me or you, or what God has put together. We are not intimidated by the enemy, but remember we are imitators of Christ. We are not afraid of the darts thrown at us, but we do need to pay attention to where they land. They may land in our minds, so we think about it like you are doing now. They may land in our feelings, so we get in our feelings, or we get emotional about it. But, we need to let them land at our feet, so we can stomp on them, and they will be destroyed. You follow-me?"
I shook my head yes. He continued.
"Just so you will know her father, Tish, is the honorable Judge WH Nash, and he was once friends with my dad. He turned out to be Judas. You understand."
I shook my head yes again. He continued again. "You see Mina it's all about politics. That's what this is all about. I love my members, I love people, I love the church God has given to me, and I love what God has called me to do. But, when people see the change in you, they get scared, (he paused), because now they can't figure you out, or no longer control you. They don't know your next move. They are confused. And if you change, then this means they will lose. But, remember this no matter what happens Mina stay on team Jesus because he already won."
I was quiet, but still, I heard and understood every word he was saying. I believe I could read between the lines. I always say I don't need to know everything, but I do need to know some things. I do know this you can start a car for someone, but anyone can figure out how to move the car into drive, and get it to moving to where it needs to go. We talked a little more. He educated me on the business called Success. I listened. He told me I was teachable. He explained the various types of businesses in the ministry and outside the ministry. I paid attention and exhorted all the information I could. It was very interesting to know the in's and out's. He kissed me on my forehead, turned and walked into the living area. He then turned on the television. The first showcase to

appear was the morning news and to my surprise the launching of **SerVant24:7**. I stood up in disbelief. It displayed me talking to a reporter. I looked so nice. They featured my work and me. I kept hearing my name, Mina Wright editor-n-chief, Mina Wright this and Mina Wright that. I couldn't believe it. The reporter begins to speak:

Last night a gathering was held for the launching of the new publication named SerVant24:7, by its founders Pastor Patrick Kincade, of the mega church A Street Called Straight Ministries and its Editor-n-Chief, Mina Wright. Everyone from all over the city was there including Commissioner Bryce Calhoun, Evangelist Kia St James, to Mayor Thomas Harry Watts, and First Lady Tish Calhoun.

I did not like the sound of, First Lady Tish Calhoun. Why did they have to mention her on my night? The sound kept ringing in my head, but I kept my cool. I listened as the reporter continued.

We had the chance to catch up with the lady everyone is talking about, editor-n-Chief, Mina Wright.

Patrick looked over at me and smiled, and there I was blushing.

Reporter: Mina tell us what do the readers have to look forward to in the SerVant24:7?

Mina: The readers have a variety of things to look forward to. We have many career opportunities, an encouraging section that will give the hopeless, hope, a word from our Pastor, and much more.

Reporter: You know we love Pastor Kincade. What's your favorite section? I looked over at Patrick, and he tried not to blush.

Mina: I would have to say Hear my Hallelujahs' is my favorite! Everyone will love that section. It will be full of testimonials.

I jumped up so high; I damn near touched the chandeliers. You would have thought I was in a circus show. Patrick was calm. But me, I was all over the place. "That's me! There I am! Look, Patrick, that's me! I have to call my baby and Mamadoll. I need to tell Naiomi. I need to tell the crew. OMG! I can't believe it. I'm on television, they're talking about me." I ran upstairs to grab my phone. He was laughing at me because I didn't know which way to run. He grabbed my hand, and we ran together up the stairs. I grabbed my phone, and I missed several calls from Mamadoll. I called her back immediately and Rylie picked-up.

We both started screaming so loud at the same time. All of us! I couldn't stop screaming. After I hung up the phone, I switched the channel and there I was again, and again. Every channel promoting the **SerVant24:7**. I needed to check my messages again. I started checking them all one by one. By now I had at least a hundred and seventy-two messages. I lost count, and I stopped writing down names. It was overwhelming. I had several messages wanting to do interviews for TV and radio not just in Charlotte but all over, in different cities. Naiomi left me three messages.

Mina Wright, I know you with that fine Pastor, but call your bff back.

#Two. Mina, please call me girl we need to talk. #Three- Mina are you married and pregnant by now? Call me.

Patrick was standing afar looking at me. I put down my phone slowly. "Is something wrong?" He had a smirk on his face. "I believe there is a time to work and a time to play," He said. That was pretty much all I needed to hear. "Should I turn off my phone?" He turned on a movie, and responded, "I turned mine off."

I turned my cell phone off also. Patrick put a movie on. I nodded a few times during the movie. I believe between the party, work, Nay Nay, and my flights with Patrick, the word called tired had indeed caught up with this forty-year-old sister. Patrick laid his head on my chest, and he too was nodding. I laid my head back, and we both fell asleep.

It was at least two hours later, and I was awakened by the noise outside. There were landscapers mowing the lawn. It was 2:30 and I believe I had received some much-needed rest. Patrick was still lying on my chest sleeping like a baby. I enjoyed seeing him rest for a change. Relaxing in my presence. He was in a different zone. He wasn't running around everywhere trying to put out fires for a change. He was actually relaxing. I rubbed my hands through the waves in his soft hair, and he begins to wake up. I slowly continued, and he woke up.

"I'm sorry I didn't mean to wake you up?" I said.

"You didn't sweetheart. Your hands felt so good I couldn't stay sleep."

"Are you hungry?" I asked.

He gave me a look.

"I was talking about food Patrick. I was going to cook for you."

"I would love for you to cook for me."

I walked over to the kitchen to prepare a meal for him. This is definitely a man with many resources. He didn't know where the seasoning was located, pots and pans, flour, sugar, and so on. He turned off the television, turned on smooth jazz, and walked into his office.

He had the finest of meats in the freezer and plenty of fruits, and vegetables. I would love a mellow, nice glass of wine before I began to cook. I know he doesn't have any wine in this house and as I began to probe, I turned out to be right. I thought I would ask anyway. I walked down the long hallway to his office. When I finally reached his office, I could hear him speaking with someone on the phone. I didn't eaves drop. I walked in to his office, and his back was turned to me.

"I can't right now and today is really not a good time. I will say this. I cannot and will not continue to endorse Bryce. Your daughter was really pushing it last night. I didn't appreciate the way she acted at all. We go way back sir, but my father is no longer here. I'll meet you sometime next week to discuss the disclosure."

He hung up with the person on the other line and fell to his knees. He began to pray, so I walked out the room and decided to let him have his time to himself. I wondered who he was on the phone with. I wondered what they were talking about. I walked back to the kitchen and continued to prepare his meal. My phone rung a few times, and I ignored the calls.

It was around 4:15 and dinner was almost done. The house smelled like a soul food restaurant. I closed the pantry door and screamed because there standing was chef Jeffery.

"I'm sorry, did I scare you?" he asked.

"Yes, you did." My heart was pounding so fast you would have thought I just finished running a marathon. I was happy I still had my robe on, if I had not been Jeffery would have caught a glimpse of all the flowers in my garden. "How did you get in the house?"

"Like I always get in the house," He said and went on to say, how did you get in the house?"

Now I know he is not trying to be smart. I gave him a look like I know you didn't just go there, I know plenty of chefs that would love this job. He spoke again.

"Patrick let me in. Do you need any help with anything? Patrick told me to check on you."

"No thank you. I think I just about did everything I needed to do here."

"It smells delicious and looks wonderful, can I stay?"

"No Jeffery, not today. You're here all the time. It's my day." I said in a sarcastic voice.

"I was only kidding. Well, I guess I'm out of here." He turned to walk out the door and then turned around again. "In the two years, I have worked for him. I don't think I have ever seen a woman in this kitchen cooking. It's always been just me. I don't know what to do with myself today." He said.

I thought to myself. "Well good to know Jeffery, and thanks for dropping that information to a sista." I have something for you to do. "Jeffery, where can I get a good bottle of Chardonnay?"

"You can get that at any corner or liquor store. I can get it for you, if you would like?"

"Great!" I gave him a few instructions and off he went out the door... He returned about an hour later, as I was finishing up. Patrick was still locked up in his office. He looked to be in deep thought. I left him to himself again. Jeffery walked to the dining room. It was exquisite. From the colors to the deep high ceilings this man has great taste. I didn't have any clothes to change into, so I ran upstairs and finally found one of Patrick's shirts that hung to my knees. I put my heels back on and sprayed some perfume. Jeffery went from being the chef to my personal assistant. It was around 5:15 and Patrick finally walked out of his office. He called my name, and I finally found me in the dining area. The lights were dimmed, and balloons were propped up all over. I stood up and screamed surprise!

There were candles lit on his huge cake along with his meal. He didn't want anyone to know and wasn't aware that I knew, but it was his anniversary day he was drafted to the NFL and also his mother's birthday.

Jeffery and I had a very informative conversation while Patrick was in his office, and Kia along with the others text messages helped also. He was overwhelmed with excitement and showed plenty of emotion. He walked over slowly with the look of disbelief. He grabbed me by the hand and walked me to one of the chairs. We both sat down. He gripped my face and kissed me.

"Wow! Thank you, baby. Thank you. Thank You. I'm not going to ask you how you knew."

"Discernment," I said.

We both laughed. "I'll take that answer. Mina, you are simply amazing." He stood up and put his hands on my shoulders. "Thank you so much for being patient with me during this entire situation. I know it's not easy for you."

I inhaled, and then exhaled. "It's not Patrick, but I accepted the situation. I just hope you will be honest and this doesn't become a permanent situation lingering on for years, I can't deal with that again. I think I'm worth more than a secret."

"You absolutely are. Remember what I told you when we first met? You would have to realize and believe you are special. It doesn't matter what I say; it's what you believe."

I smiled, and he continued.

"You bring out some type of part in me that I didn't know existed. I like the new me." He said.

"Oh Do I. Like what part baby tell me?"

176

"I will let you in when time permits."

"Ok. I can wait. Change of subject. I was wondering would you like your gift now, or later."

"I received my gift."

"You did?"

"Yes. It was you."

We both smiled and sat down at the table. We ate the meal I prepared. I fed him from time to time, and he fed me. I could stay in this place, and feel this feeling forever. I had a wonderful much needed and desirable weekend.

Once we finished eating, he hesitated and procrastinated, but we both knew it was time for me to go home. It was late, and we had church in the morning and plus I needed to go back to being a mommy. He had a certain look in his eyes from across the table as I ate my piece of cake.

I sat at the end of the table and opened my legs wide with no panties on. I begin to lick the frosting off the fork really slow with my tongue. I took my t-short off my shirt and rubbed frosting around each one of my nipples.

I then licked the frosting off my nipple. I began to perform for him. I moved my hand up and down between my legs and begin to massage my lips down below. I could see he was rock hard. As he massaged himself, I climbed on the table and crawled across to him in my birthday suit. I slid the silverware, dishes, and anything else in the way; onto the floor. The wine was working within me, yet again. Blame it on the wine, I said to myself. Once I made it to him, he licked the butter cream frosting off each of my nipples. He then opened his mouth wide and licked my finger. He sat comfortably in his chair. It was his day, and he was my king. I climbed off the table and I bent over with all my assets in his face. He slapped my cheeks, each one from behind. I then sat on his lap as his hand went everywhere on my back. I bounced and bounced and would rise up and down and all around on his manhood as he went deep and deeper. I slowed down and bent over to grab my ankles tight until he finished shaking. What a coincidence it was to hear Sade's song playing in the background, *Is it a Crime*? I was thinking to myself; if it is a crime, arrest me. I'm guilty as charged. I had to have another flight in the dining room before he took me home. Two times wasn't enough, but three is always, and will always be a charm.

We showered together again, dressed, and then jumped into one of Patrick's cars so he could take me home. The entire drive I was thinking about our relationship. What is the purpose for us meeting one another? I know it's bigger than sex, and I know it's more than the newspaper. Everything has a purpose. I also wondered, why we do; both women, and men need, to validate our relationship with titles and rules. Why? I glanced at Patrick and said to myself he has become my friend, my Pastor, my mentor, and my Man in a short period of time. But, why do I need to call him all those names? He squeezed my hand as drove to the gate. I have come to the realization when you let go, it will all fall in place. I know some people say you should not let a man pick you up for a date after nine. Or, don't give him any before ninety days. Or, better yet don't let him around your child after a certain time. And some have even put a time limit on when to tell him you love him. Well, all of that maybe true in the dating game, but I didn't have to tell this man anything to do to make me feel like a woman, or put a time limit on when he would receive my inheritance. I believe you should enjoy the moment, take your emotions out, and feelings, out. Walk by faith and see where faith will lead you. Whatever is going to be, will be.

Chapter 9: Welcome to Successville...

Lights, Camera, Success! Time flew by so fast, it seems like the first issue hit stands yesterday. It's been Six months, and we were already into summer. June was coming to an end, and elections were drawing closer and closer. Rylie finished the ninth grade and began volunteering at the local YMCA as a lifeguard. She became very popular in a short period of time because everyone knows her mom and her mom's newspaper she said often. Life could not be better. It could slow down, but I won't complain. The paper, of course, is a success just after the first five issues. We sold more copies than any other publication in its first week surpassing all major news publication was such a blessing with all the social media sites in effect we didn't know what to expect, but we trusted God, and like always he showed up for us. I shopped at the finest boutiques because I needed to look exceptional when I made appearances. And there were plenty of experiences. Every day there was deadlines to be met, and someone from the team was either doing television programs, radio, or out meeting and greeting the public. Patrick bought the staff an Escalade which read, **Servant24:7,** to drive, so we would not put too many miles on our cars. There were shirts, hats, cups, jackets, and anything else with room enough to place the **Servant24:7** name. The name became a household name. Virtually everywhere you went in the city it was **Servant24:7** this, and Servant24:7 that. People would see me and yell, "I'm a **Servant24:7**." We were all over the place. I made t-shirts that were given to every member of the congregation, which read, *I'm serving 24:7.* I had become so busy in my day-to-day life I maybe got three to four hours sleep at night. My team has been very supportive along with Mamadoll, and Patrick of course. Patrick and I were growing closer and closer each day. We sneaked around the office, closets, cars, weekends to get a piece of one another even if it was a hug, a kiss, and a rub. It became an every other day thing. As time passed, I have still longed for him to announce he is a divorced man so I could be free from sneaking. But, I will be patient because I know good things come to those who wait. Although the months have passed and seasons changed, my feelings for Patrick has not. I have felt like a very well kept secret.

    I have received a very nice financial compensation for my contribution to the **Servant24:7.** I have been able to be a blessing to my Mamadoll amongst other people that are near and dear to me. Mamadoll needed minor repairs around the house, and I had those done. We also added an extra room because I needed a bigger space for an office than my bedroom. We were able to pay off credit card debts. Both of our credit score were raised, and my savings account was looking lovely. I was everywhere from radio interviews to television interviews. I along with everyone else was all over the city. Everywhere I went people recognized me. Although I was receiving the attention, I never forgot what my purpose for the newspaper was. I sat and visited many nursing homes with Patrick and watched him conduct many funerals and visit their families. We attended wedding ceremonies from time to time together as "co-workers". It was a blessing to be in the position I was in. Kia was on fire also.

We barely spent time outside of work or on Sundays together. I begin to conduct the Sunday morning services announcements at church. And more and more people were joining.

Mamadoll still worked at Bryce campaign center but only part-time because she helped with Rylie schedule and mine as well. Zi'lah and I never really talked after the launching, and eventually, she stopped coming around. She would email me constantly to put Bryce on the cover, but I didn't because I had so many requests and it was always first come first serve. Aunt Bae and her husband bought ads for any sections of the paper mentioning Bryce and his dad practice. We were also gaining more and more members, and Patrick was becoming even busier. He was asked to make appearances everywhere, and I was too. I had a new wardrobe, a new look, and eventually a new car. I traded in the Tahoe and Patrick purchased me a Porsche Panamera, it was mine title and all. I was offered many opportunities to speak at different engagements. Everyone was experiencing successville in many different ways, but although it was a lovely feeling, I also felt something missing. What I had was what some women desired. I had a wonderful man in, and out of bed. Oh yes, he was successful and everything he touched prospered, I do mean everything. If he looked at It, It became successful, if he watered It, It grew if he wanted It, he got It. He was the man, and I begin to fall more and more for the man. I allowed him to water this garden anytime he felt the need, and I felt the need for him to do it. But don't think he was alone in Successville, remember two is better than one, and God has no respecter of persons. No baby girl was right there too. If I created a slogan the city said it, radio DJ's was saying it, and t-shirts said it.

Now let me hear your hallelujah! This was all over social media and bumper stickers. If I was at the gas pump, people and yell, *Let me hear your hallelujah, hey Mina.* If I walked into a grocery store, they went out their way for me. If I ate at a restaurant, it was free. Now, where was the owner for this restaurant when my bank account was negative? It was all-good, and Successville was a nice place to stay. And it got better.

The most important television program, the most viewed in the city, and the one I grew up watching daily as a teenager and dreamed about being on, finally invited us on the show. The show titled, AM/PM Charlotte. This was the only show we had not appeared on, but it was very important that we did. The show was so huge because it appeared in the AM when you woke up and a new episode appeared at night the PM when you went to bed. It also reached three other states. This meant spreading the gospel even more and Patrick making history. This show had never had a pastor or spiritual leader to ever appear on its stage since it debuted in 1987. But what made the show even better is it had the same host. The host I grew up watching and admiring and wanting to be like.

"Mamadoll can you please help me find my paperwork?" I yelled from upstairs just shy four hours before our appearance on AM/PM Charlotte. Patrick has prepped us all week and reminded us as big as he is; he has yet to be on this show, which I could not understand. We all were walking around on eggshells. I needed my answered questions for this interview ASAP that was sent to me from the network via email. I had created a document and rehearsed my answers. I was praying Mamadoll didn't throw it away with her mail pile from the dining room table. She didn't. I had accidently placed it with Rylie's forms to take to the YMCA. I raced to Rylie's job because this day she had to turn the forms in. I was so happy I made it in time because I didn't need any extra gossip, or someone writing about the fact we knew the questions that were going to be asked prior to our live interview. I grabbed my things and headed out the door to Rylie's job. Thank God it was on the way.

I arrived at her job in twenty minutes. I noticed there were plenty of cars already in the parking lot. I walked into the building headed for the office, and standing near the entrance door was Bryce, his running mate, and their personal assistant, Zi'lah. Apparently, he was there trying to encourage the young people, eighteen years old and up to vote. I did say trying. I didn't want him to see me, but of course, the some of the faculty members wanted to speak with me. I turned around to greet them while I was waiting on Rylie. Patrick was texting me and so was Kia, along with my staff wondering was I on my way to the television studio. I was thinking I wouldn't miss it for the world. Rylie gave me the paperwork and back to my car I headed. Standing on the steps as I walked out the front door was Bryce and Zi'lah. I was cordial to them both, but I was not about to be fake and smile as if we were new friends. I smiled and kept on moving.

"Mina, Mina can we talk to you?" Zi'lah said running up to me.

I acted as if I didn't hear her call my name. Then Bryce called my name as well. I stopped walking and turned around slowly. I remembered my Not's like always. *I do Not have time for bullsh..t. This morning.*

"Good morning, how can I help you two?" I asked.

He walked over to me holding hands with Zi'lah. I wanted to vomit. Zi'lah had a good husband. He wasn't rich in material possessions, but he worked damn hard for her and those kids, and he was rich in his heart.

"Hey Mina girl I'm so sorry about the way I acted at your party, please forgive me," she said.

She reached her arms out to hug me. Then just when I thought she was sincere, she had to prove herself to Bryce. I crossed my arms and showed no emotion to whatever it was they were about to say.

Bryce looked at her and laughed, "Zi'lah was it a party, a gathering, or business? I get so confused you know one minute Mina is on the Lord side, and the next minute you are hanging with a married man, I'm so sorry your boss." He laughed extremely loud.

I laughed even louder than he did. Sometimes you have to laugh at those twin spirits called miserable and jealous. "Well, Bryce you have the woman you want so you need not worry about who side I'm on. Anything else?"

"Well of course. Let's cut the BS Mina. Look I need your help. I need the cover page for the **Servant24:7** next edition. It is election time, and this is very important to me. You have three to four more editions before the election end, and I need more votes. I really need your help with this. I need to win this election."

I thought about everything he just said and how I could really be nasty, but it's always good to kill'em with kindness. "Bryce I really do wish I could help you, but someone has already paid to be covered on the front page. I'm sorry."

"Why?"

"Why what?" He walked over to me, and Zi'lah just looked away.

"Why are you doing this? Are you jealous of Zi'lah's and my relationship? Are you mad because you wish you could have what we have? Huh? Are you upset because you are on second base and not first?"

"Excuse me, your relationship? Look Bryce maybe if you could mingle more and spend time with the people in your community, then you would not need my newspaper to help you. Pray about it. If it's meant to be, you will be the commissioner again. And as for first or second base, I am neither one. I am the COACH. I have to be somewhere I wish you both the best."

He had so much anger in his face, and I felt a little uncomfortable. Just a little. I winked and walked to my car. He started walking behind me. I could hear his footsteps, and I begin to walk faster. I wished Zi'lah would control her man. I opened my car door and sat down to try to close it, but Bryce stopped it with his foot. He leaned over in the car.

"Hey, Mina, tell me how it feels to be as secret? Huh? You gave that hypocrite everything he wanted, more fame in this community, more members, more money, more and more sex and you still can't be with him in public."

I looked at him the same way he was looking at me and responded. "I wouldn't know what is to be kept as a secret." I then stepped back out the car. "But from what I heard your mother was very good at keeping them. Who's your real daddy Bryce?" I jumped in my car and drove away.

Once I finally made it to the studio, I was pressed for time. I sat down in the chair for my hair and make-up to be touched up. Naiomi said she was watching on the Internet and told everyone from the church I previously attended. Everyone would be watching. Patrick wanted us in the same colors. Black of course with red added to our outfits. Kia came over, and we spoke briefly. I could tell she had a lot on her mind. She seemed distant, but she also was preparing for her interview, so I didn't bother her. I was extremely excited and nervous at the same time. I was a social butterfly flying all around the studio networking. I saw everyone was in position to go on to the stage. The producer walked over to explain the procedures and the order of operation. He said Kia was to go on first and discuss *Hugs for Hope*; then I was to go on next, and last but not least was Patrick. It was thirty minutes until show time and still no Patrick. It had been at least two hours since he texted me and said he was on his way and of course I became worried. I decided to call him, but his phone went straight to voicemail. He always answers for me, and this was not like him. Kia turned to ask me did I prepare myself for the interview with my questions and answers, and of course, I said yes. I asked Kia did she know where Patrick was, and all she would say is he will be here. The producers, no one made mention or even asked where he was.

The show was on from ten till eleven a.m. and it was already 9:46. I could hear the theme music beginning to play and audience clapping. Patrick was still nowhere to be seen. He was the one who always taught us, *Arrive Early, plus, Skip Lunch, plus, Leave Late, equals Success.*

Patrick made a shirt out of this slogan, and of course, it sold very well. He is always about business, so I don't understand why he isn't here. He wanted this so bad.

I paused while the make-up artist touched my face up again. The producer walked over and began the count down. Kia walked out, and the audience begin to clap and cheer. I was up next. It was my time to shine on the biggest show in the city. I took a peep from behind the curtain to view the audience. The room was packed. I then smelled this certain aroma enter the room. I turned around quickly, because I knew that smell oh too well. Walking through the door was in slow motion was PAK, aka, Patrick Kincade. He was dressed like he had stepped off a GQ magazine runway show, looking good, smelling good, and shoes were on point. We made eye contact immediately as he was greeted by the staff. A sigh of relief came over me. It was like he walked in the room and everything and everyone stopped what they were doing. He smiled and shook a few hands. He walked towards me, and I saw his lips moving. He signaled me to come here as the staff members hurried him in the chair to touch-up areas on his face for the camera. I started to walk over to him, but was interrupted by the cameraman.

"Ms. Wright you are up next,"

I said ok and continued eyeing Patrick. He pointed to his phone, but I shrugged my shoulders letting him know I didn't have it with me. He had a strange look in his face. This was not like him. Something was definitely wrong. I could feel it. He then put his hand on his heart. I couldn't hear any of Kia's interviews from paying attention to Patrick. He signaled for me to come here, but the next thing I heard,

"Please give an AM/PM Charlotte welcome for Ms. Mina Wright."

The audience member cheered loudly throughout the studio. It felt surreal to hear my name being called on a television program like this one. I grew up watching this woman for many, many, years host this show, I thought I would love to do what she does, but I never thought I would be sitting on her couch speaking to her about my newspaper. I walked out with confidence and the biggest smile on my face. This could lead to so many more doors opening since it airs in three other states. I wasn't nervous at all because I knew I had this. I was comfortable speaking with people, and I enjoyed talking about my newspaper. In case you didn't know I love saying my newspaper. J I had my interview answers locked in my brain. Kia stood up and whispered in my ear, "You look superb girlfriend."

I smiled and waved at the audience as I walked on the stage. I gave it to them if I do say myself. I sat down, and the cheers continued to flow in. I laughed because I was flattered.

Host: Well isn't that some kind of welcome! Hello Ms. Wright and congratulations on the success of the Servant24:7. I see why they are cheering the way they are, you are very attractive, and you are giving it to us today!

Mina: Thank you, thank you so much and for having us on here. I grew up watching you every day, and I finally get to meet you. You have not aged at all.

Host: Well thank you sweetheart, or should I say thank you to your Aunt's husband.

We all laughed.

Host: Tell me something, how far do you think the newspaper will go with social media being so dominant in the world today?

Mina: I think it will go as far as God allows it to go. I have never been intimidated by the success of social media. I love social media myself, but we still have a large number of people who want the traditional way of being informed of what's happening in their community.

Host: Absolutely. I will admit I love reading it. I like to see who is getting married, and the word from the pastor is my favorite. How are you handling all this success?

Mina: I am enjoying it. I look at it like this if this is the way God is going to use me then I except the assignment. I giggled.

Host: Do you think the paper has brought people to Christ?

Mina: Absolutely. We have more and more members joining every Sunday in service and online. The sales have surpassed major magazines and local newspapers.

Host: Well Ms. Wright all that is wonderful and good to hear, but our viewers had questions for you? They want to know more about you! You know we know the professional, Mina Wright, now let's find out the personal side.

She stood up and gave me a nasty look. Her tone changed from a well-respected talk show host to a messy tabloid reporter. This was new to me. I didn't remember this part being on the interview questionnaire, but I'm ok with surprises. Kia gripped my hand slightly.

Host: Let's play a game called, Who are you Really? Audience are you ready? I was confused and didn't remember this being informed about this section. I was very uncomfortable.

Audience: YESSSSSS!

Mina: Is this a new part of your program?

Host: Yes! We added today.

Host: Where are you from?

Mina: I... I am from Charlotte. I said nervously.
Host: How long did you live in Dallas?
Mina: For fourteen years.
Host: You worked for a newspaper correct before coming back to Charlotte?
Mina: That is right.
Host: Why did you leave?
She is messy. OMG. This biotch.
Mina: I missed Charlotte so much and my family.
The audience started cheering.
Host: Rumor has it that you lived with your boyfriend, not husband. Can you tell us what happened with that?
I sat there before answering. I was thinking who paid you?
Mina: Yes I lived with my boyfriend, and we went our separate ways. (Audience was quiet) I desired what God wanted me to have, that was a husband, not a boyfriend. (The audience clapped)
Host: Rumor has it he put you out his house?
Audience: OOOHHHH
Host: In the rain?
Audience: WHATTTT
Mina: That's why they are called rumors.
Host: So are you saying it's not true?
Mina: There was a disagreement, and I moved out! I'm not here to talk about the past, but the present. (I said with anger in my voice.)
Host: Do you date now Mina?
Mina: Occasionally
Host: Do you date married men?
Mina: I don't understand your question. Why would I date a married man? I am a beautiful woman that can have her own man. No, I do not.
Host: Have you ever dated a married man?
Mina: No I have not.
Host: Many of our viewers wanted to know about Pastor Patrick Kincade. How is it to work with him on a day-to-day basis? He is so very secretive you never hear anything about him.

Oh, she is going there. I hesitated, hell I damn near broke out in a sweat, but like always I remembered my Not's. I am Not afraid of where this interviewing is going.

Mina: Pastor Kincade is a wonderful person both inside and out. He is a very giving and a cool laid back type of boss.
Host: She looked into the camera: That was an innocent answer from Ms. Wright. Like all the other sweet answers. She is so sweet, isn't she? That's why

everyone has grown to love her. When we return, we have none other than Pastor Patrick Kincade.

They went to a commercial. The lights on the stage dimmed. I stood up, and Kia pulled me back down in my seat. I was furious.

"I need to go to the bathroom, Kia."

"Mina calm down." Kia began to whisper. "Sit down. You will give yourself away. Play it cool. They are watching you, us. There have been rumors about you and Patrick. You are a fresh new face that became successful overnight. A lot has changed here. We have too much to lose. The public is looking for something. With the success of the paper and Patrick getting bigger and bigger this will happen. It's all about the ratings."

"I don't give a damn about rumors or ratings. Excuse me, Kia. That was not on the questionnaire. This is not what I signed up for. Asking me about my past? That was very humiliating. Can she do that? I thought this show was about the community? I don't recall ever seeing her throw dirt the way she just did."

"Mina, she can do whatever she wants. She didn't stay on the air for this many years playing by all the rules." Kia said.

The lights became brighter, and the music began to play again. The host appeared out from behind the camera smiling and clapping her hands.

Host: *Welcome back Charlotte. Our next guest is one of the most influential pastors of our time with one of the largest congregations around town. Former NFL star, author, husband, father, and entrepreneur. But he is not alone; he brought with him my friend, his wife, a wonderful mother, and first lady of a Street Called Straight Ministries. AM/PM Charlotte stand to your feet and please give a warm welcome to Mr. and Mrs. Patrick Kincade.*

I damn near jumped out of my seat to walk off stage. My flesh went into overtime. No double time. I was beyond upset and pissed off. I didn't remember signing on to be on the Jerry Springer show. I wanted to stand up and slap the both of them. My emotions, feelings, hormones, and all of the above were raging. My body lifted and shifted all over my seat. Kia squeezed my hand again.

She whispered, "Stay calm."

I looked back at her, "Who did this? What is this about?" I am not about to play theses type of games. But this is what happens when favor knocks at the door along with the other prizes to join it, adversity. Tish walked out smiling and blowing kisses to the audience. They barely clapped their hands. She hugged Kia and tried to reach out to hug me, but I slid my handshake in real slow and cool. Patrick hugged Kia first then me real quick. He wouldn't even look at me. The crowd went crazy. The cheers were so loud, and they kept coming. Patrick giggled a little.

Patrick: Wow! Thank you. I am grateful.
Tish: They love you, baby.

She then stood up. Flashed her ring.

Tish: Okay ladies I love him too. He has me cheering like that all the time. Ha, ha, ha,

She then gave the hostess a high-five.

Tish: Hello my favorite hostess with the mostess!!!!
Host: I'm so glad you are here my friend. (Well now we know why she's hear, they're friends) *Please tell us how it feels to be married to the influential Patrick Kincade, and also be the first lady of a mega church?*
Tish: It is a blessing, but can be stressful at the same time I love being a wife and mommy.
Host: I bet you do with that fine man. How do you two balance this life and then keeping your marriage tight and right?
Tish: You know it's all about communication and keeping it spicy in the bedroom ladies. I always keep it spicy.

The audience loved her comments. They were laughing and clapping their hands. She was giving them everything they wanted. She glanced over at me. I didn't make any facial gestures at all. I stood still. I'm feeling very uncomfortable, but I continued to remind myself I was on television.

Host: Well, Pastor, aka, Patrick, aka, PAK Kincade how are things going with you? Your wife came out here on stage and took over.
Patrick: Thank You for having me I feel so loved.
Host: I haven't seen you since Tish birthday party three years ago.
Patrick: Tish party? Was I there? Oh yes, I remember now. Has it been that long? I didn't remember?

The audience was quiet, and some laughed. The host looked shocked. She cleared her throat and made eye contact with Tish.

Host: Patrick, I do believe so. Are you being fresh with me?

What is fresh? No, he was being sarcastic with you because he knows like everyone else knows this is a mess.

Patrick: I was only teasing you; I have a sense of humor. Yes about three years ago is the last time I saw you.
Host: Let's talk about this successful newspaper you have entertained us with. I mean really what can't you do?
Patrick: To be honest I can't do a lot. Actually, I didn't do this; it was all God working through Mina. God led her back home to Charlotte and into our lives and I must tell you she had been both a blessing to the ministry and me. She has

brought her creativeness to this project, and I'm so grateful for her. She created the layout, the name, and marketing plan. All of it basically.

Bam! In your face. Kia cleared her throat, and I straightened up in my seat. Tish and this messy host became real quiet. Neither was giggling anymore. The producer also seemed confused. I could see now this was not going the way someone had planned.

Host: Well let's get a little personal with you. Can we get a little personal with you and your lovely wife?

Patrick: "It depends. Remember I'm a Pastor now."

Host: We would like to know, how you and your beautiful wife keep the marriage going so well. You have such a beautiful marriage.

Patrick paused. He seemed uncomfortable, and it seemed as though he wasn't going to respond. He moved his neck from side to side and fixed his posture in his seat. He then turned his focus on the audience.

Patrick: You must work on a marriage daily like you would on your job, or in a ministry, or as a parent. It takes work like anything else in life. But, you also have to take time from working, just as you would do on a job, and take a vacation. This is called the rainbow season, because after all the arguments, tears, fights, and struggles leave. God allows you to have season of sunshine. This is where the non-stop lovemaking happens, the calling in to work sick to lay in the bed with your husband while the kids at school time and those date night's return again. Marriage must be God ordained. It will never work if it is put together by the two m's, which is money and mansions. It is a beautiful ministry designed by God where two souls become one and nothing; I mean nothing can tear what God put together apart. I love that Mina named the section in the Servant24:7, Two is better than One for couples who are on their way to marriage. It happens to be one of my favorite scriptures.

I never knew that was one of his favorite scriptures. The audience, especially women, was engaged at his answer of course. This man could tell people to buy an expired gallon of milk, drink it, and they would. When he finished, they clapped and cheered. He knows what to say and how to say it that's for sure.

Host: I like how you said that Pastor. My husband and I would love to get with you and your gorgeous wife to have a marriage made in heaven like you two.

I just knew at any minute I was going to vomit.

Host: Well Tish let's hear from you. How do you handle being a wife of such a well-known pastor? How do you keep it all together with all the attention he gets from ladies?

Tish: I am secure in this marriage, in my marriage.

The audience went crazy with loud cheers. She loved it! She begin laughing and clapping her hands.

Tish: Let me finish ladies. No matter what happens, I know where his heart belongs. And what God put together can't no man tear apart.

She looked over at me and then reached for his hand. She then grabbed it and held it up. Patrick was wearing his wedding ring. I got all the way in my feelings. My feelings had been on the battlefield and were wounded. She continued.

Tish: Also I have nothing to worry about. I am the one with my husband on this stage. Come here honey and give mama some suga.

She and Patrick kissed. They kissed passionately. The host, Tish, and audience clapped and cheered. Kia smiled, and I clapped as well. Tish and the host ate this opportunity up! The entire plate. The show finally ended, and I was thanking God I had self-control and kept my composure. I knew it was him who kept me calm. As I walked off the stage, I never looked back. I hurried towards the dressing room, and Kia was right behind me. Neither one of us spoke a word. I over-heard the producer tell Patrick he needed to stay on stage because he agreed to take pictures with his wife and audience members. That comment by the producer answered the questions, which clogged my mind this entire show. He knew she was going to be here. Why didn't he tell me? She wanted the attention on her and him. Their; *made for the people marriage.* She wanted to take away my moment of my success, she brought mess, when I had a message, and Patrick didn't stop it. Kia and I both grabbed our things and headed for the door, but the producers stopped us. Apparently, Patrick had agreed with the network that we would also take pictures. We looked at each other then placed our things back down real slow. Just when I thought I was delivered from this fiasco, I was again face to face with mess.

I observed Kia, and she quickly put on a smile as soon as we walked back into the studio. I would soon learn that pretending has become a part of being in the public eye. So I put on a smile as well. When I walked in, several audience members swarmed me. Many of them had questions and wanted to write columns for the **SerVant:24:7**. Some asked me to come to their church and help them with their newsletters, or could I give them idea now. A few said they had reached out to me via email and was glad I responded. I had begun to put what happened on this show behind me. I was doing what I loved, and that was sharing my gift with people. I had touched so many people in just a short period of time. I was asked to take pictures, and I agreed to sign a few newspapers brought to the show. Some had me sign their **SerVant:24:7** t-shirt as well. I was ready to ease my way out the door until elderly women approached me. She was around eighty-five years old. She asked me would I take a picture with her, and Pastor Kincade. I almost said no to her I had to leave, but I couldn't, so I agreed too.

We looked around the room together and no sign of Patrick. She asked me would find him for her; she said she had known his father and mother, but has never met him. I scanned the room again and still no sign of him. I then looked over near the stage and saw him through the shear curtain sitting alone. I walked with the elderly woman through the crowd to where he was sitting.

"Patrick," I said.

He stood up immediately. He seems surprise to see me. He stuttered a little. "Mina I didn't know you were still here? I have been calling you. I called you two or three times. I wanted to talk."

"We can talk later. I have this beautiful angel here who says she knew your parents and wanted to meet you."

"Yes, ma'am. Please have a seat. How are you?"

She smiled very big. He smiled back. She placed her hand on his face. Her frail framed body couldn't stand for long.

"I'm supposed to be in the hospital, but your prayers have helped me, son. I love the way you spread the gospel. I worked with your mother at the hospital for many years."

Patrick eyes became watery.

"She loved you so much. All she talked about was you. Son, I want you to know people can tell real from fake."

Patrick listened.

"Remember Jesus kept it real; we don't have to pretend when were in Christ."

She then whispered in his ear and whatever she said to him I will never know. Patrick became overwhelmed with emotion as a tear fell from his eye. He adored his mother and loved his father very much. I pulled the tissue from my purse, and handed it to him. I didn't make eye contact with him. We took the picture and then we had a chance to sneak out the back door. We walked the elderly woman to her ride awaiting her. The senior citizen bus was parked not far from my car.

Patrick helped her onto the bus, and I instantly heard elderly woman screaming,

"There's Pastor Kincaid! Hey pastor," and so on.

He called my name, and I waved goodbye to him not in a rude way, but I needed to get away from this studio. As soon as I was able to make it to my car I let out every bit of emotion I had held in. Frustration is too nice of a word to describe the way I am feeling. An individual can work so hard to make their creation and themselves successful, and people are no-where when you are trying to make it, but they are everywhere when you finally make-it. Tish was never around. But now she is suddenly making guest appearances, and Patrick is allowing it. I saw a side of him I had not seen. He pretended so well; he gave the people what they wanted to see a good-looking, rich, married, happy, successful, couple. That's exactly what they gave the audience today, and the audience bought it. I talked and vented to myself while stuck in traffic the entire way home. I finally looked at my phone for the first time and noticed Patrick had, in fact, called me prior to the show. I had a total of four missed calls from him, and two was prior to the show beginning. I listened to the message. He did in-fact call to warn me about Tish appearance. He also mentioned he refused to have her appear, but could not back out. He said her father, the judge, needed the public to see his daughter as the good wife, mother, and first lady because he needed help to win this campaign. He then left me another message apologizing.

I realized my radio was turned off and decided to turn it to hear relaxing music and shut down the ongoing noise in my brain from the show I just witnessed. Before I could press the CD button the first thing, my ears heard from a local DJ,

Everyone listen up we have some gossip for you. In case you listeners and church going folk didn't hear our favorite Pastor Kincade was on AM/PM today and of course, he was with Kia, his associate Pastor, and the creator of **SerVant:24:7**, *Mina Wright. Now everyone knows this newspaper is hot right now, but it was hardly mentioned. What was surprising was to see his wife who is rarely seen in public on the show talking about their marriage and they were real affectionate. She went in hard. Pastor Kincade is real low key, you never ever hear anything about this brother, but that's not what everyone on social media is talking about. Everyone on social media is saying the show today was a little messy, and Pastor Kincade wife was speaking out to the ladies that come at her husband, but what everyone was asking, who is she talking too? Could it be Kia or Mina? I said he is doing the both of them. Hit us up with your opinion.*

Caller: *This is Derrick calling form Charlotte. I say she was talking to Mina, because I don't care if he is a pastor. You cannot be around all that ass and not want to hit it...you feel me?*

Caller: *Hi this is Megan calling from Charlotte. If it was me and I was working around Pastor Kincade...I would give his fine ass some too...She got her own newspaper...and I heard she just got a Porsche. I ain't mad at her.*

Caller: *My name is Teresa. She was talking about that Mina chick. It's something about that chick. She's always with Pastor Kincade. That chick always talking about God and those be the hypocrites.*

Caller: *Hey this is Shay calling from Charlotte. From what I heard, Mina will do whatever Pastor P asks her too. I saw her at a wedding with him, I saw her a fundraiser with him and his wife was nowhere around. I guarantee you if Pastor P said, "Mina I'm on my way to hell, you want anything back? She will answer, hell yeah!"*

I screamed. Unbelievable. I was looking like the bad guy. I pressed the power button to off, so hard. I really should call and give them something to talk about. It seems, our message had in-fact turned into mess.

I was able to finally make it home at a decent hour, and I was hoping and praying Mamadoll wouldn't probe about the show. I wanted someone to at least see the purpose of the show and not the pretending. I walked into the house and was greeted immediately by her, and Rylie. Mamadoll appeared to be very quiet. She didn't say much about what happened she continued to tell me how good I looked on television and how proud she was if me. Her comments felt really good, although I couldn't believe she didn't mention what happen. She had prepared a big meal for us to celebrate as usual. It was quiet as I sat down at the table and looked through my mail as Rylie sat the table. It scared me that she didn't make one comment. We had just begun to eat, and the doorbell rang.

"I'll get it," Rylie said.

I was surprised and thought surely my ears were deceiving me. I let out a deep breath and stood up to see who it was at the door. But before I was out of the kitchen, Rylie walked in and walking behind her was Patrick. I thought Mamadoll was going to jump out of her wig.

"Mama, it's Pastor Kincade," Rylie said.

I glanced up at him and pretended like I was happy to see him. "I see, welcome Patrick. Rylie, you know better than to open that door without telling one of us who it is."

"I'm sorry Mina. I thought I told you I invited him. Hello Pastor, please have a seat. Are you hungry? Would you like me to make you a plate?" Mamadoll said.

"Thank you so much. I would love to eat. I am starving. These are for you."

What is this about? He think is so smooth. Trying to charm Mamadoll. He brought her a bouquet of twelve dozen roses and handed Rylie the newest PlayStation game. Mamadoll didn't bother telling me he was coming. He sat down next to me, and I continued to look away at the television. He immediately began rubbing his hand on my thigh underneath the table. I took my hand and removed his hand to his thigh real quick. I stood up and walked over to the living area and sat next to Rylie to help her open her new game. I was trying my best to play it cool. I could not let Mamadoll know how I really felt. He and Mamadoll laughed and talked. At least an hour went by before I walked back into the kitchen. I didn't want to make it too obvious that I was not happy to see him. I begin to help her clean up.

"This is absolutely delicious. I want to take you home with me Mamadoll. You must have been the one who taught Mina to cook like this?"

"I sure did. Mina is a great cook."

"Yes, she is. Very good."

I looked over at Patrick. Mamadoll face bloomed with a smile, but sort of confused. "Have you tasted her cooking?"

Patrick didn't answer right away. "Yes ma'am she brought something to work one day."

"Really? Mina, you didn't tell me."

"I guess I forgot with so much going on," I said.

"I wasn't going to bring this up, but you too were very good on the show today."

We both said thank you as she continued.

"This newspaper has touched many lives. I was down at the campaign center, and everyone was talking about my Mina and her talent. I'm so proud of her. You know it has helped people who don't get the word on a daily basis, or if at all."

"That was the plan to reach souls and change lives. I just hate it wasn't talked about more on the show today." I said looking over at Patrick.

"Well, Mina it was mentioned. Sometimes that's all it takes. It doesn't take God long to get his point across." Mamadoll said.

"That is very true Mamadoll. It's not about how much you talk about it. It's about being about it. I can talk all day about **SeVant:24:7**, but if no one buys it, or read it, it's all in vain. Your message will be marketed and sold, but the message will not be instilled in the heart of the people."

"I disagree," I said sarcastically. He stopped drinking his tea and gave me a smirk. Mamadoll laughed.

"Mina why would you say that? Pastor Kincade has made a very good point."

In a loud, harsh tone I replied. "I feel like our purpose for being on the number one show in Charlotte, was never to sell **SerVant:24:7**, it is selling on its own, but to talk about the meaning behind Servant24:7, not solely about Patrick view on marriage or watch him and his wife….never mind…anyway, there were plenty of sections to touch on."

They both were quiet, and I suppose all those wounded feelings were just exposed.

"We talked about what the viewers wanted to talk about," Patrick said.

"And what was that? To hear about you and your wife?" I asked sarcastically.

"Yes! A survey was conducted prior to us appearing on the show, and the viewers wanted to hear...." He paused. "About my marriage and see my wife..." He paused again. "I meant to say see Tish because she is rarely seen."

"You said your wife." We both starred at one another without flinching and without smiling. He continued.

"Anyway, *Two is better than One* is one of the most popular sections in **SerVant24:7**. People want to see that love still exist." He said.

"People want to see Real love still exist," I said.

He stood in disbelief. The telephone rang.

"I'm going to answer this phone call in my bedroom and allow you two to finish your conversation." Mamadoll walked out.

I got up from the table and began placing the dishes in the dishwasher. I felt him walk behind me and his hand gently touched my waist.

"You didn't have to go there. I thought I could trust you."

"Patrick I thought I could trust you."

"Mina. Baby, please allow me to explain. Mina, look at me please?"

I turned around. "There is nothing to explain Patrick. The people wanted you to talk about your marriage, and that's what you did. You did what the people wanted you to do."

"Mina, it's not like that baby. It was last minute, and I left you several messages, and furthermore, you know the situation."

"Do I? I don't know what to believe. You were superb in your performance today; you wore your ring. You two kissed passionately and you seem to enjoy it. So how do I know you're telling me the truth?"

He began to whisper and walked close to my ear. "Because I am telling the truth, and I have told you the truth from the beginning, and you made the decision to do what you have done with me. I told you this was for the professionals. If you can't handle it, Mina I suggest you move to the sideline and watch."

"Patrick, I can handle whatever but what I do not enjoy is it being thrown in my face, on my time and a very important day to me."

"I'm sorry baby. I truly am. But that's not how the game works. Things come up. It was last minute. I didn't mean for your feelings to be hurt. So you need to get out of them."

"Patrick it's not just about me and my feelings. I looked into the faces of those people in that audience. They believed you. They looked up to you. It's a deceiving spirit to portray something to people, but in reality be something else."

"Do you think this is easy for me? You think I don't feel convicted? I fall to my knees every day and every night asking for forgiveness. I know it's deceiving, and I am working on telling my congregation, but you can't walk into my life and just think I'm going to decide to tell them because you are telling me it's deceiving."

"I don't expect you too. It doesn't matter Patrick what I say, because you don't have to answer to me, you have to answer to God.

"Let me ask you a question Mina. Is having sex with me, making love to me, or you slurping on me, is that any different than me pretending that I am still married. Sin is a sin."

He went there. "There is a difference. I'm not a leader leading followers to Christ. I am a witness. I wasn't chosen to preach the gospel, you were."

He shrugged his shoulders. "I am not going to argue with you. It is what it is. You're either with it or not. It's your play. You're either going to run with me or run from me. You decide."

We stood in the kitchen staring at one another. He turned around and walked out. He damn near slammed the front door. My emotions, my feelings, could not bring myself to give in this time to him. I don't know what came over me. I don't know if God was speaking through me to Patrick, or if my flesh was still angry from today. Then the doorbell rang. Rylie looked like what is going on. I opened it.

"One more thing. Don't forget we have the election fundraiser in a few weeks from today. This is very important. The staff for *SerVant:24:7* will be receiving an award."

He is always about business. "I wasn't aware. What kind of award?"

"We broke the record. We sold the most copies in a single week. No other publication had ever done this before in its debut. We did it."

I was quiet. "God did it!" I said.

"Yes, he did. He gave us the opportunity, and we took it Mina."

"Yes, we did." We both were quiet.

"Thank you, Patrick."

"Your welcome sweetheart, another thing. I purchased this dress for you to wear to the awards banquet."

He pulled a red full length, off the shoulders, Versace dress out of his trunk. It was absolutely beautiful.

"Thank you Patrick. It is stunning." I begin to talk to myself and continue to tell myself to not give in. I wanted to jump all over him, hug and kiss him, but I couldn't do that. He walked over to me and slowly kissed me on my forehead. His kissed stayed there for a minute as I closed my eyes. I forgot where I was and then I quickly remembered I was standing in front of Mamadoll house.

"I will see you in the morning sweetheart."

In a low voice, I whispered. "Ok in the morning."

He jumped into the car and sped away. I looked down the street around the corner, as his car left out the gate. I stood in the front yard for a minute thinking. Did I really just do that? Let him drive off? I slowly turned to walk into the house. I closed the front door and walked over to sit on the stairway. I really made the conscience decision to walk away. I have to stand for what is right, and what I believe in. I always have. I don't think in the past five months have I thought of the situation, or what happened to Damien and me. This situation reminded me of what I left back in Dallas. I was longing to do what was right but continued to allow time to past, and stayed in the same situation. I allowed it to escalate and that brought more problems than I had anticipated. I felt as if God was giving me another chance to get it right this time. Or, maybe he's using me in some type of way, or maybe both. With God, there is no confusion. Why am I confused then?

Mamadoll walked over. She sat on the stairwell. I just knew she was going to give me a sermon, But she didn't.

"Mina baby, you just left one situation. Slow down. Stop being anxious. Stop! Let the wounds heal. Let them recover. Then you can be released."

"I understand."

"And always stand for what you believe, always." She then walked upstairs.

"Yes ma'am."

"And Mina, one more thing. Get out your feelings, and play your position in the game. The rookie will always show up and have their time to shine when you least expect them to. That's why they are drafted." She stood up and walked down the stairs toward her room. "Goodnight rookie." She said.

Chapter 10. The Spirit is willing...but the flesh is weak...

"Everyone listen up," Patrick said at Friday's staff meeting.

Three weeks had passed since we appeared on the show, met at Mamadoll's, or even spoke to one another outside of work. The past weeks we avoided one another. He was in his feelings, and I was out of mine. But I was a little horny, but I surely was not going to tell him. He would give me a quiet hi, or good morning, or have a goodnight. I would reply with, *morning, or night, or hello.* Nothing more added. No more flirting, or giggling. No more coming into my office and kissing, and no more weekend sleepovers. All that came to a cease. It was silent in the boardroom at lunch because we were always the two who talked and everyone else laughed. I stayed locked in my office all day some days, and so did he. I sat farther back at church, and his sermons became quick and to the point. It was getting close to the fundraiser and also election time was approaching. We were busier than we had ever been. Not to mention the holidays were around the corner. Rylie was about to enter another year of high school. It seems everyone wanted an ad in the paper, which said, Happy Thanksgiving, or Merry Christmas, and they were starting early. It was only July. It was also more and more Christmas weddings and more babies being born than usual. Patrick wanted all of us to be on one accord, so he begins prepping us for the fundraiser as well as the election, as well as a very busy season.

"Good morning everyone, and please listen up we have a lot to cover in a short period of time, and we also have some very busy weeks ahead of us. First, I want everyone to be ready for Saturday night. Mina and Kia, I need your schedules for the week."

"I have mine, Patrick." Kia handed hers over.

"I have mine also," I said and handed over mine.

We handed our schedules to him, and he looked at them both.

"Wow! Congratulations Kia. I had no idea. Everyone, it seems Kia is receiving a key to the city."

Everyone clapped. She squeezed my hand real tight. We all begin to stand and congratulate her. We all were very happy for her.

"Kia you should be very proud."

"God is good. I'm excited. This my very first accolade. I have spoken at many events, revivals, but never thought I would receive a key to the city I was raised in. God is good. I have to say that twice."

"Yes, he is. He is throwing blessings everywhere, and so catch them. "I said.

"So where are we with the election advertising Mina?"

"I have all the ads ready for the design team."

"Does Commissioner Calhoun have the cover?"

"No sir, Commissioner Hollis does. He bought the cover two months ago."

Patrick was quiet. He walked over and gazed out the window for a moment. "Well, business is business."

I added to my response. "Commissioner Calhoun has a half page of advertising his campaign and also an advertisement in the section, "Two is better than One."

"Is that right?" Patrick said.

"Yes. He and his fiancé, Zi'lah are getting married."

"Really? Ok, then I'm fine with that? What else is going on?" He stood quietly looking at me.

The security guard came into the boardroom and spoke with Patrick silently. The boardroom door then opened and appeared Tish and Patricks' daughter. This was the first time I had seen him with his daughter. She made an entrance just for the cameras.

"Hello, Husband." She then kissed him real hard and long. Patrick didn't try to push her away. He stood there. He didn't move. She then fixed his tie and said I love you. Patrick looked but never said a word. The room was quiet. Everyone said hello to her then hugged and kissed his little girl. He was dotting all over Pasha. He tickled her and then grabbed her and tossed her up and down, and then he began singing to her. "Oh, how daddy misses you, how daddy thinks of you. Did you know that your daddy loves you?" The room was silent.

"I am so sorry to interrupt this meeting about the **ServVant:24:7**, but I have something far more important to discuss at this time. Its family time Mina." She then smiled at me.

"That was inappropriate," I said.

"What was inappropriate?"

"The kiss," I said.

"Why are you jealous?'

"Of what?"

"Mina, please relax," Patrick said.

"Listen to your master." She said.

"My what?" I said

"Can you hear?" Tish said.

Someone, please hold my hands down before I jump out of my seat and slap her. Then I would be the one called violent.

"Tish! Please get to the point." Patrick said.

"I have some visitors with me, and I don't know if Patrick told you all but my father is filming a documentary of him on the campaign trail with his beloved famous pastoral son-in-law. If he wins this term, he will have made history in the state of North Carolina."

Everyone clapped but me. My hands were still folded.

"Thanks, guys. Of course, me being his wife and the love of his life, the producers wanted to involve my family." She smiled at me, and I smiled back.

In walked her father, along with Bryce and Zi'lah. I could only laugh at the circus. Damn, did I bring some heat to these people? Am I that effective to what is going on in their lives to the point they have to interrupt meetings? Does someone see the capabilities in Mina? I mean really do we need to interrupt meetings and perform the happy song and dance and involve children? The rookie is shining.

"Well hello everyone. Patrick what a beautiful office you have here." Tish father said.

Doris leaned in my ear. "I don't think in the five years I have worked for him I have ever witnessed this man come into this office, and I have met her maybe once, maybe twice in five years."

I stood up along with the rest of the staff. I walked over to Zi'lah. "Congrats cousin when is the big day?" This heffa tried to treat me funny.

"We haven't set a date yet." I wanted to respond and tell her that means you don't have a date sweetie.

"Well, I'm happy for you Zi'lah." I could be really messy and ask her if she was divorced yet, but I will be a lady about it. "And please do not forget to invite me," I said.

She hesitated and didn't get the chance to respond because Bryce responded for her. "We will send Mamadoll an invitation Mina. I just need you to make sure I am on the cover this month. Let me rephrase that, on each bi-weekly issue until the election ends, and I know for sure you will do it."

"Bryce, unfortunately, there are several candidates running in this election, and there is not enough space for everyone, but I did manage to squeeze your ad in the section, Pathetic Politicians, I'm so sorry I meant to say Praying Politicians, forgive me, Bryce I've been so busy," I said as I winked at him.

"Mina, you probably would have your own man and not sharing with someone else, if you would put a safety pin on that mouth of yours."

"Well Bryce if I did that, I wouldn't be able to talk smack to you!"

"Mina, I don't think I have seen you since you appeared on AM/PM Charlotte? I heard you were very excited until the show started." He smirked at me. He's a dirty, miserable dog.

"Actually, I enjoyed it Bryce. Did you watch it?"

"Yes, I did. I wouldn't have missed it for the world. You seemed uncomfortable."

"Mina relax," Patrick said from across the room.

"Well, well, I don't believe we have met." Tish dad extended his hand to me.

"Hello, I don't believe so. I'm Mina Wright."

"I know who you are. I'm the honorable Judge W.H. Nash the third."

"Very nice to meet you, sir."

"You also." He glanced at over at Patrick. "She's polite Patrick." He said.

"I'm standing right here Judge Nash you can talk to me, about me." The room was silent, and Patrick began walking over my way.

"Feisty too! I like what you did with the **SerVant:24:7**. You did a good job, a real good job. Who else are you serving, sweetie?" Bryce laughed really hard, and Zi'lah giggled. I kept my cool.

I cleared my throat. "Excuse me? I missed the joke, I guess." I could feel Patrick hand on my waist.

"She's a servant of the Lord, Judge Nash? Mina, its ok the Judge has a sense of humor at times."

"She's just fine Patrick. Shouldn't you be over there with your family?" He asked Patrick.

"I'm where I want to be Judge," Patrick responded sarcastically. "They're done filming."

Her father stared at Patrick then looked back over at me. "Patrick, make sure everyone is on one accord. I do mean everyone."

Patrick turned around. "Everyone excuse me and please listen up. Judge Nash and Bryce would like to make a brief announcement regarding the upcoming election."

"Hello everyone I'm Commissioner Bryce Calhoun, and we all know its election time. This means voting for a God fearing, loving, caring, understanding, family man who is for the people and his community. Now Judge Nash and I are the only two candidates you should be concerned with when you approach the voting booth. What we are about to do will change the community for the better? We know that Mina and Patrick have brought a new type of vibe to the news publication area with **SerVant:24:7**, so me and Judge Nash want in as well. There is plenty of room left on stage. My aim is to be mayor, and

Judge Nash is going to run for Senator. Now, this information is for everyone standing in this room only. We need each of you to encourage everyone you know of, like your family, friends, and neighbors. Understood? Judge Nash your turn." Bryce said.

"Now I have something to say." Judge Nash said. "We as politicians do not have time for what people claim to be reasons why they didn't vote.

We don't need to hear your people saying, I had to get my hair done, I had a nail appointment, I don't have transportation, or I don't have the time I got paid today, and I had to cash my check. The polls will be open until eight o'clock, some nine pm. We need you to vote! Bryce and I want to make a difference in this community."

I wanted to shout out loud to him, did you say your people? What the hell does he mean by that comment? I have been voting since I turned eighteen years old, and just because he is asking me to vote, does not mean I will be voting for him.

"Does everyone understand?" Judge Nash asked.

Patrick walked over and interrupted him. "Everyone understands they must vote and they will vote."

Everyone smiled and shook their heads up and down in agreement.

"Patrick does Mina understand she must vote. She didn't shake her head."

I know he did not call me out. Does he know I don't give damn about him being a judge? Everyone looked at me, and I didn't flinch. My one eyebrow lifted up, and I was ready to respond. I felt Patrick must have known it was not going to be nice because he damn near leaped over to where I was standing and jumped right in to respond.

"She has always voted Judge Nash."

He gave Patrick the most uneasy, uncomfortable look. "But will she vote for me, is what I'm asking?"

I was thinking. I'm not sure Judge Nash if I'm able to vote that day. I have a hair appointment, and I need to cash my check that day.

"Judge Nash she will vote. Please step aside." Patrick said.

He laughed and then walked over to Bryce. He took his hand and put it on Bryce shoulder. "She will vote for Bryce too? Correct Patrick?"

I felt a certain type of feeling. Something is definitely wrong with this picture. I don't know what's going on, but it is so much deeper than pretending to be a happy family in front of the camera and people, and gaining votes.

"Judge Nash everyone will vote. Is there anything else you need from myself, or my staff?" His little girl walked over and grabbed his hand. Patrick looked down at her and smiled.

"I want to hear it out of their mouth Patrick, please let them speak."

The judge walked near Kia. "Kia, I hear you are receiving the key to the city? Is that right?"

"That's correct sir." Kia body language displayed a sign she was uncomfortable.

"Kia I really do want you to receive that key. So I hope you will do what is right darling." He placed his hand on her shoulder. He then walked over to Doris. Wait a minute I know he does not call himself black mailing people? What in the world is going on? Kia straightened her body and then exhaled deeply.

"I believe the award is God given and I will receive it no matter what."

He laughed out loud and looked over at his daughter. I don't understand why Patrick will not stop him. I looked over at Zi'lah, and she was smiling at me. I then glanced at Tish, and she had a smirk on her face as well. This is ridiculous, this unacceptable, two times in a row, the show and now this?

The judge then responded. "Kia you know now if you want that key, you better vote right, and not wrong."

Kia didn't say a word or move a mussel. I was praying he would make his way to me. Come over here, Santa Claus. I have an answer to your threats. Please Lord, let him walk over here.

But he never did. Bully. He walked to Mrs. Doris. I moved a little closer to where she was standing, and Patrick cleared his throat. Patrick and I always talked in codes. I'm really not feeling the codes right about now. I want to know why this man feels he can threaten people, or black mail them into voting for him and Bryce.

"Is it Mrs. Doris?" he asked. She responded with a yes. She seemed very, very nervous. She broke out in a sweat.

"You have worked for Patrick for quite some time now is that correct?"

Her voice trembled. "Yes, sir. I have," she said.

"Good. Well, I shouldn't have to tell you who to vote for. I know you've been praying to that God of yours and would really like him to answer your prayer to see your grand-son released from prison one day. And who knows, maybe he will be released. Maybe you will be able to see him walking around in the land of the free. But you must vote for me, or he will have another few years added."

203

"Enough Nash!" Patrick yelled. "Everyone will vote. Do you need anything else from either my staff or me? If not please use the exit door."

He giggled nervously. "Nope! I guess were all done here." He said smiling. "I love every one of you all, I really do. I hope to see you all at the polls in a few weeks and remember to vote Judge Nash and Bryce Calhoun. Let's go, Pasha, granddaddy, is going to take you to have some lunch."

Everyone walked out the boardroom together slowly. It was only Patrick and myself left in the boardroom. We both sat there across from one another in silence. At least five, or maybe more had passed, and we both were still sitting there, staring at one another without speaking. I wonder did he like the kiss. I don't know. I guess Patrick realized maybe I had figured out there was a whole lot more than pretending to be married. This story had in fact manifest itself or exposed the fact it was a whole lot going on, and I was beginning to question myself and ask, do I really want to know the truth? I stood up and walked out the boardroom back to my office. On the way to my office, I stopped by the restroom. I stood in the bathroom stall contemplating, did I want to go on this.

"Mina."

I heard someone whisper my name. I looked around because I thought I was the only one in here. I squatted slowly down to see if I could see someone feet in the other bathroom stalls. I didn't see anyone.

"Mina."

"Ms. Doris? Where are you?"

Her back was against the next-door stall.

"Mina, please don't say anything to anyone. Please. I believe you won't. Please promise me you won't."

"I promise."

"I guess I'll never see my grandbaby. I'm not voting for that man. Mina, I love Mr. Kincade. I appreciate everything he has done for me. But I can't allow him to allow those people to have their way. I don't know what they have on Mr. Kincade if anything. But my gut tells me there is something. Nash and Bryce are atheist. It's many of them. They are a part of an organization who removed prayer from schools, and they are fighting for the removal of God to be used on any news publication, store front, etc. Do you know what will happen if we were to put him on the cover? It will go against everything you believe in. It's like opening the door to what you have built and allowing the enemy to tear it down."

"Do the people know?"

"It has been a rumor for many years around the city. This is why he wants the *SerVant:24:7* cover so bad. And why they need that influential person to help them. They want the public to believe he is the upstanding family Christian man, who loves blacks because he has a black son-in-law and he is a preacher. Understand now."
"Yes, I do. And Patrick knows he is an Atheist?"
"If I know he is an Atheist sweetie, what do you think?"
I was speechless, and I was hurt.
"Mina I'm loyal to Mr. Kincade. I love him like a son. I don't ask any questions I just watch and pray. I mind my own business, and I do what I'm told. Patrick is a good man, but he has to protect what he has built, and this is not the church, this is his business. People don't understand how to separate the Pastor and the entrepreneur. Mr. Kincade is not going to allow any harm to come our way.
He will do whatever he can to protect us, but he can only do so much. Mina, you are a good Christian woman who truly love the Lord. I can see it. It's all over you. Some people Mina see business, Monday-Saturday, and that's all, and on Sunday it's about God. But, Mina you carry God with you seven days a week, I can see it, I can hear it in your voice, everyone don't carry that spirit. Do what you have to do. But at the end of the day, you are the one that has to answer to God. "
"They are going to destroy our newspaper, my reputation."
"It's not Patricks' newspaper; it's yours sweetie. Look in your desk drawer to the left before you leave. Goodnight."
Oh, Jesus. What did they do? I ran out the restroom to my office. I opened my desk drawer and saw a check made out to me in the amount of two hundred thousand. I slammed my desk drawer and rebuked that check, the amount, and whoever wrote it to me. I then opened the drawer and looked at it again, and again, and again, and one last time. I had to talk to myself. What is really going on here? What have I gotten myself into? What other secrets are Patrick holding? I grabbed my things to leave for the day. It was 4:30 and I had enough for today. I locked my office door. And turned around and jumped. Patrick leaning against the wall startled me.
"Leaving early?" he said.
"Yes I am. How long have you been standing there?"
"Since you walked out the restroom."
I was quiet.
"Why are you leaving so early?"
"I'm a little tired, and with so many activities coming up I need all the sleep I can get."
"What did you decide?"

"On?"

"The cover?"

"I decided to keep Judge Hollis on the cover. He submitted his advertisement months ago and paid very well for that cover…" I paused for a minute.

"More than Judge Nash and Bryce?" Patrick asked?

I paused. I thought about the check in my drawer. "Hollis paid very well Patrick. And I just feel he is the man for the cover. That's all."

"You sure it is a feeling?"

He is probing. "This is about business. Nothing more."

"You are absolutely right. But Mina I will make the decision of who will be on the cover this time sweetheart, ok? He walked close to me.

I turned red, blue, and purple. I cannot believe he is doing this. But I kept my cool…for a change. "Goodnight Patrick."

"Goodnight is that it? Whoa. You a little short with words Baby. You're not going to ask me why?"

"Why should I? You said you would be making the decision. I have nothing else to say."

"I do. Come over here. Give me a kiss."

"I have to be at home early Patrick." He grabbed me by my waist and began kissing me on my chest through my V-neck blouse. His hands begin moving in places that were not visible to the eye.

"I can't be alone tonight. I don't want to be alone tonight. Can I hold you all night, please baby?"

"Patrick I can't. Not tonight."

"Huh?"

"I can't keep doing the same thing over and over and asking God for forgiveness."

"I didn't ask you to do anything, and I can't either Mina. I just want to hold you in my arms baby, that's all. Is something wrong with that?"

"There is nothing wrong Patrick. Let's just pray about it, and about us."

"OOOk…"

"Ok."

"Can I walk you down to your car?"

"Yes, you can."

Patrick grabbed my hand and escorted me to my car. We hugged one another, and he held me tight like he always does, and his hugs always feel like he doesn't want me to leave. I held onto him the

same way. I didn't want to let go, but I knew I needed to. I need some things to manifest before I can continue my role.
"Promise you will call me when you arrive home." He said.
"You know I will." We stood there staring in to each other.
"Goodnight."

I was still in amazement after what Ms. Doris told me. I tried to act as if I wasn't bothered by anything, but I was. I prayed all morning that I would keep my cool. I reminded myself to stay calm and cool. Act as if nothing was told to me. But it was hard. The news of both Bryce and Nash being Atheist, and Patrick knowing about it, but still was going to allow them to be on the cover, was heavy on my heart. As soon as arrived to work the next day I began checking my email. I had several email messages I had in-fact missed. I sat in my office and responded to them all one by one. They were all complementing me on a job well done, or inquiring about a job position or interested in placing an advertisement. This is why I stay here with this ministry and tolerate the things I see going on. It's not about me. It is about the people. It is God's people. His children. His message. It is his word we must get across to a dying world. But how do you do that when you are weak yourself? How do you minister to a crowd of twenty thousand souls and your world is chaotic? Especially when the world want to be encouraged, motivated, and would like to know their leader has it all together. Patrick and Kia, these two are going through. But they must remember who they are. I begin to reflect on the first time I met Patrick when I first came back home. I wanted to sit and talk with Kia so bad. She was distant with me. I thought they had it all, the both of them. When I say the word *all*, I mean, it all out together, no problems, no worries, nothing got them down or discouraged them.

They always smiled in my presence, and Patrick always was on cloud nine. He preached every Sunday with everyone on their feet. What happened? I guess God was trying to tell me I was so busy looking at how perfect I thought man was. I should have had my eyes on how perfect he is. He will always show us what is real. It was the afternoon, and I was still working on one section of the paper. Kia knocked on my door, and I immediately invited her into my office. We rarely talk about what is going on around here, and she never mentions anything about Patrick to me. She is very different from the Kia that was my bestie. She seems distant and very introverted at times. She speaks, she smiles, and off to her office she stays the entire day. She would have lunch with us, but that stopped after we appeared on the show. She had never invited me to her house. Often times when I ask to meet her at her home she says it's too far, or it's a mess. I never addressed any of my concerns to

207

her. I figured we were grown now and no longer the close teenagers who shared everything or every situation we went through with one another. I tried putting myself in her situation, and look at it from her point of view, because she is a public figure. I have learned since being with Patrick public figures seem to be very guarded. I can empathize with her because she does have her reputation to protect. I guess that's why the *image* is to maintain in front of the public. When a person; is admired by so many people, that favoritism brings a sort of pressure on an individual. You lose yourself to become what the public portrays you to be. You focus on living up to the expectations of those individuals who didn't help you get to where you are but adores where you currently are. It seems you forget who you truly are. It explains now why she and Patrick are partners. They have something in common. I pray for them both.

"Come in girlfriend. Have a seat." I said.

"Thanks." She said as she looked to be distressed about something.

"Kia are you ok? Is everything alright?" I asked.

"Yes, I'm fine. We never really had the chance to talk after the show. I know it's been months, and it was my hard to talk with you...especially after what happen yesterday."

"It's all good. I know you have a busy life. We both do. I'm all ears sister Kia." I said to her because after what I just heard and what I just witnessed I truly don't know what to believe at this point.

"I want to apologize for the behavior that had taken place around here. I asked you to work with us, and I feel responsible for what you dealing with here in the office. What you have done with **Servant24:7** has been phenomenal. I know you probably are wondering what is going on around here and I can't blame you. Although this is a business and we are at work, God has still called us to be who we are. I know this whole thing you have witnessed may make you want to leave us, but please don't Mina. There are just a few things Patrick need to fix, and that is getting rid of his ex and her family. It's not easy for him but since you have entered the picture, it seems to be a smoother road for PAK, and he is determined to fix it. He has this ministry and so much going on, I pray for him constantly, day in and day out. I believe God will see us through it. It has been an ongoing trial for him, and he deserves so much more and far better. And more and better far is on its way."

"Well, Kia I'm glad someone has made mention of the problem. After the fiasco in the boardroom on yesterday and after appearing on the show, I must admit I was a little discouraged."

"Mina please you don't have to be it will be fixed, I promise you."

"I just don't know what to believe. I feel there are secrets. I take that back. I know there are secrets. And believe me, no one is exempt from keeping a secret. But it's almost like Patrick allows Tish to walk over him. It seems as if he doesn't say anything back to her, or her father. She came onto the show with trouble and now this I just don't get it. Why does her father and Bryce want the cover so bad?" I stood up and walked over to the window. I saw Patrick standing outside on his cell phone. He seems upset and was pacing the parking lot.

"Mina its politics, money, etc. you know girlfriend. Politicians have secrets. They both need black voters. The city is not that big and when rumors spread, it's hard to convince people there not true. And as for PAK, he can hold his own I've told you before. He has a reputation to protect, a ministry, he is not going to fight her with words Mina. You should not be concerned with that. Stop focusing on Nash, Tish, and Bryce. Just do you hunty…you have an amazing life Mina."

She will not give me any information. Nothing. I wonder how she feels about them both being Atheist. If Doris knows, I know she does also. "Thank You. I paused. "Well, I haven't been in a situation like this before. I just need to make a decision on what to do about the cover."

"I thought Patrick was making the decision."

"Yes, that's what he said. I was speaking of some other decisions I need to make. I meant." I lied. And sort of changed the subject. "I guess after the launching party incident and the way Patrick did not acknowledge her I assumed it was always going to be like that."

"What do you mean the launching party incident? What happen? Where was I?"

"You were not around Kia. I don't know where you were. I guess I didn't tell you. Tish and Bryce appeared out of nowhere when Patrick and I were having a private moment together." She said.

Kia seemed startled. She stood up immediately and walked towards me. "What…what was said? What did they say to you? What did they tell you?"

"They didn't tell me anything. They were basically trying to get me to approve Bryce campaign to be more visible, or advertised in **Servant24:7**."

"And?" She asked?

"And that's it. I introduced myself to her, and we exchanged a few not so nice words to one another, and then Patrick and I excused ourselves from their presence."

"How did PAK seem?"

"What do you mean? He seemed confident then to me at that time. But that was months ago. What I'm trying to say is he doesn't seem confident now." I said.

"Mina like I said PAK is not a confrontational person. He picks his battles, and that's how he is."

"I understand that Kia. I just would like to see him defend himself more verbally."

"He does Mina. He chose to handle it in a different way. He doesn't expose his frustration for an audience. He is a very smart man Mina. He didn't make it this far on his looks."

"I believe that Kia. I have been around him enough to know he's a very smart man. I just don't know what to believe anymore."

"Believe me when I say this, he cares so much for you and Rylie, and your well-being. He is just going through a situation, and this has made think about what he has been missing. But, now this beautiful, genuine, Christ like woman walked into his life, he is now realizing its time to move forward. Be patient with him. It will be over before you know it."

"I don't have patience for mess or drama Kia. I'm not a people pleaser Kia. I'm not a camera junky. People will not issue me my reward when I die, but God will. I must admit as a woman I was a bit jealous when I saw her on the show with him, the two of them inter-acting with one another, and also to see Patrick wearing his wedding ring, also in the boardroom; the kiss. It made me feel extremely uncomfortable."

"I can understand it. It's the woman, looking at them, "once she was his woman." But, you shouldn't be jealous, not at all. They are jealous of you. You landed on their territory, and you won. They are now a thing of the past. They had the chance, but that chance is long gone. They know they are no longer wanted and so now they are scared. I do mean terrified. So they will do whatever it take to interfere with what is now and what is going to be. I'm quite sure you know who they are?"

"Oh yes! I am very familiar with, who *they* are."

"So what are you going to do? Are you going to allow them to win?" She walked a little close to me. I could see her reflection through the window. She crossed her arms and stood there waiting for me to answer.

I turned around and sat on the window ledge, and then crossed my arms. "Like I mentioned earlier I have some decisions to make."

She walked a little closer. "That is very true. But, God also enjoys a little effort from us. You don't give in, and you surely don't give up. You don't allow the enemy to win!"

"The enemy was defeated over two thousand years ago," I said.

"That statement is very true. But, we also have to realize just because the battle has already been won, we are still in the fight until we reach eternity to be with our Lord and Savior. We are not of this world, but we are still in this world Mina. Remember we wrestle not against flesh and blood."

She walked over and gave me a kiss on my jaw, and whispered in my ear, "You are human, and your man needs you. Your man wants you. Everyone has issues. Don't let your man go into the hands of another woman Mina you are too smart of a woman to do that and your way too close."

She walked out my office, and there I stood looking out my window. One thing I know is a woman always needs another woman to talk too. We understand one another and can relate to each other without talking for hours. We can encourage one another and be straight and to the point. But my so call man has some issues, and they have become mine. I cannot allow him to put those politicians on my cover of my paper. My conscience is killing me. I glanced over at my clock, and it was 6:02 pm. The sound of raindrops falling, begin to hit my office windowpane. I was ready to make my way out the door because I had worked, listened, and witnessed enough for one day. I stayed a little longer to respond to a few more emails because I love interacting with people. I gathered my things to head out the door. If I can make it home before nine o'clock pm, I can still see an episode of How to get away with Murder I was thinking.

"Knock, knock." He said.

"Who's there?" I said.

"Patrick," he said.

"Patrick who?" I said.

"You're once upon a time man Patrick." He said.

"That's cute. What can I do for you, Patrick?"

"You can stop avoiding me." We smiled. "Seriously, I don't know Mina. What can you do for me?"

"I asked you that question shouldn't you answer?"

"I should, but I'm afraid my answer will get me in trouble." He said.

I turned around face to face with him. "What will get you in trouble?"

"You." He said. "You will get me in trouble Mina. Don't break my heart." He then put his hand on his chest and smiled.

"You sure you want get me in trouble Patrick?"

"Have I gotten you in trouble?"

"Not yet and please don't."

I turned around and kneeled down to grab my brief case. I felt him on my butt, and he was rock hard. I couldn't hold back. It had been a month since I released some stress. Not for a minute, not for a second, was going to not release some tonight. I was weak and like a dog in heat. I slightly turned around as he began to unbutton my blouse with his mouth. I walked over to my desk as he watched. I propped my body up and sat on my desk, and then opened my legs real wide. I took my shirt off slowly, then my lace bra. I was bare breast and all. I rubbed on them slowly and massaged my nipples as he watched me from afar. I then took my hands and rubbed my vagina up and down, round and round. I then took my panties off slowly. Threw them over to where Patrick was standing.

The panties landed at his feet. He picked them up immediately and moved them across his nostrils real slow. He sniffed them more, and more. Then he walked over to me slowly. He laid me on my desk with nothing but my heels on.

"I missed you Mina." He said as he laid my body down on the desk.

"I missed you too," I responded

He licked his tongue out, and it hit the bottom of his chin. That did it for me. He squatted then opened each one of my legs. He then began to lick every part of my body there was to lick. It was evident he was hungry, and I had left him starving. It was time for him to eat dinner and time for me to serve. I let him enjoy himself as I lay there on the desk. It was soon raining on the inside of my office. SPLISH, SPLASH the desk was wet. The more I gave him some juice to drink with his dinner, the faster his tongue went. He was at record-breaking speed for the fasted tongue. He was getting full, but he wasn't the only one hungry, I was too. I rose up off the desk then I dropped to my KNEES to PLEASE...him. Strokes and more strokes with my mouth, my tongue, and up and down I went. Slurp one, slurp two, slurp three, slurp four, Slurp, Slurp and here's the big one. I kept it in my mouth, no hands; arms up and....it's a touchdown. SPLISH SPLASH I took a bath... to the face and then swallowed some. I slowly moved his body on top of my desk, and then climbed on top of him as if he was my horse ready to run out the stable. I rode him like the big black handsome

stallion he was. I went for a ride. I went up and down, front to the back. He then forced my body on the desk, and he was on top.
"You ready to perform your yoga move?" He said.
I didn't hesitate. I answered him by wrapping my legs around his neck. I put my arms above my head, and I gazed into the lights on the ceiling, off to the sky I went, and the rest is history. We both let out the stress amongst other things, one-in-a-half hour later. We entered the elevator together and couldn't keep our hands off one another. He was rubbing and I was allowing him to. He stopped the elevator took his shirt off. He began to rub on my face.

Before I knew it, one of my legs was propped on the corner of the elevator, shirt was off again, and he had pulled the black python out and placed him back in my garden.

30 Minutes Later
We walked to the car slowly. It was nine o'clock. "I need to get home."

"Mina, I missed you so much. I am so sorry about everything that has happened over the few weeks. I promise you I am not lying about anything, I am telling you the truth about everything, and I want you to believe me." He said.

"I believe you Patrick. I miss you baby. I want us to be together. I don't want to deal with the blackmailing, the threats, and the pop-ups on the shows. It's about me and you, yours, and mine. I know you have a reputation to protect and know you love your members. But PAK baby you have to think about what is best for you! Not what is best for anyone else? "

We stood there gawking at one another holding hands. He kissed my hand. I wanted to ask him why, was he trying to put those unbelievers on my paper. But I didn't say a word about it.

"I will Mina. I will. I promise I will. It's not easy for me, but it will work out for me, for us. I know it will. Mina, have patience."

"I'm trying Patrick. I know I can't walk into your life and expect everything to change with-in a year but after today this has left my mind wondering all over the place. Patrick people, your congregation, want to believe they can trust you. As well as your employees, and business partners, and me."

"Just have some patience with me and don't allow my situation to affect you where you can't enjoy your success. Don't put so much focus on what happened, you know the truth, focus on what is happening between us. In time God will deliver me from what I am dealing with. I know he will. He hasn't failed me yet Mina, even if I am wrong. His grace and mercy is all around us. Just look around Mina, you have broken a record baby; you have so much to be happy about. Let's continue working on the progress. "

"Alright, Patrick your right. I will work on me, and you work on you. I trust you will handle it."

"I will. I promise, but one more thing. Baby I can't be alone tonight. I don't want to be alone tonight. Can I hold you all night, please, baby please?"

The sound of his smooth voice made me tingle. Damn it! Just when I thought I was going to be good...Bad girl Mina shows up...again. "Can you leave your car here?"

"Of course, I own the property. What are you thinking?"

"Do you have clothes for work tomorrow?" I asked.

"Can you take me by the house in the morning so I can grab me some clothes?"

"Spend the night with me. Get in the backseat."

"I didn't know your name was slick Mina. How are we going to do this?"

"If you want to be with me tonight... you have to take risk. Hang on and watch your girl in action."

He jumped in my back seat of the car, and we rode off to Mamadoll's house. I would glance in the rearview mirror every once in a while to see if he was ok. Poor thing looked like he had just stepped out of a steam bath, he was sweating so much. It was close to ten pm, so I knew Mamadoll and Rylie would be getting ready for bed.

I pulled into the gate, and I didn't see any lights on. I parked, and it seems to be ok for Patrick to sneak in with me, so we both headed to the front door. I slowly opened the door and sneaked my way in to get a look. I didn't see any sign of Mamadoll or Rylie in sight. I signaled for him to come to the door. Once he got there, I slowly unlocked the front door. I walked in the foyer, and it was dark and quiet. It seemed everyone was already in their bedrooms.

"Mina baby, is that you?" Mamadoll called out from a distance. I panicked, and Patrick did also. We laughed and slowly closed the door.

"Mina baby what have you gotten me into? What are we going to do?"

"Patrick calm down. I got you. Take this key and walk to the side door next to the garden and go up the stairs. My room is the first room on the left. I'll meet you there."

"Are you serious? Do you know who I am?" He said joking.

"I know you don't have any other transportation and it's a quarter until 10, and you are a long way from your mansion." I held the key up.

"I cannot believe I'm doing this. Something must be wrong with me."

"No. Everything is just right with you. You're living your life. You are no longer afraid. Not so structured. Not worried about what someone will say or think, you're enjoying life, taking risk."

"I guess so." He replied as he grabbed the key out my hand. "I'll see you in a minute." We kissed and went our separate ways.

Unfortunately, the minute turned into two hours. Patrick made it to my bedroom safe and sound, but as for me, it took a little longer. Mamadoll and Rylie decided they wanted to entertain me for a while by catching up on the day. Finally, Mamadoll said her goodnights and Rylie jumped in to the shower. I headed to the bedroom to check on Patrick. I opened the door and there he lay in my bed, under the covers, sound asleep.

I looked, and from what I could see, he laid his clothes on the chair and kept his boxers and tank top on. I covered him with my duvet and watched him to sleep peacefully. I checked in with Rylie, said her prayers with her and held her until she went to sleep. I then went back down stairs and checked all the doors in the house, set the alarm, kissed Mamadoll and headed back upstairs. I must say I am a woman that holds her house down. I jumped in the shower and then headed to lay down with my man. He was snoring by now. I hate to toot my own horn, but it look like the adventure on the desk had worn a brother out.

But, as I stood there watching him sleep, my heart could only go out to him. He didn't know that Kia shared with me, some details of him, since we have stopped talking. She said he leaves work at seven or eight at night to visit hospitals, only visiting members that admire him. He arrives home so terribly tired he falls asleep in his clothes still on his body most of the time. Then after what I witnessed in the boardroom, I could only empathize with the Patrick, the very well known, well-loved, well-admired, chosen minister who God has placed in a position to lead his people had lost his confidence in the God we serve. Although he preach a wonderful anointed sermons on faith, trusting God, overcoming life obstacles, and thousands of more sermons, his actions off the pulpit clearly showed a different side of the beloved pastor that so many look up too and desire to be like. It seems somewhere down the road of being chosen something, or someone moved in his space while he was answering his call, and interrupted what was supposed to be a journey for the Lord turned out to be a journey for man. He gave his members just what they wanted to see, "appearance" that word goes a very long way, and that word will destroy an individual. This is what many believers want to believe about a minister or their minister that he has it together. But not only ministers, believers in general. They want to see their minister has it all together, and who wouldn't? I mean when you think about it he is called by God to spread the gospel of Jesus Christ. He is anointed. He relays the message sent by God every Sunday, so surely he couldn't be wrestling with part of that is true, and also the other part is the minister is also still a human being just like the rest of us. I think about how he has become such an influential person in his community. But I also, see how this has allowed himself to keep truth of his present lifestyle from the public. This life he is portraying is wearing him down, and that's exactly what the enemy wants to do to you, or does the enemy want you to continue the lie in front of people, so he to keep that stronghold on you. This position in life has caused him drama, lies, blackmailing, hurt. When the life he was called to do should have had him leading, encouraging, mentoring, God's people only. I guess this where we all get confused when we feel our leaders, ministers, pastors, have it easier in there day to day life than us. That's far from truth. I know the same God that delivered me from terrible situations where I didn't know what to do can do the same for him.

But, I have to ask myself does he want to be delivered? Or, is he enjoying the performance of a perfect family? Where in his life on his journey did he feel the need to accept the worldly approach, before he accepted the word of God approach? Believing in God's word and knowing for sure without a doubt if he brought you to the situation he can and will bring you through the situation, so why lie? Why deceive your members and people who look up to you? On my other hand, I also can empathize with Patrick because I was once the same way. I also don't want to get caught up again with someone who sells me promises, but five years down the road I am still waiting on him to tell his congregation the truth, and I am still looking like and feeling like the other woman. One thing I must remember is to myself I must always be true.

The truth of the matter is I care so much about this man and his well -being, but I know I cannot continue to allow myself to compromise the truth. My spirit will not allow me too, but my flesh is telling me it's not your problem why should you care? Your successful now go along with it, smile for the cameras, shake hands with the finest professionals, show up on every television outlet there is, just do it, you have money in the bank, nice clothes, a very nice car, can get it when you want it, play along with it. All this may be true what my flesh is saying, but I can have those things along with a peace of mind without pretending because God told me he will supply all my needs and his word will not come back void. I discovered something about myself as well during this transition in my life. I believe I too have to be strong and not let my flesh move-in the way it has every time I miss Patrick, or every time were alone. I am around him. Here I am struggling on one hand, and on the other hand, enjoying every overtaken blessing thrown my way. I walked over to my bed and lay down next to him. I pulled the cover over us, and Patrick wrapped his arms around me and squeezed me tight.

"Mina I care so much about you. I need you in my life. Goodnight sweetheart." He said.

I responded with a goodnight praying to the lord he gives me an outlet to get out of this house in the morning without Mamadoll discovering the pastor slept in the bed with me and hoping Patrick will understand when he sees the cover of **SerVant24:7**.

My alarm clock went off at six a.m. sharp. I think I hit it several times before I got up. Patrick was already up and on bended knees. I got up to brush my teeth and let him have his time with God. I walked down the hallway to awake Rylie and ran downstairs to check on Mamadoll. To my surprise, she was already up with company. Of all mornings Aunt Bae decided to stop over and have coffee. We hadn't seen her in months because she claims she has been in Africa feeding the children. But, I heard different. I heard her, and the doctor were getting "plastered" from another doctor, a friend of his. I didn't make a sound. I stopped breathing. I turned to walk slowly back up the stairs and that one stair I've been promising Mamadoll I would replace squeaked so loud you would have thought I weighed a ton.

I heard a loud voice yell, "Good morning Mina is that you, or Rylie?"

I froze and took another step. "Morning," I said.

Good morning girls."

I turned around slowly, damn! "It's me, Auntie, I saw you had company," I yelled from a distance.

"Mina you better come down here and give me a hug." Aunt Bae said.

I walked slowly in my PJ's towards the kitchen area. "Good morning everyone," I said as I kissed my aunt.

"Mina, look at you girl. Heard you became a star in this city overnight and since I've been out of town." She couldn't wait. She didn't even ask, how I have been.

"I am still Mina Aunt Bae. How are you? We missed you around here."

"No, you didn't Mina stop telling that lie." She said joking. We both laughed.

"We really did Aunt Bae. How is the husband?"

"He is wonderful. We are getting ready for the election and the governors fund raiser. I know you will be there."

"I will. How did you know I was going?"

"Well you know I mingle with the best of the best Mina, it's no secret that you and Pastor Kincade..." she paused with a smile on her face.

Mamadoll looked at her with unease. She then inhaled deeply and looked me in my eye. I didn't flinch, and I was prepared for whatever came out of her mouth at this point, because I know Bryce and Zi'lah have given her an ear full. And it was too early for BS, and furthermore, I needed to handle my situation lying in my bed upstairs.

"Pastor Kincade and I are great partners with a best-selling news publication." I winked at her, "Sorry ladies I would chat with you a little more, but I got to get Rylie to the bus stop."

"Mina will you be bringing a date to the fund raiser." Aunt Bae asked.

"Why would I do that Aunt Bae, it's a fund raiser, not a couple's event."

"Well I mean a beautiful young woman like yourself should have a handsome man on her arm. I mean, everyone else will be there with their significant other's I would hate to see you all-alone. That's all."

"Aunt Bae you know me, I'm different. I don't do what others do. I do what I do. One thing I've learned about trying to do what everyone else is doing, you will end up in debt, miserable, and still alone."

I turned to walk up the stairs, but Rylie met me with my phone and car keys in her hand.

"Where did you get my phone?"

"Mom, your room, let's go, I can't be late, I have tests."

"You went into my bedroom?"

"Yes! Why do you sound so surprised, Mom? I always go into your bedroom." Rylie said with a wink.

I stood there about to pee on myself, as I cleared my throat as we walked out the front door. I wanted to pick Rylie apart. "Rylie, I can't remember did I make my bed?"

"Mom I didn't pay much attention at all. Your purse was on the dresser I just walked in your room and went over to your dresser and grabbed it."

"Ok…good girl." I began to breathe again.

Chapter 11... To much is given much is Required...

"Mom are you ready yet?"
"Yes I am sweetie, I've been ready. You have my things ready?"
"Yes, ma'am your make-up bag, your, and your keys."
"Good."
"You look good girl."
"Thanks, Mamadoll. I love you both."
"Mina we love you."
"Love you too. Riley, take care of Mamadoll."
"I will."

I drove off on my way to the fundraiser. I looked in the rearview mirror to see my two favorite people waving me good-byes. Mamadoll couldn't attend this event tonight because her arthritis in her knee was giving her the blues all week and doctor orders said she had to stay off of it. In a way I was glad, I knew it was an event for adults, and people would be drinking, and Mamadoll is not comfortable around that type of atmosphere, and Riley is too young in my opinion. I felt good. I knew the windows of heaven had opened up wide, and I had my hands out to grab them all. I must admit I was a little drained of all the partying and I still had one more to attend and that was on tomorrow, which was Saturday. Kia receiving her award for her foundation, and then church on Sunday. It seems as though it was an event to attend every weekend or something for me to do, or somewhere for me to appear. But, too much is given much is required.

I was greeted then escorted to our table as soon as I walked through the door. The entire city was in attendance once again. I waved and gave many hugs and smiles to unfamiliar faces before reaching my table. This event was held at the very elite Duke Mansion, and it was extremely nice. The chandeliers were shining so bright I needed shades. The silver ware was exquisite, and the décor in the banquet hall was mosaic.

It seem everyone had a significant other on their arm. But I came alone. I sat down at the **SerVant24:7** table which was close to the front stage and very well decorated, and spotlighted.

Ms. Doris joined me shortly after I sat down. She looked beautiful. I ordered a glass of wine, and so did she; we then noticed Kia who walked in alone.

We all were having a really good time dancing, mingling with the crowd. I was enjoying my second maybe third glass of Chardonnay.

I was probably having too much fun. At least forty-five minutes had past, and the fundraiser had yet to start.

"What's going on?" Kia said.

"Why what's wrong?" I said.

"The cameras are going crazy." Ms. Doris said.

"Look its Pastor Kincade and his wife." The waitress said.

"That's why they are going crazy," I said as I sipped on a glass of wine.

Patrick walked in and on his arm was Tish. They wore the exact same colors. She smiled and smiled as she made her way through the crowd, and so did he, smiling, waiving, and laughing with the guest. Not far behind them was none other than Bryce and Zi'lah. They all walked in as if they were the happiest couples on the planet; all four of them. The media that were in attendance had a field day. Flashes were going crazy. I looked around, and the people seem so happy to see them together. I observed Patrick, and he was smiling and laughing with his wedding ring on and they were holding hands. Everyone at the table was quiet. Kia and Doris both looked over at me. I forgot all the NOT'S. Kia changed seats with Doris.

"Mina, remember the truth. You know the truth. And remember what we are here for. It's not about her; it's not about Patrick, it's not about you or me. It's about what we have professionally did for our community."

I exhaled. "Your right Kia. I'm fine. It's our night."

She put a smile on her face, and she looked at me as if she was reminding me to smile. I responded with a big fake smile. Patrick made his way to the table with Tish, still holding hands, and again I couldn't stop noticing he was wearing his wedding ring. That's not a good look. As he approached the table, he was staring at me. I stared back. Tish was smiling with that Miss America smile, only thing missing was her crown. Once they arrived to the table he hugged each one of us as usual, and me a little tighter and closer. He sat down in a chair right next to her. I thought it wouldn't bother me, but of course, it did. I took another deep breath and another sip of my wine. I figured if I had to look at the two of them as this happily married couple all night, I was going to need a little assistance to keep me calm.

"Every one of you look great I must say, and I am glad you all or here tonight. I'm so excited about this award, and it's all because God has placed each and every one of you in my life I could not have did this with-out you guys. Please have a good night and do not pay attention to what you see, but what you know to be true." Patrick said. He then grabbed a glass.

"Let us have a toast." Everyone raised their glasses.

"Patrick, are you drinking tonight? You know how you get when you drink." Tish said as she looked over at me.

"Everyone knows I don't drink Tish. May I continue?"

"Yes, you may." I said as looked over at Tish.

"One more thing, I want to tell each and every one of you…" he looked around the table… (He paused) and looked over at me. "I love you all very much. What we have done with this news publication is unbelievable. I pray for each and every one of you every day, and I only pray we will continue to grow together. If God be for Us."

We all lifted our classes and repeated.

"If God be for Us." And in unison, we all said, "Who can be against us."

Someone touched my shoulder, and it was Aunt Bae along with Bryce and Zi'lah. I stood up and of course, put on my smile. "Aunt Bae you look great."

"Mina you do as always." She turned around in a circle for me. "Look at Zi'lah and Bryce aren't they such a good looking couple."

"If I must say so, they are simply divine together, and Zi'lah I love your dress." The both of them just looked at me.

"Thank you, Mina, hopefully, one day God will send you your own man like he sent me," Zi'lah said. She then walked a little closer over to Patrick.

"Pastor Kincade, you and your lovely wife, look so good together. I hope me and Bryce marriage is as beautiful as you two."

Did God send him to her? I wanted to choke her with that fake cubic zirconia necklace around her neck. I started to toss her a napkin so she could wipe her neck before it started turning green.

"Well thank you so much Zi'lah. Just remember to hold onto him tight and keep him away from those who can't get their own man." Tish said.

"Sweetie you don't have to hold on to anything tight when God gives it to you, because if it's from God, it's yours! There is no second guessing, no confusion, no doubting, and no pretending." I said."

"Mina." Kia said.

Aunt Bae cleared her throat. "I believe we will continue to make our rounds."

I smiled. "You all have fun." I didn't want to go there. I was doing just fine in my own world sipping on my wine. But since *they* sent for me, I went there!

It was silent at our table then before we knew it the mistress of ceremonies begin speaking. They were going to begin raising money, then handing out awards. There were at least six, or seven awards that would be presented before we were up for ours.

The waiters began taking orders for more drinks and dinner was served, and we mingled with one another while we ate. Patrick stood up to mingle along with the other guest. I stood up along with Kia and Ms. Doris, and we all headed to the ladies' room. We all had been there at least an hour and needed a break. I freshened up, and as I was leaving the ladies room Tish walked in, and I ignored her and begin to walk out the door. She immediately walked out the restroom behind me and walking towards me was her father with a few secret service look-a-like men with him wearing ear buds in their ears. I continued to walk with straight tunnel vision and pretended not to see them. He stepped right in front of me I and tried to maneuver around him and continue to walk. He maneuvered as well and stepped in front of me again. I begin to get nervous because I didn't see anyone around. All of these people in attendance and no one else was in the foyer besides me and these blackmailing crooks.

"Excuse me," I said.

"Excuse me." Judge Nash mimicked me.

"I said excuse me." I tried to walk away.

"No need to have an attitude Mina, we're just wanting to tell you how beautiful you look tonight." He then took his old, rusty, crusty pointer finger, kissed it, and began to rub it on my shoulders. I moved my shoulder out of the way.

"Now Mina, don't move away. From what I hear, you like to be licked." He then burst out laughing, along with the other secret service men and Tish. I didn't flinch or smile. I was terrified. I didn't know what they were going to do to me.

"Daddy, don't scare the poor woman. I have a question for her. Mina I was going to ask you, where was your date tonight?" She said sarcastically as they laughed again.

I turned around not one bit concerned with her question, and no matter what is going on around me, I'm still Mina and so is my mouth. I smiled, "Tish my date is the same man I was with on his birthday, and the same man I work with on a daily basis and spend all my week-ends with. He walked in with you, because he had to, that's who my date is."

"Daddy, Mina seems to think Patrick is her man. She is so funny and so deceived." Tish said.

I rolled my eyes up in my head. "Whatever, you will do and say anything at this point to make me think you and Patrick are still married, or still sleeping together."

She laughed real hard loudly. "Do you honestly think sweetie when you leave his home I don't walk in?"

"I talk to him all throughout the night Tish, don't even try it, sweetie."

"You talked to him until one a.m. in the morning. Then he hung up with you. I was laying right there next to him."

I froze and felt sick in my stomach. I yelled. "You are a liar Tish."

"Really? I'm sorry you feel that way, but it seems as though you have been lied to by; your boss, your pastor, and your lover. You have been deceived just like the congregation. And Mina, please don't thank me, but I had to have Jeffery, *our* chef clean up your mess you left on the dining room table one day."

I wanted to drop to the floor. I couldn't believe what my ears were hearing. DAMN! How would she know about the dining room table? How does she know we talked until one? OMG? What have I gotten myself into? What is this? She stood there and continued as I tried to tune her out.

"Mina, Mina, and the cake you bought Patrick was to die for; I mean simply delicious. I love butter cream frosting, and l have to give you credit where credit is due. I thought I was freaky in the bed, but you Mina, you made me step up my A game girlfriend. You made me pull out all the tricks, so I want take all the credit for his smiles these days…thank you Mina, our bedroom life is so much better now since you have joined." She smiled at me.

I lifted my hand up to slap the shi.... off her face, but I quickly remembered I was alone, by myself with no back-up, no homies to help a sister out. Mamadoll didn't raise a fool. I remembered my Not's immediately. You never ever let anyone still your joy and surely don't let them see if they did! She always told me at All times, Not some of the time, you must use Wisdom. I heard the mistress of ceremonies say they were about to take a five-minute break, and then the next award was for a record-breaking news publication. I heard cheers and jeers afar. I was thanking Jesus because I knew he would send me help that being people walking out and this show of would end.

"Tish let me say I apologize." Her eyes immediately were wide open.

"Oh my goodness, thank you so much girl for some good information. I thought you were my enemy. I am so sorry, if I have done anything to hurt you or your family. Patrick spirit is very deceiving, trying to play the both of us, and his congregation, so sad. But I think what's most important here I can see the change in you Tish. Yes ma'am.

I sure can. I mean you are nothing like people said you were in college, or during the run for Miss America." I said.

She looked very confused. "What are you talking about? You know nothing about me."

"I'm sorry Tish, but we haven't had a chance to talk like two real adult women should." I was hoping one of the doors opened quickly so I could run into the banquet hall.

"I heard stories about you as well, just like your father said he heard about me, but I didn't believe a first lady of a mega church or a first lady period would act in such away. No. Not you?" I said sarcastically.

"What are you talking about? You used and misused mistress." She said.

"Tish please, no name calling; we are here to help one another. I was recently informed that you had sex with the all the judges, including women judges to become a runner-up in the Miss America Pageant." I said to myself, *now surely she did not sleep with all the judges, including woman judges to only become a runner-up*, I mean surely you would do all that you did to win, not just to become a runner-up, right? I mean I did what I did with Patrick, and I'm a winner, that's why I am here tonight." I smiled, you could hear a pen drop in the room, and I was praying someone, somebody, anybody would help me. I've talked all this shit, and these men looked like they were going to bury me, at any minute.

She didn't say a word. She turned red as a Strawberry, tomato, cherry, or any other fruit or vegetable you could think of.

"Listen hear little girl you watch your mouth and what you say. You will not speak to my daughter, your first lady in that tone, or that way. Who in the hell do you think you are? Do you think you're going to walk into this city with your holier than thou self and things were going to change overnight? You listen real good, gal, don't know who you think you are and who you think Patrick is, but I will tell you this."

He grabbed my chin with his hand and pushed away. My heart was pounding real hard. I begin breathing hard. I was so scared. I stood there shaking thinking to my all I wanted to do was start a newspaper for Gods people and here I am fighting a blackmailing judge and his daughter. A very well-known judge at that. I only wanted to do what I love to do. Start a newspaper for the people and date my boss and pastor, who is supposed to be single, and all this came with that? Lord, have mercy on me. He wasn't finished he continued.

"What has Patrick told you? Huh? Has he confided in you Mina? Tell me?"

They are afraid of whatever Patrick knows. Very interesting. "I am the mistress remember? Why would he confide in me?"

"Your right? But whatever he has said to you and if he does decide to confide in you," he paused...." You better not ever be repeated or, I can tell you this. You listened real well to me Mina Wright. He walked close to my face and gripped my chin again, along with the Secret Service men, as they walked behind me. "I know you love that Mamadoll. And I also know your daughter is your heart am I right?"

I damn near spat on him. "If you know these things then there is no need to ask me, right?"

"Wrong little girl. First thing is this, Bryce better be on the cover of that newspaper of yours on Monday. I don't want to see Judge Hollis on that cover. Also, I better be featured in that news publication, I mean advertising for Bryce and myself better be on each page.

Or else that precious child of yours will lose another parent. Try us if you want. I will send your ass back to Dallas in a coffin." He stopped speaking. "Poor, poor Riley, she doesn't deserve to lose another parent, and she's so good in school. Make such good grades." He starred at me. "I'm not playing with you. I am DEAD serious."

I could not understand, or comprehend what my ears were hearing. Is he threatening my life? Mamadoll life? I stood there staring at him eye-to-eye and terrified of what he would do to my family. I saw people walking out the banquet hall finally. I walked away calmly, no I damn near ran back to the table to reach my cell phone to call Mason my photographer and for the *SerVant24:7.* He answered.

"Mason, its Mina. Listen to me there's been a change in plans."

"Mina, Mina calm down. I don't have a lot of time what's up. My battery is dead, and of all nights I didn't bring my charger."

"Mason, listen to Me." I saw everyone walking back to the table.

"Mina whoa, what's going on? Is something wrong?" Mason asked.

"Pull the cover photograph right now."

"Do what?"

"Just pull the cover. Put Commissioner Calhoun on the cover, not Judge Hollis."

"Mina I can't. They're already being distributed."

"What? You told me they wouldn't go out until midnight Sunday." I said.

"I'm sorry but there already gone Mina, they went out today earlier than normal because I am going on vacation tomorrow. I'm sorry Mina." Mason said.

225

"Oh shit!" I heard the mistress of ceremonies from a distance say, "Time for our next award. This award will be the first for the next recipients." People began cheering.

My heart was pounding I was so nervous. I felt someone grab my cell phone out my hand and turned around quickly and struck Patrick. "I'm so sorry Patrick; you scared me" I said, panting.

"Mina, what is wrong with you?"

"Dammit, you're what's wrong with me? This is what's wrong with me." I picked his hand up with him wearing his wedding ring. "Your damn pretend wife, or ex-wife, hell I don't know what she is, and her fake ass devil daddy threatened my life and, that's what's wrong. I just wanted to write, to create a news publication for the people. It's like your problems became my problems. I didn't ask for all of this?"

"What? When? Talk to me." Patrick seemed overly surprised. "What happened Mina talk to me baby please."

I heard, this award goes to, **SerVant24:7**. We stood there looking at one another. I was shaking I was so nervous. "I had Judge Hollis put on the cover, not Bryce."

He stood there in disbelief. He backed up but continuously stared at me. He didn't say a word.

He turned and walked in the banquet hall. The flashes from all the cameras were indescribable. Everyone began clapping. The crew was making their way to the stage. I walked behind Patrick and people were clapping, and of course, I didn't see Tish or her father. I saw Bryce and Zi'lah sitting on the front row with smirks on their faces. We made it onto the stage and Patrick grabbed the microphone. I was still dramatized from everything that took place. Kia and Ms. Doris were looking asking me, *where had I been*, I had a blank, confused look on my face and so did Patrick. I was ready to call it quits. I didn't care about the award. I wanted to get home and be with Riley and Mamadoll. Thoughts raced through my head over and over again. I don't know who to trust, what to believe. All I wanted to do is write that's all, that's it! Who do you trust? As soon the thought appeared into my head. I wanted to be excited about my award, but my excitement had vanished. I fought hard to smile as I heard my name being called. I was in an astonishment state. I saw Kia smiling in slow motion? Ms. Doris was clapping. Patrick wasn't clapping or smiling.

"Mina, please speak," Kia said.

I walked slowly to the microphone. Kia grabbed my hand and then raised it high in the air.

"This is the reason the **SerVant24:7** is what it is today. God had given this woman a gift. That gift has touched every one of you and has given all of us, including myself favor from our God, please give her the credit she so rightly deserve."

I remember the crowd went crazy with cheers. Tish walked over and stood next to Patrick, and he grabbed her by the waist. They both looked at me. Bryce and Zi'lah was staring, and next to their table was Judge Nash. He winked at me. I was very emotional and didn't know where to begin.

"Thank you, everyone. I am so grateful for this award to night. I love you all, but most importantly I love God. He is my all and all, he is everything to me. I want to make him happy, not man. I love my family and will go home tonight and share this with them. Thank You."

I walked off the stage, grabbed my purse, and headed out the door and never looked backed. I gave the valet attendant my ticket and my car could not have come quick enough. I hopped in the car to head straight for my house. I flew down the highway going 90 on a 70 mph freeway. Who cares? No one is honest anymore. I saw the light on in the foyer area. I walked slowly into the house. I saw Mamadoll sitting in the living area reading her bible. I was happy to see her but didn't want to talk. I was still dramatized from the threats I heard earlier. I felt I needed to make a decision on my career and I felt like I needed to do it soon.

I knew I had told Kia I would attend the banquet to watch her receive her award. The truth of the matter is, I don't want to attend, and I'm not. Mamadoll never once asked me a question about the night. She wanted to see the award to put it in the credenza. She said she was going to start an award collection for me. I wanted to tell her there was no need because I didn't know if I could pretend any longer like the others. I just wasn't up to acting, and I wanted out! But I didn't say a word. I hugged her, as she hugged me tightly, then I proceeded to bed.

Monday Distribution Day

I had not talked to Kia or Patrick since the fundraiser. I over heard Aunt Bae tell Mamadoll that Kia preached on Sunday in Patrick absence. She said the church was told he and his wife went out of town suddenly. I am over this whole fiasco. I reached over to grab my cell phone and saw I had two missed calls from Kia that morning, and one text message. *Call me please ASAP.* I thought I would wait, I'm sure she wants to know, but after all, I figured she might have questions. Why Judge Hollis is on the front cover and not Bryce, and also why I am not at work this morning, or why didn't I come to church on Sunday? My text message ringer went off again; it was Joshua, my graphics designer. *Please call me I need to speak with you.* Then again, this time it was Ms. Doris,

Good morning Mina, just checking on you call me please. I didn't respond to any of them. I continued to get dress to get Rylie to school on time. She had math project due the next day and figured I would help my child with her project and not focus on **SerVant24:7** for one day.

I walked into the building a quarter till 11. I was supposed to be there at 8 am sharp like the other mornings, but for some reason, I didn't care. I walked straight to my office. I didn't see Ms. Doris at her desk, or Kia anywhere in sight, or Patrick. I closed my door, but to my surprise, it soon opened.

"Good morning," Kia said.

"Good morning," I said.

"I'm sorry did I scare you."

"No." I jumped at the door opening so soon after I closed it. "How are you this morning?" I asked.

"Disturbed Mina," Kia said.

"What's disturbing you?"

"Two things, the fact that you didn't show up to witness me receive my award, you didn't respond to any of my text messages, and also, the cover of **SerVant24:7**. Have you seen it?" Kia said.

"Of course I've seen it, I approved it?" I said.

"Without Patrick knowing I was told." She said.

I cleared my throat. "You know Kia; I don't know what you were told, I did as I believed."

"Well your belief has brought the heat in this office, and this paper. You had no right to go against Patrick's orders. If he told you to do something or asked you, you do it."

"Excuse me, but the last time I remembered my father was deceased."

"But your superior and your boss is alive and well, and he instructed you to put Bryce Calhoun on the cover, no one else, then he instructed you that Judge Nash should have a full page, you didn't include Judge Nash anywhere in this paper. Mina, do you realize what you have done?"

"Yes, I do. I realize I stood up for what I believe in."

"What you believe in? Mina this is business, not belief."

"But for me it is."

"It's not about you? This is bigger than you."

"Kia I will not put a man that is an Atheist on the cover of my Christian newspaper. I won't do it. And I'm not sorry either." I paused. "Kia It surprises me that you, Patrick and this organization, would allow him on the cover," I said.

228

"Mina that is a rumor, simply a rumor. You should have told Patrick what you heard, and then allowed him the chance to tell you what route to go before choosing your own. I know by now you know this is about business. BUSINESS! Nothing more nothing less, it surprises me that you would go against what Patrick told you to do, being that he has been extremely kind to you." She said.

"Excuse me. Kind to me? I didn't want to take it their Kia, but you are out of line. You are the one who is called to be an Evangelist, and you stand here questioning my decision to put an atheist on a Christian publication? Were you called by God Kia, or did you choose yourself?"

There was silence in the room. She didn't speak another word, and I was done talking myself. I turned around and began to work. I soon heard the door slam. I had not received a text, phone call, or any other form of communication from Patrick. I wasn't surprised if this is the way it's going to end whatever Patrick and I had then so be it!

I was tired of trying to figure out why he, and Kia and the other staff members were so afraid of a man to compromise their belief. Josh was still on vacation. Ms. Doris called in sick, and the entire floor was quiet.

I continued to work on the next featured cover of the **SerVant24:7** because this would be the winner, even if it meant Bryce winning another term. Mamadoll text said Naiomi and me had been trying to get in touch with me. I had not spoken with her in maybe a month or two. She knew what was going on in my life, a little, but I never went into details of everything happening. It was the end of the day, and I was ready to wrap things up at the office. It was nearly 5:30, and I was anxious to get home to help Rylie with her Algebra project. I grabbed my briefcase and proceeded out the door. I stopped by the grocery store on my way home to pick up supplies for Rylie's project. She needed a passing grade, and this project was all she needed to help her. I had a good day today. No drama just peace. I was excited about the election and the cover even more after I heard people talking about it in the store and after I noticed **SerVant24:7** was sold out! I made a good choice for the cover I know I did. I will always support my decision. Once I arrived home, I smelled the good cooking smell coming from the foyer.

"Good evening," I said.
"Well hello, there you are home early my dear." She said.
"Yes, I am. I wanted to sit down and have dinner with you two and help Rylie with her project."

"Oh, that's good Mina. She had been really trying to get it together. I'm so glad you are here to help her."

"I am too. She will be fine." I said.

"I know she will. Were you able to speak with Naiomi." She asked.

"No, I am going to sit down and call her tonight."

"Good. I wanted to tell you I love the cover of the **SerVant24:7** this week. One of your finest covers Mina."

"Thank you Mamadoll. I wasn't sure of myself on this one."

"Why not? We need someone new. God does new things?"

"That's true Mamadoll. So true."

"So don't doubt yourself. Judge Hollis belongs on the cover."

"Thank You Mamadoll. Others would have like to see Bryce on the cover, so that makes me even happier to hear you say you liked the cover."

"Forget what others have to say or think. Bryce needs to sit down somewhere. I'm sick and tired of him and his cockiness. It's not of God. He could care less about the people. He can't control his self, so I know he can't help run a city. You know Mina you can work around someone and learn a whole lot about that person." She said.

"Oh do I know," I said. I was also a little surprised at her comments regarding Bryce, but then again I wasn't. Mamadoll had strong spirit of discernment.

"It's time for a new thing Mina, a new thing. God always does something new. Remember when you are a "new" creature in Christ, remember what he says in Isaiah, "behold I do a new thing." Keep allowing God to use you. I'm proud of you and I love you."

"Thank you Mamadoll. I needed to hear that." We sat and had a nice peaceful dinner, with just the three of us. Something we had not done in a while. After dinner, Rylie and I worked on her project until midnight. I continued to work on it after she went to bed. It was finally completed, and I decided to lie down to get me some rest.

Tuesday

It was the next day after distribution, and I still had not heard from Patrick. I wasn't tripping because I knew the decision I made was right. Although my feelings was a little hurt at the realization of he and Kia's behavior regarding the cover, I realized now it's about Business over Belief with those two, but it wasn't for me. I woke up after a peaceful night sleep. It was around 6:45 a.m. I turned the television on while I got ready for work. I knew I had to get Rylie to school early because she wanted to be first to show off her project.

We headed downstairs, and to my surprise, the doorbell rang.

"Good morning Uncle Henry."

"Good morning you see your friend on the news?"

"My friend? What friend?"

"That Evangelist friend of yours. Somebody been keeping secrets but they are out now...ha, ha, ha!"

"What are you talking about Uncle Henry?"

"They say she was shacking, oh I'm sorry, living with a man, or was it a woman. Well anyway, she wasn't married to him or her and was preaching in the pulpit. Lord have mercy I said I knew that church had some secrets."

I walked over and turned the television on immediately. There were commercials and at least ten minutes of stories I didn't want to hear about, and Uncle Henry talking and talking. It was time for me to get Rylie to school and suddenly that story appeared.

"We have breaking news, and if you haven't heard already the very popular and local Evangelist Kia St. James had not been telling her congregation, and followers the truth about her lifestyle. A young man by the name of Myles Monroe came forth and is claiming he and the Evangelist have been living together for two years, although they were not married, and even though she preaches against living together before marriage. The gentleman also said he has never worked, and she has supported him financially with church funds, but what is most disturbing about this story the gentleman claims, Evangelist St James, made him and demanded him to perform sexual acts, with other women, and men, while she watched. The twenty-three year old young man has obtained a lawyer since he has told his story."

"Twenty-three years old!" Mamadoll yelled from the kitchen. "Now she need her forty-five-year-old ass whooped for that," Mamadoll said. "Lord forgive me," she added.

I was tripping. I couldn't believe my ears. This explains why she never invited me over to her house. OMG. I couldn't speak.

"So the so called Evangelist like to watch men and woman. She's a freak. How did I miss hooking up with her all these years she's been around us? Damn, Damn, Damn...ha, ha, ha." Uncle Henry said.

"Stop it Henry," Mamadoll said.

"I have to get to work. Rylie lets go."

"Mina."

"Mamadoll please not now I have to get Rylie to school."

231

I rushed to the car. On the way to taking Rylie to school, on every station, the topic was this Myles Monroe and Kia story. I don't believe it for one second. I just don't. Kia is too anointed. It seems everyone had a comment.

DJ: *If you are just tuning in and haven't heard the very popular Evangelist Kia St James of a Street Called Straight Ministries is said to have been living with a twenty-three year old man and supporting him with church funds for at least two years. But the story even gets better according to the young man she is not only a cougar, but she is fifty shades of freaky...enjoying watching him with other woman and men. Ha, ha, ha, hit me up tell me what you think.*

DJ: *Caller you on the air.*

Woman: *Hi this is Shey from Birmingham; I knew it was something about her. I saw her speak hear about a year ago and that same young man was with her, and they said it was her bodyguard. He was doing more than guarding her body. God is going to get her for this. She has put the church to shame. Shame on her.*

Man: *Hey this is Lonnie out of Virginia I watched her on tv all the time and even paid my tithes to that church faithfully, do you think I get my money back?*

Man: *Hello I am a single twenty-three year old man, Kia call me please I will give you something to watch.*

I turned the radio to the AM station. It was even worse. I pressed the CD button. I looked over at Rylie, and she was staring at me.

"Rylie you can't believe everything you hear. Understand."

"I understand."

"People are innocent until proven guilty."

"Why would he lie on her mama?"

"I don't know sweetheart. People make up things all the time. Money. Success brings on a whole new level of Devils. And people don't want to work for what you have worked for. He probably wanted money or something. But I need to get to work and find out the truth."

We made it to Rylie's school. I jumped out the car to help her with her project. "I know you are nervous but you are going to get an A, so text me and let me know how it goes." I kissed her and off she went.

"Good morning Mina."

"Hey girl," I said to Naiomi.

"Girl, what have the Evangelist done? Lord, have mercy what's going on down there I Charlotte."

"Nai I don't know yet. I am on my way to the office as we speak. This is surprising."

"I'm not surprised. This is why she never allowed you to get close to her."

"You think so?"

"I know so.

"Mina I told you to be careful around those people. Be careful. You knew her in high school. People change. You don't know what a person is doing behind closed doors."

"That's true. I mean if he was younger than her, so what."

"So what is she wasn't ready for the opinions from the church folk. She wasn't ready to lose that position. I guarantee you he is going to sit her down."

"I'll call you later. I am at work now."

I arrived at the church, and it was chaotic. Reporters were all over the streets outside the gates. An employee had to open the gate for me, and after I parked the car, he had to escort me in the building. On the way in the building I saw Patrick's car, but not Kia's. I made my way up the elevator and the first person I see when I stepped out the elevator was Patrick. Our eyes met. "Good morning Patrick, welcome back."

"Good morning Mina. Thank you it's good to be back. Can I see you in my office please?" Patrick asked.

"Of course," I said.

I followed him to his office. On the way, I saw Ms. Doris on the phone at her desk. I spoke to her, but it seems her conversation on the phone was very disturbing, so she didn't speak back. Once inside Patrick office, I saw Kia sitting on the couch. I glanced at her. Her eyes looked to be swollen as if she had been crying for days. She looked away.

"Mina, have a seat. I know by now you have heard the rumors are allegations against Kia."

"Yes, I have. I know they are rumors."

"Well part is, and part isn't. Kia was living with someone, but I'm not going to get into all of that. Anyway, the only person that would have been able to influence Myles to go to the media would have been Bryce or Nash."

"Bryce!"

"Yes, Bryce…. Mina. If you would have did like Patrick told you to do we wouldn't be in this position."

"We? Excuse me are you trying to say it's my fault this young man exposed a lifestyle you preached against?"

"This is my life that is about to be destroyed. I am still human. I am human. It was you alone who decided to put Hollis on the cover, and now he is winning by more than enough votes, and Bryce is losing, and now Bryce is out to destroy us. Patrick's reputation, don't you understand? You are out, way out of your league here! You have destroyed my reputation!

"You destroyed your reputation Kia by living two different ways. You did this." She had a look of anguish, embarrassment, and shame on her face. "If you had not done what you did, Bryce would not have anything to blackmail you with," I said.

She stood up and walked over to me. I stood there and didn't move. Patrick stepped a little closer in between us. "I wonder what you will say when he comes for you. This magazine will not sell another copy if the congregation knew how you screwed and screamed Patrick name all over this building for months and months."

"Kia enough! You are upset. It is not Mina's fault. We need to fix this. We have to meet with the press and give them a statement. This is not the time to point fingers. Not now. "Patrick yelled.

"Just so you both know, I tried to remove Judge Hollis from the cover, but it was too late." I looked over at my purse and briefcase. I didn't want to be here today, and I'm thinking I don't want to be here anymore. Kia walked into my office and closed the door.

"I owe you and apology." She began to speak from her heart, and her heart told me what her mouth couldn't say. Although words were speaking out her mouth, it was evident she had struggled in her very own walk of being an evangelist.

"It was about two years ago I had just begin my journey and entered another phase of my life. I had just answered my calling to become an evangelist. I knew I always wanted to preach the gospel, but I didn't know how to walk away from him. I had just lost daddy, and I was extremely lonely. I was asked to speak at a domestic violence shelter, although, a man has never physically abused me, but I had been mentally. I spoke from my heart, and the Holy Ghost showed up and showed out. I didn't know who I was that night or what I was saying. God begin to speak through me and souls were saved. I had never felt like this and knew then I was to spread God's message. I met Myles that very same night. He was only twenty-one. He had lost his mother was seeking love and guidance. I began counseling him and gave him a job doing minor things around the house like cleaning the pool, and my landscaping. I would cook for him, and the more I spent time with him I became enlightened with him and he with me. I knew I was attracted to him but I thought I was walking under the anointing and my attitude was, *you can't get any of this if you begged me*. I was wrong about him, and I was wrong about me. The more and the harder I tried to avoid the temptation I was only left to realize I was trying to fight my flesh on my own. I used the, *I* syndrome. *I can do this, or I can do that. I was using the scripture, I can do all things through Christ who strengthens me,* and also was reminding myself that Jesus died for my sins, and we don't operate under the law anymore, we now operate under grace. And all of that is very true. But, I also was forgetting I was in a fight every day, a spiritual warfare, and was no longer dealing with a small enemy and his troops, but a commander and chief and his army. He comes to steal, kill, and destroy and I didn't see him coming. I was praying, I was fasting, and I thought I was prayed up, but I was operating in me, and not in God. Before you know it, you're living with a very young man that's not your husband and doing the things you said not to do until your married and things you're preaching against.

Many may believe you are instantly saved and sanctified and filled with the Holy Ghost instantly. That's true I was. But, my flesh wasn't ready to surrender, and the battle began.

I soon forgot this is an everyday fight we fight against spiritual wickedness and the more I avoided Myles, the more he approached me until I surrendered. I wanted to be loved after giving people so much love. I wanted to please him. He began manipulating me, and when I tried to leave him alone, he did what so many people do when you are a local public figure he threatened to go to Patrick and the media. He met Bryce while doing some landscaping at his house. Bryce got the women for him. He would sleep with women in my house and asked me to watch while he had sex with them. There were never men. So I watched him. He would look at me the entire time he had sex with these women. It was like he had so much control over me, and my mind." She stopped. Then she continued.

"Remember I was a babe in Christ and I was still preaching to people telling them you can ask for forgiveness. You can ask forgiveness, and God will forgive you, but God would often take me to the scripture in *Hebrews 10:26* which read. "*If we sin willfully after we have received the truth, there no longer remains sacrifice for sins.*" I wanted out the relationship so bad. He always threatened to tell the media and the congregation. He wasn't good for me. It was as if he was jealous. But, just like Patrick, I was growing so fast in the ministry, and the ministry was blowing up. People were hungry for God's word. They were joining the church, I mean by the thousands. I would often tell Patrick if we weren't ready, then God would not have called us. But, the truth is, Patrick called me. I could speak very well about the gospel, and he saw the way people were drawn to me, but they were drawn to Gods word. I felt so good when I ministered God's word, but I felt like a hypocrite when I walked off that stage. When I accepted the strength to walk away that God had given me, I begin to seek my own place to live, and I told Patrick. While I was living with that man, I told Patrick I would not be on that pulpit preaching. And he no longer allowed me to go on there.

That's why I never preached. He understood without questioning me. I may have preached a few times, but I refused to continue to spread the gospel and live that type of lifestyle knowing I was wrong. God reminded me today, even in my sin, my God showed me grace, amazing grace, and he used you to do it. Myles wanted to destroy me after I paid him to move out and go away. I never gave him church money. I gave him money from my book sales. But, God is always looking out for us Mina even in our sinful nature." A tear fell from her eye as she gazed out the window. "God will give us away to escape, and I found it."

I didn't know what to say, or how to respond to the information I had just received from her. I felt at this time I would just be quiet and listen. You think you know a person, but really and truly you don't. I believe as a Christian sometimes we forget the people who spread the gospel, or still human and sometimes fall short just like we do. I must say at least she didn't want to continue to preach knowing her lifestyle didn't line up with God's word. She continued to talk, I related to her, and her situation. It also explained why she didn't want me to visit her home. Part of me is still in the same boat I floated into Charlotte on. I couldn't point fingers at her. I felt the guilt of what Patrick and I did with one another as well for months.

The door to my office opened. "Kia its time," Patrick said.

The look on Kia's face was a look I would never forget. She began to cry as I quickly grabbed a Kleenex for her to dry her eyes. She refused.

"I need to go clean up myself before I go before the cameras."

"No, you do not. That's exactly what the people need to see." Patrick said.

Whether I agreed with it, or not, I kept quiet. That's Patrick for you, always camera ready. I decided to make my way home shortly after they left for the news station. I knew it would be televised on the evening news and I wanted to hear what Kia would have to say to the people. But then again, I didn't. She needed prayer. The next day it dawned on me that Naiomi was correct, Patrick removed Kia from the pulpit. Over the next few weeks, Kia couldn't go anywhere in public. Her CD's stop selling. Her billboards came down, and her non-profit organization was put on hold. Patrick sent me a text message one night which read, "See why I'm not ready, to tell the truth."

Now Me:

"Mamadoll, Rylie, I'm home," I screamed from the foyer. No answer. "Hello." I heard nothing but a little noise coming from Rylie's room. As approached her room it sounded as if someone was crying. I opened the door and saw Mamadoll rocking a very emotional Rylie.

"What's wrong, what happened?" "What's wrong with my baby?"

"Mina she failed. She failed her Algebra class."

"Whaaattt!" I worked all night on that project."

"You wanna know why?" Mamadoll didn't hesitate.

"Why?" I asked nervously.

She reached in Ryle's backpack and handed me Rylie's Algebra folder. I slowly opened it. There were some photos. They were not just any photos; they were photos of me. Not only me, but Patrick and me. The photos showed me performing oral sex on him in his car. I was speechless. I was embarrassed, ashamed, humiliated, and finally tired, sick and tired. I sat on the bed.

"I'm soooo sorry Rylie and Mamadoll. I will fix it! I promise baby I will fix it."

"Mina, what is going on? Thank God the photos were in her Algebra folder, so when she pulled them out, she went to present her project, she noticed them and wouldn't do it. She didn't want to expose you or embarrass you or herself, so she failed Mina. She didn't do it! She told the teacher she didn't have it. She called me to pick her up. I called the police. The photos were in her backpack and Mina this scares me. This means someone was in our house, our house Mina. This baby is innocent."

She stood up and approached me with anger in her voice. "Mina, I'm not going to play these games. I am Not!" She sat down on the bed and continued to rock Rylie.

I looked over and on the chair, and there was my uncles shot gun. Mamadoll was not playing...and I wasn't either.

I proceeded to walk down the stairs. But that walk came to an abrupt stop.

"I'm sorry Mina, but this has got me very upset." Mamadoll said.

"Mamadoll you have nothing to be sorry about," I said.

"Oh no. I know I don't, but you do." She said.

"Mamadoll what are you talking about. I have just been humiliated in front of my daughter and you. Do you know how I feel? I'm so hurt, I want to hide."

"You are hurt, I'm hurt, and Rylie is hurt. Kia is hurt. Hell everyone is hurt. It's not just about you. I am embarrassed to know that I raised someone who has not healed from one bad relationship but walks into another relationship and think she's going to change them by sleeping with them and in reality became one of them."

"I stood up for what I believed, and I never became one of them Mamadoll."

"You stood up after you saw that something was wrong. That's true. Yes, you did that. But before all that happened, you slept with him, ate with them, smiled for the camera with them, worked with them, was on time for them, created a best-selling news publication for them, won awards for them. Just like your last job in Dallas. Now, look what has happened Mina. Your child was affected."

"I didn't mean for Rylie to be affected. I left Patrick alone." I said in a distress tone.

"No Mina. No!" She screamed. "He left you alone. After you didn't do what he wanted you to do, he left you alone. After you stood up for yourself, he left you alone. You were perfect for him and the business until you went against what he wanted you to do. Hell, you even started pretending with him while he held his wife hand and waived. Ask yourself this, when was the last time he wined and dined you honey. What happen to the late night phone calls and text messages? What happen to the sleepovers on the weekends? The gifts where are they? Actually ask yourself this, since you and Kia were exposed and embarrassed, why haven't anyone told his secret? Huh? Wake up Mina, when will you ever learn how to wait on the lord? When will you stop jumping in and out of relationships, and the bed at every handsome man, with a nice house and a nice car, nice bank account, because they smile at you? You saw how he pretended to be married so you should have kept it strictly business and told that negro to holla at you when he was a divorced man who didn't want to pretend in-front of the public and his congregation. Mina, I thought what happened in Dallas taught you something. We are to learn from our mistakes. God is going to keep putting you through the same test until you pass. It will come in different forms, but it will always be the same lesson until you pass. Repent, and ask the Holy Spirit to help you with your weakness baby. You are getting to old for this shit Mina. Lord, forgive me. Close those legs, Mina. Make him chase after something. Don't be a yes woman all the time. Yes I'll be at your house, yes I'll be at work early, yes I'll spend the weekend with you.

Yes, I'll sit in this section at church, so on and so on. Mina, I have always told you, God first, you second, and you third. Now grab a Band-Aid cover up your wounds and keep it moving... Goodnight."

The very next morning after pleading with Ryle's teacher, and paying off a few of her bills, she agreed to give Rylie a passing grade and also keep her mouth close. I was finally was sick and tired of this and that, secrets, and lies. I didn't know who to believe and frankly, I didn't care. The feelings for Patrick were long gone, and after witnessing the tearful plea from Kia to the public, I still wasn't moved. As a matter of fact, I didn't believe a word she had to say.

     Patrick sent a group text with staff member and asked for us to arrive at work for an important meeting by 9:00 a.m. sharp. I arrived at noon, and I didn't respond to any of his text messages, hell if you really want to know, I deleted them before I could read them. Therefore, I don't know what time the meeting started ☺!

Chapter 12... Secrets Revealed...

Over the course of weeks, the phones were ringing off the hook at the office. The media was going crazy over Kia's apologetic speech of course and the fact that the honorable Judge Hollis was indeed winning. I stepped off the elevator and walked towards the boardroom. I heard voices talking from a distance.

"I believe the people have wanted change for many years now, but they didn't know how to bring about a change in their community. Lack of knowledge is why people perish. They were demanding change, but no one was out there in the neighborhoods demanding people to go and vote, not even myself. I encouraged my members, but I didn't push the issue like I could have. The ***SerVant24:7*** has brought so much positive change to this community. The article Mina wrote on voting rights and what it means to vote was phenomenal, and I believe it pushed people. This news publication had been so influential."

I opened the door, and he stopped talking.

"Good morning Mina I didn't think you were going to join us."

"I'm not. Patrick here is my notice. I am resigning. I will see you in court regarding the ***SerVant24:7*** future."

I walked into my office and slammed the door. I began to pack my belongings. At least twenty minutes past and I didn't hear any more voices.

The door opened and in walked Patrick. "Mina, I know I can't talk you into staying, and I thank you for staying with me this long and giving me what I needed the last few months, it will be over before you know it if you will stay."

"STAY! Are you serious? Summer, fall, and winter has passed, and hell it's almost time for winter again and you want me to stay with everything that's going on around us. The parties, the awards, interviews, secrets, blackmailing photos of us, the rumors about Kia, it's too much, I didn't sign up for this."

"Photos of you and me? What are you talking about?"

"There were photos of me and you that night before you went out of town. Remember in the car? There were in my daughters Algebra folder. Someone had to put them there in the house or in her school. I don't know but she is innocent, and this shit has to end. I am humiliated in front of my daughter, Mamadoll, the teacher?"

"What? Pictures? What teacher? Mina, I can't believe it. Why didn't you tell me?"

"I just did. Because it just happened."

"When?"

"Why? Why Patrick? Does it matter? Are you going to fix it?"

"Teachers saw us who else? Why didn't you tell me about this?"

"Ha! That's all you are concerned about, what people think, what people have to say. Who knows about us? Why should I tell you? Jesus, when will you be true to yourself and stop being so caught up in people? You know what Patrick, if success causes this many problems then I don't want it."

"And sometimes it happens that way, Mina. Success will one day show up, or it will take its time. You have to be ready for it in season, and out of season, at all times. I can say for myself I was blown away these past few months with everything that has occurred. I didn't think the success of a newspaper, me dating you, would bring out so much hatred in an individual, or individuals." He stopped and again we both were quiet.

"What individual would you be speaking about, I don't believe the success of the newspaper is the only problem? Or me and you dating?"

"What do you believe is then Mina? What is causing so much hatred toward and animosity between us? Huh? Tell me please I would like to know."

"You tell me, Patrick. You don't see it? You tell me why once I didn't put an Atheist on a news publication, secrets are exposed, but not all secrets? Why are we being co-hearse into voting for a judge and commissioner, and also blackmailed by people who we know is not for us, or our community, and who don't believe in the God we serve. Patrick, you are a minister! And I understand this is a business, but as a minister, you have been called by God almighty to lead his people to Christ. People are watching you, Patrick, your every move, you are admired, and you don't want people to see your failures, or your flaws. Yes, you are human, but you are equipped to lead, not follow, not be afraid when the wind blows a little, or when it starts sprinkling a little rain. How can you be a witness? You told me no more secrets, but we both know that's far from the truth. How bad is it Patrick? Why is it that Kia and I are humiliated, and you are not exposed? What does the judge have on you? What?"

He became extremely angry and began yelling. "Maybe they have enough on me, Mina, to end everything I fought to keep. There I said it. You happy now…are you happy now?"

He said it. I knew it! I sat down in my seat and folded my arms. I didn't flinch at all, not a mussel.

"Are you happy Patrick?"

241

"What does that mean?" There was a knock at the door. Patrick shouted. "Who is it?"

"Its Ms. Doris may I come in?"

"Ms. Doris, of course. Come in." We both said in unison.

"I'm sorry I didn't mean to disturb you two."

"Ms. Doris, your fine, come in." We both said, again.

"Hi.... I hope I'm not interrupting you two?"

"Of course not." We both said again at the same time again.

"Ms. Doris, how can we help you?" Patrick said.

"I heard some shouting and wanted to see if everything was ok?"

"Everything is fine Ms. Doris. Could you hear us? Could you hear us talkin from outside the door?" Patrick asked.

She hesitated. "Just a little sir."

"Could you hear what we wear saying?" Patrick asked in a nervous voice.

"No, sir. I could only hear voices."

"We are just fine Ms. Doris, thank you for your concern," Patrick said looking at me.

"You are welcome Mr. Kincade. I just wanted to tell you both; I Love the both of you. Mina, please don't leave us. We needed you, and we need you. We all are waiting to see who wins tonight. I'll see you both tomorrow." She smiled and said as she walked out.

I waited for Patrick to continue. He walked out of the office into the main lobby to make sure no one else was around. Everyone was gone home early. Patrick said the past two weeks had been very difficult for Kia to work and not only did she need a break but we all did. It began to drizzle and then the rain fell and from what I could see from a distance on the lobby television Bryce was losing the election...early, but there was still a few more hours left.

Patrick continued. "You and me and the entire ordeal with the talk show, and the situation with Bryce and the judge, and my ex-wife. The pretending, the performance in deceiving people, God's people, and my people, just all of it, and more. I know where all of this started but, it was like I couldn't stop it and now I know I have to stop it. I heard Kia's cry. I finally had the chance to listen to a sermon of hers this morning as I was driving into work. "It's Finally Completed, Now Delete It." I loved when she said when it's over, it's over, and you throw that thing away, recycle it, and don't pick it back up. The past is what she was talking about. She was talking directly to me. I said to myself Kia was on fire. That message blessed me. Anyway back to where I was going with all this. Mina, you have been so heavy on my heart. I missed spending the past few weekends with you, like we often did. Waking up seeing you peacefully sleep, our lunchtime together, and just being around you, a woman. I had to ask myself have I allowed deception, and the opinions of what others would think about me, or what the aftermath would be if I did reveal I was divorced. This deception has kept me from someone so good for me? After years of pastoring to others, encouraging others, praying for others, marrying others, and so on, I finally realized I needed deliverance in an area of my life I didn't even recognize had been there for so long..." He looked all around the room. "I think it's called, fear." I'm going to share something with you because I know the truth will set you free. I'm speaking from my heart right now, and I will never speak of this again, and I pray you want either. I trust you Mina, and you are right about what you said, and the answer to your question is yes they do have something on me."

"PAK it's between you and me, like everything else. I am not a vindictive person. I am not someone who will blackmail you, I am not made that way, and I know you know me better than that. What will I gain from seeing you, and what you have built destroyed? What will I gain from watching what we built, the *SerVant24:7* fall? Patrick, don't go there with me. You either speak now or forever hold your peace." I said.

"Follow me." He said.

I followed him. We walked around the office as he was looking around to confirm if we were in fact alone. We went into his office as he closed the door behind him. He pulled a chair out for me at the table next to his desk. "Have a seat please this is going to take some time." He said.

"I remember growing up all I ever wanted to do was play football, and be just like the great Walter Payton. That's all I would say when people would ask me what I wanted to be in life. It's funny, because my mother would always say that's what you want to be son, but what does God want you to be? Then she would kiss me at the top of my forehead. Even as an adult she would still kiss me right there." He then took his finger and pointed at his forehead. "I loved my mother, and she loved me. She was my heart, and I was hers. You would think my dad would have been jealous, but he wasn't, he loved me the same way. I didn't want for anything. I was so blessed Mina with those two parents. So you can understand why I made every effort my entire life to make them proud of me. My dad always wanted me to play football, but my mom always said God gives us more than one gift, and I would one day share my gifts with the world, but the gift would mean more than me carrying a football in my hand. And boy was she right. She spoke it into existence. She was a praying woman who faith in God was exposed with every trial she went through."

He stopped speaking for a moment and then he blew out a deep long sigh. A teardrop fell from his watery eyes as he began to explain his life long journey as Patrick Allen Kincade and the secrets that have kept a stronghold on him for some time.

"I only wanted to please my parents. If they were not satisfied with my work, or with me, then I wasn't satisfied. I was born in 1967 to Patrick Charles and Mara Ilene-Kincade. I was their first child and would eventually become their only child. My dad came out the wound blessed. His father, my grandfather, was handed over acres of farmland from generations before him. His great -great -great- grandfather was left the land after his slave owner died. He left my great -great- great grandfather everything. This was before 1900, and my family was the richest African American family in the south. My dad went to the best schools and prestigious college. My dad hung with the best of the best back in the 1960's even with all the segregation, riots, blacks being killed, with everything that was going on my dad was so blessed. He had white friends; he was the first minority at his company, which he would eventually become CEO of. Remember this was in the heart of the 60's. My mom was a gorgeous woman. Cocoa complexion, fine hair, she stood about 5'6 and had curves, like yourself." I blushed. "She was a sister indeed. She wasn't as fortunate as my dad was while growing up. Her dad died when she was five years old, and she watched her mother struggle with five other children in the house. She and her brothers and sisters would eventually drop out of school to help my grandmother out around the house. Mom started working at the age of fifteen, and although she didn't have a lot of book sense, she had wisdom over smarts. There is something about a person who knows the real meaning of the word struggle. My mom was more of a survivor than my father and didn't have half the education he had. Mama knew how to open her bible read, fall on her knees, and call on Jesus when problems arise. My dad, on the other hand, knew how to talk his way out of situations with his wallet, or he would write a check to solve the problem. They met when my dad went into a drug store where my mom was working. He had a headache and needed some Tylenol. That was 1966. I guess the rest is history because here I stand 47 years later." He walked over to his refrigerator and grabbed two waters. He then glanced over to the television, which was on. Bryce was losing by one thousand, five hundred votes, and it was three hours until the polls closed. Judge Nash was winning; it was a close race, a very close race. I could see the election was bothering his mood. Three hours left and nearly half the voters haven't gotten off work yet."

He said. Patrick handed me a bottle of water and continued. It was the summer of 1983, and I was a few months shy of my 16th birthday. It was time for this very popular football camp held by the, "who's who" of Charlotte. It was fourteen days long with extensive training for the best football players around the city. It was seven hundred and fifty dollars per person including room and food. Of course, back then that was a lot of money to send a one sixteen year-old to camp for fourteen days at seven hundred and fifty dollars, that's a whole lot of money today, in 2015 for that price. I had attended the camp the prior year and did not enjoy the way I was treated. I was young. My parents had kept me sheltered. Away from racism, well at least they tried. I was the star at the camp, and I scored all the touchdowns, and it was fun, but I was the only black teenage boy there, and the other teenage boys treated me like I was from a different planet. I experienced racism, first hand. I knew racism was relevant in our lives back then, but I had not experienced it this way because I grew up in the same neighborhood and played with the same white children, who fathers worked under my dad. So you know if they were going to mistreat me in any way, their daddy wouldn't have a job any longer. I had two cousins on my mom side of the family, and they moved out of the south to the East coast, and my dad only had one sister on his side of the family, and she didn't have any children. At the camp the guys there wouldn't talk to me, they acted as if I didn't exist off the field. At dinner I ate alone, after dinner none of them would hang out with me, they all played games, watch television, etc. I would stay in my room and read my bible. I enjoyed reading about Jesus, I felt like I was like him in many ways, and I could relate to him, he was often denied by others and persecuted, but he didn't stop, he knew he had a purpose to fulfill. And that's how I have always felt. So I went back every summer. I wasn't going to let another race run me off. This particular summer would be different and one I would never forget. I was so excited. My dad was concerned about me the previous summer and reassured me I would enjoy this summer. He sponsored three teenage boys from the "other side" of Charlotte who parents couldn't afford to send them, and all three were black. Dad said he refused to allow me to experience what he did because I was a blessed black man. That was daddy. He would always pull the wallet, write the check, but sometimes money still doesn't cover the scars you've endured. Anyway, these three guys were the all-around best football players in the state, and they were coming to camp. I was so excited because I knew I wouldn't be alone, but I also knew I would be around my own. It's something about being around your own culture when you are never around them. We all hit it off from the moment I stepped into the room. We were like long lost brothers. God knew what he was doing when he put us four together, and we were the same way on the field. Jeffery was the baddest quarterback out of all the high schools, I was the baddest wide receiver, Matthew was the baddest running back, and Deek was the baddest corner back, we called him Dee-Baby because he was the youngest of the crew, we all were fifteen. So, of course, we won on offense because of the three of us, and then we won on defense also, because Deek intercepted every ball thrown in his direction. We kicked butts every day we played a game against them. We walked around after dinner, had fun, and played games just like they did, and they did not enjoy seeing this. We couldn't understand if they were more upset at the fact that we were winning every game, or the fact we were black and winning, or all of the above. I guess that why I'm so calm when it comes to haters, they are not new to me."

Patrick went on to say, "We would try to talk to the other teenage boys, but the tone they used when they spoke to us was condescending. It was two days before we were to leave camp to go home. 48 hours. One night around nine p.m., we were in our room playing dominoes, eating popcorn, teenage boy stuff, just chilling. We had grown so close to one another in such a short period. There was a knock at the door, which surprised us because no one ever knocked on our door. Jeffery jumped up to answer. It was Dilan. He was a seventeen years–old 272lb. 6'4, white, rich kid, from Myers Park. His dad was the top heart surgeon in the state. He was going to avoid going to college and going straight to the NFL the next year after he graduated. He was the linebacker from the other team. He came every year just as I did. He started acting a fool and cursing at Jeffrey as soon as he opened the door, real rude, and I could only hear him continuously calling him "boy." Dilan was rambling on and on. We didn't like what we were hearing, but we all were raised right by our parents, and we just wanted to get alone with those guys. The calmest, and me being the oldest I stood up and walked over next to Jeffery. I asked Dilan was there a problem, and to my surprise, he had at least six of his teammates standing behind him. I gasped and placed my hand on Jeffery stomach to push him back away from the door. I noticed from Jeffery's body language he was getting real angry with Dilan, and in any moment something was going to happen. I remember asking Dilan, what was the problem? He responded and said several of the teammates belongings were missing and some of their money out of their drawers and luggage, and some very expensive tennis shoes. I was surprised and thought he was coming to warn us. I remember asking, *Are you serious. Did you report this to the coaches and staff?* He responded, *yes we did, and we told them we know one of you niggers took our things.* My brain froze for a minute. I couldn't breathe, or grasp the word he used to refer to us black men as, or the accusations he was making toward us. Before I could say a word, Jeffery, Deek, and Matthew all stood up and lunged towards him, and Dilan and his crew reacted. We all began to argue back and forth. I stood between the both of us, and as I turned to tell Matthew to go downstairs and get one of the coaches before I knew it Dilan hit me so hard on my jaw, I fell to the floor. I was struggling to get up. Everyone begin hitting one another. Punches were coming from everywhere. He jumped on top of me and with every strength I had in me to fight him, I did. We were tossing and turning on the floor, and somehow I got the best of him. I caught my balance and stumbled up. Deek went to hit him, but I stopped him. I saw the others had left the room and it was only Deek, Jeffery, and myself. I tried to tell Dilan to let it go, let's end this, and he was so angry he hit me again. I turned around, and my fist met his jaw. I hit him so hard he stumbled, and stumbled and stumbled and began panting fast, and hid eyes were blood shot red. He was breathing so hard, and he couldn't catch his balance." Patrick hesitated, and his voice began to tremble. "Before he hit the floor his head hit the corner of the window ledge. The ledge corner punctured a nerve in his forehead. He died before the paramedics got there." Patrick put his face in his hand.

"Oh my God Patrick. I...I...I'm so sorry." I grabbed some tissue and wiped his face off for him, but the tears wouldn't leave. They were flowing like a river. He grabbed the tissue and continued.

"Once the police arrived, paramedics, and our parents that was only the beginning. The police arrested not only me but also all four of the black teenage boys. They said witnesses said they saw us stealing from those guys' rooms and I just knew I was going to be ok because it was self- defense, and I knew we didn't steal those items. I was wrong. Dead wrong. We were four black young men, and it was 1983, and we lived in the south, and those were white boys, and Dilan's dad was the finest doctor in Charlotte and Dilan was on his way to the NFL. Our career, our future, our life was over at fifteen years old. I had never in my fifteen years-old witness my parents cry the way they did, until that day. I felt like it was me who should have died. I had killed a man."

"You defended yourself, and it was an accident," I said.

"That's very true Mina, but it took me awhile to realize that myself. My father and mother believed me. They immediately began planning to save me from all of the mess, the turmoil, and the situation, whatever you want to call it. But I didn't see a way out. My mother never stopped believing in God. Her faith never swayed. We all were thrown in juvenile detention until our court date, two days later, where we would appear before a Judge. When word got out around the city about four black men, a fight, and a dead white teenager, no one cared to hear the story or the facts. They wanted us executed right then and there. The media had a field day, and while they were having a field day, my dad immediately obtained a lawyer and begin to handle the situation anyway he could. That meant doing anything he needed to do for me to have freedom. Jeffery, Matthew, and Deek, as well as myself, were all terrified. There were so many threats against our home's, and our parent's and us. We were all hit with a one hundred and fifty thousand dollars bail. When I say all, I do mean all. The judge said Jeffery, Matthew, and Deek were all in the room at the time Dilan fell and did nothing to stop it, according to witness testimonies. The only witnesses were the other teammates, who started the fight in the first place. The judge also stated since none of them, Matthew, Jeffery, and Deek, tried to stop the fight, according to witnesses, they also would be charged with first-degree murder of Dilan, like me. But, when I tell you I had a praying mother who knew who she was, whose she was. She told me from the minute she wiped my tears off my face and said, *Patrick Jesus has already won the battle for you. He came to give you life and life more abundantly, and life you shall have, and your life will not be in a prison cell. You have been chosen by God, and he will use you.* To a teenage boy, that statement was confusing, because I was thinking if Jesus came to give me life, and if God had chosen me, why was I in the situation I was in? My mother said, *Remember there is an adversary who walks around like a roaring lion. You kill the adversary with the word of God.* She turned me around to face the mirror, *I want you to look at yourself and say these three scriptures until you get it deep down in your spirit. I am more than a conquer through Christ Jesus. I can do all things through Christ who strengthens me. If God be for me, who can be against me.* Then she would say, *repeat it again.* I repeated it again. Then she would yell, *repeat it again.* I repeated it again, and again, and again until I begin to say it all day long, every day. Then she would say, *Now believe it?*

"She sounds like someone I know." We both giggled.

"I agree. Mamadoll and my mother should have been sisters. LOL."

"LOL. That's how we have made it this far, by those praying women."

"Yes...Yes...those faithfully praying women. She always knew Mina, what I would be in life."

There was a knock on the door. "I thought we were locked in," I said.

"We are, but we have to eat my dear." I glanced at the television, Rylie had texted me, I Believe Uncle Bryce is losing the race, with a sad face. I responded, Sorry to hear that, with a straight face.

"I have us some Chinese food here. I ordered your favorite."

"Good! I was starving. Great timing PAK."

"Anything for my baby." He then squeezed my hand. "Shall I continue?"

"You sure can, and my ears are ready to listen."

"My dad bailed me out of jail. He helped the parents of the other three as much as he could, but they weren't able to come up with the remainder of the money, so they had to stay in there until the trial. Those were the most humbling months leading up to my trial in my entire life, and that's when I begin to seek God and build my relationship with him. I had just turned sixteen years old. When teenage boys were chasing girls and playing sports, I was on my knees praying for myself and the other guys sitting in a cell. I felt so bad when I thought of them sitting in a jail cell for something they didn't do. I would have fail in a deep depression if I didn't have a praying mom, or if I didn't remember my scriptures, and learned how to pray for myself. I couldn't go anywhere in public, because of the media, and all the hatred from people that came along with the trial. It was almost unbearable. I believe in my waiting period before the trial I finished the entire bible. My dad knew people, who knew people in the judicial system and this is one time his wallet showed up. Daddy was always a mover and shaker. He never accepted the word, no, or the word maybe! If he was told No, he found the answer Yes from somewhere else. While dad was moving and shaking and making deals to seal my freedom, mom was praying and praising to help my future."

Evening had approached quickly. He stopped for a minute.

"Take your time Patrick, I'm in no hurry."

He began to eat a little, and we both watched the election come to an end.

"It seems Bryce lost the election. Judge Hollis is very happy I'm sure. He deserved it." I said.

"Yes, Judge Hollis did. Time was up for Bryce just like the others. The community voted, and Bryce got his answer."

I began to clean off the desk. And he started again.

"My dad moved us ninety minutes from Charlotte to Advance, away from all the madness. *The State of North Carolina verses Patrick Allen Kincade*, I remember that sound of the judge voice, like it was yesterday. The trial went on only one week before I was found not guilty. My mom yelled Hallelujah! And my dad screamed Hell Yeah! But, my boys, unfortunately, were found guilty. They weren't charged with Dilan's accidental death, but they were charged with robbery for the missing items and were each sentenced to twelve years in prison. I was sick in my stomach and saddened. I cried as if it was I going to prison because part of me was. I kept in touch with my boys through letters and regular visits." He stopped then wiped a tear from his eye.

"I watched them become men in there, and I become a football star and one of the biggest pastoral leaders of our generation. Their parents hated my dad. They felt he could have done more to help their boys. Believe me, my dad tried, but it was the 1980's, we were black boys, and a white boy was dead, there was little my dad could do. I went on through the years watching my boys grow up as men in the judicial system. They were my heroes. Their strength and will to survive, and one day be an upstanding citizen in this community was impressive. I went on to high school, and of course, I made the varsity team my freshmen year. I played with passion because on the inside I was fueled by anger. I think every time I saw a white boy approach me to knock me down on the field, I gave every bit of me to knock him to his knees on that field. I was determined to make a difference in my race, and in my life. I wanted to be more than an athlete, and I knew God was taking me far beyond football. I went on to graduate from high school and gained a scholarship to none other than Duke University. I was popular from my first day on the field. Mama always kept me grounded. No matter how much success I obtained, mama always said your purpose in life is to serve God. It is favor from God, but don't you get the big head, God loves humbleness. So I stayed humble. She and God kept me that way. I was everywhere on the campus, but I always s felt different, like I didn't belong there. It wasn't the color of my skin. I was growing in Christ. I was always invited to parties but never went. I often times were studying or in my room reading my bible. I never really had a relationship with anyone but maybe one girlfriend in high school. She went back to her hometown after I took her to the prom and after graduation. I loved women. I loved women. I wasn't a player or anything like that. I just wanted one woman, the woman. I finally met her my sophomore year. My name was all over the campus and the newspapers by now because of football. I was always approached my girls, always, but I believe I was still traumatized by what happened to me years prior, but the people weren't. It's as if the situation was erased. Gone. And as for me, I stayed away from anything that looked like it would get me in trouble. If that meant staying away from girls. I stayed away. I decided to finally attend a fraternity party one Friday night. It was crazy how the cheerleaders and their friends, friend, were all on me. If you name it, I could have it, or them. I was approached by this girl; by the name of Daniell Childs. She was maybe eight out of ten sister's that attended the university. She was fine too. I'm talking Nia Long, boy's n the hood fine. Cocoa complexion, hips, little waist, nice hairstyle, and she stood about 5'4. Oh yes I was all over her, and she was all over me. We slow danced to Michael Jackson's, *Lady in My life*. I didn't know how to dance, she taught me. We left the party and went back to my dorm room. I gave her me, and I got a lot of her. I was in love after that. She was the second woman I had ever been with. We begin to date. My first girlfriend and my first heartbreak. We dated the whole school year, she went back home the summer and she began to date her high school sweetheart. She got pregnant and didn't return to school. I begin my junior year single, and heartbroken. I concentrated on football and my bible. While people were partying, I wanted to study my bible. I was definitely different. Even back then everyone would call me preacher. I would laugh, but truth be told they were right. I was always in my dorm room, locked up studying. I had this finance class which kept my in the library, or begging for someone to tutor me. There was this one particular young lady who would often flirt with me everywhere I went. She would pop up out of nowhere in the library, cafeteria, after my games, parties, I mean everywhere. She would practically throw *it* at me. Her name was Tish Nash. I wasn't afraid of her. I was cautious. I really wasn't interested in dating her; I sort of still had the memory of what happened that summer, so therefore I stayed with my own. One night everyone was going to a movie then out to dinner with their girlfriends. Tish asked me to join them but I declined the offer. I stayed in my dorm room feeling lonely and empty. The only real friends UI had were gone, and the girl that I first loved had gotten pregnant. I remember I grabbed a beer out of my bag that my roommate brought me and drank it. It was good so I drank me another one. I was drunk before I could drink another one. Tish had called me all night, maybe two or three times to see if I was going to join them. I had turned her down hoping she would give up but she was so persistent and after two beers I decided to allow her up in my room. The rest is history and we became girlfriend and boyfriend after that."

"Did you fall in love with her?" I asked.

"You know the funny thing is, I never fell in love with her, but I loved her." That's where all this animosity, and jealousy of you and me both is coming from. I dated her for many years. She was always there for me. I mean everything I did; everywhere I went she was always there. I didn't know our parents, well our father's, knew one another, but they did and knew one another very well. They wanted us together.

They played golf together, socialized with the people, went to the same community functions, everything. I was approaching my last year in college, and an NFL team had already had their eye on me and wanted me to sign. I tried to separate myself from Tish then and also her family, but my father was determined for me to be with her. My father would always tell me she was the best thing for me, and her dad this, and her dad that. My mom and I were not feeling her that way to spend the rest of my life. I wanted a change, and also I was still growing in Christ but my dad was so eager for us to be together. I wanted to make my dad happy, so I continued to see her. I also wanted my mom and dad to stop fighting over the situation. I saw what the enemy was trying to do in their marriage through my problem, and I couldn't allow that. I began to minister to others and myself about faith, and seeking God, and leaning not to your own understand. I was at the top of my NFL career, and they were pressuring me to marry her, our dads. I loved her and never allowed her to see any different from me, but I knew I had a calling on my life, and I never felt she was going to be part of it, but I was wrong. If anyone had a plan, it was her father and mine."

"I'm, a little confused Patrick, are you saying her father and your father made you two marry?"

"No, what I'm saying is her father, and my father made me stay in the marriage. I went on to the NFL, and I was still obsessed with ministering to people. No matter how big of the contract I wanted to preach. Even more so once I became a professional athlete. I believe it was because what I saw money and fame do to some people. I had a passion to preach and always wanted to have my church one-day. Years went by, and I ended up retiring from the NFL, and I had a game plan to start a ministry. I had never seen my mother so happy. But, she would often ask me was I ready. I always said yes because I felt like I was. I still was single, and I had dated here and there when I was in the league, but Tish was always around. She never dated anyone else she was like obsessed with me and of course my status, and financial stability."

"I'm sure she was," I added with sarcasm.

"LOL. Yeah, well, I felt like the right thing to do was to marry her. Again I loved her, and I was starting my ministry and I most importantly I was tired of fornicating. So we married around the same time I was building the ministry. My mom was happy I did what was right, but she never felt that Tish was the one for me, and she also didn't like the fact she wasn't black, but she accepted my decision. One year into the marriage and six months into the ministry. It was small back then, but it was growing at a rapid speed. I mean I never expected so much favor from God or people. I was overtaken with members, I mean

Sunday after Sunday; non-stop people were joining. I didn't have anyone, but the boys helping me. I didn't have an associate pastor, no one. The choir was members who joined. The choir director was a musician my father knew. It was crazy. It was just fast paced. I had spent so much time in building the ministry I wasn't even paying attention to the fact that I was a husband. I sort of put all my time in the ministry, not sort of I did. I gave it my all because it was my call. Tish wasn't feeling it. She was feeling the notoriety and the attention, but she wasn't feeling the fact that the ministry had all my attention. I put God first and his kingdom. She felt we were lacking in our relationship, and couldn't understand how I could counsel others on marriage and not take care of my own. Then after time passed, she became pregnant. After being together off and on for eleven years and only being married for two, we were now going to become parents. Our parents were ecstatic! My mom was so happy. I was also. I tried not to give the church all my attention, but it was hard. I blew up! I mean I couldn't go anywhere in public. People loved the anointing on me, and everywhere I went I was wanted. People wanted my autograph. They wanted to take pictures. I had to do interviews, travel. It was chaotic. But God kept me doing what I was called to do. Tish was pregnant, and the pregnancy brought about a lot of rumors. There was a time period when we went without sex, so I was curious about the rumors."

My mouth dropped to my feet. Where was he going with this?

"Pasha was born healthy and beautiful. Curly dark hair, light brown skin. She was a beauty. I had to know if the rumor was true, but that would be hard because my dad continually told me to ignore the rumors. *Son you have the life your mother and I worked so hard for. You are a famous preacher, beautiful wife, new baby, number one congregation, money in the bank, and people love you. You have it all son, don't mess it up. Smile and let it go. The people like what they see. Remember your mother and I went through a lot for you to become successful.* That's what he always told me. Same speech. I never told my mom about the rumors because I couldn't bare the disappointment it would bring her. We were all in a good place with the success of the ministry, so I let it go, in a way. I remembered this one particular brother always hanging around. He and Tish became friends. He was a, nobody, and he wanted to be somebody. He worked in the ministry for a short period of time until I fired him. You know him Mina, its Bryce."

I damn near peed on myself. I couldn't speak or talk.

"One sunny day it was only me and Pasha at home. She was only three months old. I had to babysit her while Tish and her friends were out shopping. I was too noticeable around the city to have a DNA test performed at the hospital, and the press would have had a field day with the story, and I did not need that. I still had to protect what God had anointed me to build, that was my ministry, and I was just at the top of my game. I knew doctors, nurses, etc. So I had my doctor come to my home. He put that swab right in Pasha's mouth, and the rumors became truth right in that bathroom that day."

I stood up slowly in disbelief. "Are you telling me what I think you're telling me?" he didn't answer right away.

"It was confirmed. Pasha was not mine. She was Bryce Calhoun, daughter." Tears were streaming down his face. He would never look at me.

"Patrick. Jesus. I'm so sorry…OMG…PAK." I was at a loss for words and began to cry myself. I could feel his pain. "The incident as a teenager, and now this?"

"When I first heard the rumors of those two, he still worked in our ministry. I had my people gather every cup, spoon, straw any object he touched with his mouth was placed in a Ziploc bag awaiting to be tested. I could have avoided knowing, but Mina I had listened and did everything my father asked me to do." He hit the desk with his fist and shouted. "I mean everything. Because I felt like I owed him for keeping me from going to jail. I didn't know who Tish truly was until it was brought to the surface. I had never felt so betrayed in my life. I had a spirit of murder all over me, and I wanted to kill Tish. I immediately wanted her out of my house and away from me, immediately. I filed for divorce and immediately her dad was notified. He and my dad acted as if I was wrong. That's when my dad confessed what I had always discerned anyway. My dad owed Judge Nash one, and it was time for him to use that "one". See Mina Judge Nash was the Judge on the case when I was arrested. He covered up certain things from the press; he silenced the press, and was paid very well by my dad. He kept the press off me. The man has and will always do whatever he wants to do in this community. He made sure I was found innocent. He and my dad negotiated and negotiated until my dad got what he wanted. Although the jury wanted to bury in the prison, my dad sold himself to the devil for me. So this time he needed my dad, and he was not going to allow his daughter look bad in the public, or loose a lifestyle that people dreamed of. No sir. She was the beautiful daughter, mother, and wife and that's the way the public would forever see her as long as he lived, and there was not going to be a divorce, because the black voters and the black community enjoyed seeing that Judge Nash wasn't prejudice, and Judge Nash wasn't an atheist, not when his son-in-law was black and a pastor. And if I did divorce her, he was going to re-open the case back from 1983, because there was new evidence, new witnesses and from the witnesses mouth Dilan death was not an accident. Nash said to my father and me. I agreed to do whatever I needed to do to keep my name clean. I was afraid. So I agreed and pretended, only if I could divorce her. They weren't getting everything they wanted. I didn't want her near me. I forgave her, but I wanted her to stay away from my house, my life, my everything." He turned around. "You understand now Mina, why I was pretending?"

"Words cannot express or explain how sorry I am Patrick. If I judged you, I'm sorry. So this is how they control you?" I said.

"That's exactly how. Control. Have you ever met anyone who had absolutely no belief or fear in God, no fear at all, and they used what they had on one of Gods children because you hate the light, which lived in me? And I hated the fact that my dad made a deal with the devil that would be a part of my life forever. I wished I would have been found guilty and sent to prison, because although I have lived on the outside, I have never been free from what happened that summer. I can't break free from the chains that have me bound, and my daddy is not even hear anymore, but yet I'm still paying the price for an accidental death that was not my fault."

I walked over to take hold of his hand. He continued to look out the window. "Patrick baby, why didn't you give Bryce, or Nash what they wanted? Why didn't you just put them on the **SerVant** cover? Why did you allow me to not include them if it was this deep? Why PAK? If I would have known all this maybe I would have put them on the cover."

He turned around and faced me. "Mina I wasn't going to allow you to do that. It's not you. It's not your thing. You stand for what you believe in. Maybe that's what I needed to see. **SerVant24:7** stands for something, Servants of Christ, and his people. His people. Nash is an Atheist. It was time. Time for me to take control and say enough is enough! Time for me to face that fear, and if it took God using you and you walking into my life and showing me what I have been missing in a woman, or in life, or to take a good look at myself, then I am thankful for that. There is a purpose behind everything. I had to bear this cross for so many years. If it took you not knowing the truth and doing what needed to be done, then I needed that. If you had known all the details, they would have continued to have control, because we would have put them on the cover, and Bryce would have won. I needed a reality check of who I was, and who I am in Christ."

"And If Bryce would have won the election, and if we would have put him on the cover then they would feel like they still controlled you, and now me."

"Exactly. That's all the enemy wants, is control. That's why so many people fall victim to his strategy, power, money, lust, greed, titles, so on, and so on. We live in a world surrounded by what you have, and how much you have this is what people are impressed by. People seem as if they don't have integrity anymore and I don't want to be that type of person. All of these are tactics used by the enemy to keep people in bondage. The bible told us in Timothy that men would become lovers of themselves and lovers of money."

"They couldn't control you with money, because you've had it all your life."

"That's correct! They used my weakness which was my dad, besides blackmailing me."

"Unbelievable. So does Bryce know about…Pasha?" That was so hard for me to ask.

He exhaled. "Yes and he saw it as an opportunity, he like pretending, because it's in his nature, and could care less about Pasha."

"What? What kind of man would allow someone else to raise their child, or pretend it's their child? Well, now I think about what I've just asked, we are talking about Bryce Calhoun."

"Bryce took advantage of it. That's how he became county commissioner."

"I should have known. I knew it was something." I said.

"He had no political knowledge or history. He partied all the time and slept around with whatever looked decent. His father and mother paid all his bills because he couldn't keep a job. He was offered a deal to become something in the community, and he ran with it and has been running ever since. If he kept his mouth closed, he acquired a label, a name for himself, another one of Nash puppets. They are all over the city, and I was once a part of that team. There I was ashamed, disappointed, upset, humiliated in marriage on one hand, and on the other hand, I was the #1 pastor in the city admired by many, with ten thousand members in my congregation, and a #1 best-selling book on every book store shelf, *Living a Guilt Free Life*. But, I learned so much from this trail, this giant, this mountain that refused to move in my life. This is why all success is not always good success. It brings out the best, and the worst in people." He said.

"You don't have to be ashamed. You were protecting yourself from a past situation, and you obeyed your fathers' request. If you are speaking of your marriage, Patrick she made the decision to do what she did. We have the freedom of choice, to be faithful and work at our marriage, or to cheat on our spouse and seek what we are lacking from somewhere else. Her dad did what he did because his daughter would have looked so bad to people, not only the congregation. Don't you feel better now you have released that heavy burden and told someone?"

"Yes Mina. The truth will set you free. Whatever happens at this point happens. I am confident now as I was reading my bible last night God spoke to me from *Isaiah 54:4, Do not fear, for you will not be ashamed. Neither be disgraced, for you will not be put to shame.*" When God says something twice, it's a done deal."

"So it's a done deal? I have a question for you? Well, two."

"Ask my dear, and I will tell you." He said smiling.

"Did Tish ever deny who Pasha's father was? What happened when she finally was revealed?"

"It's funny you asked me that. Even with the proof in front of her face, she denied ever sleeping with Bryce. Then when she did finally admit to it after all the evidence was brought forward, she blamed me, of course. She said I was never there for her and I loved the church more than her, and it was all about the church."

"Of course she did Patrick. It's easier to put the blame on the other person. Have you forgiven yourself?"

"I just forgave myself recently for pretending to be married and deceiving people. I know that God knows our intentions, and I know I gave my best effort to be truthful. Next question dear."

"LOL, whatever happen to Jeffery, Deek, and Matthew?"

"Deek is director of my band, remember the band on the yacht and the organist at church. He also works the security system along with Matthew, who is also my driver, and of course, you've met Jeffery."

"I did. Jeffery?"

"My personal chef."

"Oh my goodness yes, yes, Jeffery."

"Remember your personal assistant?" He said as he winked at me.

"LOL. Of course, I remember Jeff. You didn't tell me it was your birthday that weekend. Jeffery went out for me and purchased a beautiful cake." We both were quiet. "I'll never forget that week-end. I had such a beautiful time with you that week-end."

"I can't wait to have those type of weekends every day and more permanent." He cleared his throat then smiled at me. "You feel me?"

I shook my head yes that I understood every word he was saying.

"If you feel me then tell me what I need to do Mina. Tell me baby girl."

"I need for you to be honest with yourself about me and you, honest about this entire situation regarding you and your ex, and the congregation. Are you ready to face those giants in your life? Are you ready for the consequences that will follow behind the truth? Are you PAK?"

"Mina I can't answer your question at this very moment. What I will say is every piece of information I just gave you was the truth and from my heart, but you cannot change the way I handle the situation no matter how you preach, teach, lead, guide or anything else used to persuade a person's decision in his situation."

"Patrick I was never trying to persuade you! I...I thought you were telling me what you told me because you were ready for a change. I assumed..." he quickly interrupted.

"You assumed. That's you. I never told you I was going to do anything. You and I both have experienced a lot of negative reaction in this relationship, but we stayed down with one another. I know you didn't want to see me wearing a wedding ring. I know you didn't want to see my ex on my arm at those parties, and also know that it seem deceitful to you, but it is what it is, it's going to be whatever it's going to be until I'm ready sweetheart. When I'm ready, not you, understand?" He said with an aggressive tone.

"Oh, I understand. You are not ready, because you don't know what the Judge will do. Where is your faith in God Patrick? Huh? Where is your faith? What about all the talk about, "The truth will set you free" What about that comment?"

"I have faith, and I told you the truth. Mina you know sometimes you come across as hypocritical. You really do. And I'm not judging you at all, I listen to you and I'm thinking this woman make love to me on tables, in the shower, but I'm at fault because I haven't told my church that I'm divorced? I don't understand you or your theory of what is right or what is wrong?"

"Hypocritical! I'm not a sheep feeding God's flock as I've said to you before. There is a difference. Here we go again, back and forth. But, I blame myself, because I operated in the flesh, and here I am trying to preach to you about being a preacher and teaching one thing and doing another. I am a witness and yes we all fall short, all of us. To be quite honest Patrick, this isn't me. Never was. Never will be. It's never ending, never ceasing drama with your ex, secrets, lies, black mailing, and only God knows who's married to who for real, and who's not. We are supposed to be; you know what never mind. I have done enough talking about this situation. "

"So...what are you trying to say Mina? Just say it. I told you the truth. I didn't hold back. I told you absolutely everything, now is your time. Here's the red carpet... walk it out Mina."

"I decided to take a different route this time. I thought you knew Mr. Kincade. I like to skip the red carpet because I don't enjoy pretending to be happy for the cameras, and I'm really miserable on the inside. My two weeks' notice still stands. Goodnight Patrick. Take care of yourself and thank you for everything. I'll be in touch regarding the **SerVant**."

Chapter 13...1 Step Closer to the End...

In earlier news today the infamous Pastor Patrick Allan Kincade announced, he will be holding a press conference during his Sunday morning service in a few weeks. There have been rumors that he will be going into politics after the loss of county commissioner Bryce Calhoun. We will keep you posted on the actual date of the press conference. Or, will he and his lovely wife announce the renewing of their wedding vowels? Also, speaking of former commissioner Bryce Calhoun he has released a statement saying that he planning on starting a ministry of his own. We will all sit back to see how that plays out. Well last but surely not least what will Mina Wright do with all that talent, since she has left **Servant24:7?** *Everyone is asking what happened and why did she leave? She won nearly every award and invented a very receptive news publication. She declined to comment when we reached out to her. Rumors have been all over the web and town that Pastor Kincade is no longer giving her those private sermon services...LOL. We will have to sit back and see what happens with his story to. LOL But we wish her well.*

"Ha, ha, ha...I mimicked that messy reporter laugh. I nearly hit the car, which sat in front of me as I stalled on the freeway searching for my exit. I wasn't sure if I was surprised at what she said about me, or after I heard the reporter speak on Bryce opening a ministry. The only thing I could do was shaking my head. I'm not surprised at all, the devil knows the word also, and I'm quite sure he will have nothing but women as members. LOL. I haven't heard much regarding he or Zi'lah's wedding. He had virtually disappeared and she had also since the election. It had been 3 months since he lost and since I had decided to make very heart breaking decision. I felt I had built the **SerVant24:7**, and to be quite honest I did. God gave me a gift and I used it. My position there was like a relationship, that had gone sour, and therefore I had to leave. The **SerVant24:7** and my influence was greatly appreciated by many and they couldn't understand why. Although, I gave them plenty of notice I was avoided until my last day. Kia was devastated along with the rest of the crew, and Patrick was distraught. He was so upset with me he has yet to speak to me since I left his office that election day. He didn't give me a hug, didn't say good-bye have a nice life, see you later, nice knowing you, nothing. Some former employees told me that, even though I was no longer an employee my office is still the same as I left it. Roses are still delivered freshly in a vase with "M" engraved in the glass, and my coffee is brewed freshly daily. Ms. Doris place the items on the desk like I'm coming into work. I miss them so much; I cried the entire way home on my last day of work. You know you build a relationship with your co-workers because you are with them eight to ten hours, if not more. I had to take a chance, again, and make a decision to protect my family and me. Mamadoll was very suspicious at the rumors from the media, and the ones fed to her from Aunt Bae and Bryce, along with Zi'lah. She knew about Patrick and me; but the rumors were exaggerated endlessly.

The fact that I had received flat tires on my Porsche after the day of the election although, and after the photo incident, it disturbed her because the toy cop sits right at the entrance gate of the community, and didn't see a thing. I thought that was enough but, my laptop was hacked and someone tried to transfer money from my account to another one. After a lengthy investigation from the bank, I was informed there was nothing they could do. I changed banks along with changing everything else. The suspicious phone calls on the house phone did not help either. Patricks' burden and issues with the greedy, controlling in-laws had become my issues as well, so I had to leave those issues where they began, with him. I also decided to stop attending, *A Street called Straight Ministries*, but I continued to watch online.

Mamadoll never asked me why I was leaving **SerVant24:7**. She didn't know how deep the situation with Patrick was. She cried and shared her concerns with me. She told me it was a decision I had to make and so, therefore, she chose to stay out of it! That was fine with me. She also said something's, or better left unsaid. She knew whatever the reason was for me making a change, there had to be a problem, or I would not have ever left. Even she knew that. Four months had past, and I had a strong desire to get back to work. I missed writing and going into the office every day. I missed all of those employees at the **SerVant**. I read issue after issue. I thought to myself. We really had something.

I had been offered many opportunities to begin another news publication once word got around town that I was no longer with **SerVant**, I declined them all at first. I had networked and networked during the duration while working with **SerVant24:7** and the love was still there for it, and had not left. It was my first baby. I did respond to a few interviews via email, and other options thrown my way, but never committed to any of them. After further consideration and the fact I was beginning to be bored with nothing to do but shop, I begin responding to some offers. One invitation in particular, which caught my eye, was from a local businessman by the name of Ethan Walden. He owned Wall-to-Wall publishing company and wanted to meet with me for lunch to talk about some options regarding starting up a magazine. I accepted the invitation, because I was curious and I'm always looking for new business adventures. I acquired the Patrick spirit. Before we met I decided to do a little research on him. I don't need any more surprises. I met him on a Tuesday evening at a very chic restaurant.

I liked his profile and the history of his company so I was very interested to hear what he had to offer. I finally came to my exit. This was a restaurant I had never been to before, secluded on Daniels Island. I had the car valet because my Jimmy Choos had already started eating away and my big toe, the price we woman pay to look cute. I slowly walked in to the restaurant and noticed no one else was there. They opened at eleven o'clock and it was 11:03. This seemed a little strange to me, and after all I had seen and been through I wasn't going to scream Hello any more. I turned to walk back outside and then all of a sudden a hostess appeared out of nowhere.

"Hello, Mina Wright, correct?"

"That's me. I am here to meet Ethan Walden."

"Yes, ma'am I know. He will be here at 11:15, he is just leaving another appointment, and with traffic, it is taking him a little longer. Please follow me. I have a table prepared for you."

"Sure, thank you."

She then walked me to the very back of the restaurant. She brought out my favorite bottle of wine, Chardonnay of course. How she knew I have no idea. She then brought over a bouquet of flowers and a box of chocolates. I was a little confused by the flowers and the chocolates. She then poured me a glass of wine.

"Thank you! I'm flattered, who is this from?" I laughed a little nervous.

"Mr. Walden madam."

"Oh! Thank you." I was surprised and confused and didn't quite understand what he was doing, but I continued to accept the gifts and sip on my wine. I guess he was maybe trying to take the approach Patrick did?" I let out a long sigh, and I was ready to go at this point. I'm tired of the bribing method, really tired. I looked through my phone a few times, and text Naiomi back. I told her what was happening and her response was, listen to him, pray, and give him an answer at a later date. ☺

I heard footsteps approaching my table, and I immediately looked up. Walking towards me was a well-dressed, tall, muscular, Caucasian gentleman. His dirty blond haircut lay low and matched well with his tanned smooth skin. I smiled a little as he made his way to my table.

"Mina Wright, how are you?" He asked as he extended his hand for me to shake it. I stood up immediately to greet him as well.

"I'm doing well, let me guess, Ethan Walden."

"You guessed right. Sorry, I'm late, traffic is becoming a headache around this city."

"Tell me about it. It's ok, I've only been here a few minutes prior to you arriving."

"Wonderful. Wonderful. How's the wine Ms. Wright?"

I smiled before I responded. "The wine is wonderful, and the wine is my favorite. How did you know?"

"Know what?" He asked confused.

I cleared my throat. "Never mind let's get down to business, the real purpose for this lunch."

"Is that the reason for this lunch?"

"That's the only reason I could think of."

"Sense of humor. I like that in a woman." He then looked at me up and down slowly with his eyes like an edible arrangement. I continued to talk about the reason I was there.

"In your email Mr. Walden, you stated you wanted to start a magazine, but you didn't state what kind of magazine. What type of magazine would you be interested in starting?"

The waitress walked over to take our orders, and he didn't answer right away.

"Can you please bring me a coke with a shot of vodka inside?" he asked her.

"Vodka inside your coke? I have never had that one. I usually do sprite and vodka."

"That's a good combo as well. But I prefer dark sodas with a shot of light added to it. I like the color dark, dark chocolate, dark coffees, with a little cream inside. I like the taste of cream on my tongue. Do you like cream on your tongue Mina?" He licked his lips and asked.

He's a freak. He is sitting here flirting with me. I almost answered, but I refuse to play this game again and open this door the devil is a lie.

"Mr. Walden let's keep this lunch about business please."

"'I'm sorry Mina your right, strictly business. I apologize."

"No need to apologize…just don't do it again."

As he smiled, he went on to say, "I understand, and I will turn *him* down." He then glanced down at his trousers.

"Back to the purpose of this lunch Mr. Walden."

"Oh yes, yes, yes. Mina what you did with the **SerVant24:7** was wonderful. When I first took a look at the publication, I was taken back. I was so impressed with the layout, the design, the articles, and the fact that it was a religious publication, was the icing on the cake. You did an outstanding job, and that's why I want you… I'm sorry that's why I would like for you to help my company and me out. And sorry, my initial comment came out the wrong way."

He is on a role. "I understand what you were trying to say. Thank you for the compliment, but of course, it wasn't all me, as I've said many times before. May I ask you, what kind of magazine are you interested in?"

"I'm glad you asked that. What I want to do is not what you did with the **SerVant**...perse. I want to do a religious magazine similar with the same flavor as the **SerVant**."

Interesting. "Are you a religious man Mr. Walden?"

"I knew you would ask me that question. I am not a religious man, but I am a believer in Jesus Christ and know he died for me. I don't like to call it religion because religion has manmade rules. God gave us commandments to follow, and the number 1 commandment was to love him, and I do, and that's all people need to know. That's how I run my company, and that's how I run my life."

"And that's all I need to know. So what is the plan for the magazine?"

"My plan is to have a monthly publication and website. I like money, so I want it geared towards money topics. I know people want to believe money is the route to all-evil, and it is if you let take over you. But I'm speaking of teaching those that are religious, or in church, or whatever you choose to call, or however you see it, on how to invest their money wisely. Yes we know, as believers, we should, and are to pay our tithes and offerings, but once you have received your blessing for your obedience, don't they need to know how and where to invest their financial blessing wisely? You follow me, Ms. Wright?"

"I see where you are going, Mr. Walden. So you want a financial, religious type of magazine."

"Yes, and I want both pastors and spiritual leaders from not only Charlotte to share their experience and advice with other believers on ways to invest their blessings, but those from cities and other states around as well."

"Mm.... I see where you are going with this, and to be quite honest with you, I like it. So you want the magazines based on spiritual leader investors and where they put their money, and they invest it such as real estate, time-shares, stocks, bonds, profit sharing opening businesses, etc. Not just how to buy a house but how to own a house."

"Yes. Yes. That's it! Mina, you got it! I knew you would. You are a sharp woman. They were right." He got a little excited.

"Who are they?"

"Mina...Mina.... they are everyone around town who knows your work. That's who they are. That's all. No need to be defensive."

"Excuse me I am very cautious...when it comes to my work."

"As you should be. Protect your gift Mina work hard, and then start living."

"And what will I get in return for creating you a best-selling magazine?"

"I like your confidence. Well, you will receive a nice compensation. The magazine will sell at $5.99 a copy, and you will receive $1.00 per every issue sold, and you will, of course, receive credentials on all that you do, and..."

"There is an *and* to it."

"Yes. If you can create the name for it, I will write you a bonus check before we end this luncheon for ten thousand."

"Mr. Walden money doesn't move me. It's the love for writing, creating, and wanting to help others."

"Twenty thousand, before we leave today."

"Mr. Walden, it doesn't work that way. I need time to think..."

"Twenty-five thousand before she brings the check."

"You have a deal."

"But, do I have a name?"

"The lunch isn't over yet Mr. Walden."

We both laughed at the top of our voices as he poured himself a glass of wine.

"I like not only your looks, but your brain is very attractive as well. Let's toast."

"What are we toasting to?"

"Good question what are you two toasting to?" A voice came from out of nowhere and asks.

"Patrick?"

"Mina."

"Wha.... What a surprise to see you. What are you doing here?

"I had reservations, and when I pulled into the parking lot I thought that was your Porsha parked outside but wasn't sure, then I heard voices laughing extremely loud, and I knew I recognized that voice.

"How are you, Patrick?"

"I was just about to ask you the same thing. I'm well thank you, and you?"

"I'm doing well." Quiet is always awkward.

"Patrick I'm sorry, this is Ethan Walden."

Ethan extended his hand. "Mr. Kincade very nice to meet you."

Patrick was cordial, not polite, but cordial. "Mr. Walden very nice to meet you." Patrick put his hand on his chin like he was thinking. "Where do I know that name from? Walden?"

265

Ethan smiled. "Wall to Wall Publishing Mr. Kincade."

"Yes. Yes. I knew I heard the name from somewhere. Are you two doing business together?"

I straightened up in my chair. "Patrick I believe that's a little personal and private. Don't you think?

"It was just a question Mina."

"Patrick are you ready?" A very young woman approached him and said as she touched his shoulder. I saw the look on Ethan's face. He was smiling like a reporter of a tabloid magazine. She was a tall black woman, maybe 6'1, a lean, and model look. Patrick seemed startled.

"I will be a few more minutes and I then I will be over shortly I'm just finishing up some business here. Go ahead and have a seat with the others."

"Kia wanted me to see where you were?"

"Kia is here?" I asked.

"Why yes she is Mina." Patrick seemed a little nervous as he responded.

"Well tell her I said hello." I then turned to the young woman. "Better yet, I'm sorry, I didn't get your name sweetie."

"My name is Nina, and you look very familiar."

I let out a sarcastic laugh after hearing her name. "I'm Mina."

"Mina! Mina Wright? OMG. I am a huge fan. And boy, I've heard, I have some big shoes to fill."

"Do you? I'm sorry. What do you mean by that?"

Clearing his throat, "Mina she is our new editor and chief at **SerVant24:7**. We are here to celebrate."

"Wow, Patrick! You are something else." I said with a look of concern.

"You had Mina, and now you have Nina, what a coincidence Mr. Kincade," Ethan chimed in to say.

"I do believe it is a coincidence Mr. Walden, only because we love and miss Mina so much." He then rubbed my shoulder slowly.

Ethan stopped smiling, and I start feeling a little awkward at Patrick's behavior.

"Well just so you know Wall to Wall Publishing now have Mina, so we are celebrating as well." Ethan looked over at me with a smirk on his face.

I don't think Patrick was ready for that. He was quiet. I reached for my purse; now it was time to leave.

"Wait, wait, wait a minute. Mi…" Patrick stuttered as if he was stunned and couldn't find the correct words to say.

"If you're asking if she is going to work for us, the answer is yes," Ethan said.

"She can answer for herself." Patrick looked at Ethan and said.

"Congratulations Mina. Don't tell me, are you writing a book?" Nina asked.

Then suddenly appeared Kia before I could answer. "Patrick what is taking you two so long? I thought you two ran off on another one of your rendezvous…LOL," No one laughed but her. She then noticed me sitting at the table. "Mina? I didn't see you see sitting there how are you?"

I didn't move. I didn't smile. Did she say rendezvous? This Mutha Fu… as for her she hasn't once tried to call me, to see how I was doing. "I'm great Kia, and yourself."

"I can't complain."

"Me either." It was quiet, and they all stood there and didn't attempt to walk over to their table.

Ethan was smiling and looking at them; then he looked over at me, then he would look at them then back at me.

"Um, excuse me ma'am, we need the check please," I said to the waitress.

"Are you ready to go Mina? Please, let's have more wine, my dear." He then rubbed my hand. I thought Patrick was going to jump out of his clothes if he straightened his tie one more time.

"I guess we could stay a little longer," I said.

"Why not. I'm free today, and you're free today. I'm single, and you're single. And we need to celebrate." Ethan said.

Boy is he enjoying this segment of messy.com. And why will they not go back to their table?

"I'm sorry, I didn't catch your name?" Kia asked.

Before I could respond, Patrick did it for me, while he starred at me gritting his teeth. "That's Ethan Walden Kia, of Wall-to-Wall Publishing."

"Oh very nice. I've heard of you before. So what are you two doing, writing a book together?"

"That is what I would like to know?" Patrick said. "What are you two doing together?"

"The same thing you two are doing together…ha, ha, ha," I said.

"Actually Mina is going to be the Creative Director, Editor and Chief of our new religious magazine."

I do believe Patrick world stopped spinning at that point.

"You are doing what?" Kia asked.

"A magazine for them," I said.

"Oh wow! Good for you. What will it be about?" Nina asked.

"It will be strictly educating believers on how to maintain the blessings you obtain from the heavenly father. More like an investment magazine from pastors and spiritual leaders, and how to make money and save money. More than just buying cars and having a five year car note, or buying a house and having a thirty year mortgage, but how do I make it a twenty year mortgage, then rent the house out, while I purchase two more and pay those off. And how to make that five-year car note into a three-year car note? How to own your blessings, not rent them, own them. It's yours, you ask for it, he gave it to you, now watch it grow, and watch it increase."

They all were silent. Maybe they will make their way back to their tables now.

"I love her. I knew she was the one. WHEW! YES!" Ethan said in a smiling voice.

"I'm sure you do Mr. Waldo," Patrick said.

"It's Walden, Mr. Kincade," Ethan said.

"What's the name?" Patrick asked.

"What's the name of what Patrick?" I asked

"You know of what Mina?"

Ethan stopped smiling, and I felt like Tupac, all eyes were on me. I cleared my throat and noticed they were all not going to move until I gave them a name. I've told them this much, so what the hell.

"Tenfold Magazine. That's the name of it." I smiled nervously at Ethan, and he smiled back. Patrick stepped back in disbelief. I stood up. "I think we should be leaving now. It was good to see you all."

As we walked out the restaurant, I skipped speaking to the rest of the crew. Ethan was not far behind me. I handed my key to the valet. Ethan walked up beside me. "How did you come up with the name that quick?"

It's a gift. Now, may I please have my bonus check?" Ethan smiled and handed me over the check.

"I'll see you in two weeks."

"No, Mina please let's meet before then," Ethan said.

"Call me. Perhaps I'll see what I can do." I said.

"I will." He then walked over to me and grabbed my hand. I pulled back from him.

"Like I said before Mr. Walden, let's keep it professional."

He smiled. "Of course, of course."

It only took me about two weeks to finish the first issue of the new magazine *Tenfold*. The investors who put money behind this project were watching the **SerVant** numbers, and I cannot lie after all that I had gone through to make it successful, I was also. It was still doing very well and selling at the same rate. And I was like a proud mama still happy for the success, because it was still owned by me. Patrick had yet to sign his paperwork, and I had offered him an amount to keep the name, but he didn't respond. I was not ready to sign over my rights, and no one knew but Patrick and me. But, I did have to give it a little competition. I wasn't scared this time like I was when I started the **SerVant**. I had grown and learned the hard way that this was business, not pleasure. I took all the emotion out of it, and that helped. I didn't have to work as hard either, because it seems the gift of writing and creating ad manifest itself. Creating had become quite natural for me. Ethan had lots and lots of money to put up, and he did just that.

From the color, the texture, the layout of the magazine everything was simply eye catching. The magazine was to debut this upcoming Sunday on shelves in three different states. Instead of hosting a launching party we decided to have a press conference with the unveiling. We announced and invited reporters, gossip columnist, and radio personalities from all over the three states. And of course many spiritual leaders and pastors, and politicians. Ethan had also paid a few news stations to talk about the release more and more. With all the hype surrounding me and Patrick secret, unknown what to make of it relationship, and also his hiring someone new with a name so similar to mine, we gave the media exactly what they wanted. Not to mention the fact I created the **SerVant** and then left with no one knowing why helped the debut as well. I was seen around town with Ethan more and more. The media followed us more than usual and begin rumors about him and me secretly dating. Some said I left Patrick for him, and I made sure they had plenty of photos of me seen smiling and laughing on every picture that appeared in every newspaper or on the newsstands. I felt good finally about my decision of leaving **SerVant**. I'm evolving and growing. I now own not one but two news publications, a bi-weekly, and a monthly both name sakes mine, to name a few. The press conference was the Saturday before Patrick's big press conference, and his announcement at the eleven o'clock A.M service.

"Hello," answering the phone as I headed into my new office.

"Why did you do that? Why?" Patrick asked.

"Whatever happened to how are you, my dear? And why did I do what? I'm sorry or you sure you're calling Mina or Nina?

"Mina, now you know I don't play games, and I've dialed this number a many of times. I know who I'm calling."

"I can't tell with the unknown question you're asking, can you please make yourself clear."

He let out a long sigh. "Like I asked. Why did you do that Mina? Huh? Why did you name this new magazine the name we were going to name our new magazine? Remember? You and I thought of that name together. I know you are still upset about some things that have happened, but Mina to take it this far? Really? Sweetie, it's not that serious to me."

"I don't know what you are talking about."

"Well let me remind you." He began shouting. "You and I were laying in my bed after you had just rode this big black horse. You rolled over and lay there for a minute to catch your breath. I asked you were you ready for round two and you said not yet...and we begin talking about starting another news publication, possibly a magazine."

I interrupted him..."Patrick you don't sound like a pastor right now. Hello is this Pastor Kincade, hello?"

"Ha, ha, ha. I see you want to play Mina, I don't care what, or who, I sound like to you right now. All I know is, I created that name. It's mine, not yours and you weren't permitted to use it."

"*SerVant24:7* I created. Were you permitted to continue using it?"

He was silent. "Mina." He paused. "You don't want to do this baby. You're an amateur sweetie. You can't handle what is out here. They will eat you up and swallow you, Mina."

"You've been with me Patrick, I can handle whatever ball is thrown to me, and they may get swallowed."

"You think you can handle whatever ball is thrown to you? You are in denial Mina. You are delusional and disconnected with reality if you think you can handle this. Do you really want to go there?"

"I'll take my chance," I said.

"You know what, I'm done talking. It's whatever at this point Mina."

"Then it's whatever."

The phone call ended, and I couldn't believe how I handled it. I was proud of myself on one hand and on the other hand part of me didn't like what I had become, or the negative emotion toward Patrick. It was as if part of me wanted to see Patrick fall, for deceiving people, and me. But, the Christ that lives in me reminded me that I have skeletons as well, and someone forgave me.

It was a few days prior to the press conference. I had diligently put forth extra time and effort into this project, more so than the **SerVant.** I wanted a successful magazine, and I was determined to have a successful magazine. I was walking into the building to meet with Ethan prior to the unveiling of *Tenfold*.

"Mina, welcome."

"Thank you. Sorry, I'm running late I had a phone call to take care of."

"I notice you were on the phone from my window. Who were you talking with?"

"Excuse me! I don't think that's any of your business Mr. Walden."

"My apologies, I can be a little nosey at times." He said with laughter in his voice

"Shall we start the meeting?"

"Yes, we should."

"I called this meeting today between you and me, because what the others think really doesn't matter to me. I speaking of the other writers, editors, and the design editing team. But, I wanted to let you know first that we have changed the date for the unveiling of *Tenfold*. Instead of the unveiling being televised Monday morning, I've decided to have it televised on Sunday at eleven A.M."

"Sunday!" I said surprisingly. "Why would you want to hold it on a Sunday?" That is the same day as Patrick's big announcement. I wanted to hear the announcement. Damn it! Why would he change the date?

"What's the problem, Mina?" I guess I was in deep thought longer than I realized.

"I was sitting here wondering why you would unveil a religious, financial magazine on a Sunday, while church services are going on. We need to sell the magazine."

"My goal is to sell the magazine, but that is not my main focus."

"I thought the focus was not only to help people, or believers, with their finances, but to sell the magazine. We have not done any marketing and we have not promoted the magazine enough; in my opinion, to gain readers, we haven't done anything Ethan. If our focus is on helping believers and as I said this is a time when they are at church then how will it sell?"

"I never asked you for your opinion, Mina. And I'm not sure if this is about the magazine or the date of the unveiling." He stopped speaking and began pacing the floor. I didn't respond right away. I listened to see where he was going with this.

"Is it the fact that you will not be able to hear Mr. Kincade's, I'm sorry Pastor Kincade's announcement? Is that why you are a little agitated?"

"Who said I was agitated?" I said quickly. "And who said I cared about an announcement that has nothing to do with me?"

"Are you sure it has nothing to do with you? Weren't you two an item Mina? I mean everyone knew."

I stood up and almost allowed that comment to get to me. But, I would always remember my Not's. Not today or any day will allow me to entertain his comment.

"Ethan my private life should not be your concern. This is business, and I prefer to talk about business, not whom you think I was once an item with. Like I mentioned before, it doesn't make any sense to have a magazine unveiling on a Sunday that gears towards believers, we need to sell."

"Mina all of what you are saying maybe true, but quite honestly I really don't care about selling. This is a magazine that will sell itself. You will see Mina. I have the best of the best working behind the scenes. I'm not some pastor trying to sell to a community. I am a businessman who will sell to several communities abroad. As I stated we will go live Sunday at eleven A.M., and that is final. Please dress to impress. No clothes are allowed if they look like you are going to church. This is not church Mina. I'll see you Sunday."

"I know how to dress. And you know Ethan you have mentioned Patrick name one too many times in this conversation. Why are you so concerned with him?"

"I'm confused Mina. I don't know what you are speaking of?"

"Well let me remind you. You mentioned you heard we were an item an then you made the comment, *'I'm not some pastor,'* and for you not to know him, but know of him, that's a little surprising to me."

"Mina, he is our competition baby. Wake-up sweetheart. Everyone plays to win, and after you win, you want to continue winning, you know that."

"You're right Ethan, and I love winning."

"Don't, we all."

"Yes we do. Until Sunday Ethan, have a great weekend." I turned to walk away.

What the hell is all this about? He was throwing Patrick name around, and pastor this and pastor that. This is more than just about a magazine. This is far more than just selling. Damn what secret is his ass holding hostage? What is really going on? And who holds an unveiling of a magazine on a Sunday, when you are trying to sell a new magazine. I refuse to be in any more mess. I have two days before the unveiling. I'm feeling like part of what Patrick was saying was true, but I wouldn't dare let him know that. I can walk away at any time from this and my spirit is telling me maybe I should.

"Mina, can you I see you for a second?" Mamadoll asked as I walked in the house.

"Yes ma'am, whew that smells good. What are you cooking?"

"Oh, you know just throwing something together. How is the new job coming along?"

"It's coming along. The unveiling of the cover will be on Sunday."

"On Sunday?"

"Yes ma'am. Ethan changed the date on me. I thought it was going to be televised on Monday."

"Why would he do that?"

"I don't know Mamadoll. I asked him, but he would never give me a complete answer."

"I'm not in the publishing business, and even I know that you don't hold something like what you two or doing on a Sunday. Tell me Mina, do you really know him well?"

"Well enough to publish a magazine. I don't know any of his personal business. Why do you ask?"

"Well with everything that went on Mina, I have kept my mouth closed and ignored a lot of what I've heard your Aunt Bae talk about and other people. But, this rumor about you leaving the church for this white man, and rumors of you sleeping with the pastor, is too much for me Mina. I have had enough. It makes you look bad, and me too."

"I thought you didn't gossip Mamadoll?" She stood up and walked real slow, and stopped right at my back. I could feel her breath on my neck. I just knew she was about to literally slap it.

"Turn around and look at me, Mina." I turned around slowly with my hands in guard.

"Don't you dare use that kinda tone with me, Mina Wright? First of all, I do not gossip and will never gossip. I tell the truth. I tell what I know, and what my eyes have seen. Your tires were slashed, your computer was hacked, you decided to change jobs all of a sudden from a newspaper you prayed for and received, you changed churches; that's not gossip, which means something is wrong. I never said one word. You and Zi'lah don't speak to one another, you don't talk to Kia, and you want even try to talk to your Aunt Bae. Mina what's the problem? What happen? What went on between you and Pastor Kincade? You were so fired up about the job, and a year later you give it all up. You walked away…honey that's not like you, what made you walked away from your dream?"

273

"Mamadoll you wouldn't be able to handle everything I'm going through, or everything that went down with the position I held, or between Pastor Kincade."

"It looks very bad Mina. It really does. Aunt Bae said at the salon, they were saying mean and hateful things regarding you and Pastor Kincade and his wife, and Bryce, just a bunch of mess. I have ignored the rumors I've heard, I mean I have put them away in the trash, but this has got to stop. This makes you look bad."

"Look!" I yelled. "I am so tired of everyone worried about a look. What about the truth?"

"What about the truth Mina? That's what I want to know, the truth. I feel like as your aunt I have that right. Mina, you have a child. You are placing yourself in the public eye as being a sort of home wrecker."

"Oh is that what it look like Mamadoll? Did you concern yourself with the look when your sister got married five times? Where you concern with the look when you volunteered at the center with Bryce who has slept with half the women in this city, and they were married? I wonder, Mamadoll?" My heart stopped beating at the look she gave me. I always thought looks could kill me and I was right. I was looking at death right in the face after I glanced at Mamadoll fist gripping tighter and tighter. I could envision her fist on my jaw and me in the operation room trying to get my jaw repaired, but it wasn't repairable.

Mamadoll let out a long and laugh and I laughed back.

"Mina, I love the woman you have become. I love how you are protecting yourself, defending yourself. I like it."

"You do?"

"Yes, I do... But not with me little girl." She said sternly with a mean, very mean look in her eye and teeth grinding.

I stopped laughing, and so did she. We both stared at one another for a minute.

"Mamadoll there are certain things I can't talk to you about and don't feel comfortable doing. And I know you want to know what happened, but I'm not ready to talk. When I'm ready to talk, I will, trust me."

She was silent. She walked over to the living area and sat on the couch. She then turned on the television to watch the five o'clock news like she often did. I walked over and sat quietly next to her, because as a mother I know she was only concerned about me, because she loves me.

We are interrupting our normal news program to bring to you a press conference called by the well-loved, influential, admired Pastor Patrick Kincade of Street called Straight Ministries, where he has begun to speak to a crowd of reporters amongst others who are anxious to here this big announcement. We now join the program in progress.

Mamadoll and I looked at one another in shock. I couldn't believe he was having a press conference earlier than the date he originally scheduled. It was Friday evening, not Sunday morning service. He dropped the bomb on everyone. *Patrick, what are you up to?*

"Turn it up Mamadoll, turn it up please," I shouted because truth be told, I wanted to hear, what needed to be said by him.

"Calm down child, please"

"Okay, okay."

He walked to the podium slowly with the look of a tall melting chocolate ice cream dream bar ready to be licked. I missed him. I had to stop lying to myself and admit that I wanted to wrap my legs around him and give my...

"Mina?"

"Oh! Yes ma'am."

"Mina, what is wrong with you?"

"What are you talking about Mamadoll?"

"Child, I called your name twice can you hear?"

"You did? What did you say?"

"I said turn up the volume on the surround sound?"

"I'm sorry. Where's the remote?"

"Turn your eyes toward your lap…, and that's your answer."

I grabbed the remote from my lap and turned the volume up.

He started to speak, but hesitated and then cleared his throat. He's nervous. I know him. He was alone with no one else with him.

"Hello everyone and thank you for attending this press conference on such short notice. I called you all hear today to make an announcement that I have been holding on the inside of me for some time now. I am not the Pastor you all have viewed me as. Well, let me say I am not the trustworthy Pastor that many of you have thought I was. I am a Pastor, but I'm also a human being who forgot who I was, and whose I was. But, If any of you know our Lord and Savior Jesus Christ, he will always put something in your life, like an event, storm, situation, or a person to remind you that you are his, and no matter what you do his grace is sufficient, and his mercy endures forever. But I didn't come to preach today, but when I think about what God has brought me through and his goodness my soullllll cry's out Hallelujah!" He stopped, briefly…"I really don't know why I have been so afraid…of them…"

He stopped speaking again. I know this must be hard on him.

Take your time Pastor Kincade. Someone yelled form the crowd of reporters. He wiped his eyes, and I wished I were there to wipe them also.

"God put someone in my life; someone who wouldn't put up with deception, lies, or pretending. Someone who knew that there is no, in-between, when you're living for God and have accepted a calling to lead his people."

Mamadoll and I looked at one surprisingly. We both had a look on our faces wondering where Patrick was going with this.

"And she was right. I want to let each, and every one of you hear today know that I am divorced from Tish Kincade, and have been for some time now. I want to say I am genuinely sorry for pretending to be someone I'm not, but something I preached and encouraged people, and married couples to be. I am ashamed of my actions, I am guilty of my actions, but although all of this may be true, I want every member of as Street Called Straight Ministries to know I love you and I am truly sorry for deceiving you all in any kind of way. I ask for your forgiveness, and I want you to know I did this ignorantly and in unbelief that my father could see me through and bring me out of the situation, I was in for many years. But, I stand here today to tell every one of my enemies I am not afraid of your faces anymore and if God be for me who can be against me! Thank You, and may God continue to bless and keep You!

The reporter speaks: *You just heard Patrick Kincade big announcement that he was in fact divorced. I am surprised myself, but I suppose, all those rumors were true. He just admitted to pretending to be married, and he wasn't. What happens now with his ministry? Will he loose many of his members? I mean you trust someone to bring the word of God and to find out they have deceived you? What would you do? Many people have taken to Facebook and Twitter to post comments. What will happen to the* **Servant24:7**, *and was the "she" he referred to in his speech, Mina Wright? What do you think? Post your opinion on our website at….*

Mamadoll pressed the off button on the remote. We both sat on the couch quietly.

"Lord have mercy, they cannot talk about that man, without mentioning your name. I'm so sick and tired of them doing that. You have a child. They're, just about tearing a person down. I dislike those reporters and that's why I have to pray for them." Mamadoll said.

276

Me, myself, and I, were still in disbelief at Patrick's speech. I was surprised he went forth and told the truth. My cell phone went off. I answered it, as I walked to the kitchen. "Hello there, stranger?" I said
"Surprise! How you like that?" Patrick asked.
"I liked it."
"I'll be watching yours on Sunday. Goodbye."
He then hung up the phone. I laughed out loud to myself and thought, what is he up to? I then walked back to the living area.
"Who was that, Pastor Kincade?"
"Wha? Wha? What made you think that?"
"Mina I'm not crazy. I'm old that's true, I may not have a Facebook page, or twitter, or that gram thing, all that's true, but I have a wisdom thing and wisdom tell me you leaving your news publication amongst other things made that man wake up and recognize he better get it together with God and with you."
"I know you're right Mamadoll." Aunt Bae walked in the house and said.
"How did you get in here?"
"I opened the door." Aunt Bae said.
"It was lock."
"I have a key; this is my sister house."
"And mine's too Aunt Bae."
"You don't need to have attitude Mina, and I want to know what you did to Patrick Kincade that he would risk losing those m's?"
"Those m's! Huh?"
"Yeah, money, ministry and members" Aunt Bae said with a smile in her voice.
"Aunt Bae please, I haven't did anything."
"Child, please. I was only asking because I would like some excitement to wake my husband up at night so he will stop going to sleep on me."
"Really? He's eighty-five years old, and that's just nasty. Well Aunt Bae I wish I could help you, but I can't. Pastor Kincade was my boss and pastor."
"Mm...Okay, okay...I see you want to keep it a secret. It's all-good. It seems like that's what you all do over there at the church."
"Aunt Bae that's not nice and…. I am no longer at that church, you know that."
"I was only teasing you, honey. I know you don't attend the church any longer. I have decided to not attend also anymore after what I heard today."
"He's human Aunt Bae."

"I know Mina…and you are too."

She let out a loud laugh. I wonder does she tease Bryce like this.

"How are wedding plans coming for Bryce and Zi'lah. I haven't heard from either of them in a long time."

She grew silent. "They are both fine I assume, but I haven't seen Zi'lah in about a month, and Bryce is doing Bryce as usual."

"Isn't he trying to be a pastor?"

"Mina to tell you the truth I don't know what Bryce is going to do next. All I could do is pray for him."

Isn't it funny she can't remember anything about Bryce? "Well if you do see either one of them, I would like to give the both of them an invitation to the unveiling of my new magazine."

"A new magazine?"

"You didn't know?"

"No, I didn't. Mina, you are everywhere. I mean one minute you're at the **SerVant24:7** and the next minute you are doing something else. I'm not mad at you at all girl."

"Thanks and I would say this…I believe you should always seek other ways to use your gift. If the opportunity presents itself, go for it." I handed her the invitations.

"I heard that. I will pass the invitations on to them both."

"I would love to see them both and you too."

"Oh Mina I wish I could, but I can't miss church."

I knew she was going to say that. "Of course you can pick up a copy when you're out and about on Monday."

"I sure will. Mina, I have a question dear, why did you leave the Servant?"

I hesitated at her answering her question. "Who said I left?"

"Ha, ha, you're something else…" she said.

"Ha, ha, you are to Aunt Bae."

I left her and Mamadoll in the living area and headed to the patio with my glass of Nay Nay. I returned Naiomi's call immediately, because I know she wanted to talk about Patrick's announcement.

"Yes BFF, you rang?"

"Yes I did girlfriend I saw the big announcement, and I must say I can't believe he did it."

"I'm surprise to girl and at the same time wondering where he is going with all this, but who knows."

"Well I thought about that as well, and I wanted to make sure that you still own the **SerVant24:7** right?"

"Yes, I do. I'm not giving that up, and he isn't either."

"How are you going to do this Mina? How are you going to be part of two magazines that compete with one another sweetie? Have you thought this through?"

"It's a little late for that question now Naiomi. I will be fine."

"I know you will BFF. Please be careful Mina. It's just so much going on, and I don't want anything to happen to you. Rylie needs you here. I'm praying for you girl."

"And I need for you too. It will work itself out. I know it will."

"We'll talk tomorrow." She said.

"Until tomorrow my friend," I said.

We both hung up the phone.

Sunday 11:00 AM

I smiled for the non-stop cameras flashing in my face. I have been down this road before, and I really wasn't as excited as I was when the **SerVant24:7** launched. Maybe it's because the first is always the best and most memorable; first love, first kiss, first time, first job, first kid, first husband, so on and so on. I believe I had so much on my mind that I couldn't give Tenfold the attention it needed, and I must be honest I had Patrick to work with every day and Ethan is not as an eye candy, and not really my type of male figure, but he has opened the door for me to advance to another level in this news publication industry. I noticed Ethan once I walked in the pressroom first. There were a lot of businessmen there as well as numerous reporters from all over the surrounding states. I hope they don't think I'm speaking because I'm not. I told Ethan I would stand beside him only. I walked over and slowly took the cover off for the unveiling of the magazine. It was a one million dollar bill with the writing, "In God, we put our trust, and you should to," written in the form of a scripture. In small print it read, "Give, Gain, Invest, and Inherit." That was my idea of course. We heard all the applause and the more and more cameras snapping.

"Thank you very much for being here. Ms. Wright and I are truly glad to have had this magazine in your presence and just, so you all know, each one of you will be taking home a copy today before they even hit the stands." We heard more and more applause again.

"Everyone who knows me, know I really don't speak much, so enjoy, network, and have yourself some mimosa's while you eat your brunch, it's on us, but only this time, because we need to save and invest, not spend our money and issue our money…ha ha…ok? Please, please enjoy."

We both smiled and smiled and begin to walk off. Ethan said we would not be answering any questions because this was not a press conference like Patrick held. I heard my name being called by several reporters and I turned around and waved.

"Mina, will this be a magazine as popular as the **SerVant24:7**?" I immediately turned around and approached the microphone. Ethan gripped my arm, but I continued to proceed to answer the question. "I cannot tell you what this magazine will do. I can only hope for it to sell as well as The **SerVant24:7**. Tenfold and **SerVant24:7** are two different publications, but they both bring something unique to the reader, and I believe it will do just as well, if not better."

"How is that Ms. Wright? I don't think you can get better as the **SerVant24:7**?" I heard a familiar voice from a distance yell from the crowd. I couldn't see from all the flashing. I responded with a slight but devious smile. Because Pastor Kincade, the reporters went crazy with their flashes. "This is a publication about financial stability and financial gain. Also, everyone wants to know how they can make more money and also save their money. The **SerVant24:7** did not discuss finances."

All the attention turned towards Patrick as he walked closer and closer to the stage. Lord, why isn't he at church? *What is he doing here*, I asked myself.

"Well tell me how did **SerVant24:7** do?" He asked.

"It was about unity, about love, about the community needs, and not just about our needs. It focused on the community."

I paused, and he and I stood there staring at one another with the flashes going crazy. Patrick looked at me like why are you doing this, although he knew why? Before I could say another word or answer another question, Ethan interrupted.

"This has been very interesting and entertaining, but it's over and again; thank you for attending, enjoy your Sunday."

Ethan then grabbed me by my arm and walked me over to the back of the stage area of the conference room, then pulled me aggressively down the hallway to his office.

"What was that?" He yelled and became very angry. He was pacing the floor back and forth over and over while he spoke to me.

"What was what? I yelled back.

"I specifically told you we would not be answering questions, and you continued to answer his question as if I did not instruct you otherwise. Can you hear? Do you understand?" He walked closer to my face, and I stepped back.

"I can hear perfectly fine, and get an understanding of what is needed of me, because if I couldn't do either one of these, I wouldn't be and editor and writer for your brand new publication. I don't think a businessman like yourself would take that chance."

"Your right about that, I wouldn't. So why would you answer the questions."

"Ethan I didn't want to be rude. I wanted to respond to the question. What is the problem? I answered the question very professionally, and I don't think I owe you an explanation, you are not my father Ethan, and I don't know why we are having this discussion."

He turned around swiftly, "You are right Mina. But where you are wrong is when I tell anyone who work for me something to do, I expect them to do it. I don't expect them to get all hot and excited, because a deceiving pastor shows up at a press conference and smile."

"Oh, I see what this is about. This isn't about me answering questions; this is about Patrick Allan Kincade. Isn't it?" I said.

He didn't flinch or move a mussel. He then began to pace the floor again and run his hand on his head back and forth real fast. He started sweating.

"You…you are very clever Mina… you think you are doing something here, but you're not sweetheart, I'm the one that invented this, not you. You know I sat and thought for a long time about you before I approached you with an opportunity, where you could advance your career for beyond **SerVant24:7**, but you were not to be trusted." He yelled.

"What? Trusted?"

"You told Patrick I moved the unveiling date didn't you?"

"I'm going to address to issues with you, and I don't want to talk about this anymore after today. First of all, we both invented this, and I don't understand why you are accusing me of telling Patrick anything. Secondly, I don't appreciate you speaking to me the way you are, and placing your jealous issues of Patrick on me. If I smile at anyone, that should not be your concern and, if I answer the question correctly, you should be glad and not accusing me if anything else. This is ridiculous Ethan."

He smiled sarcastically. "I might be a little jealous Mina. Just a little bit. I mean you screwed that man over and over again, and he left his wife for you. Who wouldn't be a little jealous?"

I laughed historically to agitate him even more. "So I'm a little confused. Are you admitting to being jealous of Patrick, or not?"

"It's a good jealous. You see, I'm only jealous at the fact that I didn't get to feel it like he did. I mean, that's what I heard, but I don't like to gossip Mina…shhhhh….I want tell sweetheart, or is it, my dear." He then placed his finger over his mouth.

"You don't know shit. I'm leaving Ethan. And you know what Ethan I will let you know if I want to still be involved in this project, I really don't think this is for me. You are extremely unprofessional, and I don't enjoy working with someone as talented as yourself when comes to business, but so messed up when it comes to his personal life. Well, now that I think about it you don't have one because you are too interested in mine. I mean Ethan you built a company but, yet is so concerned with a pastor and his success."

"Ha, ha, ha, Mina, you are hilarious." He laughed even harder. "My only concern is that I didn't get him slurped on." He then looked down at his pants.

"Ha, ha, ha, I'm sorry Ethan; let me be the first to inform you...I don't know what you heard and could care less. I don't slurp on blow pop suckers with bubble gum in the middle. I go big, the bigger; the better. I enjoy slurping and swallowing a double dip waffle ice cream cones, and that's not big enough.

He glared at me like I was from another planet. I guess he couldn't believe the response I gave him.

"Mina let's hope this magazine is a success. Because if it's not, I don't think your tongue is going to be so quick to respond with those types of comments."

I was suddenly feeling a need to leave. When I say leave, I do mean leave. I knew I didn't want to continue talking to Ethan. I knew that for sure. I knew I didn't want to mingle with any of his guest that were invited, or reporters. What I did know is I was at the point where I needed to do some soul searching. I can't keep running from situations every time I'm fed up. And I surely didn't want to continue running from every situation, because it will never show me what God can truly do in my life. But how am I going to continue to work with this half man, half hater. I wondered why Patrick was all of a sudden presenting himself at social activities. I wonder do they know each other in some type of way. This was never like him. He was always a brother who was very private, and a pastor that refused to miss his church services. I walked towards the conference area where reporters and several others were gathered. I was hoping to catch a glimpse of Patrick on my way out, and I did. I still liked the looks of that smooth chocolate skin, and those deep waves, which lay on his head. He was leaning against a wall with cup of coffee in his hand, dressed in the finest suit just like when I first met him. He was looking like Charlotte sexiest man in the city. It had been several months since I had touched his body and he had touched mine. How I missed his touch.

I waved good-bye at him from a distance as I begin to walk at a faster pace. I didn't want any pictures of him and me together. He acknowledged the fact that I waved at him by nodding his head. As I moved closer to the exit door, I quickly noticed another very familiar face, or two. It was Bryce and Judge Nash mingling with reporters. Interesting, I thought immediately to myself. I didn't concern myself as to why they were in attendance. I didn't want to re-open that door. I had no desire to speak with Bryce or the Judge. That door had been closed for sure, and I wasn't going to go there with either them or Patrick. I rushed out the exit door even quicker than when I started walking towards it. My hand went to open the car door and from behind that hand that I longed for touch mine.

"Mina." He said my name in a deep, seductive voice like always did.

I didn't turn around. "Patrick not here. Not now. It's too much going on, and it's going too good right now. Let not mess this up."

"I doubt that. It can't be going that good, or you would be in there mingling with reporters and not rushing out a side door. It's me, sweetie."

"Patrick please let my hand go." I still didn't turn around. I could feel him breath on my neck.

"We need to talk about you selling the **Servant** Mina."

I paused, and his body came closer to my backside. He touched my neck with his hand as I damn near jumped out of my skin. I calmed down and realized what he was trying to do. But, before I could speak, he spoke again.

"Mina, you left. You don't have to do this. If you're trying to get me back; then my dear you won. I'm showing you I am ready to move forward. I told my members, I told the city, the world, that I deceived them what more do you want from me? Come back home Mina, where you belong. You told me if I wanted it, I had to work for it. Baby, I missed church, wouldn't you say I was putting in overtime. Sweetheart, I'm sorry for everything that I have put you through."

That was probably the first time I ever heard him say, I'm sorry since the day I left. He had never admitted to any wrongdoing. I took a deep breath as he continued to put his body closer to my backside, and my hands still gripping my key tight. I guess he forgot we were standing in the parking lot, and I did too for a brief second. My body wanted to toss him in the car, and take him on a long hard ride. But I knew I couldn't.

"I'll be in touch Patrick," I said as I pushed the button to the car door.

Chapter 14: The First will be Last and the Last will be First...

I arrived at work early in the morning the week after the debut of **Tenfold**. I had managed to avoid Ethan all week. I had to some extensive soul searching all week long, and I must admit to myself and be honest with God, not like he didn't know, that I fell in love with Patrick. I was strong all week long and avoided many of the text messages and phone calls from him during that week. I also avoided the emails he constantly sent me during the week. I had decided to allow God to work, and that's exactly what God did, this time for real. I reflected back on all my relationships and thought to myself as a woman how we give so much of ourselves, and I know God gives us added strength from day to day when we don't have a significant other present in our lives, but sometimes it gets rough and tough on a sister. I mean I sure desire to feel his touch, and long to go back to my invention, my creation, and a news publication that may not have meant a lot to someone, but sure meant a lot to me. I looked at myself and quit pointing the finger at Patrick. One can always put the blame on someone else, but never admit to their selves what they did wrong. I love the relationship I had with Patrick, oh how I loved it, but I couldn't take another day of the pretending and lies and that was so hard to walk away from, but I did it. Some women would have stayed and did it for twenty plus years. But I wasn't that kind of woman. I thought about my relationship with Damien. Some women shack for ten years, or more, and more. But I wasn't that woman. I then reflected all the way back to my relationship with Rylie's dad, may he rest in peace. Some woman would have allowed a man they were married to constantly cheat and let that go by for years before they decide to leave, if they ever left. I wasn't that woman either. So, some may ask me and I may ask myself then what type of woman are you Mina Wright? I answered to my inner soul and my outward man who may wonder about my life and me. And the many that view me from a distance, and of course the reporters who wrote about me and those who pointed their fingers at me over the past few months in a negative way, I tell them, I am a beautiful woman in which God created in his image and he knows the plans he has for me!

"Ms. Wright these are for you."

Ethan secretary then handed me over a fresh bouquet of a dozen roses. They were in a vase with an M engraved on it. She placed a cup of freshly brewed coffee on my desk.

"Where do you want these?" she asked.

"Leave them on my desk for now. Thank You."

There was a card attached, and it read...Congratulations on your debut success. I have often heard actions speak louder than words.... am I loud enough yet Mina?"

Love Patrick

I nearly melted. Calgon, please take me away. Damn it Mina get a grip. Now he wants to act right.

"I see someone is loved Ms. Wright. Everyone should be loved like you. I wonder to myself at times; what does it take to be loved that way." Ethan said.

"You have to give love, to receive love Ethan." I said as I placed my flowers closer to my belongings."

"Are we going somewhere, Mina?"

"Yes, Ethan I was going to talk to you on today because the past week have been hectic for the both of us and I didn't want to intrude on your busy schedule."

"Mina, I guess great minds do think alike. I know you have been here only a short time, and I'm proud of your effort to produce such a great news publication. I am also very extremely happy that it debut at number one, but I wanted more for this publication." He began to pace the floor like usually does. "I wanted this publication to knock **Servant24:7** off its high horse. I know you are probably wondering why? So, let me explain. You were brought here to do a job. You did that job. Even with everyone saying they didn't think you could do it, you did it, for yourself, for me, and for the company. And many others, although you didn't know it, you were being constantly watched. I mean we are in the business to make money. We could care less about helping people invest."

I rudely interrupted him while he was speaking. "Who are they?"

"Well those who have helped me on this adventure or journey to produce a magazine."

"You still didn't answer my questions, who are they?" I put inference on it.

"Those who have invested in **Tenfold** Mina, that's who they are. Please allow me to continue. As I was saying, we are in the business of making money, and we made a little money with the first debut, but we wanted so much more, and I thought since you did so well with numbers and money with the **SerVant24:7**, then you would for sure do well with **Tenfold**."

"I did do well. We debut at number one Ethan. I really wish you would get to the point."

"Well I would like to, but you continue to interrupt me and I cannot. So, may I finish?"

"You may," I said as I crossed my arms standing in front of him.

"Anyway, what we were trying to do, was break records, and we were surprised we didn't. **Tenfold** sold one hundred and twenty-two thousand copies its first week. The **SerVant24:7** sold one hundred and seventy-two thousand copies its first week, and the same week we debut **Tenfold,** the **SerVant24:7** still sold one hundred and eighteen thousand copies. Only one hundred and twenty-two thousand were distributed. That means only two thousand people didn't buy the **SerVant24:7**." He cleared his throat. "So, my colleagues and I were discussing the numbers, and we tried to understand why **Tenfold** wouldn't do better than **SerVant's** debut? I mean the **SerVant** sold one hundred and seventy-two thousand copies! Why is the **SerVant** still doing so well and the person that put it all together is no longer creating it week by week?"

"I have no idea Ethan, maybe there are many more servants that are concerned with helping others than saving a dollar or two."

"So that's your answer? You are not concerned about how your competition is still hanging on when you were the It factor, and mastermind behind it?"

"No, not at all Ethan. I have come to a place in my life where I refuse to, worry about things or situations I have no control over. That being said I think we should start focusing on our news publication and not someone else's and maybe we can sell as many as them."

He didn't smile, and the facial expression was a look of disgust, of what I wouldn't agree with what he was saying.

"Someone?" He said.

"I'm sorry, I didn't catch that."

"You said someone else's, who is someone Mina?"

"Whomever is helping them now Ethan, remember the girl Nina, she replaced me. We met her at the restaurant."

"Really? Oh, yea, yea...I remember her. But, no it's not her Mina."

"Wha.... Well I don't know, and I really don't care Ethan, and frankly I'm tired of talking about the **Servant.** I have an appointment at my daughter's school, and I need to wrap things up here so I can make it on that side of town by noon."

"Why are you running?"

"Running? Who said I was running? I have an appointment. I'm a busy woman Ethan." I laughed

"That laugh sounds nervous to me." He said

"Nervous? Ethan please I don't have time for this. I have somewhere to be."

"Please have a seat Mina, I will only be a few more minutes, and you can go to your appointment. Please, please sit down. A few of my colleagues and I want to talk to you about expectations, and so forth, real quick."

What is he up too? I asked myself as I starred in his eyes. I'm am not feeling this shit, not at all, and I am ready to run up out of here at the first door that opens, I am going to ease my way closer to the entrance door to my office. I know this man is not crazy enough to do anything stupid to me in this building with all these people. But, then again he is sweating and turning red as a tomato as he walks the floor of my office. He seems like he is ready to explode on someone and Lord knows I wasn't trying to go there today, or any day. I do not want to be the one he loses it on. I know for a fact I will be as humble as a bird, if this man says one more word, It will be yes sir and no sir. I slowly reached for my cell phone. I mean he is really giving me a preview of what the devil looks like right about now, and it's ugly. I reached in my refrigerator for my small single bottle of Chardonnay. I opened the desk drawer for my champagne glass. I poured me a glass of wine, because he had a sister's nerves so messed up right now, I didn't know if his head was going to start spinning around and around like he was in the movie Exorcist, or if he was going to become Jeffery Dommer and chop me up. Which- ever way it went I was having me a drink…. Or two.

"Hello Mina."

I recognized that voice oh so well.

"Hello Bryce. What are you doing here?"

"Well, Mina I'm doing great. Thanks for asking. I have no complaints at all. Successful magazine, beautiful daughter, and a winner at everything I do!"

This two-faced, messy mutha-fudge cake. I knew his trifling ass was up to something. I knew deep down in my spirit. But if they want to do it this way, I was ready for whatever at this point. What Ethan didn't know is I never trusted him from the beginning of this project. I see now we do have a game, people! Take your seats and enjoy.

"What brings you here Bryce?"

"It's funny you ask that question, Mina? I was driving around the neighborhood, and I thought to myself I should stop and say hello to Mina. So, hello Mina."

"I thought the same exact thing, Bryce." A white hand was placed on Bryce's back.

"Hello Mina, I know you thought you wouldn't see us again."

"No Judge Nash, you have it all wrong, I mean all wrong. I didn't give any of you much thought." I said. "Would any of you like a glass of wine?"

"Mina we are here to conduct business, not drink glasses of wine," Ethan said.

"Oh excuse me for being polite. How can I help you?"

Judge Nash pulled a chair up to my desk, and sat down, and so did Bryce. Then Ethan.

"Surprise Mina. We're back. I bet you thought you got rid of us since you left Patrick."

"No Bryce. I knew you would come back. The bible said the enemy only leaves for a season."

"Ha...I see you are still the same Mina. I thought by now Patrick would have taught you the game, and also married your fine ass by now for all you did for him? What a sorry, ungrateful, man."

I didn't flinch at his comment. I had my gun, aka, my tongue ready to fire at all the words, phrases, sentences that came out his pathetic mouth.

"Everyone is not ready to get married Bryce, That's not everyone's dream or goal. Something's, happen naturally, and something's are just given to us from God. We don't have to lie, connive, or kiss ass to get it. We work for what we want. We don't need pay-offs, or to be someone's' flunky."

Ethan sat down in the chair he had placed closer to my desk. "Let's cut the bull-shit Mina. We want you to tell the press that Patrick was lying about the fact he left his wife. We want you to tell them that he was sleeping with you and he told the press in fear that you would come forward."

Is this man crazy? What the hell. They are trying to sabotage Patrick. I knew it. They are trying to destroy a successful black man. Patrick has did a whole lot of wrong, but at the same time Patrick has did a whole lot of good to his community, And also, he has been through a lot during his years of teenager, and adult, and he has had so much lost.

"What's in it for me?" I asked.

Judge Nash immediately spoke up. "Whatever you want Mina. You can have. I want Patrick out of sight, out of mind. I don't care at this point."

Wow to hear those types of words about another individual was frightening. "Again what is it that you want from me? He was married to your daughter, cant she do what needs to be done to get rid of Patrick, to get him out of your, whatever it is you want him out of?"

"My daughter is not a part of this, but you are. Are you going to help us or not?" He said.

"Not," I said as I sipped another glass of wine. They all were extremely quiet and staring at me. "Would any of you gentleman like a glass of wine? We need to celebrate the debut of ***Tenfold*?*"

"Is this a game to you Mina? Do you think we are playing a game here? That's your problem, Mina, you are the one playing while we are serious." Bryce said.

"I don't think anything. No, I take that back. I think you all are a bunch of haters towards Patrick. And you Bryce.... you are a black man helping the other man bring another black man down. It's so sad. They don't need to bring him down. They have you. It's so sad that you would limit yourself and the little talent you have on trying to bring another black man down. Use your gift on something else Bryce. Please. You are boring me, and everyone else in this city. You are following behind a judge for what? You lost the election anyway? He is using you son. Open the eyes God gave you."

"She's trying to manipulate you Bryce don't listen to her. She is not smart and will never be smart to tell anyone what to do."

"I was smart enough for Patrick to tell the city he wasn't married," I said.

"I'm sick and tired of you gal. I mean sick of you. Now I will tell you one last time you help get rid of Patrick, or you are going to leave back to Dallas on the next plane out of here. I know you're background sweetie and it ain't as sanctified as you try to make it be. Now you or going to help us, or you're going to go right where Patrick is going, and that's down, and I mean below the dirt. I warned you once, you have destroyed my family, and it's over and it's finished. Now you will do as you are instructed to do. You will admit to having an affair with him, and the wanted to continue the affair, and you didn't want to."

"Mina."

"Don't say a word to me Ethan. Not one word." I walked over to him, and there I stood face to face with him. "You used me. You used me. You used me." I stood up and shouted again, "You used me...BUT...I was one step ahead of you and your colleagues."

The door opened, and Patrick walked in. The look on their faces, were as if they had witnessed a dead man walking in the flesh. They all stood up at the same time in pure amazement.

"Gentleman, please sit down, we have some business to conduct," Patrick said.

I walked near to where Patrick was standing. Ethan went to reach for his cell phone.

"Put the cell phone down, or I am going to call every media outlet, and will have them televised what I am about to say," I said.

"What's going on Patrick? What is this boy?" Judge Nash asked.

"This is a meeting with colleagues," Patrick said as I smirked at each one of them.

"You weren't invited, Patrick," Bryce said.

Patrick began pacing the floor as the mystery of his arrival made them all sweat more and more. They were all breathing heavily and seem quite nervous.

"Bryce it's always a pleasure to see you. God forgive me, for telling that lie. You have been keeping a low profile since the loss of the election. What are your plans now for the future, since you are no longer commissioner?" Patrick asked with a sneer.

"Well, Patrick I thought I would start by grabbing some of your dedicated members after you are exposed. I then will have the largest church in the city."

Patrick shook his head from side to side. "Bryce, Bryce. You always wanted what God gave me instead of knowing him for yourself and believing what he said in his word, that he is no respecter of person. But, since you don't believe in him, you never gave him a chance to show you. You always wanted what I had. I must admit you got that from Tish, but that was all you took from me, and actually, I gave her to you."

They all gasped at his comment. "Patrick, what the hell are you doing?" Nash said.

"I am doing what I should have done many, many years ago Nash. But it's all about timing, and now it's my time. I'll let Mina have the floor."

"Thank You Patrick. Judge Nash I did some background on you as well, on all of you. Ethan I was prepared for you to offer me a job. I had a list of all Judge Nash connections, thanks to Patrick and the envelope left at my doorstep, you were one of the many colleagues listed. You were never that interested in a magazine; you were only trying to get to Patrick. You have been following me for months and months. I saw you and I remembered from the launching of **Servant24:7**. Bryce you had my tires sliced in my driveway. You then tried to pay the gate attendee in out sub- division for the videotape, no let me re-phrase that, you did pay him, and he accepted your dollars, after he came to me first and allowed me to make a copy! Bryce you also paid someone to hack my computer. He was the janitor at your campaign headquarters fresh out of prison, the brother had a gift of hacking into computers and when you found out, you paid him to hack mine. But! There is always a but, when the young man figured out how you and Judge Nash were behind sending him to prison, he came running to me and told me everything, when I say everything, I mean everything. Judge Nash you have destroyed so many lives. So many. And if I was not ahead of the game you were going to try and destroy mine, but I couldn't allow you to do that. So, I did my research on you. A little background check."

"Gal, you have nothing on me. And, if you did, it's not going to affect me in anyway. Your, not the first to try and take the judge down, now is she Bryce?"

Bryce wasn't laughing, or Ethan.

"This piece of information may affect you. Do you know a woman by the name of Martha Danielle Taylor?" It was "drop a pen" on the floor type of silent. I looked at Patrick, and he nodded for me to proceed.

"Who…who… are you talking about?" He stuttered and looked extremely confused.

"Let me help you Nash, because you have did so much dirt you probably don't even remember her. Tall, brunette, slender, but athletic build, very pretty. She gave you what you needed sexually from time to time, or more like every other day when your wife was in the hospital fighting for her life after being in a car accident. You and her would get high together, sniff a little cocaine here and there, and other drugs. She also distributed it for you to those who needed a hit, and your colleagues. She supplied you and your friends both sexually and in other ways. She was passed around. You remember Nash? She was diagnosed with ovarian cancer and shortly afterward found dead in her apartment three weeks later. It was awkward to me because after I researched and researched this case, I thought about how after she died all of a sudden, her apartment was ambushed with gunshots through her bedroom window. But, she didn't have any family in Charlotte, she was a former prostitute, run-away, so who would care about her, so you assumed. After requesting her medical records, dental records, and conducting my own investigation I discovered that Martha Danielle Taylor never had ovarian cancer, because he didn't have ovaries. Martha was in-fact Marvin Daniel Taylor, a man."

The pen dropped. Even Patrick sat down on this one. "That's right everyone Nash had a sexual involvement that went on for years and years with Marvin aka Martha. And he didn't want it to be exposed. From what I hear he would kill before he was exposed. Therefore, he had him killed after Marvin threatened to go to the press in exchange for 2.2 million dollars, offered by Nash opponent in the election. He went to Nash thinking Nash was going to beat the amount and give him more money to keep his mouth closed. Nash immediately ordered the hit on Marvin Taylor because he didn't believe Marvin wouldn't tell the press even after he paid him. Nash paid a very wealthy known forensics pathologist to alter the autopsy report to read Martha Taylor, aka Marvin Taylor died of ovarian cancer. Therefore, the gunshot wounds were never mentioned, but Marvin was truly shot to death in his apartment. Nash had the body removed, police were paid, the cleaning crew who cleaned the apartment were paid, and everyone was paid. Just another life wasted. It reminds me of the behavior and treatment you have handed over to Patrick all these years by using your judicial influence and position by abusing it with control. You have to control everything Nash and everyone it is your nature, but, I refuse to allow you to do that to me and my family, especially those I love." I looked over at Patrick to see the response on his face. He was in a daze. "You knew Patrick had a lot to lose once he became a professional athlete and when he became a well-known minister. You used that against him all this time, you, Bryce, and your daughter. You saw you could not control me so you wanted me to destroy Patrick. If I would comply that way you could hold that betrayal over my head; all because you wanted control. So, after I learned of Marvin Taylor's situation, It made me curious to know what really happen that day back in 1983, so I had the case re-opened involving Patrick in 1983."

"You did what?" Nash shouted.

Patrick mouth opened, and he was overly confused and in disbelief. He wasn't aware of this scenario or piece of information I had discovered as well pertaining to his case. I couldn't share everything with him. I had to save some for myself.

"You heard me Nash. I re-opened the case of The State of Carolina verse Patrick Allen Kincade."

"There is no way you could have did that… Without…" Judge Nash stopped in the middle of his sentence.

"Without what? I'm sorry I don't understand? Is it because you weren't notified from your inside snitches? Insiders from the forensic labs, insiders from the police station, and insiders from whomever you will pay to watch me and Patrick going and coming. It didn't work this time, because Nash you are not the only one with long money. Now back to where I was going with all this. I re-opened the case, and I had the body of the young man who Patrick had the altercation with, exhumed."

"Mina, you did what?" Patrick yelled.

"She did no such a thing," Nash said.

"What is she talking about Nash? Tell me?" Bryce asked.

"All these years you had Patrick, along with his father, believing he pushed that young man to his death from a head injury. Well, I had another autopsy conducted. Since you paid the medical examiner who worked this case back then, you know the one you had on your payroll over the many years. This autopsy discovered the truth, what really happened that fatal day back in July 1983. Your pathologist report said he died from a fatal head injury. That was a lie."

"You illiterate whore, you are a liar!" Nash screamed. He then turned to Patrick. "She's lying to you, Patrick. She's manipulating you. She is nothing but a pathological liar. She will never be nothing."

"Shut-Up Nash!" Patrick yelled. "SHUT-UP!"

"Here you are, Patrick." I handed the photos and new autopsy report to Patrick.

Patrick snatched the report and photos and slowly squatted down in the chair.

"Look at the photographs real well Patrick. Look at the paragraph which reads the cause of death for me out loud so everyone can hear, especially Nash, not that he doesn't already know what it says."

Patrick turned the pages faster and faster until he reached the very last page of the report. He also engaged himself deeply in each photo. Back and forth he studied each photograph slowly making sure he didn't look over any important details.

"The cause of death determined this by The State of Charlotte North Carolina is determined and confirmed that...was killed due to a massive heart attack, not...not...a fatal head injury."

WHAT! HE DID WHAT!" He turned and began walking toward Nash. "I want to know, what did you do? You are PATHETIC! PATHETIC." Patrick screamed.

Nash backed up towards Bryce.

"I will tell you exactly what he did Patrick. Your father paid Nash to find you not guilty. Your father did what he had to do to protect his son. You were aware of that piece of information. But, what Nash failed to mention to your father was the young man you had the altercation with really died from a heart-attack."

"No way, No way, no way. Mina where did you get this from?" Patrick was truly disturbed.

"Patrick the young man's body went into shock after you pushed him, he did not die from your push. He became overwhelmed with fear after you pushed him and he realized he couldn't catch his balance. His brain reacted instantly sending shock waves through his body to his heart causing a heart attack. That's exactly how he died

Patrick, not from you pushing him to his death like you have thought for so many years. It's in the report."

"Your father knew," Nash screamed. "HE KNEW!!!!"

"YOU LIAR…You Liar! My father would have never paid you, or had to pay you for my freedom if he knew he died from a heart attack." Patrick yelled.

"You were a black teenage boy who killed a white teenage boy in 1983, with a promising future. Understand me; you would have been found guilty Patrick if I didn't rule it self- defense. No one wanted to accept the truth about that boy dying from a heart attack Patrick. The white community wanted you gone because you did hit him and he fell to the floor regardless. His parents wanted you gone; death threats were being made against my family, police officers, etc., the investigators were paid by people; by the time your father came to me. Your father came along with more money to offer, and we agreed to keep the story of the fatal head injury. Everyone said it was a fight. Everyone saw the fight. I had people to pay as well Patrick. It was a fight. There was people wanting you dead regardless. Your father and I did what we had to do Patrick. Don't you get it, son?"

I didn't believe a word Nash was saying. It sounded like bull…t! Patrick turned towards the window head down. The room was silent, and a somber mood was in full effect. He was in deep thought and looked to be disgusted with what he was told.

"I have and will never been your son. Don't call me that. I don't believe a word you are saying. YOU LIAR LIAR LIAR!!!! My father paid you because that's what he had to do. You weren't paid by people to say it was a head injury. YOU DID THIS! YOU PAID THE Medical Examiner. My father never knew that young man died from a heart attack. My father loved me too much to keep that piece of information from me. He would have never allowed you to black mail him, or me all these years. You did that to have control. All these years, All these years, All these years I have carried the emotional guilt and shame on my shoulders from that young man death. My boys did all those years in prison. The struggles I have had with not walking away from you and Tish. The pretending to be something else, pretending and pretending, and lying, burden after burden I have carried. I used to cry myself to sleep from the emotional anguish after his death.

"ALL THESE YEARS!!" Patrick continued to yell and scream and became overtaken by his anger and the thought of what Nash did for so many years. The look of disbelief on his face made room for the tears, which also flowed down his face.

He sobbed and sobbed until the anger within him took him over to Nash, and the next thing I saw was Nash laying on the floor, and a few teeth landed with him. ONE PUNCH! No one moved. No one walked over to Nash to see if he was ok. No one reached to help Nash off the floor either. Nash screamed, moved, and squirmed in pain. He tried getting up off the floor with one hand over his mouth. While stumbling to catch his balance, he didn't have a chance. Patrick punched him in the same place... again and this time I saw blood. Bryce went to make a comment as he slowly made his way towards Nash, and before he could open his mouth, his top two left teeth had found them a new home also... on the floor.

Ethan stepped in front of Patrick. He then turned around and snatched a gun from his pocket. Everyone hands up in the air. We all put our hands up in the air. He then raised his badge and placed his gun in his pocket. He grabbed his phone and began speaking.

"This is detective Walden requesting back-up." He took some handcuffs out of a duffle bag.

I was in shock. Ethan was a detective. All this time. We all looked surprised except for Patrick.

"Pastor Kincade, are you ok sir." Ethan asked.

Patrick shook his head yes. I continued standing there, although the police officers had arrived, more detectives, DA, along with Patrick and my attorney walked the floor and did what they needed to do. They had been on stand-by the entire time listening from the wire attached to Patrick undershirt. The police grabbed Nash off the floor in his handcuffs and read him his rights. He yelled and wrestled with the officers until finally he was taisered. Simply evil.

"Wha...wha....wha... thi...?" Bryce tried asking the police officer, "What is this?" as he placed the handcuffs on his wrist.

"Bryce he can't understand you, wait until after your teeth are replaced," I said giggling.

The police officer continued. "Bribery, extortion, blackmail, falsifying information to become County Commissioner, accessory to murder for Marvin Daniel Taylor."

"Accessory to murder?" I said.

"Yeah Mina. Apparently, Bryce was the recruiter for the forensic pathologist that lied on Marvin Daniel Taylor's autopsy report." Patrick said.

"Recruiter? Wait a minute I'm confused, Patrick. What are you talking about?"

"Mina you know you women keep stuff from us men all the time. I couldn't tell you everything at once." He winked at me. "Bryce had to have a role in this somehow, someway, because he was a flunky. He was the person who scouted the college campuses and talked to the professors to retrieve the best forensic students they had. Once they graduated from college and received their license to work, Bryce would offer them a deal. Of course, you had those who rejected him and those who accepted what he had to offer. Those who had student loans and other financial obligations didn't realize they were selling their souls to the devil."

"I'm not surprised. Just more lives wasted thanks to Nash. Patrick, I must say I didn't see that coming. I never knew Ethan was a detective. Didn't have a clue. You are a smart man."

"Thank you. Ethan and I have been trying to get Nash for the past three years, and I never had enough evidence, or any evidence, and I was always scared that he would tell what my father did for me. All these years believing I killed that boy. This is deliverance for me." He dropped his head. "It was scary. I didn't know if you would take the job offer from Ethan, if you didn't, it would not have worked. You are a smart woman, but I couldn't share all the information with you." He said.

"Well, you did very well. Now, Nash and Bryce will be roomies and Nash won't have to hide that other sexual side he has anymore... Ha, ha, ha. They all can become one big happy family in cellblock #666. I may visit them and make them apart of my prison ministry...after they are delivered."

"You're laughing Patrick. At a time like this, and you still can laugh." I said.

"The joy of the Lord is my strength, Mina. I'm tired of crying. I have been crying for far too long. And in case I didn't tell you. Thank You. Thank You. Thank You. Thank You. We make a great team. I could not have done this without your help and the help of the detectives. My mom always told me I would win. What a great team I had behind me. We are so good together." He said in a low tone voice as he began to get emotional.

"We sure are Patrick and always have been."

"And we always will be my dear."

We starred at one another for a second. "Always?" I asked.

He responded as he walked near me and placed his hand against my chin. "Your office has always been there? Your roses have always been delivered fresh. Your coffee has always been freshly brewed, and you have always been missed since the day you walked out the door."

I responded, "And I have always missed my roses being freshly delivered, and my coffee freshly brewed and most of all you and everyone else." I said.

"Well while you are thinking about it lets make our way out of here. Can you have dinner with me tonight?"

"I would love to Patrick, but I already have plans."

He cleared his throat before responding,"Oook...."

"I'll call you," I said.

He stuttered again. "Oook." We both headed towards the exit door of the building together.

"I think you both need body guards," Ethan said.

"Trust me they are outside in position waiting for the both of us."

"Ethan you tricked me," I said smiling.

"I know Mina that was the plan…ha ha ha" He said.

"It was great working with you," I said.

"Are you sure about that? I believe someone was getting irritated with me."

"You think?" I said smiling.

We all made our way to the exit door. "So what happens to **Tenfold** now?" Patrick asked.

Ethan looked over at me. "Nothing. It will still sell, probably more so now, with all the media attention. I own it, and **Servant24:7**. They both belong to mama."

"So does this mean I will see you at work on Monday?" Patrick asked.

"Yes, you will," I said.

"Church on Sunday, dinner on Monday?" Patrick asked.

"Let's take it one day at a time. Hold on wait a minute. I just thought about something, where's Nina?" I asked in a sarcastic tone, with a smile on my face.

He looked over at Ethan, "Ask him, it's his wife."

"Oh my goodness. Nina is Ethan's wife?"

I touched him with my pointing finger on his shoulder.

"Boy, you're gone give me heart attack. Patrick, what else do I need to know? Seriously, come on let it out. Before I come back to the office, I need to know now, absolutely no more secrets, Patrick. I refuse to work like that. No More. I mean it!"

"I'll let you two talk this out. Excuse me." Ethan said as he walked away.

"Woman calm down!"

"Calm down? You're telling me to calm down after all this!"

"Ok, ok, Mina. Since you must know everything. This is the only secret I have not shared with you. I promise."

"I'm waiting," I said as I folded my arms.

He took a deep breath. "I Patrick Allen Kincade Love You Mina Wright." He said and turned and walked away. He stopped and turned around,

"Don't forget church on Sunday and dinner on Monday, with you, Rylie, and Mamadoll."

Chapter 15: Deliverance is available...

New beginnings are always fun. After the storm surely comes a bright ray of sunshine. I often keep that piece of information tucked away deep with-in my soul to keep my faith plant, watered. Life has become extremely peaceful since I have been delivered from various strongholds that I felt I was keeping me from my purposeful life. I often told God I was going to wait upon him, but would always fall. I would always sing the, *I'm only human* song that is now played out, and no longer holding the number one position on my music chart. I am now singing a different tune, and that is, I will wait, trust, and believe God is going to do what he said he is going to do in my life and he does not need any help from me, and especially not from my flesh. I went back home and began working at the **SerVant24:7** again. Home is truly where the heart is. I have also been working on **Tenfold** at least two to three times a week. It is selling quite well but could never sell more copies than **SerVant24:7**. Even after all the negative press.

I am truly blessed these days, and have entered a great place in my life. Glory be to God for that. I am now following him and can see things so much better now. I have been abstaining from sex for eight months now, which is great for me. Many people may say that's not a long time, but to me it is when you are working very close to a very handsome, respectful, prosperous, popular, Godly, single man that told me he loves me and someone I once had a relationship with. It's not easy. Lord but it's worth it, if I do it God's way. I started searching for Rylie and me a house. I completed the renovations while at Mamadoll's, so I knew I was walking into a new season of my life and it was time to move forward. It is two months before my 42nd birthday. Whew! I can't believe it's been two years since I made it here to Charlotte. I look back on it and laugh now, but back then nothing was funny. I think about all the growing pains I have experienced and all the lessons have been taught. But, I can't say it wasn't worth it. I guess I had to go through all the mess to finally say enough is enough, and this gold mine I'm sitting on will be shared only with my husband. FORREAL! That's what I vowed to God before, and before, and before I met him. But, this time I can work around *him* daily and continue to keep my covenant between God and me, with no self-gratification, for the first time in my life.

Patrick and I have been spending a lot of time together, and we are currently working on our testimony for Nash and Bryce trial. We are praying for the best sentencing the state will issue them. We are building a solid foundation called friendship this time. We have been to a few social functions together surrounded by others. After the arrest, we were overwhelmed with interview request, book deals, and movie deals. Patrick, of course, has been offered millions of dollars for a book deal, as well, as movie. But, he turned them all down. He said if they want to know his story they could come to church service, or watch it on the Internet. We both are growing, just like the ministry. All the members he lost came back. Tish is under investigation for *recruiting* as well, like Bryce.

Patrick has decided to still be the father in Pasha's life, that's the only father she has ever known. He said it doesn't make since for her to lose two parents and a grandparent. Rylie babysits for Patrick, as well as Mamadoll and myself. She has become part of our family. And as for the **SerVant24:7** team, we all are still here.

Patrick and I are both keeping a low profile to protect us, as well as our family. It has been none stop media coverage leading up to the trial. It's all the radio stations talk about as well as news commentators. I looked at my calendar and realized the day before my birthday, I will be testifying against Bryce and Nash. Some people have said Nash has paid many judicial officials off, and will probably be found not guilty. They have also said me and Patrick should be afraid. But, I say who cares about what people say. It's whatever God says. Plus we had enough evidence against that man to build a prison just for him alone.

"Good morning sunshine here are some messages for you," Doris said.

"Thanks, lady."

"Mina."

"Yes, ma'am."

"If I never told you… welcome back."

"Thank You, Ms. Doris. It feels good to be back."

I walked towards my office, but before I made it to my destination, I stopped by to see Kia. I haven't had a chance to talk with her much since she has been traveling so much, spreading the news and promoting, *Hugs 4 Hope, Everyone needs a hug, it leads to hope.* She also has moved forward and away from all the negative attention. She looked as though she was on the phone so I decided I would come back later.

I walked into my office to witness a room surrounded by at least twenty plus dozen of roses, sun shining bright through the windowpane with soft music playing from the surround sound. It feels like home, and I want to stay here and continue to grow. I have sinned here and at the same time been delivered here. I forgave here, and also have been forgiven here.

"Miss Mina."

"Hello there, Gregory."

I stood up to hug him. Gregory was the young intern that started working at the Servant two weeks before I left. It was his birthday, and he had just turned twenty-four!

"It's so good to see you. I have boxes and boxes of mail from the prison ministry for you madam."

"Thank you so much. How have you been? I missed you."

"I missed you also. Every day I came in here, and I would sit and look out the window. I would often wonder how you were doing, you and your family."

"We were fine. I had to be about my father's business, and serve others."

"I understand. Mr. Kincade told me you would be back. Although, he was a different person after you left Mina."

"Is that right? Different how?"

"Well for one, he wasn't talkative. He was to himself. He was off to himself frequently, every day, and he never socialized much with any of us. He seems to be happy now that you are back. It's like old times. When you were here, he was always smiling, joking, and concerned about what was going on with his business. It's amazing what a woman can do. I think I want to try it?"

"Interesting. I think the happiness comes from winning a battle he has fought for so long. He has a burden lifted off his shoulders that has weighed so heavy after all these years. Not to change the subject, but changing the subject, what are you going to try?"

"I realized I like older women. It seems like women or world changers. You can make a man do some strange things sometimes."

"Well God made a woman in a very special way, and he uses us in different ways in the world. We are home changers, job changers, relationship changers, and church changers. Remember a woman gave birth to our savior, and he changed the world."

"I know, and I want to see what it's like; I am for sure I like women, no I am for sure love woman. And I am ready to go forth, and see what it is like to be with a woman."

"So you are a virgin?" I asked.

"Yes.... I am"

"Wow Gregory, how old are you if you don't mind me asking?"

"I'm twenty-four."

"That's wonderful. You are probably the only virgin in Charlotte. Well, I'm happy for you Gregory. Do you have anyone in mind? Have you met someone?"

"I have someone in mind."

"Who do you have in mind? Do I know her? Is it someone at the church? Where you live? Sit down and tell me all the details. I won't tell PAK." He had a look on his face as if he didn't believe me. "I promise," I said.

"She is…beautiful…."

"I know she is." Patrick walked in my office and said. "Good morning my dear, beautiful roses, who sent them?"

"I don't know, some random admirer. I think he likes me."

"I know for a fact he does. Good morning Gregory." Patrick then kissed me on my jaw.

He has been quite the gentleman that I have longed for him to be. He is so happy these days, and it feels good to see him happy, and so am I.

"Good morning Mr. Kincade."

"Gregory, what are you trying to keep this beautiful woman from telling me? We can't keep secrets anymore, right Mina?"

"That's right Patrick. I think Gregory is keeping this between him and God."

"You are correct Mina. So let me get to work now, I have a busy schedule." Gregory said.

"You don't have to run Gregory. I was stopping by to speak to Mina. I know I have to share her."

"Ha ha, ha...how sweet of you to say. And you do have to share her Mr. Kincade…haha"

Patrick didn't crack a smile. "Is that supposed to be funny?" Gregory looked horrified. "Ha ha ha, I was only kidding…"

"Patrick, give him a break. How are you this morning love?"

"I'm doing wonderful I have no complaints. Life is good. And is about to get better."

"Oook. What's going on Patrick?" I asked.

"Are you ready for this?"

"Yes, I am."

"I was informed by our lawyers today that Bryce Calhoun pleaded guilty to all charges. God is good."

"All the time."

"And all the time."

"God is good."

"This is great news for us PAK."

"And he is doing much more Mina than I can think or ask. I spoke briefly with Tish this morning; she is going to give me sole custody of Pasha. She knew some things that her father did illegally, and she pled guilty today. It's all over the news."

"I haven't turned the television on or radio this morning. Patrick, that's wonderful news. Wow! You're going to be a full-time father. I'm happy for you."

"Thank you sweetheart. Things are about to change for sure in my life Mina. I'm about to change some things that needed changing a long time ago. I didn't see this coming."

"I didn't either. What do you think she admitted to? What did she help her father with?"

"Mina, to be honest, I believe everything. I believe she knew about so much that she had to admit to it. Tish would have never admitted to anything that would hurt her father. They were too close for that. I believe she didn't see a way out."

"How much time do you think she will get?" I asked.

"She said maybe three to five years. Good behavior she'll be out in two."

"Two years?"

"Yes, Mina two years. Her dad knows people."

"I know that, but he is the biggest criminal. What about Bryce? How much will he get?"

"You really want to know?"

"Yes, I really want to know?"

"Rumor has it six to ten years."

"OMG! After all, he did. Someone died. He knew about it. Geez, I'm afraid to ask about Nash."

"We will find out today. We're not afraid of anything. Whatever happens, God is our refuge, Mina. Put the flesh to rest. We are fighting this in the spiritual realm."

"You are right Patrick."

"Gregory, I forgot you were standing there."

"Sir I'm sorry. I was looking at you two together. It's as if you two were meant to be."

Neither one of us said a word. "Well like I said earlier I have a lot to do, let me get to work."

We were still quite. "Let me get out of here I need to meet with my lawyers and get Pasha situated," Patrick said.

"I understand Super dad. So what's on the menu for tonight's dinner?"

"The norm, unless you and Riley want to come over and join us."

"MMM, and who's doing the cooking?"

"MMM, you?"

"Really? I don't think that was on my schedule."

303

"It is now my dear so what time do I need to expect you two?"

I paused and thought about it before I spoke. "Patrick let's take it slow this time. Let's pray about it and be sure that this is God, and not our flesh this time. Our kids are involved now. We need to be careful."

"We always should be careful. I understand our children are involved, that's why I asked for you both to come over. Mina if it was my flesh, I could easily hire a nanny today and have Jeffrey the chef, prepares a meal for Pasha and me. I can ask you to come over, or pick you up around 11:30 pm, once both of the kids are sleep. Come back home and walk you into my bedroom and workout on something other than my free weights. It's not my flesh my dear. Maybe you should ask that question about yourself, Mina? Is it your flesh?"

I stood there for a moment after I was put in a coma from his tone of voice. "Is seven o'clock too late?"

"Seven o'clock is perfect. I'll have everything waiting for you, thawed out and fresh on the counter."

Dinner at Patrick's with our girls...

We arrived at Patrick home around 6:45. Rylie have been here before, but it's been awhile so of course she was excited to take another tour. I pulled through the gate to see a few cars there that I didn't recognize. The closer we approached the front door I noticed one car that stood out amongst the others and it was Kia's. I was a little surprised. Maybe she stopped by to speak with Patrick but who were the other cars. I didn't expect this and I was not ready for any more surprises. Rylie mentioned the fact that she thought it was just going to be us four, and so did I.

I rang the doorbell and the housekeeper whom cleaned Patrick's house from time to time opened with a better smile than she usually wore when I came over. Patrick and Pasha were walking down the stairs as we entered.

"Welcome my favorite girls. Make yourself at home."
"Hey Pasha" Rylie and I said in unison.
She smiled and giggled a little. "Can we walk around?"
"Of course you can Rylie. Make yourself at home sweetie."
"Thank You."
"I'll show her my room daddy."
"Okay Pasha, show her your room darling."

I walked towards the kitchen area to begin to prepare for dinner. "Who does all those cars belong to outside?" I asked as I turned on the lights.

"SURPRISE!!!!!!!" Was yelled from many familiar voices. I was appalled, astonished, and emotional. I was also confused, because my birthday wasn't for another few weeks. Pasha and Rylie both ran over to the kitchen.

"Are you surprise mommy?"
"Yes. What is this about?"
"Well baby, Patrick asked us to be here." Mamadoll said as she grabbed my hand.
"We wouldn't want to be anywhere else." Kia said.
"Hey Girlfriend." Aunt Bae said waving.

I looked back at Patrick. I smiled but nervously. "Ok what's happening...?"

"Mina we forgot to tell you?" Gregory said.
"Tell me what? Mamadoll. Kia. Ms. Doris what is going on?" I looked at around the room and everyone was smiling at me.

Patrick tapped me on my shoulder. I turned around slowly. He just stood there looking at me.

"Mina Wright I love you more than you know, and more than I show. I loved you from the moment you almost knocked my head off running out the restroom." We all giggled.

"But seriously, all joking aside. I knew you were the one meant for me, the one sent to me by God. I knew God was going to send you; I was waiting on you in anticipation. I hold you in my arms when you are not even with me. I smell your scent even when you're gone. I still see your smile even when you're frowning.

I can taste your kiss even when I haven't kissed you. God looked beyond my faults and he saw what I needed. I needed you. Will you marry me sweetheart?"

I stood there in pure disbelief. This was unexpected and caught me off guard. I didn't answer right away which made my audience gasp at my brief delay to respond to Patricks' question. I looked over at everyone staring at me waiting.

"Yes, of course, I will marry you Patrick."

Everyone clapped and cheered and begin to hug the both of us. The girls were excited as well. Pasha called Rylie her big sister immediately and held her hand as we headed to the dining room.

"I'm so happy for the both of you. I'm so glad you waited on the lord Mina. I knew he would answer your prayers. You just had to wait. You both did." Mamadoll said.

"I understand now Mamadoll. I truly understand."

"I do as well. I know that waiting on the Lord brings the best results in any situation, especially when you can't see your way out. I preach it, I teach it, but sometimes you have to sit back and use your own advice." Patrick said.

"Amen to that comment." Kia walked over and added to the conversation. She hugged the both of us as we took pictures.

"Congratulations Mina and Patrick." Gregory said.

"You knew?"

"No ma'am. I thought I was coming to dinner."

I smiled and tears rolled down my eyes as I watched our children get along and my co-workers and soon to be husband getting along, with the woman I loved so much like a mother. Ms. Doris walked over and wiped the tear that fell on my face.

"This means you will be the first lady of the church?" Ms. Doris said.

"Yes I believe so."

"You are ready Mina."

I was quiet.

"If you weren't God would not have given it to you. He doesn't bless mess sweetheart. You know that."

"Yes I know Ms. Doris. I'm afraid. " I let out a long sighed. "I hope and pray I am the first lady God has called me to be for the church. The members need that, they need someone who genuinely love Christ and have the love of Christ that is in them."

"You don't have to worry about that sweetie. God will show you the way. He will teach you how to be the wife and first lady you need to be. Allow him to do that Mina. Don't question him, just follow his lead."

"I will. Thank You. I won't let God, the church, or my husband down." *I said, my husband, I believe I am ready.* "Did you just hear me say my husband?"

"LOL. Yes I did sweetie."

"I'm ready. I'm ready for my husband. I'm ready. I'm ready." I shouted loud and the room grew quite and all the attention turned towards me."

"And he is ready for you." Patrick walked over to me and said to me.

"And I for him." I said as we stood in the kitchen face to face holding hands gazing into one another's eyes. It seemed unreal to me and as if we were in a movie, or a dream. Mamadoll with her spirit of wisdom gently grabbed my hand and squeezed it. She lifted my hand high while it was still gripped to hers. She grabbed Patrick hand and lifted his as well. There she stood in the middle of the both of us, holding each one of our hands high up to the ceiling.

Mamadoll began to speak loudly to the guest who was present. "You both are champions. You both are more than conquerors. You both are believers. You both are the heads and not the tails. You both did not grow weary in well doing, so therefore you will reap because you didn't faint. Walk into your season that was given to you by no other than God himself. Be blessed Patrick and Mina, and be a blessing to others."

There wasn't a dry eye in the room. Mamadoll hugged us both and we hugged her tight. All the wisdom and advice she was instilling in the both of us for the past two years was now manifesting. I whispered in her ear a simple, "Thank You."

We began to eat the food prepared by the Chef and socialize with one another. We turned on the television to hear the latest news.

Patrick and I walked into the formal dining area because he wanted to give me my ring. He placed the thirty-two carat diamond ring on my finger, and then he kissed it. We then joined everyone again.

"I have one question." Gregory said.

"Go ahead ask." I said. He paused and looked over at Patrick.

"Ask son." Patrick said.

He took a deep breath. "What date is the wedding going to be?"

"Yes Mina, what day?" Mamadoll asked.

I paused. I looked at Patrick. I smiled. I looked at the girls, and I smiled. I winked at Mamadoll, and she winked back at me.

"May seventh. My mother's birthday."

"May seventh?" Gregory yelled from the family area.

"Yes May seventh." I yelled back.

Gregory looked mortified.

"What's wrong with you son? Why do you have that look on your face?" Patrick asked.

"Six months. That's what the news just announced Judge Nash sentence would be. If all goes well with him, he will be released on May seventh." Gregory said.

The End